Modeling Creativity and Knowledge-Based Creative Design

edited by
John S. Gero and Mary Lou Maher

Design Computing Unit
Department of Architectural and Design Science
University of Sydney

IEA
1993

LAWRENCE ERLBAUM ASSOCIATES, PUBLISHERS
Hillsdale, New Jersey   Hove and London

Lawrence Erlbaum Associates, Inc., Publishers
365 Broadway
Hillsdale, New Jersey 07642

Library of Congress Cataloging-in-Publication Data

Modeling creativity and knowledge-based creative design / edited by
John S. Gero and Mary Lou Maher.
    p.   cm.
Includes bibliographical references and index.
ISBN 0-8058-1153-2
1. Architectural design—Data processing.   2. Engineering de-
sign—Data processing.   3. Computer-aided design.   I. Gero,
John S.   II. Maher, Mary Lou.
NA2728.M6   1992
721'.0285—dc20   92-17655
                                                        CIP

Books published by Lawrence Erlbaum Associates are printed on
acid-free paper, and their bindings are chosen for strength and
durability.

Printed in the United States of America
10 9 8 7 6 5 4 3 2 1

Contents

Preface

Chapter 1   Introduction   1
             J. S. Gero, M. L. Maher

PART I: **Creativity**   **7**
Chapter 2   Social aspects of creativity and their impact on
             creativity modeling   9
             T. Heath
Chapter 3   A computational view of design creativity   25
             W. J. Mitchell
Chapter 4   Emergent value in creative products: 43
             some implications for creative processes
             S. McLaughlin
Chapter 5   A neuropsychologically-based approach to creativity   91
             T. Takala

PART II: **Knowledge-Based Models of Creative Design**   109
Chapter 6   Creativity in design using a design prototype approach   111
             M. A. Rosenman, J. S. Gero
Chapter 7   Creativity and design as exploration   139
             B. Logan, T. Smithers
Chapter 8   A connectionist view of creative design reasoning   177
             R. D. Coyne, S. Newton, F. Sudweeks
Chapter 9   A genetic approach to creative design   211
             R. F. Woodbury

PART III: Knowledge-Based Creative Design   233

Chapter 10   Creativity enhancing design environments   235
                G. Fischer

Chapter 11   Knowledge-based systems for creativity   259
                E. Edmonds

Chapter 12   Inducing optimally directed non-routine designs   273
                J. Cagan, A. M. Agogino

Chapter 13   Computer supported creative design: a pragmatic approach   295
                R. F. Coyne, E. Subrahmanian

Chapter 14   Dynamic associations for creative engineering design   329
                M. L. Maher, F. Zhao

Subject index   353

List of contributors

Alice M. Agogino, Intelligent Systems Research Group, Department of Mechanical Engineering, University of California at Berkeley, Berkeley California 94720 USA

Jonathan Cagan , Department of Mechanical Engineering, Carnegie Mellon University, Pittsburgh Pennsylvania 15213 USA

Richard D. Coyne, Department of Architectural and Design Science, University of Sydney NSW 2006 AUSTRALIA

Robert F. Coyne , Engineering Design Research Center, Carnegie Mellon University, Pittsburgh Pennsylvania 15213 USA

Ernest Edmonds, LUTCHI Research Centre, Department of Computer Studies, Loughborough University of Technology, Loughborough Leicestershire LE11 3TU UNITED KINGDOM

Gerhard Fischer, Department of Computer Science and Institute of Cognitive Science, University of Colorado, Boulder Colorado 80309 USA

John S. Gero, Department of Architectural and Design Science, University of Sydney NSW 2006 AUSTRALIA

Tom Heath, Faculty of the Built Environment, Queensland University of Technology, Brisbane Queensland 4000 AUSTRALIA

Brian Logan, Department of Artificial Intelligence, University of Edinburgh, Edinburgh EH1 2QL SCOTLAND

Sally McLaughlin, Department of Architectural and Design Science, University of Sydney NSW 2006 AUSTRALIA

Mary Lou Maher, Department of Architectural and Design Science, University of Sydney NSW 2006 AUSTRALIA

William J. Mitchell, Graduate School of Design, Harvard University, Cambridge Massachusetts 02138 USA

Sidney Newton, Department of Architectural and Design Science, University of Sydney NSW 2006 AUSTRALIA

Michael A. Rosenman, Department of Architectural and Design Science, University of Sydney NSW 2006 AUSTRALIA

Tim Smithers, Department of Artificial Intelligence, University of Edinburgh, Edinburgh EH1 2QL SCOTLAND

Eswaran Subrahmanian, Engineering Design Research Center, Carnegie Mellon University, Pittsburgh Pennsylvania 15213 USA

Fay Sudweeks, Department of Architectural and Design Science, University of Sydney NSW 2006 AUSTRALIA

Tapio Takala , Department of Computer Science, Helsinki University of Technology, Espoo 02150 FINLAND

Robert F. Woodbury, Department of Architecture and Engineering Design Research Center, Carnegie Mellon University, Pittsburgh Pennsylvania 15213 USA

Fang Zhao, Department of Civil Engineering, Carnegie Mellon University, Pittsburgh Pennsylvania 15213 USA

About the Editors

Dr John Gero is Professor of Design Science, Director of the Design Computing Unit and Director of the Key Centre of Design Quality, University of Sydney, and Adjunct Professor of Architecture at Carnegie Mellon University. He is editor/author of 19 books and over 200 papers and chapters on computer-aided design, design optimization and artificial intelligence in design. He has taught at universities in Australia, France, UK, and USA.

Dr Mary Lou Maher teaches and researches in the area of engineering design and artificial intelligence at the Department of Architectural and Design Science at the University of Sydney. She is the editor of five books on expert systems and civil engineering, and over 60 papers and chapters on artificial intelligence and design.

Preface

Design is one of the most significant of the purposeful acts of human beings. It creates a new, artificial world for us to inhabit and as such changes us all. The burgeoning ability to model and implement design processes as reasoning systems, making use of artificial intelligence research and techniques, has given new impetus to the study of design theory and methodology.

There is general acceptance that design activities can be categorized as being either routine or nonroutine. The distinction being drawn by this categorization is to separate design processes, in which the functions (i.e., goals or requirements) are known as are the available structures and the processes which map function to structure, from those in which one or more of function, structure or mapping is not known a priori. This allows us to begin to address one of the fundamental issues in design: that of creativity. Dictionary definitions of creativity are too imprecise to provide either a formal or operational definition that is useful.

An operational definition of creativity in design that has been found to be useful states that creativity involves the introduction of new variables into the design process, variables which were not originally considered by the designer or design system. Such a definition begs important questions related to the value of artifacts designed by such processes.

The problem-solving paradigm used in artificial intelligence appears to preclude the introduction of new variables because it was initially concerned with finding ways of achieving predefined goals from a specified initial state while passing through known states in some state-space representation.

Because creative design involves exploration (i.e., finding new goals, new states, and new state transition processes), it would appear that the original ideas of problem solving are applicable only to routine design. However, the concept of problem solving can be readily extended to encompass the notions involved in exploration.

Over the last decade research into design processes utilizing ideas and models drawn from artificial intelligence has resulted in a better understanding of design as a process, particularly routine design. Most of the current research activity directly or indirectly deals with routine design only. Not surprisingly many practicing designers state that the level of understanding represented by models of routine design is only of mild interest to them because of the lack of any ideas about creativity embodied in them.

This book provides a set of chapters in the areas of modeling creativity and knowledge-based creative design which examines the potential role and form of computer-aided design that supports creativity. The objectives are to define the state-of-the-art of computational creativity in design, and to identify research directions. This book is published at a time when the field of computational creativity in design is still immature, hopefully it will assist the field in reaching maturity and influence the directions of growth.

The shape of the book is very much a function of Fay Sudweeks who developed the LaTeX style to produce a consistent whole. As always, special thanks are due to her.

—**John S. Gero**
—**Mary Lou Maher**

1 Introduction

John S. Gero and Mary Lou Maher

Modeling creativity and knowledge-based creative design is a topic that invokes both positive and negative responses from designers and researchers in artificial intelligence and design. The topic is a difficult one given our current understanding of creativity and potential computational models of creativity. For some, the notion of understanding creativity is in itself a contradiction of terms. In this chapter we raise some of the issues in proposing that creativity can be modeled and that knowledge-based approaches have the potential to provide computational models of creativity.

1.1 Creative design

Design distinguishes itself from other human activities in a variety of ways. One of the most important ways is that the resulting artifact is expected to be different, albeit even if only slightly, from previous artifacts. This places design within a social context because the differences are evaluated within that context. The magnitude and quality of these differences are commonly used to separate artifacts into two categories although the boundary between them is fuzzy and constantly changes. These two categories are labeled routine and nonroutine designs. The labels can be applied equally to the processes of design that produced them as to the artifacts or designs themselves. The interest in drawing this distinction lies in the implications it has for articulating computational processes that support design activity. The inference is that processes for routine design are likely to be different from those for nonroutine design.

Routine designs may be defined as ones that are recognized as not being different from previously produced designs in their class in any substantive way. Thus, in structural engineering, designing a reinforced concrete beam for a given span and load subject to the normal goals and constraints generally will result in a rectangular cross-section of particular dimensions with certain reinforcement sizes and placement. Whereas another designer may produce a design that has different dimensions and reinforcement sizes and placement, the two designs will be recognized as being remarkably similar. Furthermore, the same designer designing another reinforced concrete beam for another span and load may produce a design with a rectangular cross-section of different dimensions and reinforcement sizes and placement and this design is also recognized as being similar to the previous design.

What makes these designs similar, it can be argued, is that they all exhibit the same properties but with different magnitudes. More formally, we state that these designers all chose to use the same design variables to work with and produce different values for those variables dependent on their perception of the situation. They may well have used similar processes as well to produce the values of the variables. Two processes are of interest. The first is concerned with the selection of the variables of interest and the second is concerned with producing values for those variables. The design variables with their values describe a design.

Nonroutine designs may be defined as ones that are recognized as being different from previously produced designs in their class in some substantive sense. We describe how we understand and interpret these differences later. It is convenient to draw a further distinction within nonroutine design. We label these two subcategories as **innovative** and **creative** design.

In innovative design we recognize that the substantive difference has come about from a particular set of values for the design variables that are outside the commonly used range. For example, in designing a camera with a zoom lens, the focal length of such lenses is normally 35 mm to 105 mm, however a designer may wish to use a range of 28 mm to 135 mm. This is likely to result in a longer, heavier lens but may well not produce any other changes. The camera would still look, feel, and work like any other similar zoom lens camera. This design could be considered innovative. A structural engineer may choose to design a reinforced concrete beam that was very deep compared to the normal depths for beams in order to emphasize the beam's load bearing function. The resulting design will not have any new design variables in it, only unusual values for those variables. However, a user of the design may evaluate it as being different from previously produced designs.

In creative designs we recognize that the substantive difference has come about from the introduction of new design variables. For example, in designing telephones the normal way of allowing the user to move away from the location of a telephone cradle has been to provide a long, extensible cord connecting the handset to the cradle. The introduction of an alternate means of connection of the handset to the cradle based on radio waves produces a design that is seen as being creative.

However, for a design to be evaluated as being creative the criterion of novelty is insufficient, utility and value are also required. Assuming all designs are novel and all designs are useful because designing is a purposeful act, value remains the important distinguishing criterion in the evaluation of the creativeness of a design. It has been suggested that value is related to two ideas *transformation* and *concentration*.

One property present in some products but absent, or less obvious, in others is the power to transform the constraints of reality. Some objects combine elements in ways that defy tradition and that yield a new perspective. They literally force us to see reality in a new way. These products involve a transformation of materials or ideas to overcome conventional constraints.

Products that warrant close and repeated examination are those that do not divulge their total meaning at first viewing. These products offer something new each time we experience them, whether they are great works of art or highly developed scientific theories. They have about them an intensity and concentration of meaning requiring continued contemplation.

The implication of these ideas is that the creativeness of an artifact can only be evaluated after it has been designed. This leaves us with the questions: Are there processes that are capable of producing creative designs and are these processes different from those that may be used to produce designs that are not considered creative? Further, are there computational analogs of these processes? Can we write computer programs which are capable of producing creative designs? Can we write computer programs which aid the production of creative designs? Can we write computer programs which support the production of creative designs? Finally, can we conceive of computational support for the evaluation of the creativeness of a design?

1.2   Implications of knowledge-based creative design

The introduction of knowledge-based systems as an approach to developing computer programs that support or simulate design processes has provided new insight into understanding and/or modeling creative design. Although the knowledge-based approach does not answer many of the questions raised in the previous section about the nature of creativity, it does provide some techniques that can be used to explore the questions themselves and possibly to propose some answers. In this section we highlight some of the implications of knowledge-based creative design, where the concepts of knowledge-based systems and creative design come together and complement each other.

The basis of knowledge-based systems is that knowledge is represented in an explicit form and used to reason about solving a problem. This explicit representation of knowledge provides a means for reasoning that differs from the mathematical models that preceded knowledge-based systems in computational problem solving. The distinguishing features of knowledge-based systems are the separation of knowledge and control and the predominance of symbolic modeling. The separation of knowledge and control in modeling creative design implies that we can discuss the role of the knowledge-base in creative design separately to the role of reasoning in creative design. This relates, in a loose way, to the difference in creative processes versus creative products. Creative processes implies that the reasoning process itself is creative. Creative products implies that the knowledge provides the basis for creativity. In a knowledge-based system the two work together so that knowledge can be used to produce a creative product independently of whether the reasoning process was creative. If this is the case, we can produce computational models of creativity by providing an appropriate combination of knowledge representation and reasoning.

The role of the knowledge base in creative design is to provide the content and organization of design knowledge that can be used to generate a creative product. This is similar to the role of experience and extensive training in human designers. Creativity is rarely the result of naivety, but rather it results from the ability of a highly intelligent person to put different ideas together and recognise their value. The knowledge base serves the purpose of providing such knowledge. In knowledge-based creative design we are able to explore the role, content, and organization of suitable knowledge bases. We come across terms such as *memory organization, indexing, flexible retrieval,* and so forth. These concepts allow us to explore the issues of knowledge-based creative design. In this book models of creative design based on the knowledge-base organization and content are presented.

The role of reasoning in creative design raises issues related to modeling design processes. In some cases it is difficult to distinguish between design and creative design, because the result of designing is to produce a new object. When we discuss the role of reasoning in design we refer to various process models such as decomposition, search, exploration, analogy, and mutation. These reasoning methods provide a basis for exploring creative design and the knowledge needed to support the processes.

1.3   Approaches to knowledge-based creative design

Researchers are beginning to explore various ways in which knowledge-based systems can support and/or produce creative designs. These approaches include:

- the development of better user interfaces to knowledge-based design systems can support creativity because the knowledge-based approach to design can be flexible and provide justifications and knowledge resources;

- the development of bigger knowledge-bases can support creativity because creativity depends on knowing a lot;

- the type of knowledge required for creative design differs from the type of knowledge required for routine design, so knowledge-based creative design implies a different knowledge representation scheme;

- creative design processes are different to routine design processes, understanding the difference allows us to implement such processes; and

- creative design requires a computational model that has a more flexible search mechanism.

These approaches vary in whether the knowledge-based system supports human creativity or attempts to model human creativity. Another distinction in these approaches is whether the content and organization of the knowledge-base is different for creative design or whether the difference lies in the reasoning mechanism. The chapters in this book explore many of these approaches in more detail, highlighting the role of the knowledge-based system for creative design and the actual or potential implementation.

1.4   This book

This book is based on a workshop held in December 1989. The submitted papers were reviewed where the basis for acceptance was the relevance to the topic of the workshop rather than demonstrated results in producing models of creativity or implemented knowledge-based creative design. The workshop served as a forum for discussing the various issues raised by the accepted papers. The presentation was in the form of a round-table discussion which provided the basis for the organization of the book. The book does not follow the proceedings of the workshop but is an afterthought of the participants. Each author had the opportunity to revise their submission based on the experience of the workshop.

The book is organized into three parts. Part I deals with creativity itself. The notion of creativity has an historical component and an aura of mystery. The chapters in this section raise issues related to understanding or to being able to understand creativity. Part II takes a more computational view of creativity by considering how artificial intelligence or knowledge-based approaches can provide models for creative design. The chapters in this section present models and then either support them or show how they cannot begin to address the creativity issues. Part III is even more oriented towards computer creativity where computer programs have been implemented that demonstrate some aspect of creative design. The chapters in this section propose a computable model of creativity and describe an implementation of this model.

The issues addressed in this book center around the fact that creative design is an important and timely topic. Understanding creativity and providing support in the form of computer programs and environments are goals that the participants in the workshop strive to achieve. Whether such goals are achievable and whether this book provides the seeds for achieving these goals is yet to be seen. The conclusions to be drawn from such a discussion are left to the reader.

PART I

Creativity

Part I considers creativity from both a human and computational perspective. The first chapter, "Social aspects of creativity and their impact on creativity modeling" by Heath, presents the concept of creativity from a historical perspective in which creativity and mysticism are synonomous. The second chapter, "A computational view of design creativity" by Mitchell, discusses the areas in which computer-aided design fails to support creativity, such as shape emergence. The third chapter, "Emergent value in creative products: some implications for creative processes" by McLaughlin, looks at examples of creative design and considers the issue of automation in producing or supporting such designs. The fourth chapter, "A neuropsychologically-based approach to creativity" by Takala, looks at a model of human creativity as a basis for a computable model of creativity.

2 Social Aspects of Creativity and their Impact on Creativity Modeling

Tom Heath

Creativity is not solely a matter of individual abilities or behavior. Creativity implies an innovative outcome. This depends on opportunity, which is social. Within a constraint model of design, this social aspect of creativity can be represented in the form of an 'index of opportunity.' This 'reality principle' is required if creativity is not to degenerate into fantasy.

2.1 Creativity and the tradition of individualism

'Creative' is one of the keywords of our time (Williams, 1976). Liam Hudson has remarked that creativity applies to all those qualities of which psychologists approve (Hudson, 1966). This draws our attention both to the strongly honorific sense of 'creative' and to its rather careless use. Its importance is so established that a concept originally intended to apply to artists only, and to distinguish them from artisans and technologists, and also from commercial hacks, has been appropriated by the very people it was meant to exclude. Everyone now agrees that scientists are creative. Poincare's book on mathematical creation has become a classic of the literature on creativity (Poincare, 1908). An important section of Wertheimer's book on productive thinking (Wertheimer, 1945) is devoted to Einstein's recollections of the path by which he came to his major discoveries. By the time of the post-Sputnik explosion of creativity studies, it was accepted that even quite prosaic technical and commercial innovations involve creativity (Schön, 1963). Williams (1976) lamented that advertising copywriters "officially describe themselves as creative." Such extensions of concepts are historically common. However it often happens, and has happened in this case, that associated ideas and assumptions, derived from the original historical context of the idea, are dragged along with it, so to speak. These assumptions then become accepted without much, or perhaps any, critical examination. Among the subsidiary ideas that form part of our conception of creativity is the assumption that creativity is essentially individual and not social. This assumption is examined here in relation to modeling creative design.

Creative, Williams suggested, has "a general sense of original and innovatory, and an associated special sense of productive" (Williams, 1976). Whether change and innovation in cultures are products of individual genius and activity, or, rather, of fields of ideas and social figurations that are not dependent on any one of the individuals who constitute them, is a hotly debated issue in cultural anthropology (Brady and Isaacs, 1975). Although not conclusive, the common occurrence of simultaneous discovery gives color to the social field hypothesis (Ogburn and Thomas, 1922). It raises the possibility that the individual, or psychological factors in creativity may be relatively widely distributed and commonplace. The social factors, the *opportunity* to exercise whatever abilities are involved in an effective way may on the other hand be restricted or even determined by the social field. The creative *outcome* then depends on both sets of factors. This does not diminish the importance of simulating individual productive performances, but it does add a dimension to the task of modeling creativity.

The notion that social factors have a positive contribution to make to creative work runs counter to the conventional wisdom. Our ideas in good currency on the subject are strongly colored by the romantic individualism and primitivism of the early 19th century. In romantic theory, the socialization process in general, formal education and civilization stifle creativity. Wordsworth, in the preface to the Lyrical Ballads (Wordsworth, 1800) argues that it is not specialized knowledge of any kind, but knowledge that is naturally possessed by everyone, which is necessary to the poet. Similarly, children and people from less technologically advanced cultures than ours are thought to be more creative because their natural ability has not been repressed. In this context, attempts to encourage creativity by social action have concentrated on avoiding or eliminating the supposed ill effects of early learnings of one kind or another (Hudson, 1966). Educational theory, from Rousseau (1762) to Dewey (1916), and Wertheimer (1945), and down to the present, has been preoccupied with this perceived problem. One can see Gordon's 'synectics' (Gordon, 1961) and Osborn's 'brainstorming' (Osborn, 1963) also in this way.

As already implied, this chapter takes a somewhat different view of the influence of social figurations. It will be assumed that mental process of the kinds identified by Coleridge (Richards, 1934), Wertheimer (1945), and Schön (1963) are essential for original or productive thinking, and indeed for mere survival. It will also be assumed that personality factors such as those identified in architects by Mackinnon (1962) and Schmidt (1973), and particulary a certain toughness, or inner-directedness, are important. Such abilities are of course individual, and it is extremely interesting and important to be able to model or simulate them. On the other hand it will be argued that these abilities do not become effective, or creative, unless they are harnessed in an appropriate social figuration or field. Creativity in its full, honorific sense requires opportunity. The distribution of such opportunities in design, particularly architectural design, will be investigated through the discussion of a constraint model of the design process.

2.2 Constraints in design

Design, according to Zeisel (1981) consists of three elementary activities, imagining, presenting, and testing. Design is distinguished from fantasy by the existence and application of tests. These tests are the constraints that the design must 'satisfice' (Simon, 1969). The knowledge-base in terms of which the process is carried on finds its main expression in terms of these constraints. The constraints may be pictured as defining a larger or smaller space, the solution space. If the solution space is a point, there is only one satisficing solution. However such a case is not a design problem. Design problems are characterized by imperfect closure of the goal state (Wade, 1977). They thus necessarily have a large number of satisficing solutions. It is also possible for constraints to be contradictory, which produces a negative solution space (Heath, 1984).

Constraint models of design are currently receiving considerable attention (Gross et al., 1988). However constraint models can easily be interpreted as allowing no scope for originality, except perhaps in making an arbitrary selection from the final solution space. There is a mistaken tendency to treat constraints as inherently 'fixed' (Gross and Fleisher, 1984). This is contrary to experience. Constraints are to a large, even a predominant, extent socially defined. They are rarely based directly on 'laws of nature.' Rather they express the resolutions, the aspirations, and sometimes the speculations, of people. Even constraints that appear to be physical may have a large social element. In architecture, for example, site constraints might be taken to be physical. On further investigation, however, such constraints turn out to be based on assumptions of many kinds. It is assumed that *this* site *must* be used, that the boundaries cannot be changed, that certain trees or buildings must be preserved, that exceptions cannot be made to regulations, and so on. These assumptions in turn depend on further assumptions about the likelihood of delay, cost, embarrassment, and other purely social factors. In reality then constraints turn out to be strands in a more or less closely woven social web of values and beliefs. If the weave of the web is not too tight, they can be relaxed or even sometimes eliminated. Very few designs would be completed if this were not so, for contradictory constraints are discovered at some stage in almost every design process (Heath, 1984).

In designing, an architect, for example, will make use of constraints derived in several different ways. Some constraints will be based on general professional knowledge of the explicit kind embodied in formal education. This will include knowledge of the 'knowledge domains' in which constraints may be found (Goldschmidt, 1983). Other constraints will be derived from personal professional experience: "I'll never use Gallow's locks again." These too will usually be transparent and explicit. However not all the necessary constraints will be present in the architect's memory or even the 'external memory' of reference material. Some will have to be elicited from consultants, clients, users, or others. Some may have to be discovered by observation. Constraints therefore have to be derived in terms of some overall knowledge structure. Further, the success of a design process, in terms of achieving a satisficing design within a reasonable time, depends heavily on the order in which constraints are discovered. An understanding of the hierarchy of constraints is essential if backtracking is to be minimized (Zeisel, 1981). Knowledge of the rules governing constraint hierarchies and decision sequences in architectural design is almost entirely a product of individual experience and is largely inexplicit. Procedures for investigating and representing these rules have been discussed elsewhere (Heath, 1984). However even in the present restricted state of our understanding, some points are clear. Just as one does not discover 'facts' by observation alone, but in terms of some theory for the testing of which those facts are required (Popper, 1963), so design constraints can only be discovered in terms of some initial picture of the task, in relation to which those constraints would constitute relevant tests. In the case of an architect, such an initial picture may be quite concrete, a literal physical model, or it may be some quite abstract general concept such as those detected by Darke (1979). Such initial schemas serve an heuristic purpose, although their necessarily tentative nature is not always recognized. Changes to the designer's initial idea that might seem to be required by the constraints which it unearths are often vigorously resisted. When changes do occur, the outcome is not necessarily less 'creative.' Le Corbusier's 'Pavillon Suisse' was radically modified to avoid serious foundation problems, under great pressure from the client, but is nonetheless recognized as a masterpiece (Curtis, 1981). However, the disposition to test constraints themselves in this way, a product no doubt of the personality factors mentioned earlier, is obviously important for a creative outcome. The struggle between the schema and the 'reality principle' is often fruitful rather than destructive.

2.3 Creativity and design

Under a constraint model of design, then, innovative or original thinking and decisions are possible at every stage of the design process. The initial concept may be close to or far from some existing type or stereotype. As constraints are discovered, the initial concept may be modified in ways that are minimal and predictable, mere variations, or radical and unconventional, true inventions. Quite possibly the initial concept may be abandoned and a new guiding scheme adopted. Alternatively, the constraints may be modified, with consequent changes to the social figuration. Undergoing growth, development, differentiation, and even mutation through a succession of discoveries of constraints and responses to them, the design homes in on the solution space—if all goes well, that is. Zeisel has represented this in his spiral model of the design process (Zeisel, 1981). In practice, however the scope for creativity in architectural design is limited (Blau, 1984). In our society it is generally the case that the more commercialized the particular form of production and type of product, the less departure from stereotypes will be permitted in the initial concept and in adaptation to constraints. This is not a consequence of some malign power associated with capitalism. It is because highly commercial large volume markets evolve in interaction with a multitude of social pressures and demands, including consumer choices. These pressure demands and choices form a tightly woven segment of the social web and engender relatively precise expectations. Variation is permitted, certainly, but it tends to be superficial, marginal, and fashionable. Inevitably, the greatest volume of design work, in architecture as in other fields, concerns itself with products that are near to the commercial end of the scale. As one moves away from this well-defined, near-routine activity towards the experimental, the exploratory and the symbolic, the demand for innovation increases, and with it the opportunity for creativity. However, such opportunities are necessarily rarer and the chances of the design being realized smaller.

Looking across fields of productive activity, we find this same range in each. In literature we have thousands of romances written to a formula, and very few 'serious' novels, and fewer again that bring their authors anything other than fame. In painting we have advertising art and illustration, academic portraiture, and avant-garde gallery paintings. In music there is a particularly clear range; from the 'reproduction' of the performer, which is nevertheless regarded as 'creative' through the improvisation of jazz or the raga (Johnson-Laird, 1987) to the dubious permissiveness of John Cage. In architecture the range extends from the 'commodity' building, which may be only one step away from being standardized, through the 'systems' building, which is designed to meet emerging or changing social demands, to the symbolic building, in which the designer seeks to provide a metaphor for certain value systems (Heath, 1984). In science there is a like range from engineering application and applied research through 'normal science' (Kuhn, 1962) to fundamental research and the development of theory.

The so-called 'fine' arts, design, science and technology are juxtaposed here with a purpose. Despite the extensions we have made to the original concept our accounts of creativity are still confused by the original romantic notion of a special domain reserved for artists, aesthetic and metaphysical. The fact that art and design conspicuously involve aesthetic constraints does not distinguish them from technology, which invariably also makes use of aesthetic constraints, if only those which result in 'useless work' (Pye, 1968). Science and mathematics notoriously make use of aesthetic tests in the selection of theories. Nor are aesthetic constraints metaphysical or arbitrary in some sense in which other constraints are not. They have a psychobiological component, but this is far from being metaphysical. Like other constraints they also have social elements, which we call style when many strands of the contemporary sets of ideals and values are implicated, and fashion when only a few are. Our society assigns priority to economic constraints and treats aesthetic constraints as weak, but history provides many examples of opposite priorities: medieval Japan, and Islam throughout its history.

2.4   Social opportunity and creativity

The process of commercialization in our society is thus only one example of the way in which particular productive activities mature, become deeply embedded in the social fabric, take on the character of routine, and lose much of their possibilities for innovative action. In our society, but not in those of ancient Egypt or Byzantium, the 'fine arts' are among the less constrained activities. This means that today the arts have, in Hegel's term, retreated to the margin. Centrality is here best defined in a systems sense. What is central is what has the most links to other elements of the fabric. The densest nodes of the net are the most constrained. Places, groups, individuals that are marginal in this sense have, conversely, the greatest scope for creative action. In this context it is interesting to note that as science becomes more central to our society, so various groups increasingly seek to restrict the freedom, that is, the creativity, of the scientist. The center-margin relation is often represented by modernists and progressives through the metaphor of the frontier. This is a good metaphor because on the frontier much is permitted and authority is weak. The avant-garde, the scouts, can even go beyond the pale of civilization and return, if they do, with altogether new technologies, ideas and customs. It is also a metaphor based on fact. The vast majority of innovation in human history has resulted from 'cultural borrowing' across geographical frontiers (Murdock, 1956).

Major innovation is only possible at the periphery. Change also takes place in more central activities, as a result of variation (Murdock, 1956). Variation is of two kinds, random and directed. Fashionable change is in its nature random. It is change for the sake of change. This lack of substance distinguishes fashion from creative innovation. Nevertheless a major task of designers today is to meet the ever-growing demand for such fashionable changes. The whole process of modernization has imposed progressively stricter and more pervasive discipline on the citizens of modern societies (Weber, 1930; Foucault, 1975). The obverse of this trend is the search for socially permissible means of escape, the 'quest for excitement' (Elias and Dunning, 1986), of which the cult of the new is a significant element. In recent years, with the rise of so-called 'post-modernism,' even architecture has become involved in fashionable variation. Insofar as buildings become 'commodities' (Heath, 1984), they have to conform to the requirement of marginal product differentiation for advertising purposes. However, the low regard in which fashion is often held should not be allowed to obscure its role as a facilitator of other kinds of change. Just as the stimulus seeking drive on which fashion is based causes animals to vary their habitual behavior patterns and thus sometimes make beneficial discoveries (Berlyne, 1960), so fashion acts as a form of social inquiry that from time to time discovers forms and ideas that have more enduring qualities. A selection of random fashionable variations is subjected to directed variation.

Change to central ideas, institutions, and technologies may be due to

external force: war, plague, famine, culture shock, or other disaster. However, major change and even revolutionary change are also produced by
evolutionary changes: directed variation. Guided by dominant values of
the society, and proceeding by incremental steps too small to alert effective
opposition, such changes may in time create a totally new situation. To
take a remote historical example, but one not without relevance today, Elias
(1969) explained how the introduction of large quantities of precious metal
from the Americas in the 16th century acted as the catalyst for the rise of a
money economy in France. This in turn over time made the nobility more
and more dependent on the cities and the Crown. This economic fact found
physical form in the enforced centralization of this class on Versailles and
Paris. Significant changes in architecture followed: not only the construction
and extension of Versailles and its gardens, but also the invention of a wholly
new and highly sophisticated architectural type, the hotel or noble town
house. A more recent example of the same process is provided by the
progressive development of the Boeing 707 series. Later members of this
type had twice the range and payload of the earliest, a 'species change'
with wide implications for the sociotechnical system of air travel, and its
associated architecture. (Encel et al., 1975).

At any given time, then, our culture provides opportunities for the
exercise of creative abilities in three different ways. There is the opportunity
to contribute to fashionable changes. There is the opportunity to work in
socially marginal areas where experiment is permitted or even encouraged.
And finally there are minor and major 'frontier shifts' that come about
as unintended consequences of long term directed variation, or, more rarely,
under the pressure of external events. The possibility of a creative outcome is
greater in the third category than the second, and greater in the second than
the first. It is the frontier shifts, the revolutions, the **paradigm changes**,
to use Kuhn's (1962) term, that create the greatest opportunities. However,
as previously remarked, the number of opportunities tends to be in inverse
proportion to their importance.

Buildings that have achieved historical importance or critical acclaim in
this century seem to fit this broad model of the distribution of opportunity.
The majority of such buildings are houses. In modern ideology, the house
belongs to the private sphere, which is 'free' and therefore marginal (Berger
et al., 1973). In principle the house owner may and even should pursue an
individual 'lifestyle' in a correspondingly idiosyncratic setting. In practice, of
course, domestic life is governed by many conventional constraints, and the
home owner who departs too far from local norms will experience hostility
and even legal action (Rapoport, 1982). Nevertheless house design is an
accepted area of tolerance. Buildings for the arts and entertainment would

appear to offer the next best opportunities, followed fairly closely by 'up-market' office buildings and shops. Buildings for activities that depend on advanced technology, such as major hospitals, airports, and laboratories also provide opportunities for creative innovation, but the possibilities are restricted by the presence of relatively rigid technical constraints. A systematic analysis of this apparent distribution might prove helpful in constructing a model of opportunity. Such a broad model may have importance for schema selection. Design work based on a divergent schema will be rejected if such divergences are not socially acceptable.

2.5 Modeling the social aspects of creativity in design

Identifying the opportunity for adopting a divergent schema is the first step in modeling the social aspect of a creative design. An architectural design process will often begin with a search for examples that have been produced in response to a similar problem. These are potential sources for an initial schema. If there are many examples in the literature or easily identified in the environment, and if they have many common features, this indicates a strong social consensus. This will be confirmed if the literature identifies some instances as exemplary, and still more strongly supported if the client or user group agree on exemplars. Conversely, the absence of examples, significant differences between examples, or widespread criticism of those that exist indicate weak consensus and relative lack of constraint. In general the presence of debate and contradiction indicates weak constraint. Where constraint is weak there is opportunity to produce a solution that will be recognized as exemplary and itself become a precedent for later design. There is also a high risk of failure. It may be difficult to gain agreement and the proposed solution may not be accepted.

The principles that apply to selection of the initial schema also apply to the progressive modification of the schema by the discovery and application of constraints. If there is debate in the user organization about the operating procedures to be adopted in the new building, there is corresponding opportunity for creative innovation in the physical form. Similarly, if a building is to be built on a site over which there is much contention, or on a site that has characteristics not usually encountered or even desired, such as a steep fall, opportunities for innovation arise. Dissatisfaction with the performance of existing materials or technology, or the introduction of new materials or technology with socially desired characteristics, such as greater economy, durability, consistency, or visual interest, also enable innovation at the detailed level, and may support more fundamental changes in form. The mere availability of a wide range of possible techniques encourages experiment.

When on the other hand the range is narrow or limited by convention or law constraint is increased and the chance of innovation reduced.

Variety, dissatisfaction, and debate are the qualitative indicators of opportunity for creative design. Where they are present, the social web of constraint is loose textured and weak. If we may indulge in a metaphorical use of Freudian terminology, at the points the ego, the 'reality principle' is weaker and the 'primary process material,' the ideas and values of individuals, can break through. This may apply to the whole design task, or to parts of it. In either case, it will be desirable for modeling purposes to be able to quantify the opportunity for creative innovation, at least in a rough way. Clearly the strength of the constraint web over any given area depends on the strength and flexibility of the individual constraints and their number. The strength of an individual constraint is equivalent to its reliability. Some kind of probability function will be able to be estimated or perhaps calculated, although estimation is the more likely case. The flexibility or elasticity of an individual constraint is proportional to the number of satisficing instances that that constraint will permit. This too will in most cases be a matter of estimation rather than calculation. The connectivity of the constraint is the number of other constraints that would be affected by a changes in that constraint. In modeling a design process this could be expressed as an actual number; this is implicit in Alexander's early work (Alexander, 1964). This would indicate the local density of the web in relation to the individual constraint. The index of opportunity for an individual constraint is then a function of these three quantities. Given that two at least of them are measured on ordinal or interval scales, there will be mathematical difficulties in combining them into a single index, and the resulting measure will need to be tested empirically. However, there is no difference in principle to the modeling tasks that occur in economics and the social sciences generally.

In the design process, the constraint set is constructed progressively. Therefore the 'index of opportunity' must also be calculated progressively. In principle one might decide to calculate the index for every constraint. This is likely to be costly in terms of data collection and computation. It is also likely to delay or prevent the discovery of a satisficing design. In practice there are two cases in which such an index could be helpful in modeling creative design. The first is the case in which a constraint is discovered that would require the rejection or radical modification of the current schema. This is more likely to arise in the case of a schema which is not based on exemplary precedent; a 'creative' proposal. Then the determination of an index of opportunity for that constraint will indicate whether the constraint or the schema should be modified or abandoned. The second is the case in which two or more contradictory constraints are discovered. Here the index of opportunity will help in deciding which of the contradictory constraints should be relaxed or abandoned.

In summary, then, a model of design must be able to select a schema, discover constraints in terms of that schema, and progressively modify or vary the schema and the constraint network until an acceptable or satisificing design is reached. It is probable that any such model must incorporate operators that simulate the fundamental human creative abilities in order to function. However to achieve creative outcomes the model will have to be able to select initial and revised schemas on the basis of a wide range of analogies, and to prefer the less literal analogies. This is equivalent to the exercise of imagination. The model must also seek to maintain its schema in the face of contradictory constraints, by questioning the reliability of the constraints or exploiting their imprecision. This is equivalent to the bloodymindedness and pigheadedness which are so characteristic of creative designers. However, in order to prevent its imagination and determination from leading it into mere fantasy, the model must also incorporate a 'reality principle,' which relates the design to the sociotechnical matrix, or constraint web. This is the 'index of opportunity.' Without such a representation of the social aspect of creativity a model will not operative realistically and may not be able to operate at all.

2.6   Summary and conclusion

The basic human abilities involved in creative design are not distinct from those that enable people to construct a lifeworld, imagine possible courses of action, and evaluate them. There is no separable mental function, 'creativity.' This is not to say that there are no characteristics that distinguish the 'creative' person. Frequently they are strongly inner-directed, tolerant of ambiguity and uncertainty, and provided with an unusually broad range of knowledge and experience. However at any given time there are many people who possess these characteristics but who are never identified as 'creative.' Creativity is recognized by a kind of outcome, innovation. Innovation occurs when individuals with abilities, knowledge, and personality characteristics that are relatively common encounter more or less abnormal circumstances. The abnormality of the circumstances lies in the fact that the web of social constraints which constitutes the culture and keeps it going is weakened and the social figurations rendered unstable. This way of looking at things is consistent with the widespread belief that 'creativity' is somehow repressed by social forces. It is however, opposed to the prevailing individualism, the notion that creativity characterizes persons rather than social situations.

Culture is by definition a learnable system. Thus it resists change and tends to repeat itself. The way in which things go on is highly determined by a web of interdependencies. This web is far too robust to be readily changed by the deliberate action of individuals or groups. Attempts to change it in fact generate resistance in direct proportion to their scale. Culture operates homeostatically. It is in this sense that we can speak of culture or society as a web of interdependencies or system of constraints. Strands or fibers of the web include the state of knowledge and belief, the available technology and organizational skills, the resources and above all the intentions, in the philosophic sense, of people. None of these general systems is the 'fundamental' system. Economic constraints, for instance, are not in any sense privileged. Social figurations of mutual interdependency and the constraints that arise from them are structural and organizational, and communicative, in that they all depend on exchange of information, and economic, involving exchanges of goods and services, all at the same time.

Nevertheless culture is not a *closed* system. Change occurs, but largely as a result of the dynamics of the system, rather than as a result of insight or choice. Again this contradicts the voluntarism that is characteristic of modernist thinking. Modernism tends to take an engineering view of things, to regard the world as 'makeable' (Berger et al., 1974). The whole notion that 'creativity' is something that one can and should encourage is part of this belief. The contrary view, taken here, and more commonly found in those social sciences that make use of history, can be illustrated by considering the cases of the safety razor blade and the personal computer. As is well known, the safety razor invented by Gilette and patented in 1896 rapidly became an enormous commercial success. However, this was not the first safety razor. A razor with a safety guard was invented in 1828, not long after relatively cheap high quality razors first became available. Other designs were proposed in the 1880s and received some support from various public figures, but did not sell.It would appear that, for the safety razor to sell, other changes had to occur. Changing fashions, changing standards of hygiene, an ongoing relative fall in the price of razors, an increasing tendency of people to shave themselves rather than be shaved by others, and rising concerns about safety were all perhaps implicated. The 'creative' technical invention was of relatively little significance.

The safety razor blade proved difficult to introduce despite its 'obvious' advantages and despite its apparently minimal impact on the total system. Shaving went on much as before. Conversely, the introduction of the personal computer was, commercially speaking, unexpectedly successful. Its history is comparable to that of the Ford car or the Boeing 700 series aircraft. Rapid technical improvement in design and production of components and systems

made possible the extension of a technology to a wider market. The result
in each case was major social change, much of it unanticipated. A positive
feedback loop was created, which rapidly involved the entire social system.
The driving force in the case of the personal computer was the stuff of
interdependency itself,the drive for increased communication. Even though
this is a central value of modernism, we can be sure that had the likely
effects been widely understood, efforts would have been made to contain or
prevent then. This happened in the communist bloc countries. Even in some
Australian universities attempts were made to maintain the centralization
of computing on the old mainframes. In a relatively free society this was of
course futile.

Despite the inherent conservatism of culture and the difficulty of predicting its timing and effects, the modern world has to some extent in-
stitutionalized change. It has done this through the invention of specific
social figurations that mediate and promote change, even though they cannot
control it. Among the most important of these institutions are 'art,' 'science,'
and 'design.' All of these, as words, as activities, and as subsystems of the
social system, are inventions of the late 18th and early 19th centuries. In
these institutions, 'creativity' in its secondary sense of actively challenging
the status quo, of *enquiry,* is encouraged. People working in these fields are
believed to have a duty to innovate. Although they have been and to a great
extent are still socially marginal, and generally poorly rewarded, they enjoy
a certain social standing and regard. This privileged but marginalized status
shows signs of disappearing as research and innovation move from affordable
luxuries to an official strategic role in corporate and government policy. They
are becoming more 'accountable,' that is, subject to an increasing variety
and number of social constraints. In terms of the thesis proposed here, this
can be expected to lead to fewer and less radical innovations.

'Art' and 'science' promote change. Design both promotes change and
seeks to manage it. Design is an instrument of policy in its nature. It
represents a conscious effort to stop things going badly wrong when a need
for action is perceived but the goals are ill-defined. The existence of a
perceived need for action and the poor definition of goals are symptoms
of a breakdown in the social constraint web. Some kind of conflict has
arisen between activities or intentions. A constraint model of design focuses
our attention on the exploratory character of design processes. More or
less systematically, designers probe the situation with which they have to
deal. They locate constraints or demands that are relevant to defining the
goal and identify conflicting or contradictory demands. Where these are
contradictory demands some constraints must be relaxed if the project is to
proceed. The tools by which this exploration is conducted are schemas or

models that are progressively adapted through a series of partial or outline proposals, so that the design and the constraints are derived interactively. Design is thus creative in the sense of *inquiring*. The apparent constraints are not necessarily accepted. Design can be seen as a way of exploring the scope for social action and innovation. In order to model creativity in design we must be able to simulate not only individual behaviour, but also social behavior. Creativity is social as much if not more than it is individual.

References

Alexander, C. (1964). *Notes on the Synthesis of Form*, Harvard University Press, Cambridge, Mass.

Berger P., Berger, B., & Kellner H. (1974). *The Homeless Mind*, Pelican Books, Harmondsworth.

Berlyne, D. E. (1960). *Conflict Arousal and Curiosity*, McGraw-Hill, New York.

Blau, J. R. (1984). *Architects and Firms: A Sociological Perspective on Architectural Practice*, MIT Press, Cambridge, Mass.

Brady, I., & Isaacs, B. (1975). *A Reader in Cultural Change*, Wiley, New York.

Curtis, W. (1981). Ideas of structure and the structure of ideas; Le Corbusier's Pavillon Suisse, 1930–1931, *Journal of the Society of Architectural Historians*, **XL**(4): 295–310.

Darke, J. (1979). The primary generator and the design process, *Design Studies*, **1**(1): 36–44.

Dewey, J. (1916). *Democracy and Education*, MacMillan, New York.

Elias, N. (1969). *The Court Society*, Basil Blackwell, Oxford.

Elias, N., & Dunning, E. (1986). *Quest for Excitement*, Basil Blackwell, Oxford.

Encel, S., Marstrand, P., & Page, W. (1975). *The Art of Anticipation: Values and Methods in Forecasting*, Martin Robertson, London.

Foucault, M. (1975). *Discipline and Punish*, Penguin Books, Harmondworth.

Goldschmidt, G. (1983). Doing design, making architecture, *Journal of Architectural Education*, **37**(1): 8–13.

Gordon, W. J. (1961). *Synectics*, Collier-MacMillan, London.

Gross, M. D., & Fleisher, A. (1984). Design as the exploration of constraints, *Design Studies*, **5**(3): 137–138.

Gross, M. D., Ervin, S., Anderson, J., & Fleisher, A. (1988). Constraints: Knowledge representation in design, *Design Studies*, **9**(3): 133-143.

Heath, T. (1984). *Method in Architecture*, John Wiley, Chichester.

Hudson, L. (1966). *Contrary Imaginations*, Penguin, Harmondsworth.

Johnson-Laird, P. N. (1987). Reasoning, imagining, and creating, *Bulletin of the Council for Research in Music Education*, **95**: 71–87.

Kuhn, T. (1962). *The Structure of Scientific Revolutions*, University of Chicago Press, Chicago.

Mackinnon, D. W. (1962). The personality correlates of creativity: A study of American architects, *Proceedings of the Fourteenth Congress on Applied Psychology, Volume 2*, Munksgaard, pp. 11–39.

Murdock, G. P. (1956). How culture changes, *in* H. L. Shapiro (Ed.), *Man Culture and Society*, Oxford University Press, New York, pp. 247-260.

Ogburn, W. F., & Thomas, D. (1922). Are inventions inevitable? A note on social evolution, *Political Science Quarterly*, **37**: 83–98.

Osborn, A. F. (1963). *Applied Imagination*, Scribner, New York.

Poincare, H. (1908). *Science and Method*, trans. F. Maitland, Dover, New York.

Popper, K. (1963). *Conjectures and Refutations*, Routledge and Kegan Paul, London.

Pye, D. (1968). *The Nature and Art of Workmanship*, Cambridge University Press, Cambridge.

Rapoport, A. (1982). *The Meaning of the Built Environment*, Sage Publications, Beverly Hills.

Richards, I. A. (1934). *Coleridge on Imagination*, Kegan Paul, London.

Rousseau, J. J. (1762). *Emile* (1911 edn), J. M. Dent, London.

Schmidt, H. E. (1973). Personality correlates of the creative architecture student, *Perceptual and Motor Skills*, **36**: 1030.

Schön, D. (1963). *Invention and the Evolution of Ideas*, Associated Book, London.

Simon, H. A. (1969). *The Sciences of the Artificial*, MIT Press, Cambridge, Mass.

Wade, J. (1977). *Architecture, Problems and Purposes*, Wiley-Interscience, New York.

Weber, M. (1930). *The Protestant Ethic and the Spirit of Capitalism*, trans. T. Parsons, Unwin, London.

Wertheimer, M. (1945, 1959). *Productive Thinking*, Greenwood Press, Connecticut.

Williams, R. (1976). *Keywords*, Fontana, Glasgow.

Wordsworth, W. (1800). Preface to the 'Lyrical Ballads', *in* T. Hutchinson (Ed.), *The Poetical Works of Wordsworth* (revised A. de Selincourt, 1946), Oxford University Press, Oxford.

Zeisel, J. (1981). *Inquiry by Design: Tools for Environmental-Behavior Research*, Brooks-Cole, Monterey, California.

3 A Computational View of Design Creativity

William J. Mitchell

This chapter explores the interrelationships between intending, seeing, and doing in design. It argues that design intentions evolve through the course of a creative design process, that these intentions determine how emergent shapes in drawings will be recognized, interpreted, and reinterpreted, and that interpretation (and reinterpretation) of emergent shapes plays a crucial role in directing design explorations. Traditional computer-aided design systems do not effectively support creative design because they provide only very limited and inflexible ways of interpreting shapes. Computer-aided design systems can, however, be developed on an alternative foundation that provides the necessary flexibility.

3.1 Creativity

'Creative' design appears to be a residual category: it encompasses all the things that designers do for which we cannot specify an effective and efficient mechanism. This presents a paradox. Any successful attempt to describe the mechanics of some 'creative' design activity will have the immediate effect of redefining that activity as 'noncreative'. The more success we have, the more we can be accused of dealing only with the noncreative aspects of design. Undaunted by this, my aim here is to reduce the residue—not to nothing, but to something rather smaller than it is usually taken to be.

3.2   The process of designing

First, some definitions. *Designing* is a complex cultural activity, and often becomes a practice (in something close to the religious sense of this term) that can offer profound personal satisfactions, but for our purposes here I simply want to consider it instrumentally—as the computation of shape and material information that is needed to guide fabrication or construction of an artifact. This information normally specifies artifact topology (connections of vertices, edges, surfaces, and closed volumes), dimensions, angles, and tolerances on dimensions and angles. In addition, symbols may be associated with subshapes to specify material properties.

Sometimes material properties are taken as given, and a designer is concerned solely with shape. Sometimes (as in materials design) shape is irrelevant. And sometimes a designer may be expected to provide more than shape and material information—to specify the details of a construction process, for example. But I shall take it that the usual outcome is a specification of shapes and materials.

The process of designing takes different forms in different contexts, but the most usual computational operations are transformations (unary operations) and combinations (binary operations) of shapes in a two-dimensional drawing or three-dimensional geometric model. An initial vocabulary of shapes, together with a repertoire of shape transformation and combination operators, establishes the shape algebra within which the computation takes place (Mitchell, 1990a).

The computation terminates successfully when it can be shown that certain predicates are satisfied by a shape produced by recursively applying the transformation and combination operators to the initial vocabulary. These predicates are normally stated in symbolic (verbal or numerical) form. Thus determination of whether a predicate is satisfied usually involves producing a numerical or verbal interpretation of a drawing, then deriving inferences from this interpretation by applying rules or formulae (Mitchell, 1990a).

Distinctions are frequently drawn between well-defined and ill-defined design problems, and between routine and nonroutine design processes. Different theorists have formulated these distinctions in different ways, but they basically have to do with the assumptions that we can reasonably make about stability and monotonicity. A well-defined design problem is usually thought to be one in which a given shape vocabulary and repertoire of shape operators jointly determine the domain of formal possibilities that is to be explored, the requirements for a solution (that is, the predicates to be satisfied) are predetermined, and there is a test that can be applied to establish whether a given formal possibility satisfies these requirements. Assumptions of monotonicity—that the axioms structuring a design problem are consistent and stable—are usually an important factor in making a problem well-defined (Mitchell, 1990b). Solution of a well-defined problem of a known type (sizing a steel beam, say) is routine when we have an adequately efficient algorithm for producing formal possibilities that satisfy the requirements: We merely apply the algorithm to what we know in order to get what we want.

On the other hand, a design problem (such as 'design a house for a poet on a rocky bluff') is ill-defined in respect of the domain of possibilities when new vocabulary elements and operators may be introduced at any time, or established ones may be forgotten, so that there is no fixed set of design variables to consider. And the problem is ill-defined in respect of the solution criteria when the requirements are not predetermined, the nature of a 'solution' is ambiguous or controversial, and there is no clear way of telling whether a given proposal really is a 'solution.' Such problems typically cannot be solved in a routine way, because production of a solution cannot be separated from formulation of the problem—making it difficult or impossible to tell whether a given algorithm will do the job. A solution is interesting not just because it shows a way of satisfying some requirements, but because it crystallizes and expresses some intentions. Production of an interesting solution to an ill-defined design problem (presumably by nonroutine means) is usually thought of as a creative act—a valuable contribution to culture.

3.3 Describing and manipulating shape

Traditionally, architects and other designers have used drawings as the primary vehicle for creative design: They produce drawn ideas for consideration, then discuss and analyze them. In recent decades, computer-aided design systems have replaced hand-drawing techniques in many of the routine aspects of design, but they have not proven capable of providing effective support for creative design. Designers tend to develop ideas through hand sketching, then use a computer-aided design system for recording and developing established concepts. Technophobia is, no doubt, partially responsible for this pattern. But a more fundamental difficulty lies in the way that computer-aided design systems describe and manipulate shapes. Let us consider this.

A computer drafting system (or three-dimensional modeling system) models some shape algebra in essentially the same way that a four-function electronic calculator models the familiar algebra of real numbers. The calculator's display shows a number in the set of numbers that carries the numerical algebra, and the drafting system's display shows a shape in the set of shapes that carry the shape algebra. The calculator's keyboard provides a set of operators (addition, subtraction, multiplication, division) for manipulating numbers, and the drafting system's menu provides a set of operators for manipulating shapes (insertion, deletion, translation, rotation, and so on). The calculator is useful because we can employ numbers to represent balances in bank accounts, or areas of rooms, and we can then employ operations on numbers to represent operations on bank accounts or rooms. The drafting system is useful because we can use shapes to represent spaces and construction components, and we can then employ operations on shapes to represent operations on those entities. For this to work, however, it is essential that the formal properties of the algebra that is modeled correspond appropriately to the structure of the situation that we wish to represent (Stiny, 1990b).

The standard approach to formalization and computer implementation of a shape algebra was developed in the earliest days of computer-aided design. It is founded on the idea that a straight line segment can be described by the coordinates of its endpoints. A shape can thus be described as a set of lines, or equivalently as a set of vertex coordinate pairs or triples together with a relation of connection in that set. Basic editing operations follow directly: Lines can be added by specifying and associating endpoints, and deleted by disassociating endpoints. It also follows that translation, rotation, reflection, scaling, shearing, and perspective transformations can be performed by multiplication of coordinate vectors by transformation matrices. This idea provided a foundation for Ivan Sutherland's pioneering Sketchpad system, and a quarter of a century later it is still the basis of popular computer drafting systems such as Autocad.

The idea of describing a geometric element by specifying its boundaries can be generalized (Mitchell, 1991). Just as a zero-dimensional points bound one-dimensional lines, so one-dimensional lines bound two-dimensional surfaces, and two-dimensional surfaces bound three-dimensional solids. This insight provides the basis for the data structures of surface modeling systems and solid modeling systems, with their extended sets of editing operations— sweeping to create surfaces, and the spatial set operations on closed solids.

This provides a basis for parsing and interpreting a drawing. The drawing is treated as a set of geometric primitives (lines, surfaces, or solids), and subshapes are thus subsets of primitives. A structural description of the drawing can then be produced by picking out and classifying subshapes and specifying their relationships. Interpretation becomes a matter of establishing the references of subshapes and considering their relationships. A CAD system may automatically produce interpretations of various kinds by reporting from a database structured in this way, by applying analysis procedures to data extracted from the database, or by performing inference based on extracted facts.

In a retrospective article, Sutherland (1975) suggested that "the usefulness of computer drawings is precisely their structured nature." The behavior of such drawings, he noted, "is critically dependent upon the topological and geometric structure built up in the computer memory as a result of drawing operations." Traditional drawings, by contrast, have no inherent structure, and are merely 'dirty marks on paper'.

3.4 Maintaining structure

It is a short step from recognition that structure is important to the idea that a CAD system should automatically *maintain* specified aspects of topological and geometric structure (and hence preserve some interpretation derived from that structure) as a designer manipulates a geometric model. If a designer shifts an element, for example, neighboring elements should be adjusted to maintain specified alignments and attachments. (If a column is moved, a beam that it supports might be correspondingly lengthened, so preserving an interpretation of the assembly as a frame capable of supporting a roof.) Sutherland introduced the idea of constraints that could be specified by a designer and thereafter maintained by a CAD system. Eastman (1978) later explored it in the context of three-dimensional solid modelers. More recently the idea of generalized constraint programming languages has emerged (Leler, 1988), and has found some application in computer-aided design. Gross (1990) has implemented an interesting prototype CAD system built around concepts of constraint maintenance.

The idea of modeling in terms of geometric elements, combined with maintenance of explicitly-specified relationships between elements, proved to be a useful and durable one. But its inherent limitations began to show up when attempts were made to use CAD systems for design exploration, rather than just representation of completed designs.

3.5 Emergent shapes

First, the structure that a designer puts into a drawing or geometric model by virtue of input operations is a limiting one. The only subshapes that it allows the designer to indicate or manipulate are subsets of the elements. Emergent subshapes are, from the computer's viewpoint, unrecognizable. Designers, however, frequently recognize emergent subshapes, and subsequently structure their understanding of the design and their reasoning about it in terms of emergent entities and relationships—ones that they never explicitly input. (It has been shown (Finke, 1989) that emergent subshapes can be recognized even when shapes are *mentally* combined.) When this happens there is a mismatch between the way that a CAD system is explicitly structuring the design and the way that the designer is implicitly structuring it, so the explicit structure becomes a hindrance rather than a help.

Consider, for example, a forty-five degree right triangle. Addition of just one straight line produces a shape containing three such triangles (the original one plus two smaller ones). If the figure is described, in the usual way, as a set of four lines (one vertical, one horizontal and two diagonal) specified by their endpoint coordinates, then the large right triangle can be recognized by looking for subsets of lines in appropriate relationship but the two smaller ones cannot. The large triangle can be selected and transformed but the small ones cannot. The problem is not solved by restructuring the description as a set of six lines—a horizontal, a vertical, and four short diagonals meeting at a point. This move certainly makes the small triangles recognizable as subsets of three lines, but it turns the original large triangle into a four-sided figure.

The difficulty can be overcome by equipping a CAD system with operators not only for instantiating shapes from some vocabulary, but also for recognizing emergent instances of shapes in that vocabulary (Stiny, 1989; Stiny, 1990a; Tan, 1990; Nagakura, 1990). This allows the designer not only to put instances into a drawing, but also to get them out—perhaps in unexpected ways. (Recognition is the converse of instantiation, and the two play a complementary role in many intellectual processes.) Thus the designer can restructure and reinterpret drawings through application of the recognition operators. Recognized emergent instances can be selected and transformed, their structure can be maintained as the drawing is edited, and their properties and relationships can be analyzed. Analysis of the two emergent triangles might, for example, yield their areas and the fact that their areas are equal.

Recognition operators must, however, be applied selectively or combinatorial explosion will result. Consider, for example, the squares that emerge from the overlay of four horizontal lines on four vertical lines. There are nine one-by-one squares, four two-by-twos, and one three-by-three. Clearly this sort of thing can rapidly get out of hand.

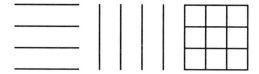

Furthermore, recognition operators can be applied in different sequences to yield different hierarchies of subshapes within subshapes. Let us suppose, for example, that we have recognition operators for the following:

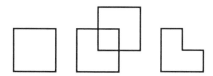

We might apply them to decompose the three-by-three square grid into two overlapping subshapes as follows:

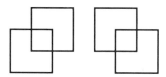

Then we might decompose each of these subshapes either into two squares or into two L-shapes.

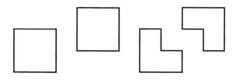

This yields a variety of alternative hierarchical decompositions such as the following:

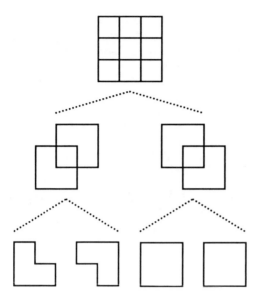

In other words, a drawing typically has many possible structural descriptions in terms of instances from a given shape vocabulary and relationships of those instances. The instantiation operations performed by the user of a CAD system to construct a drawing have the effect of picking out one of these descriptions, but there is no strong reason to believe that this is the most appropriate one for a designer's purposes. Recognition operators can be applied to produce other structural descriptions. Production of the right structural description for the design task at hand is a crucial design act.

An impatient practical man might reply that this is all very well, but indecisiveness about structural description is just a bad thing—precisely the sort of sloppiness that a CAD system, built on sound engineering principles, should root out. You should just take the commonsense course of deciding what a thing is, assigning it an appropriate structure, and sticking with that. But design is not description of what *is*, it is exploration of what *might be*. Drawings are valuable precisely because they are rich in suggestions of what might be. To blind oneself to these suggestions by imposing a rigid, Procrustean structure on a drawing is to impoverish the creative imagination.

In sum, the meaning of a drawing is not adequately captured by imposing *one* structure on it. The last thing that I want, as a designer, is a clanking mechanism doggedly maintaining some structure that is, for me, irrelevant and forgotten. Perhaps an analogy with word processing will make this clear. It would be absurd if your word processor allowed you to change *Time flies like an arrow* into *Time flies like a boomerang* but not (because of the syntax that you had assigned to the sentence by virtue of your input actions) into *Australian flies like a sheep.* Maintenance of structure is useless, and perhaps actively detrimental, unless a system also provides for convenient, fluid restructuring, and for parallel maintenance of alternative structures.

A further twist is given to the problem if different designers operate on the same representation—a possibility that is often claimed as an important advantage of CAD systems. What if they all see a shape as different things? What if some of them are 'aspect-blind', and cannot see the shape as others see it? (Wittgenstein raised the question of aspect-blindness in *Philosophical Investigations* (1968), and suggested that the aspect-blind would have "an altogether different relationship to pictures from ours.") What if, by virtue of the particular structure that it imposes, the CAD system itself is significantly aspect-blind?

3.6 Instability and discontinuity in structural description

The effect of allowing variation in a drawing's structural description is most dramatically illustrated by so-called ambiguous figures, such as the famous one that can be seen either as a rabbit or as a duck (but not both at once). More 'creatively' it can also be seen as a front elevation of an asymmetrical Cyclops (if that sort of thing is in your shape vocabulary). Which structure should be assigned and maintained—that of a rabbit, that of a duck, or that of a Cyclops?

Ambiguous figures might be dismissed as bizarre anomalies but, in fact, any figure has potential competing readings, and can become unstable once these are pointed out to us (that is, once we are equipped with the necessary recognition operators). (There is, it should be noted, a substantial psychological literature on alternative structural descriptions of figures and the roles that these play in cognition (Hinton, 1979; Kosslyn et al., 1983; Palmer, 1977).) The following, for example, can be seen as two large triangles, or as four small triangles, or as two parallelograms, or as a pair of vertical bowties, or as a diamond bracketed by an epsilon and a reflected epsilon, or in many other ways as well, and we can force our minds to oscillate between these possibilities (Reed, 1974; Stiny, 1989).

Notice that the variety of possible structural descriptions, and hence the degree of instability of a figure, depends on the richness of the shape vocabulary that is brought to bear. If the vocabulary only includes triangles, for example, there are few ways to describe this figure. But if the vocabulary expands to include parallelograms, bowties, diamonds, epsilons, X-shapes, V-shapes, and W-shapes, then the possibilities grow dramatically.

3.7   Shape recognition as constraint imposition

Application of a recognition operator assigns a shape to a class. That is, it implicitly establishes which of the shape's properties are to be taken as essential and therefore maintained during design manipulations (if the shape is not unintentionally to become a thing of another kind), and which of its properties are to be taken as accidental and therefore subject to variation. Thus, in effect, it imposes a set of constraints on parametric variation of the shape.

If you classify the following object as a square, for example, you may translate, rotate, reflect, and scale it, but you cannot change its proportions without turning it into a nonsquare. If you see it as a rectangle you may change its proportions without violating your conception of it, but not its vertex angles. If you just see it as four lines you can shift and resize these lines in any way that you want.

Conversely, if you translate, rotate, reflect, or scale this object you are tacitly treating it as a square. If you scale it unequally you are treating it as a rectangle. If you shear it you are treating it as a parallelogram, and if you otherwise shift and resize the lines you are just treating it as a line figure. You may want to treat it in different ways at different moments.

Different decompositions of a shape lead to different treatments. We noted earlier, for example, that the following can be seen either as two squares or as two L-shapes:

Thus translating the top subshape one module leftward can produce either of the following results:

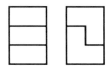

The implication for CAD systems is that application of different shape recognition operators should evoke different sets of shape transformation operators—the sets of transformation operators that are closed in the types in question. This induces development and refinement of designs in different directions. What can you make out of this next shape by transforming its parts?

It should depend, first of all, on what you take the parts to be. Are they triangles, parallelograms, or diamonds, and epsilons?

Furthermore, it should depend on what you take as their essential properties and relationships. If we treat the shape as two triangles, are these just triangles, or are they isosceles triangles with collinear axes?

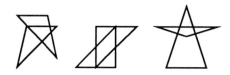

3.8   Restructuring search spaces

This arrangement allows the search spaces explored by designers to be re-structured freely in a way that seems characteristic of creative design investigation (but not of traditional CAD systems). Consider, for example, an exploration that begins with a shape like an exacto knife blade, and is structured by a shape vocabulary that includes blade-shapes, squares, and right triangles.

We might start by copying and applying isometric transformations to produce a composition of blade-shapes—for example, a pinwheel as follows:

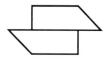

Then we might flip, rotate, and copy the whole thing, preserving the symmetry, so that a square and two right triangles emerge.

Next we might rescale the emergent right triangles to fit within the emergent square.

Finally, we might double the sizes of the corner squares to produce an interesting plan *parti*—one that contains no blade-shapes, but which interlocks squares and right triangles in a tight structure of clear and simple relationships.

Clearly we cannot describe this process (in the way that conventional CAD systems assume to be appropriate) as one in which the design is represented as a set of shape primitives, and new states of the design are produced by applying operators from some fixed repertoire to primitives and subsets of primitives. The search space is restructured whenever we focus our attention on some newly emergent subshape. This often happens when some kind of singularity develops, so that something new suddenly seems to crystallize: lines become collinear, lines reduce to points, lines cross over each other or separate, higher degrees of symmetry appear, and so on.

3.9   Recognition and replacement

Recognition should also control the application of shape replacement rules, and hence the way that a design is developed by transforming and combining shapes. The following rules, for example, specify that squares can be replaced by circles and L-shapes by triangles.

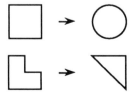

They might be applied to the following shape:

Depending on how this shape is decomposed into squares and L-shapes by application of recognition operators, and on the sequence of replacement rule applications, any of the following shapes can result:

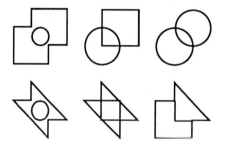

These are all expressions in the same shape language, in the sense that they are all produced from the same initial shape by recursive application of the same set of shape replacement rules. This can be demonstrated by reversing the generative rules, so that they become reduction rules, and applying them to reduce these shapes back to the initial shape.

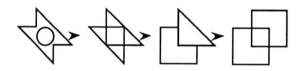

3.10   Shape grammars

The shape replacement rules of a shape grammar relate what you can recognize to what you can get: *if* you can recognize in a drawing an instance of a shape that appears on the left side of a shape replacement rule, *then* you can get what appears on the right side by applying the rule. A CAD system can support design within the language specified by a shape grammar by providing recognition operators for shapes that appear on the left sides of rules and instantiation operators for shapes that appear on the right sides.

Think of the right sides of shape rules as subgoals—shapes that you may want to achieve in a design because you value their formal or functional qualities. (Note the similarity to Christopher Alexander's (1977) well-known idea of 'patterns' that should be achieved in designs.) These right-side shapes *depict* rather than *state* what is wanted, but the difference is not fundamental: The interpretation of a shape can be extended to include any functions or predicates of the shape that might be of interest, so you can state subgoals in terms of values achieved or predicates satisfied if you wish.

In the development of a design, you have *put* yourself in a position to achieve a subgoal when a shape rule with the appropriate right side is executable—has a left side that matches something in the drawing. You can *see* that you are in a position to achieve a subgoal when you can recognize in the drawing an instance of the left side of an appropriate rule (just as a chess player may see that she is in a position to achieve a checkmate by recognizing a configuration of pieces that allows this through selection of an appropriate move). A CAD system can potentially *tell you* that you are in such a position by automatically recognizing and reporting that the left side of an appropriate rule can be matched in the drawing.

The different designs in the language specified by a shape grammar achieve different combinations of subgoals. We can regard design within the framework of such a language as search for combinations of subgoal achievement that match the designer's intentions. These combinations may be achieved in complex and unexpected ways by overlapping emergent shapes. If the shape grammar is not arbitrary, but encodes practical knowledge of how things must be put together in order to work properly, it will structure that search by establishing what combinations are, in fact, possible. A designer might want to find out, for example, whether a particular set of area and adjacency requirements is consistent with a symmetrical plan, or whether a particular choice of structural system can be reconciled with the need for a basement parking structure. These questions can be explored by attempting to find designs that simultaneously achieve all the relevant subgoals. Such designs may or may not turn out to exist within the language. If they do not, then the designer is faced with the meta-problem of specifying a new or extended language that captures what is needed within its net.

3.11 Formation of intentions

This assumes, of course, that you know what you want before you set out to get it. But this is not always the case in design: Intentions may be very vague at the outset, then may evolve and sharpen as the design process unfolds. When you work in this 'window-shopping' mode, the rules applicable at any point present a range of things that can be achieved. By choosing one, and not another, you define what you value. As economists are fond of pointing out, we express values by making choices among alternatives.

Emergent shapes and conditions may structure unexpected alternatives for consideration as a design develops. You might never have imagined something that suddenly shows up, but once you see it you can decide whether or not you want it. A sequence of such choices results in a design that may be regarded as a complex assertion of what you value—a set of stands on the issues as they have presented themselves. If viewers of the design know something of the language to which it belongs they will be able to understand this assertion—hence much of the cultural importance that we attach to designs.

When shape grammars are related to design intentions in this way, you can regard the right sides of the shape rules as an exhaustive summary of all of the things that you might want to achieve (temporarily or permanently) as you develop a design. This is too much to think about all at once. Conversely, you can think of the left sides of the rules as an exhaustive summary of all the conditions that might merit your attention. This is also too much. You need some way to sort out the relatively few rules that are relevant to your goals and interests at a particular moment from the many more that are not.

This issue can be attacked from both sides. First, the system can refer to the current structural description of the drawing to find what shape types have been recognized in it, then can automatically deactivate all the rules that do not have currently recognizable shape types on their left sides. (These rules will not be applicable anyway.) Secondly, if right sides of shape rules are classified by the sorts of subgoals that they achieve (e.g., symmetry, structural support and so on), and the system maintains a list of currently interesting subgoals, it can automatically deactivate all the rules that do not achieve interesting subgoals. (These rules will not get you to where you want to be.) The remaining rules will link the things to which you have (for the moment) decided to pay attention to the things that you currently want to achieve.

3.12   Syntax-directed graphic editing

A CAD system structured to handle emergent form in the way that I have now outlined would have the capacity to support extremely efficient syntax-directed graphic editing. The style of interaction might be something like the following:

A goal shape is selected from among those on the right sides of the shape rules in the system's repertoire, then a selection rectangle is moved freely around the drawing. If instances of the goal shape already exist within the selection window (perhaps as emergent shapes) then these are recognized and presented for consideration. If no such instances exist, or if those that do exist are somehow unsatisfactory, then the system looks for matches to the left side of the rule that produces the goal shape, applies the rule wherever matches are found, and presents the results for consideration. If no satisfactory instances are produced in this way, then the system tries sequences of rule applications (to some specified depth limit) in an effort to produce what is required. This is goal-directed design.

The alternative mode is context-directed design. In this mode, the system looks for all the places within the selection window that a shape rule may be applied. (That is, it looks for matches to the left sides of rules.) Then it enumerates, and presents for consideration, possible ways to develop this part of the design by applying sequences of shape rules.

Constraint maintenance can be integrated by allowing any instance of a goal shape to be identified as one that must be preserved (that is, its essential properties maintained) as shapes in the drawing are transformed and replaced.

3.13 Conclusion

Design is a matter of the hand, the eye, and the knowledge and intentions relating the actions of the two. Traditional CAD systems have concentrated on automating the work of the hand. I have proposed that it is equally important to automate the work of the eye, and shown how this capability may be integrated into a CAD system. Creative design depends not only on the *coup de main*, but also on the *coup d'oeil*.

References

Alexander, C. (1977). *A Pattern Language*, Oxford University Press, New York.

Eastman, C. M. (1978). The representation of design problems and maintenance of their structure, *in* J.-C. Latombe (Ed.), *Artificial Intelligence and Pattern Recognition in Computer-Aided Design*, North-Holland, Amsterdam.

Finke, R. A. (1989). *Principles of Mental Imagery*, MIT Press, Cambridge, Mass.

Gross, M. (1990). Relational modeling—a basis for computer-assisted design, *in* M. McCullough, W. J. Mitchell, & P. Purcell (Eds), *The Electronic Design Studio*, MIT Press, Cambridge, Mass.

Hinton, G. E. (1979). Some demonstrations of the effects of structural descriptions in mental imagery, *Cognitive Science* **3**: 231–250.

Kosslyn, S. M., Reiser B. J., Farah, M. J., & Fliegel, S. L. (1983). Generating visual images: units and relations, *Journal of Experimental Psychology: General* **112**: 278–303.

Leler, W. (1988). *Constraint Programming Languages*, Addison-Wesley, Reading, Mass.

Mitchell, W. J. (1990a). *The Logic of Architecture*, MIT Press, Cambridge, Mass.

Mitchell, W. J. (1990b). The uses of inconsistency in design, *in* Y. Kalay (Ed.), *Evaluating and Predicting Design Performance*, John Wiley, New York.

Mitchell, W. J. (1991). Uses in Architecture, *The Macmillan Encyclopedia of Computers*, Macmillan, New York (in press).

Nagakura, T. (1990). Shape recognition and transformation—a script-based approach, *in* M. McCullough, W. J. Mitchell, & P. Purcell (Eds), *The Electronic Design Studio*, MIT Press, Cambridge, Mass.

Palmer, S. E. (1977). Hierarchical structure in perceptual representation, *Cognitive Psychology* **9**: 441–474.

Reed, S. K. (1974). Structural descriptions and the limitations of visual images, *Memory and Cognition* **2**: 329–336.

Stiny, G. (1989). What is a design? *in* C. Yessios (Ed.), *ADADIA 89 Proceedings: New Ideas and Directions for the 1990s*, University of Florida, Gainsville.

Stiny, G. (1990a). What designers do that computers should, *in* M. McCullough, W. J. Mitchell, & P. Purcell (Eds), *The Electronic Design Studio*, MIT Press, Cambridge, Mass.

Stiny, G. (1990b). The Algebras of Design, *Unpublished manuscript*, Graduate School of Architecture and Urban Planning, University of California Los Angeles.

Sutherland, I. E. (1975). Structure in drawings and the hidden-surface problem, *in* N. Negroponte (Ed.), *Reflections on Computer Aids to Design and Architecture*, Petrocelli/Charter, New York.

Tan, M. (1990). Saying what it is by what it is like, *in* M. McCullough, W. J. Mitchell, & P. Purcell (Eds), *The Electronic Design Studio*, MIT Press, Cambridge, Mass.

Wittgenstein, L. (1968). *Philosophical Investigations*, Basil Blackwell, Oxford.

4 Emergent Value in Creative Products: Some Implications for Creative Processes

Sally McLaughlin

In this chapter it is proposed that the key to understanding the nature of creative processes lies in investigating the nature of creative products. Emergent value is identified as a necessary condition of creative products. The implications of this requirement of product in relation to creative processes are explored. It is proposed that a necessary condition of a process that can in itself be called creative, is recognition of emergent value. An argument is presented for the separation of generation and recognition processes.

4.1 Introduction

For some time now there has existed a belief among design professionals, particularly in the area of architectural design, that attempts to formalize the design process in terms of logical operations or computational techniques fail to capture what is really going on in the development of a designed product. This attitude arises, at least in part, from the perceived incapacity of such formal systems to yield creative outcomes. An implicit objective of much design activity is the development of a creative outcome. The highest achievements of most design disciplines are those products acknowledged to be creative. Even the lesser achievements within those disciplines seem to be the products of processes that lie beyond those that have been characterized as routine. If formal or computable systems do fail to yield creative outcomes then their applicability as models of design activity must be seriously questioned.

Determining whether or not formal models or computational models can yield creative products is far from straight forward. Part of the problem lies in the diversity, inconsistency, and incompleteness between and within various theories of creativity. Another part of the problem lies in the degree of contention that surrounds attempts to characterize the limits of computational and even formal logic based models. This contention is reflected in often encountered claims that current limitations will be met by the development of better representations, the provision of more information or the development of more powerful computers.

Within artificial intelligence and computer-aided design research questions of creativity typically focus on questions of originality. The reason for this would seem primarily to be that there is a general perception that the outcome of computational processes are not creative and are not original. The effect is essentially a definition of creativity by exclusion—current computational models do not produce creative products, current computational models do not produce original products, therefore the key to creativity must lie in an ability to produce original products. One of the implications of this view is that creative processes become a moving target, as computable models of various processes are developed, belief that these processes embody fundamental aspects of creativity declines. This may be seen most recently in the development of computational models of analogical reasoning and parallel distributed processing.

In this chapter we present a fundamentally different view of the nature of creative processes. We start by arguing that developing any understanding of what is meant by the term creative rests on the development of an understanding of the nature of creative products. We then attempt to underscore the fact that a creative product must be both original and valuable. The requirement of value in a creative product implies a dependence on existing values, attitudes, and knowledge. The requirement of originality imposes a constraint that the value embodied in the product cannot be fully stated at the outset of the process of developing that product. If this were not the case the valuable aspects of the product in itself would be known. We refer to the value that presents itself only during the course of the development of a creative product as emergent value. We attempt to characterize emergent value emphasizing the fact that it is grounded in but not identical to existing knowledge and that it is societally determined and subject to change.

This elaboration of the kind of originality required in a creative product paves the way for the presentation of an argument for a subtle but important shift in the way that we characterize creative processes. The only necessary conditions of a creative process are recognition of emergent value and a generation process that is not circumscribed to the extent that the value of its outcomes is predefined. Thus processes such as mechanical generation may yield candidate creative outcomes. The problem from a computational point of view lies in recognizing the original value of those outcomes.

The issue of the computability of creative processes hinges on the question of whether of not we can develop adequate models or approximations of the way that societies evaluate newly presented information. The issue is not so much one of the development of sophisticated generation techniques, as it is one of the development of a capacity to model human value judgements, to automate aesthetics. Although issues such as these must remain unresolved, it is clear that we are a long way from developing such capabilities.

Finally we return to the question of what the implications are, in terms of the utility of formal models and computational models in relation to design activity, if they cannot in themselves yield creative products. First the separation of generation and evaluation processes creates the possibility of using computational techniques in the generation phase while delegating recognition of emergent value to the user. The viability of such an arrangement would be dependent on the perceived benefits to be gained by actually attempting to separate the development of a product into distinct generation and evaluation phases. Research issues would include the identification of appropriate processes for use in specified circumstances. Second, there may be some benefit to be gained from developing computable post facto accounts of the development of creative products from related information. Such exercises may be useful in identifying the scope and limitations of computational techniques. Third, there is considerable scope for the development of support environments for the human user engaged in the development of a creative product. Evaluation of a product requires visualization of the product and the implications of that product. Graphic simulation and other computable simulation models may contribute significantly in this regard. Some aspects of the evaluation of a product may be able to be approximated by computable models. Finally support may be given to the generation of proposals through the provision of convenient editing facilities, and databases of potentially relevant information gleaned from existing artifacts.

4.2   Defining the term *creative*: Product, process or person

Common use of the term creative is such that it is applied to products, processes, and people. We are primarily concerned with identifying the nature of creative processes, however there is some contention as to whether the term *creative* can properly be applied to processes at all. We consider the assumptions that lie behind each of the various uses of the term with the objective of showing that some necessary if not sufficient conditions may be established for processes that may properly be called creative.

Adopting an etymological approach to the definition of the words *creative* and *creativity*, leads back through the root *create* to *make*. The implications of emphasizing this association, most clearly articulated by Gotz (1981), may be described as follows:

1. Creativity is a form of making and is thus a public activity as distinct from private mental activities. It is not about the thoughts, feelings, or mental processes of the creator but about concretization.

2. Creativity is about an act, the act of making, it is about process rather than product. A proviso should be added here. Mitias (1978), pointed out that create, although a verb and thus referring to action, is an achievement verb. In order for a person to create he must achieve results and these results must be encountered in the finished product.

3. Creativity is about the act of making rather than the capacity to act.

4. It is sufficient to make a product in order to be creative. Originality is not a necessary requirement of creativity.

5. Only the results of deliberate manufacture should be considered to be creative.

The unintended fortuitous results of action should not be regarded as creative. Clearly an etymological account of the meaning of the terms *creative* and *creativity* fails to capture the special qualities implied by these terms, the most fundamental of these being the requirement of originality in the final product (Hausman, 1981). It is interesting to note that despite Gotz's insistence that originality of product should not be a condition of a person's being regarded as creative, he went on to define creativity as "the process of deliberately concretizing insight." Insight would seem redundant if originality were not required.

We have briefly presented the etymological argument in order to illustrate that the term *creative* has acquired a meaning that is distinct from its origin.

Use of the word *creative* implies products, processes, and persons possessing special qualities. It is precisely the identification of such qualities in which we are interested. Our attention should therefore be directed towards the use of the term rather than its origin. In particular, arguments about the status of the verb create in relation to product and process are irrelevant.

One of the most influential characterizations of creative processes, particularly in experimental psychology, was originally proposed by Wallas in 1924. Wallas (1970) identified four stages within the creative process: preparation, incubation, illumination, and verification. Preparation is characterized by conscious investigation of a problem and includes the entire process of education. Incubation is an unconscious working out of ideas, often accompanied by time spent away from the problem. Illumination is defined as the sudden appearance of a new idea together with the psychological events that immediately preceded and accompanied that event. Verification is similar to preparation, involving conscious regulated thought rather than the wild ranging of ideas that characterizes incubation. Beardsley (1965) criticized the notion that these stages are distinct. Current proponents of the theory allow interaction between stages (Armbruster, 1989).

Other characterizations of the creative process have focussed on the issue of control, and more specifically on the nature of control in art. Here a distinction is drawn between finalistic and propulsive theories. The finalistic theory is essentially a means-ends view where the artist works towards a preexisting vision of the final product (Ecker, 1963). This theory includes definitions of art as clarifying emotion (Collingwood, 1938). The propulsive theory, by way of contrast, advocates that control is exercised by means of critical assessment at each stage of the developing work (Tomas, 1958; Beardsley, 1965). Beardsley highlighted the distinction between the two views in the following explication of the nature of the propulsive theory:

> as the poet moves from stage to stage, it is not that he is looking to see whether he is saying what he already meant, but he is looking to see whether he wants to mean what he is saying.

Khatchadourian (1977) suggested that Beardsley and Tomas differ in the nature of the control that they advocate. Tomas spoke of control manifested in the fact that the artist "can say that certain directions are not right." Beardsley suggested that the exercise of control is accomplished by comparison of an addition to the work as it stood before, accepting the addition if it improves the work, rejecting it otherwise. This distinction between negative and positive modes of control seems arbitrary, and Beardsley obviously intended to encompass Tomas's account. Khatchadourian suggested that there is evidence of the use of both finalistic and propulsive views in the development of art works and suggested that many variants exist between the two extremes.

Popular works on creativity, such as Koestler's (1964) *The Act of Creation* and de Bono's (1967) *The Use of Lateral Thinking*, have drawn a distinction between the type of thought that makes creativity possible and 'normal' thought. Koestler characterized creativity as the intersection of two normally distinct matrices of thought. de Bono distinguished between vertical thinking and the domination of particular concepts, and lateral thinking, which recognizes and moves away from dominant concepts. Rothenberg (1979) presented a similar but perhaps more restrictive theory, suggesting that creative thought stems from either simultaneous opposition, referred to as Janusian thinking, or the conception of two or more discrete entities occupying the same space, referred to as homospatial thinking.

Partly in reaction to those that attempt to distinguish creative processes from normal thought processes, Weisberg (1986), Hebb and Donderi (1987), Murray (1986) and Schön (1969), are among those that insist that the processes that make creative achievements possible permeate much of our thinking, although they differ in their accounts. Weisberg essentially maintained that creativity is problem solving and that the difficulty lies in acquiring the right information to work with. Hebb and Donderi suggested that creativity, or insight, is a function of mediating processes, that lead to the recombination of ideas to produce new ideas. They cited as examples of activities that require the function of such mediating processes the monkey who uses a stick to reach otherwise inaccessible food, or the dog that must take an indirect route to reach food that he can see through a fence, illustrating the necessity of certain types of experience, that is, the use of sticks in play (but not for retrieval), or experience of barriers in solving these problems. They extended this argument to suggest that activity based on indirect experience of relevant information permeates human thought. Murray presented an argument, based on the philosophy of Hiedegger, that our world is essentially a world of our making, that all perception requires imaginative thinking. Creative thought is thus fundamental to the construction of a mental world that makes any thinking possible. Schön argued in a similar vein but was more explicit about what he believed to be the nature of 'normal' thought that makes creativity possible. He suggested that the tendency to visualize concepts as abstract templates that allow us to determine whether or not individual items are instances of that concept is inappropriate. He suggests that any notion of a concept is grounded in individual experiences and that recognition of the applicability of a concept is by resemblance to individual experiences rather than conformity to some abstract type.

Given the degree of contention between the various characterizations of creative processes, is it possible to say anything conclusive about such processes? Does it even make sense to talk about the existence of a creative process? As an initial step towards addressing these questions we consider the basis on which these various theories have been developed.

In the introduction to his presentation of his preparation-incubation-illumination-verification model, Wallas addresses the problem of identifying aspects of creative thought:

> we take a single achievement of thought—the making of a new generalization or invention, or the poetical expression of a new idea—and ask how it was brought about.

Wallas's model appears to have been gleaned from introspective accounts of persons recognized for their creative achievements. He quotes Helmholtz, the eminent scientist, in the presentation of his ideas. It is interesting that Patrick (1937, 1935) attempted to investigate Wallas's model by (a) selecting person's acknowledged for their creative achievements—poets and artists versus a control group of nonpoets and nonartists; and (b) asking them to develop a product, a poem or drawing, given a picture/poem as subject and to talk out loud about their thoughts.[1]

If we turn our attention to Tomas's theory of artistic control the basis of the argument is somewhat different. Tomas's argument is a philosophical one based on the notion that a creative product must be original and valuable. Tomas explores the implications of the requirements of originality in a creative product in the following statement:

> When we congratulate an artist for being creative ... we congratulate him because he embodies in colors or in language something the like of which did not exist before, and because he was the originator of the rules he implicitly followed while he was painting or writing.

Both Ecker and Beardsley claim to have drawn on the introspective accounts of artists, coupled with examination of art works and the notes and sketches that accompanied their development.

Although the basis on which Koestler and de Bono arrived at their theories of creativity is not explicitly stated, the presentation of their ideas involves the use of information about the circumstances surrounding the

---

[1] Patrick concluded that these stages can in fact be distinguished. Beardsley (1965) however suggested that the material collected indicates the opposite—that all the activities are mixed together, that they are consistently (or alternately) going throughout the whole process.

development of significant inventions in the case of Koestler, and the solution of insight problems, in the case of de Bono. This suggests that their theories were gleaned primarily from consideration of product. Indeed an important criticism of de Bono's work is leveled at its use of insight problems in relation to discussions about creativity. Bailin (1988) observed that there is a fundamental difference between the insight problem that has a predetermined solution, and the situation with which artists, scientists, and others are faced prior to the development of creative products. Interestingly, Rothenberg appears to have developed his account of creative thought, primarily through discussions with a poet, over a three year period, about his dreams, thoughts and experiences, and an examination of the development of particular poems over that time. He extends the presentation of his ideas to include examination of the appropriateness of these ideas to introspective accounts of eminent scientists. For example, he links Einstein's conception of the dependence of electro-magnetic fields on the relative motion of electrons with respect to a magnetic field, to a janusian formulation of simultaneous antithesis, a simultaneous conception of motion and rest.

Weisberg drew heavily on the historical circumstances in which particular innovations, such as Watson's and Crick's discovery of the structure of DNA, took place. Hebb and Donderi, in their study of creativity in animals, compared the tools and conditions to which the animals have been exposed to their response to a new situation. Both Murray and Schön based their theories on introspective accounts of the processes involved in extending our knowledge. As such they concentrate on the relationship between that which is newly presented and that which is already known.

All the theories of process considered depend on reference to either introspective accounts of person's acknowledged for their creative achievements or investigation of the achievements and the circumstances surrounding those achievements themselves. This observation underscores the dependence of an examination of the nature of creative processes on a capacity to identify creative products or creative persons. The identification of processes that may be called creative presumes the capacity to identify creative persons or creative products.

The objective underlying much of the research relating to identification of creative persons seems to be the isolation of criteria that indicate a capacity to be creative. Early work in this area focused on individual cognitive abilities—in particular divergent thought (Guilford, 1967) and ideation fluency. The method employed seems to have been (a) the postulation that a particular cognitive ability has some correlation with creative ability, (b) the construction and execution of tests identifying this ability and (c) a comparison of the characteristics of the divisions that the tests yielded.

Bailin (1988) criticized this approach, pointing out that although such a procedure may reveal some internal consistencies, it indicated nothing about the cognitive abilities employed in the development of creative outcomes. In particular she argues that ideation fluency has little to do with achievements such as those of the author Dostoevtsky or Einstein. She stated that Dostoevtsky's work was characterized not so much by the generation of many combinations of words and images but by the development of particular combinations of words and images that have come to be highly valued. She argued similarly that Einstein's work was characterized not so much by the generation of many alternative theories but by the development of consistent and unifying theories. Mansfield and Busse (1981) claimed that there is not necessarily any correlation between divergent thinking, long touted as the principle indicator of creative capacity, and creative achievement. Hayes (1989) suggested that the key to overcoming the limitations of these types of investigations is to study the actual production of creative works. Hayes commented on the success of the Westinghouse science talent awards, run since 1942, in identifying young scientists that later went on to accomplish significant creative achievements. Interestingly, the awards were based on assessment of self-initiated projects rather than grades or IQ.

Another approach to establishing the nature of creative persons has been to study groups of people recognized for their creative achievements and look for the presence of characteristics common to members of such groups as opposed to members of noncreative control groups. Characteristics investigated have included IQ (Haensly and Reynolds, 1989), independence of thought, drive for originality and flexibility (Hayes, 1989). Alternatively biographical accounts of acknowledged creative achievers such as Einstein, Van Gogh, and Mozart have been examined in attempts to extract consistencies in personality or background. Bailin (1988) criticized such investigations on the basis that different endeavors require different personal attributes. Furthermore Hayes (1989) suggested external factors rather than inherent aspects of personality may contribute to personality traits such as low sociability, evident among scientists who spend long periods of time working in isolation.

We have seen that investigation into the nature of creative processes requires first a means of identifying creative people or creative products. Although early investigations into the nature of creative people seemed to neglect product, there seems to be a general awareness that these kinds of studies were inappropriate. Other strategies, of drawing on the biographical details of persons acknowledged for their creative achievements or looking for consistencies in the personalities of such persons, are explicitly dependent on identification of creative achievements, of creative products. Gotz (1981) criticized the use of the term *creative* to refer to a capacity stating that in applying the term *creative* to a person, we are typically referring to the potential of the person to achieve results of a particular order. Designation of the term may be based on observation of the results of the actions of that person but this is no guarantee that that person will continue to produce appropriate results. The only way in which the term *creative* can be properly applied to a person is in a retrospective sense, on the basis that they have in the past produced results that are regarded to be creative.

Classification of either a process or person as creative then, must start with a classification of product. It seems imperative that any definition of creativity must include a specification of the basis on which we judge a product to be creative. Consideration of the nature of creative products has its own problems. Creative products are societally defined. As societies change so do the products to which they apply the term *creative*. Furthermore there may exist considerable variation across those products that individuals regard to be creative. In the following section we attempt to characterize the use of the term *creative* in relation to products.

4.3   Emergent value in creative products

4.3.1   Originality and value

It is generally accepted that a creative product exhibits the quality of being original. Beardsley (1965) described creativity as the "power to summon into existence things hitherto unseen and even unthought." Pfieffer (1979) stated that for a piece of work to be properly called creative "requires first of all that it be to a significant extent new, original and unique."

Hausman (1985) correctly pointed out that the sense of originality must be restricted if it is to act as an adequate precondition for creativity. In particular, (a) objects that are new in the sense that all things are new, by the singularity of their location in space and time, but otherwise not significantly different from existing objects, should not be regarded as an original product in the sense implied, and (b) a product that is original in the trivial sense that it lacks resemblance to any existing thing, should be excluded from consideration. The sense of originality must be restricted in such a way as to ensure the unique value of the product introduced.

The requirement of value in a creative product introduces the need to consider the basis on which we assess the value of a product. The first point to be made is that value judgements are integrally linked to understanding. Newly presented information must be in some sense meaningful if we are to regard that information as valuable.

Research in the area of natural language understanding (Schank, 1982) has yielded important results with respect to the extent of the knowledge required to understand newly presented natural language sentences. Young (1987) indicated a similar dependence on existing knowledge in understanding visual information. If the value of a creative product is to be ascertained, consciously or unconsciously, it must be in terms of the existing knowledge of the processing system to which it is presented. The condition of originality, however, means that that relationship between the newly presented information and the existing knowledge cannot be one of identity.

What then is the relationship of the information presented in a creative product to that which is already known? We attempt to answer that question by consideration of a specific example. The example is taken from Beardsley (1965) a well known authority on art and aesthetics. It is particularly instructive as both product and criticism have been selected and presented.

Consider the following line from a Wordsworth sonnet:

> Dull would he be of soul, who could pass by
> A sight so touching in its majesty.

The critic, Knight (1963), offered the following evaluation of the contribution of this line of poetry:

> The peculiar pleasure of that last line—though the pleasure is independent of conscious recognition of the source—comes from the movement of mind by which we bring together in one apprehension 'touching' and 'majesty'; feelings and attitudes springing from our experience of what is young and vulnerable, that we should like to protect fuse with our sense of things towards which we feel awe, in respect of which it is we who are young, inexperienced or powerless.

The words *touching* and *majesty* both reinforce and conflict. Both words can be traced through thesaurus entries to the words *strength* and *power*. Similarly both words can be traced to the word *influence*. Majesty may be traced to words such as *dominate*, whereas touch may be traced to *reciprocate*. Here there is a conflict in the distribution of control implied by each of the words. *Majesty* has connotations of a biased distribution of control, touch of a much more balanced distribution. A second conflict arises from the sense of intimacy and scale associated with the two words. Majesty may be traced to words such as *endless, boundless*, and *measureless*; touch to *no distance, contiguity*, and *inseparable*.

Although we do not wish to trivialize the complexity of the process of understanding and appreciating poetry the aforementioned example serves to indicate the nature of some of the component processes involved. Our understanding of the line derives from our notion of the meaning of each of the words considered individually. The power of the line derives, in part, from the distinct set of relations and conflicts set up by the juxtaposition of the two words.

Recognition of the value of a creative product is thus dependent on a capacity to process the information presented in at product in terms of information that is already known. But clearly the process of establishing the value of a product involves more than the exercise of such a capacity. If this were not the case it would be expected that the greater the match with existing knowledge the more highly valued the newly presented information. As we have seen originality is fundamental to the concept of a creative product. We refer to this notion of value, that is dependent on but is not identical to existing knowledge, as *emergent value*. Furthermore we characterize recognition of emergent value as a function of the construction of a distinct set of relations between aspects of existing knowledge, facilitated by the presentation of a creative product.

4.3.2   The necessity of original value in a creative product

The term *emergent value* implies that the value of a creative product must be original. Surely it could be argued that the value of the product may be predefined and that it is sufficient for a creative product to be an original means of embodying that value.

Such an argument would be based on an artificial distinction between a product and the value of that product. In order to explore the integral relationship between a creative product and the value of such a product we consider three categories of creative products: new scientific theories; works of art; and inventions.

Kuhn (1970), in an examination of the way that new scientific theories are constructed and ultimately accepted, pointed out that the data that is attended to in the belief that it is relevant to a particular scientific enterprise, is very much theory driven. He examined the nature of natural histories, the fact gathering that occurs prior to the development of theories, highlighting the fact that such endeavors tend to produce a morass of information and may fail to include observations later deemed relevant in the light of accepted theories. Furthermore he strongly rejected the notion that new scientific theories are accepted or rejected on the basis of their capacity to explain available data. Kuhn suggested that new theories invariably fail to explain all the known data and that much of the relevant data can be collected only by the systematic and often detailed investigations that succeed the introduction of a new theory. If we accept the idea that ultimately the acceptance or rejection of a scientific theory is in a large part due to its perceived consistency with relevant data, we can see a strong temporal dependence between the product, the theory, and an aspect of its value, the data identified as being relevant to that theory.

If we turn our attention to works of art, a similar phenomena may be observed. Art criticism has a long history of attempts to formalize the basis on which the artistic or aesthetic quality of an artifact should be determined. It is generally accepted that such endeavors are inappropriate, that the appreciation and evaluation of a work of art can proceed only through individual evaluation of a given artifact.

The interdependence of an individual artifact and the basis that it is evaluated is demonstrated by the impossibility of adequately paraphrasing a line of poetry. Consider the line from the Wordsworth sonnet quoted earlier:

> Dull would he be of soul, who could pass by
> A sight so touching in its majesty.

The critic Knight focussed on the juxtaposition of a feeling of wanting to protect with feelings of powerlessness. Other interpretations may emphasize a feeling of intimacy coupled with a sense of vastness. Many interpretations are possible, and any attempt to paraphrase the line would eliminate some of the possibilities. The line of poetry is unique and not open to some alternative statement. Thus the interpretive possibilities of the line, which constitute the value of the line, are integrally linked to the line, the product, itself.

In order to illustrate that a similar dependence between value and product exists in the case of invention, we consider some of the circumstances surrounding the development of an individual invention, the light bulb. Derry and Williams (1960) described the situation that existed prior to the development of the precursors of today's light bulb as follows:

> The possibilities of incandescent-filament lamps attracted the attention of inventors from the 1840s: That some thirty years elapsed before such lamps came into use was due to the technical difficulties of their construction. Two major obstacles had to be overcome. Firstly, the filament had to be constructed of an electrical conductor that could be heated to incandescence without melting, and this severely limited the choice. Secondly, as almost all substances combine with oxygen when so heated, the filament had to be enclosed in a high vacuum, and satisfactory means of achieving this were not available to the early inventors.

A means of achieving an appropriate vacuum was made available in 1865 with the invention of the mercury air pump. The principal remaining problem was to find a suitable material for the filament. In 1880 Swan constructed the first incandescent light using a filament of carbonated cotton. In the following year Edison patented an incandescent light with a filament made of carbonated bamboo. Identification of appropriate filaments must have conformed to one of two scenarios. Either the relevant properties of the required filament could be fully articulated and the problem was one of simply selecting a material that exhibited those properties; or identification of an appropriate material rested on recognition of the potential relevance of some aspect of an existing material—the relevant properties of which were only fully determined by application of that material to the task at hand. In the first case, selection of an appropriate material must be seen as a routine step, the creativity of the final product being no more contingent upon the execution of that step than the creativity of a building is contingent upon selection of appropriate beam dimensions from a span table. We suggest that this was not the case in Swan's and Edison's identification of an appropriate filament, primarily out of consideration of the time required to achieve this final step. In the second case, the required properties of the material cannot be fully stated at the outset, their identification proceeds only with the development of a particular product. Thus we see that the value of the product, the relevant properties of the material, emerge only as the product is developed. This is the only case in which the creativity of the light bulb may be regarded as contingent upon the development of an appropriate filament. Original value is again seen to be a necessary condition of a creative product.

4.3.3   Consistency and conflict

A question remains as to the nature of the sets of relations that should be regarded as significant. In the example taken from the Wordsworth sonnet there were a number of instances of both reinforcement and conflict. Many theories have been proposed linking aesthetic experience to the simultaneous presentation of competing influences such as harmony and tension, conflict and resolution, order and disorder. Sheppard (1987) offered the following characterization of the work of the artist:

> The successful artist plays with his audience's expectations, satisfying some of them while disappointing others, using his work to modify existing expectations and create new ones.

Although clearly stated in the context of art, this statement conveys something of the nature of establishing the value of any novel information.

In order to support this claim we briefly consider the nature of the way that new scientific theories are evaluated.

Kuhn (1970) distinguished between normal science and revolutions in science, which lead to the introduction and acceptance of new paradigms. Normal science is essentially cumulative, it is about maintaining the internal consistency of an existing paradigm, while elaborating and if necessary extending that paradigm to account for various phenomena. Revolutions in science however, are of a different nature. In particular, a new paradigm often conflicts with existing paradigms. Kuhn gave much consideration as to the basis on which such paradigmatic changes can come to be accepted, rejecting the notion that this is necessarily because they immediately offer a better explanation of phenomena or solve the problems of the previous paradigm. He pointed out that the adoption of a new proposal by the scientific community is not one of an all or nothing process of acceptance or rejection but one characterized by the acceptance of the new proposal by a few scientists, who then work within normal science to develop the paradigm and show what working within that paradigm would be like. The activity initiated by a few scientists, if the paradigm is destined to survive, brings about an increasing shift in the distribution of professional allegiances. He ultimately concluded that it is sometimes only personal and inarticulate aesthetic considerations that lead to the adoption of the new proposal.

The scope in the nature of the way that scientific breakthroughs are recognized may be illustrated by consideration of the basis on which Einstein's theory of special relativity was adopted as opposed to the acceptance of Watson's and Crick's model of the structure of DNA. The first point to be made is that Einstein's theory conflicted with existing theories. In his account of the circumstances that led to his development of this theory, Einstein spoke of the "unbearable thought" that the phenomena of electromagnetic fields should be explained by two different theories depending on how those fields were created (Einstein, 1919). It is obvious that an aesthetic notion, a notion of symmetry and simplicity, was important in providing the motivation for the development of his theory, and we suggest these same ideas were also important in providing the basis on which the theory was ultimately accepted. In the case of Watson's and Crick's proposal for the structure of DNA (Watson, 1968), the circumstances were considerably different. Conflict with existing information and scientific models was minimal. It was precisely the consistency of the model proposed with available information and theories that led to it's acceptance as 'the structure of DNA.' Perhaps a similar crystallization of existing thoughts, beliefs, and attitudes is sufficient in art. As we have stated emergent value may be seen as a function of the construction of a distinct set of relations between aspects of existing knowledge. We have attempted to show that in some cases these relations will indicate consistency, but in other cases, such as Kuhn's scientific revolutions and much if not all art, these relations may indicate strong conflicts. Perhaps the acceptance of the theory or artwork depends on a subjective evaluation as to whether the consistencies outweigh the conflicts. Such evaluations would be idiosyncratic, there is no basis on which objective evaluation may take place, yet somehow scientific theories and potential art works are either accepted or rejected and some level of societal consensus is maintained.

Why should the process of disappointing some expectations and satisfying others lead us to modify our existing beliefs and create new ones? Assuming that the aesthetic experience is primarily a pleasurable one, why should we want to have our expectations satisfied, or both satisfied and disappointed? Although definitive answers to these questions may not at the current time be formulated, some tentative suggestions may be made through consideration of the theoretical and biological research that has taken place in relation to the nature of emotions and motivation.

The first issue that is addressed is the notion that cognitive activity can be sources of pleasure, or conversely, displeasure. In 1954 Olds and Milner reported the results of an experiment where electrodes were planted in various parts of the brains of rats and electrical stimulation could be delivered to the electrodes by pressing a wide peddle. Many but not all of the rats were found to continually press the bar, and thus deliver stimulation to the electrodes, for extended periods of time, often to the neglect of eating and drinking. Subsequently it was found that by placing electrodes in areas of the brain stem, cats very quickly learned to activate a switch that would terminate electrical stimulation via these electrodes (Delago et al., 1954). The location of 'reward' and 'punishment' areas in the brain have since been more precisely defined (Olds, 1977) and the stimulation of reward areas linked to feelings of satisfaction in humans.[2] Furthermore these reward and punishment areas are literally at the center of the brain and are linked to the systems in the brain for arousal and memory. It seems possible then that there may be a physiological basis to claims such as those of (Scheffler, 1982) that a relation exists between emotions and cognitive activity.

If we turn now to behaviorist theories of motivation, Festinger's theory of *cognitive dissonance* is relevant (Festinger, 1957). Petri (1986) summarised the theory as follows: Beliefs about ourselves and the world around us can be related in one of three ways; they can be consistent, irrelevant, or dissonant

---

[2]Young (1987) stated that electrical stimuli are sometimes applied by surgeons to the basal ganglia during operations for the relief of pain. Patients have reported that while the current was turned on they experienced feelings of pleasure, sometimes of a sexual nature.

(inconsistent). When beliefs are dissonant, a negative emotional state is produced that is aversive, which in turn triggers mechanisms to reduce dissonance. Dissonance may be reduced in a number of ways: one of the beliefs may be changed; behavior may be changed; or additional information may be introduced. Cognitive dissonance theory has been applied to such areas as postdecisional behavior. Wicklund and Brehm (1976) suggested that research in this area generally supports the theory. Another interesting application was the prediction of the behavior of a group of 'believer's' when a prophecy that they believed in failed. Their reaction was to supplement the prophecy with additional information, in this case that their belief had saved them from the destruction prophesied, rather that to question the validity of the prophecy itself (Festinger et al., 1956). The principal objections to the theory have been directed at its lack of precision, both in predicting which beliefs will conflict and how the dissonance will be resolved (Aronson, 1968), but these kinds of objections do not seem sufficient to reject the theory as it clearly relies on the interaction between the subjective beliefs of individuals.

Also relevant to our discussion are the many experiments suggesting that we tend to seek some degree of novelty or complexity. Butler (1954) reported that monkeys will push open a heavy door for hours on end if this enables them to see out of a box in which they are confined. This behavior is more eager if a moving train comes into view. Bexton et al., (1954) have documented the aversive effects of confining human volunteers to sensory deprivation chambers. Piaget (1952) found that patterns differing just a little from well known patterns seem seem most attractive to infants whereas Hebb (1946) found that mixtures of familiar and unfamiliar elements can be violently disturbing, even terrifying. Crandall (1967) found that word combinations that were intermediate in the extent to which they satisfied expectations as to the words that would follow were rated higher both than those which allowed no prediction to be made and those which left no doubt as to what was to follow. Berlyne (1971) explained such results by claiming that there exists a point up to which we obtain increasing pleasure from novel information but after that increases in novelty result in increasing displeasure. Such explanations have their origins in the work of Wundt (1874).

Our presentation of research in relation to motivation and emotions has been selective, but if the theories presented hold they have important implications in relation to characterizing the basis of emergent value. The first of these is that the reward centers of the brain seem to be literally the center of brain activity with many types of signals both incoming and outgoing distributed all over the brain. This would support a theory based on monitoring the relation of incoming information to an information base considered as a whole. Secondly, there appear to be two balancing tendencies that should be considered in relation to the presentation of new information: (a) a tendency to maintain consistent world views; and (b) a tendency to seek new experiences, new information. Finally, a tendency to seek new information coupled with a need to maintain a consistent world view would explain the motivation behind developing this world view in such a way that new information that conflicted with the old world view was consistent with the updated world view. A theory based on the notion of competing tendencies provides a motivational basis for modifying our expectations.

4.3.4   Discrete or continuous relations

In our description of the impact of the combination of the words 'touching' and 'majesty' we traced thesaurus entries associated with the two words—revealing consistencies and conflicts. A representation of the network of thesaurus entries employed is illustrated in Figure 4.1. Each word is represented as a discrete node and thesaurus entries indicating a direct association between two words are represented as an arc between the nodes representing each word. Thus the thesaurus entry touch: excite, be related, be situated is represented as arcs running from the word touch to each of the words excite, be related and be situated (two nodes are used to represent be related in order to simplify the diagram). Double lines are used to represent relations between words not explicitly represented in the thesaurus entries but which should be able to be established given sufficiently elaborate dictionary definitions. The solid double lines represent consistent relations between the words that they join, the broken lines conflicting relations.

In a very limited sense the emergent value associated with the combination of the two words is reflected in the distinct set of thesaurus and dictionary style relations that the two words bring into play. Perhaps recognition of emergent value can be modeled as a monitoring function operating over large databases of interconnected information, evaluating features such as the number, proximity, and type of relations involved. Such a model would be dependent on the idea that adequate representations of information can be developed by constructing discrete relations between discrete units of information. Creative outcomes would be those combinations of discrete units of information that by their predefined relation to each other, brought into play desirable patterns of relations. The notion of creative outcomes as the combination of discrete units seems to underlie theories of creativity such as those of Hebb and Donderi (1987), Weisberg (1986), de Bono (1967) and Koestler (1964). The notion that adequate representations of information can be developed by constructing discrete relations between discrete units of

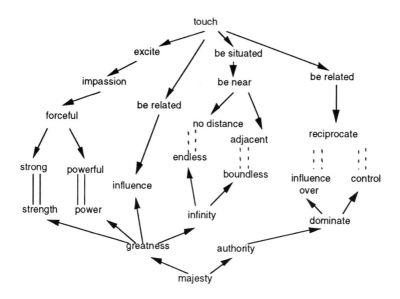

Figure 4.1. Diagrammatic representation of thesaurus entries associated with the words 'touch' and 'majesty'.

information is a fundamental assumption of artificial intelligence research. Perhaps the most succinct observation of the implications of this view is that made by Schank and Abelson (1977) in the context of automating natural language understanding where they state that in order for a computer to understand the meaning of a sentence, that sentence must ultimately be able to be represented in terms of a small set of primitives. In other words, meaning is a function of the capacity to construct a representation of new information in terms of existing information.

An important alternative to this view is based on the idea that knowledge is grounded in specific experiences. Atrens and Curthoys (1982) observed that everything we see is a function of the eye and brain's ability to construct that information from the light sources that reach the eye. Furthermore, they state that the coding capacity of the brain is essentially infinite. This suggests the possibility that information may be stored in the form that it is perceived, and that information of the complexity and detail of that perceived can be stored. Such an idea contrasts sharply with the highly abstract and simplified representations that have generally been employed in artificial intelligence research. Viewed in this way, assimilation of the meaning of a word may be seen to be a product of the entire context in which it is used. The proposition of relations between words, as may be found in thesaurus and dictionary style entries, may be seen as an artificial construct made possible only by our experience of the use of the words concerned in particular contexts, rather than the basis of a representation that allows the meaning of a word to be interpreted strictly from its relation to other words. The arguments presented by Schön (1969) and Bugelski (1983) against the notion that our thinking is dominated by the interpretation of information via the application of abstract concepts are based on similar grounds.

If we accept this alternative view, what are the implications in terms of characterizing and developing models of the process of recognizing emergent value? The first point to make is that by analogy to the idea that the meaning of a word derives from its being grounded in any number of complex experiences, the value of a creative product would similarly be derived from its relation to any number of such complex experiences. Furthermore this relationship would not be one composed of simple discrete relations, but would be of a complexity and indefiniteness equivalent to the representations of experience to which the product was being related. Second, there must still exist a basis for establishing the value of new information in relation to that which is already known, we contend that there must exist some kind of monitoring function that allows significant configurations of relations between aspects of information to be identified. Finally, it should be pointed out that the implications of adopting this alternative view in relation to developing computational models of the process of recognizing emergent value are not straight forward. Perhaps it is just a question of scale and at some level that which constitutes our knowledge of the world is of the form of discrete units and discrete relations between those units. Furthermore it may not be necessary to replicate the way that humans recognize emergent value. In the following section we discuss the notion that the value of a newly presented product is societally determined. If a computational tool could be developed that were capable of anticipating that which a society would deem as relevant without replicating the way that humans operate, then such a tool would be capable of recognizing emergent value and thus creative products.

4.3.5   Emergent value is societally dependent

In a discussion of the nature of genius, Hershman and Lieb (1988) pointed out that conference of the title of genius on an individual is contingent on a relationship, the relationship between the products of that individual and a particular society. They articulate the implications of this dynamic relationship between product, person, and society as follows:

> ... there are no unrecognized geniuses. A genius is someone who is
> acknowledged as such, even if only by those who work in, or have been
> trained in his field, and who pass their verdict on to society.

Similarly we would argue that there is no such thing as an unrecognized
creative product. The term creative is designated to a product on the basis
of a relationship between the product and a particular society. This is
reflected in the importance placed on reconstructing the values and beliefs of
particular societies in assessing the contribution played by specific products.
It is also reflected in the fact that those products regarded to be creative
may change as societies change.

By emphasizing the societal dimension of a creative product we do not
wish to imply that there are not significant differences in the products valued
most highly by individuals within a society. Kuhn (1970) highlighted the
important role played by individuals and small groups of individuals in
introducing new scientific theories—they adopt the new theory, elaborate
it and show what it would be like to work with that theory, thus providing
information that contributes to the ultimate acceptance or rejection of the
theory by society at large. We have already explored the idea that a work
of art may be open to a number of different interpretations. We must
therefore accept that the same work of art may be valued differently by
different individuals. The societal determinedness that we refer to then, is
that determined by the pooling of judgements of a society of individuals. We
do not attempt to account for the way in which some degree of consensus
is achieved, but simply observe that such a phenomenon does occur. Some
scientific theories ultimately survive within a society, others are rejected.
Some artifacts are ultimately accepted as being of high artistic or other
merit, others are not. It is in this sense that we speak of the emergent value
of a creative product being societally determined.

4.4   Creative process

As stated at the outset of this chapter our principal concern is with process.
In the previous section we developed a characterization of creative products
because we believe such a characterization to be fundamental to any exploration of the nature of creative processes. Although we are now in a position
to set some limits as to the nature of creative processes, we also wish to say
something about the possibilities that exist within those limits. In order to
pave the way for such a discussion we introduce four categories of activity:
mechanical and random generation; selection; reminding; and the merging
of retrieved ideas and experiences.

4.4.1   Mechanical or random generation

Mechanical generation may be described as the production of elements or sets of elements by some predefined procedure. Although outcomes are implicitly defined in the procedure, the significance of certain outcomes may not be recognized until they are actually generated.[3] This kind of activity is evident in the following passage written by the sculptor Henry Moore (Ghiselin, 1952):

> I sometimes begin with no preconceived problem to solve, with only the desire to use pencil on paper, and make lines, tones and shapes with no conscious aim; but as my mind takes in what is so produced a point arrives where some idea becomes conscious and crystallises, and then a control and ordering begins to take place.

Similarly, the architect Arata Isozaki (1972) outlined various strategies for the production of elements that he finds useful in the development of designs. These include 'slicing,' the cutting or exposition in section of the hypothetical boxes, cylinders or other shapes that exist in the architect's mind; 'projection,' the generation of interior lines and points using a 45-degree triangle and compass, producing meaningless shadows of the original form; 'transferal,' transferring a simple form image, altering the scale, position or meaning of the form image; and 'amplification,' the investigation of forms within a space using a basic unit of 90 by 120 centimeters. Utzon (Zodiac 14) discusses the subdivision of space by a process of projecting forms from basic geometric shapes and allowing the intersection of the forms thus produced. In particular he discusses the use of the sphere as a basis for the shells of the Sydney Opera House (Figure 4.2), suggesting that a harmony between the shells is established due to the fact that they have their origin in the same sphere, of the same radius, that they "intersect in accordance with a certain law." Random generation also involves the production of elements via a procedure, but the procedure is such that control of the procedure is external to the creator. An example of such a procedure is the incorporation of chance in many of the works of the Dada movement. Flicking through books and magazines constitutes another such procedure.

4.4.2   Selection

In research concerned with the generation of new ideas, new types or new information, the role of selection in the development of a creative product is

---

[3] A well known example of such a phenomenon is described by Stiny (1986), where two squares with overlapping corners form a third square in the overlap.

Figure 4.2. The Sydney Opera House.

often overlooked. Selection is used here in the following senses:

1. identification of conditions that require resolution;

2. as ideas are generated, the decision to pursue various lines of development rather than others;

3. the identification of the final product, that is, deciding when to stop;

4. recognizing relevant information in sources external to the creative system; and

5. identification of relevant aspects of information being dealt with.

The importance of selection can be seen when we consider Einstein's (1919) account of the events that led up to the development of his special theory of relativity. In particular consider his comment that "the thought that one is dealing here with two fundamentally different cases was, for me, unbearable." Here we have explicit acknowledgement that it was a perceived inconsistency that motivated the search for a unifying theory. Just how the theory was arrived at is a matter of speculation but the focussing of attention that resulted from the selection of the particular theories and phenomena concerned obviously played a fundamental role.

It is interesting to note that even in the case where he starts with no explicit problem to solve, Moore (1976) acknowledged that eventually "a point arrives where some idea becomes conscious and crystallizes, and then control and ordering begins to take place."

The development of the Sydney Opera House, a public building designed in response to a public competition, provides an illustration of the important role of selection by parties other than the architect. It thus provides a means of externalizing our discussion of the role of selection. Baume (1967) stated that of the six disqualification clauses in the entry form to the competition for designing the Sydney Opera House, Utzon's entry was liable for disqualification under four. These included the fact that the proposal exceeded the site limits, would probably be of excessive cost, did not provide a main hall that satisfied the minimum seating requirements, and finally was submitted as sketches rather than the more detailed specifications outlined in the competition conditions. Nevertheless the proposal was awarded first prize from 222 other entries. Baume's account of the circumstances that lead to the selection of this particular entry—that when looking through the proposals initially rejected by the other members of the judging panel, Eero Saarinen, a highly respected American architect, was "immediately struck" by Utzon's proposal—suggests that it was in part the immediate visual appeal of this proposal that motivated the judges to override the original competition conditions. The proposal was sculptural: It was designed to be viewed from all sides as well as from above, an important consideration in relation to the exposed site.[4] It was expressive of the site, its forms relating strongly to the peninsula on which it was to be built and reminiscent of the sails of the small craft invariably seen in the surrounding harbor. It also offered interesting possibilities for dealing with the programmatic requirements of the project: in particular circulation requirements, the need to avoid dead space for fire stairs; and the requirement of housing a number of different functions including an opera hall with a fly tower. In notes accompanying his competition entry Utzon (Yeomans, 1968, p.44) made explicit reference to Grecian theaters, comparing the approach of the audience to a "festive

---

[4]Bennelong Point, the site of the Sydney Opera House juts into a busy harbor. It is surrounded on three sides by water. The Sydney Harbour Bridge, the bridge that links the main business districts of Sydney is sprung from Dawes Point, which is immediately adjacent to Bennelong Point. The Opera House site is thus viewed from boats on the harbor, from apartment blocks on the adjacent banks, from traffic on the bridge 55 m above sea level and from city office blocks as well as from the approaching land entrance.

procession" and suggesting that the "whole exterior radiates lightness and festivity." He thus highlighted aspects of the proposal intended to evoke general notions of theater. At the time that Utzon's competition entry was selected it was not known that the design could actually be constructed (Figure 4.3). It was not until work had progressed well into the construction of the podium that the problem of how to construct the 'shells'[5] was resolved. Selection of Utzon's proposal was based on the way in which he dealt with other aspects of the program. A significant factor influencing the selection of Utzon's design must have been the endorsement given by Saarinen, who himself employed forms not dissimilar to Utzon's in his design for the TWA airport terminal in New York.

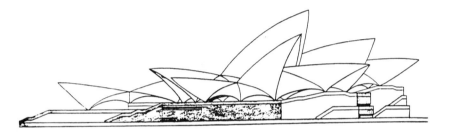

Figure 4.3. Diagram from Utzon's original Sydney Opera House competition drawings (Ziegler, 1973).

It is important to recognize the nature of the criteria that have been used by various historians to evaluate the appropriateness of Utzon's proposal. The appropriateness of a sculptural form on a site such a Bennelong Point that may be viewed from all sides and above is obvious after the presentation of Utzon's proposal but 'sculptural form' was certainly not an explicit criteria outlined in the competition conditions. The appropriateness of this specific form in its reference to the harbor, as an abstract expression of the notion of theatre and in the resolution of circulation and other programmatic requirements are likewise criteria that could not be specified at the outset of the competition, but that had a quality of obviousness[6] once this specific proposal had been presented.

Resolution of the problem of constructing the 'shells' provides a second instance of the importance of selection in the development of a creative

---

[5] Although originally conceived as concrete shells the shells of the Sydney Opera House are not true shells but assemblies of precast concrete components meeting at a central ridge.

[6] Bruner (1974) suggested that creative products in general have a quality of obviousness once presented.

outcome. From 1957, the engineers of Ove Arup and Partners, the structural engineers retained for the project, attempted to establish a means of constructing shells of thin concrete that would conform to Utzon's specifications. Principal among these specifications were that the shells should rise fairly sharply from the base and that the rise should decrease dramatically to form an almost horizontal roofing structure. These requirements were motivated by the need to allow for adequate wing and gallery space as well as acoustic requirements. In 1962 Utzon proposed an alternative precast rib roofing system. Utzon had adopted an approach whereby he investigated the possibility of creating the 'shells' from segments of a regular form so as to allow the 'shells' to be constructed from consistent precast elements. The resulting 'shells' differed considerably from the original specification, the spines of the 'shells' were smooth curves. It is likely that the engineers of Arup's had not considered such a departure as one that they would be justified in making.

Utzon's final proposal was in clear violation of some of the criteria given to Arup's engineers but it represented a remarkable resolution of other criteria: ease and cost effectiveness of fabrication; and the provision of sculptural forms and surfaces that held uniform quality finishes. The decision to pursue this specific resolution of the problem of constructing the shells was based on tradeoffs between criteria that could not be made at the outset of the search for an appropriate means of construction.

The critical point to be made in relation to the two situations presented is that holding onto particular ideas once they have been generated plays a significant role in the development of a creative outcome. When Utzon's competition entry was selected there was no guarantee that it could be built. When Utzon started working on the idea of carving up shapes of regular geometry there was no guarantee that this would yield a solution to the problem of constructing the 'shells.' Furthermore both situations are examples of situations where selection is based on criteria that could not have been adequately articulated prior to the development of the particular solutions proposed.

4.4.3   Reminding

Reminding may be characterized as retrieval of information in the form that it was stored. Mechanisms for such retrieval may range from direct indexing to retrieval via very loose associations with available information. One of the principal arguments of this chapter is that reminding is often fundamental to the development of creative outcomes and that reminding coupled with processes that allow merging and other adaptations of retrieved information are sufficient to explain the sensation of ideas arising fully formed. This argument is essentially one that acknowledges the importance of precedent in the development of new ideas, and the impossibility of developing new ideas without drawing on the old. For a discussion of precedent in relation to scientific developments see Weisberg (1986). For a similar discussion in the domain of architectural design see Moore (1976), Darke (1979), and Foz (1973). We confine our discussion to sources of the principal ideas governing the development of the Sydney Opera House proposal.

Utzon (Zodiac 10) in an article entitled "Platforms and Plateaus" discussed notions of platform and the interplay of roof and platform, that he had derived from precedents across a broad spectrum of cultures. The article was written after the development of the design for the Sydney Opera House, and could therefore perhaps be viewed as a post-rationalization of that structure, however it is interesting to note Utzon's explicit acknowledgement of his debt to an experience of an existing structure:

> The big mosque in Old Delhi is an outstanding example (of a platform that forms the backbone of an architectural composition). It is surrounded by the markets and the bazaar buildings, placed in a pell mell of traffic, people, animals, noise and nervous buildings. Here, raised 3 to 5 meters above this is an enormous red sandstone platform ... On this square or platform, you have a strong feeling of remoteness and complete calmness. An effect, no client or architect would have dreamed possible in advance, has been achieved by so few means.

Utzon suggested that his notion of platform and its capacity to evoke a sense of strength and calmness has been gleaned from sources as diverse as Mayan architecture and Chinese houses and temples. He explicitly acknowledged a relationship between precedents such as these and the strong platform element in the Sydney Opera House. Furthermore he drew attention to the interplay between roof and structure in Chinese and Japanese traditional architecture, commenting that a flat roof is insufficient to express the flatness of a platform. If we accept that this notion of platform coupled with the notion of a floating roof structure (Figures 4.4 and 4.5) provided the basis for the Sydney Opera House design, then the final proposal may be seen as a masterful adaptation of these elements to the specific context. The use of the strong platform element to evoke a feeling of stability and permanence has been coupled with its use as a means of providing uncomplicated circulation. The visible part of the complex is essentially a series of spaces sitting on top of a large staircase. External circulation and the platform element have been combined in a way that evokes notions of Greek theater, a precedent appropriate in its capacity to evoke notions of theater itself. Finally the use of concrete shells to create a form that provides adequate contrast to the flatness of the platform is consistent with the use of these forms to create a dynamic sculptural proposal that may be viewed from all sides.

Figure 4.4. Diagram from Utzon's article "Platforms and Plateaus" indicating that the required interplay between roof and platform was to be achieved by creating a floating, almost ephemeral roof structure (Utzon [Zodiac 10], Plate 9).

Figure 4.5. Diagram from Utzon's article "Platforms and Plateaus" indicating that the required interplay between roof and platform was to be achieved by creating a floating, almost ephemeral roof structure (Utzon [Zodiac 10], Plate 10).

How is the generation of a form that represents such a unique and remarkable synthesis of such a wide variety of considerations possible? We have suggested that the starting point for the design was a notion of platform and the interplay between roof and platform. These ideas are a recurrent theme in Utzon's early work, featuring in his scheme for a school near Elsinore, Denmark (Zodiac 10) and the Zurich theatre (Zodiac 14). This observation would seem to lend credence to the notion that designers may draw on a short and idiosyncratic list of concepts as the basis for proceeding with the development of a design proposal. Perhaps the uniqueness of Utzon's Sydney Opera House is largely a product of the uniqueness of vision that allowed him to select, from his experience of buildings and building types, the platform as an important element in establishing a feeling of strength and calmness. Also important would be the selection of the roof element and particular characteristics of that roof element as important in emphasizing appropriate qualities of the platform. Finally the decision that the qualities that could be evoked through the use of a platform element, would be appropriate qualities to bring to a proposal for the complex of spaces required in the brief for the Sydney Opera House, was an important and selective decision.

The notion of the platform as a giant staircase and the possibility of incorporating aspects of the form of Greek theaters, although not straightforward developments, are clearly much more evident once the selection of a platform as an important element of the proposal has been made. Similarly the retrieval and selection of shell construction as a means of building the upper part of the structure would be facilitated by identification of criteria such as the roof being a contrast to the flatness of the platform. The sculptural possibilities of this form of construction, once retrieved seem almost self evident.

Unlike Weisberg (1986) we do not wish to suggest that the development of a creative product is akin to problem solving. However we do wish to emphasize that the development of such products is often incremental, the possibilities of a partially developed product and the evaluation criteria that should be applied to that product emerging only as the initial ideas for the product are proposed and developed. Further we do emphasize that the generation of initial ideas for a product and the developments on those ideas are firmly grounded in our experience of existing products. What is remarkable about the development of a creative product is the capacity of the creator to make appropriate selections in identifying the aspects of past experience that are relevant to the generation and evaluation of the product.

4.4.4 Merging of retrieved ideas and experiences

In the previous section we emphasized the role of experiences that were (a) essentially intact and (b) could, at least in retrospect, be associated with conditions that may prompt their retrieval. Introspective accounts of the circumstances that have lead to the development of creative products, however, abound with references to fully formed ideas occurring spontaneously, often when not specifically focused on the problem to which they were relevant. In this section we argue that even these fully formed ideas are grounded in selections from past experiences.

Spence (1962) discussed the means by which he came to the idea of having zig-zagged walls in Coventry Cathedral (Figure 4.6):

> My dream was wonderful. I was walking through the Cathedral and it looked marvellous, with light like Chartres. The altar looked tremendous, backed by a huge tapestry, but I could not see the windows until I went right in and turned half back—the walls were zig-zagged! ... I can truly say I had not considered using this type of wall before I saw it in this dream. Of course, it may have been in the back of my mind, for the zig-zag is a well-known way of directional lighting. It certainly fitted in with the plan, as the windows would then face south-east and south-west; the coloured shafts of light would streak to the altar.

A number of aspects of this account are worthy of note. First, the degree of development of the idea. Spence is able to visualize himself walking through the cathedral, to the extent that he could perceive the quality of light, the altar, a tapestry and the windows. The idea of zig-zagged walls does indeed appear to be fully integrated into a proposal for the cathedral. Second, the idea has a precedent, Spence acknowledged that the zig-zag was a well-known way of directional lighting. Third, once presented, Spence was able to recognize and articulate the value of the idea, it was workable and the effect would be appropriate. We consider each of these points in turn.

Much of the expertise of the architect lies in his ability to visualize an as yet unbuilt project. A skill often actively cultivated in the course of architectural education is that of visualizing what it would be like to be in a proposed space or to walk through such a space. The way in which the idea was presented in the Spence's dream is consistent with the exercise of such a skill, possibly already exercised in visualizing tentative proposals for this specific project.

Another skill that the architect generally attempts to cultivate is a memory of the experience of being in particular places. From the beginning of his account of the process of designing Coventry Cathedral, Spence emphasized his experience of traditional churches and cathedrals. His description of one such experience emphasizes shafts of light as a dominant feature:

> I was alone and entered York Minster through the southern porch. Shafts of light shot the Gothic mouldings with ruby and gold.

Figure 4.6. Sketch of interior of an early proposal for Coventry Cathedral, looking towards altar. Light enters from the zig-zagged walls to the side (Spence, 1962).

The mere fact that the project that he was involved with was to develop the design for a cathedral should have been enough to recall such memories. Furthermore, given the architectural climate of the time, it is likely that the recreation of abstract qualities such as the effect of light in older examples of church architecture although not directly imitating the means employed in those older examples, would be a dominant goal in the development of the new cathedral. Thus the idea presented in the dream may be seen as a merging of a number of ideas:

1. the quality of light in traditional church architecture;

2. the use of zig-zagged walls and windows as a means of directional lighting; and

3. knowledge of pragmatic constraints required to manipulate natural light.

It is significant that Spence was able to recognize the value of the idea once it had been generated. Perhaps the seemingly inexplicable nature of the way in which some ideas appear to be generated is in a large part due to indirect retrieval of relevant past experience. It seems eminently reasonable that the same criteria that are used to evaluate the quality of a creative product should also be involved in retrieval of information relevant to the generation and development of that product. By appeal to our argument that these criteria, by definition, cannot be adequately stated at the outset of the development of the product, indirect reminding is based on criteria that can only be vaguely articulated is likely to be prevalent in the development of a creative product.

4.4.5   A general characterization of creative processes

A number of process categories have been introduced which, from introspective accounts, appear to play some role in the development of creative products. Some consideration will now be given to what these roles might be. In particular the questions of which, if any, of these process categories are necessary to the development of a creative product, and which if any combinations of process categories are sufficient to yield such products, will be addressed.

Consideration will first be given to the sufficiency of mechanical generation as a means of developing creative products. Mechanical generation has been defined as the production of elements or sets of elements by some predefined procedure. Perhaps the easiest way to visualize the scope of this type of activity is to take a computational example. Consider an automatic generative system that is such that each of a range of colors could be generated for each pixel of a standard graphics screen. The output of this system would be the set of all text and pictures that can be displayed on the graphic screen. Some of the screens thus generated would be original, it is unlikely that every picture and text combination that could be displayed on the screen would correspond to a previously experienced image. Some of the original screens may also be valuable but it would be a small proportion of the total number of screens generated. The process of exhaustively generating all possible representations cannot be regarded as a creative process, as even though some of its outcomes exhibit the qualities of originality and value, the processing system has no notion itself of which of those outcomes are valuable and which are not. The processing system does not have the capacity to select from the screens generated so that only those of originality and value are finally presented.

The aforementioned example illustrates a characteristic of mechanical generation in general. Mechanical generation can yield creative products but it will typically also produce many worthless products. It seems then that a necessary condition of a creative process that involves mechanical generation is a capacity to select from the products generated. By appeal to the argument already presented for the necessity of emergent value in a creative product, mechanical generation coupled with selection based on recognition of emergent value would be a sufficient set of processes to yield a creative product.

Consider now the process category random generation and the question of the sufficiency of processes falling under this category with respect to the development of a creative product. A pixel generation system similar to that described earlier may be defined, with the exception that instead of exhaustively generating all possible combinations of pixels, pixel combinations are generated randomly. Some of the resulting screens may exhibit emergent value, but again the problem arises that a discrimination between those products that do so and those that do not, is not incorporated in the process of random generation. Random generation coupled with selection based on recognition of emergent value would, however, be a sufficient set of processes to yield a creative product.

Is selection in itself sufficient to yield a creative product? Consider a situation where the technical resources of a photographer were limited to the extent that all parameters other that the selection of a photographic subject were fixed. It is conceivable that selection of a subject could be made such that the resulting artifact came to be regarded as a creative product. If this were the case then the artifact would, by definition, have to embody some aspect of original value. If this value were not included inadvertently, then the process of selection would have had to have included recognition of such value. If the original value were included inadvertently, then it would be inappropriate to refer to the selection process undertaken by the photographer as a creative process—even if the process yielded a product later determined to be creative. The creative process must be considered to include that recognition of original value that occurred after the product had been generated that allowed the product to be identified as being creative. Thus a necessary and sufficient condition of a creative process is selection based on recognition of emergent value.

Thus far we have referred to generative processes that can be externalized. When we turn to the issue of reminding and the role of reminding and subsequent processing in the development of a creative product a higher degree of conjecture is involved. We restrict our attention to a single thesis: that reminding, combined with merging of information thus retrieved and selection based on recognition of emergent value are a sufficient set of processes to yield a creative product. Consider again Spence's claim that the idea of the use of angled windows in his Coventry Cathedral proposal, came to him fully formed in a dream. Some potential sources of this idea have already been suggested: previous experiences of the quality of light in traditional churches and cathedrals, the use of zig-zagged walls and windows as a means of directional lighting, and a knowledge of orientations relevant to the use of natural lighting. Clearly, if valid sources, they have been integrated to a high degree. Although we are unable to adequately account for the processes involved in such an integration, they have been classified under the category of the merging of ideas and experiences. Reminding and the merging of ideas and experiences would seem to be a sufficient set of processes to account for the phenomenon of ideas seeming to arrive fully formed as suggested by Spence's introspective account. We include selection as a necessary condition of processes that can account for such phenomena, in the belief that a high degree of discrimination must be integrated into the processes of reminding or merging or quite possibly both. For example, the retrieval of a means of achieving directional lighting would seem to be integrally related to a desire to create a quality of light comparable to those of traditional churches and cathedrals. Similarly the incorporation of this means of achieving directional lighting into the plan in such a way that the light source is hidden from the viewer and the orientation of the windows is appropriate, indicates a high degree of control. It seems eminently reasonable that the same capacities that allow us to recognize emergent value would also play a role in reminding and the merging of information retrieved.

Whereas the aforementioned characterizations are not exhaustive of processes that may be regarded as creative, they are sufficient to provide a basis for drawing some general conclusion about the nature of creative processes. The first of these is that many different kinds of processes fall into the category of creative processes. In this chapter we have considered processes that have been characterized in terms of a number of different combinations of process categories: mechanical generation coupled with selection based on recognition of emergent value; random generation coupled with selection based on recognition of emergent value; selection based on recognition of emergent value in itself; and finally, a combination of reminding, merging of information retrieved and selection based on recognition of emergent value. The second general conclusion that may be drawn is that a necessary condition of any process that can in itself be called creative is selection based on recognition of emergent value.

In order to clarify the implications of this characterization we compare it to the theories of creative process presented in Section 4.2: Wallas's preparation-incubation-illumination-verification model; the finalistic and propulsive theories of control; Koestler's interaction of matrices; de Bono's lateral thinking; Weisberg's problem solving approach and Murray's emphasis on imaginative thinking.

If we consider first Wallas's model, the characterization proposed here immediately underscores the importance of preparation, and as a corollary verification. Recognition of the value of a proposal is integrally linked to the knowledge of the processing system to which the proposal is presented. Clearly a well developed framework of existing knowledge has to be available in order to compare the new information to that which is already known. In some cases this framework will be sufficiently complete so as to dispense with subsequent verification; in others the framework and the newly presented information will indicate potential deficiencies in the framework, the elaboration of which may be seen as verification.

More interestingly the emergent value model says something about the nature of illumination and why it may be difficult. Consider the line of poetry from the Wordsworth sonnet given earlier:

Dull would he be of soul, who could pass by
A sight so touching in its majesty.

Say the poet at the outset of the development of that line was able to identify that he wished to express simultaneous feelings of power and intimacy. A quick glance at the number of thesaurus entries associated with each of these words should indicate the number of word combinations that could be explored in finding an appropriate combination of synonyms. Furthermore additional considerations such as the development of an appropriate rhythm and tone, considerations possibly only emerging as the line develops, would similarly have to be taken into account. Smithers et al. (1989) have identified exploration, the search for the goals that define a problem, as an important characteristic of design activity, but even if these goals can in part be defined it is the nature of creative products that their value relies on their relation to a complex body of information—only as a product is proposed can the implications of that product start to be recognized.

The characterization of creative processes developed here is such that it admits the inclusion of processes that do not incorporate illumination—at least in the sense implied by Wallas—much less incubation, as creative processes. Illumination may be seen as a necessary condition of creative processes in the sense that the emergent value of a product must at some stage be recognized, but Wallas's characterization clearly entails illumination as a necessary condition in the generation of a candidate product.

Finally the emergent value model suggests that it is inappropriate to make a temporal distinction between the stages proposed by Wallas. Many combinations of processes may lead to the development of a proposal that seems promising. Furthermore it is not necessary that illumination occur as a single stage, insight as to the value of a developing proposal may be a gradual process, as with the scientist who adopts a new paradigm and then works within normal science to explore that paradigm or the artist who analyzes an existing artifact.

If we consider now the theories that deal with the issue of control, the finalistic and propulsive theories and their variants, it should be evident that the emergent value model admits both types of control. The possibility of including both types of control is perhaps best drawn out by considering the variable role of emotion in relation to the development of a work of art. T. S. Eliot (1975) described the relation between art and emotion as follows:

> The only way of expressing an emotion in the form of art is by finding an "objective correlative", in other words, a set of objects, a situation, a chain of events which shall be the formula for that particular emotion.

Hasburg (1987) has criticized this characterization of art on the basis that it assumes that the art work is an external realization of a particular feeling or emotion, of some inner entity. It assumes that an answer to the question "What is the emotion conveyed by this painting?" can be given. He suggested that often the only answer to such a question is "That emotion"—that emotion evoked by that particular painting. Furthermore he suggested that this view of art, art as the translation of emotion, excludes the possibility that manipulations of the materials of the artist's medium may be something more than a vehicle for the expression of emotion, it eliminates the possibility that such manipulations may be a source of artistic meaning in their own right. This argument reveals an interesting dichotomy that is perhaps reflected in the ways that artifacts may be developed. It is possible that the development of an art work has been guided by an attempt to construct an entity that will inspire a reaction that approximates a previously felt emotion. It is also possible that the work developed with very limited intent behind it, but that as it developed the artist found that he was developing a particular response to the work and perhaps used his understanding of that response to guide future development of the artifact.

An extension of this argument leads to a notion of the independence of the value of an artifact from the intentions of the creator of that artifact. The commonly held view that the intentions of the creator are important to the appreciation of a work of art is reflected in the following passage form Le Corbusier's Vers une Architecture (1923):

> My house is practical. I thank you, as I might thank railway engineers or the telephone service. You have not touched my heart. But suppose that walls rise towards heaven in such a way that I am moved. I perceive your intentions ... By the use of inert materials and starting from conditions more or less utilitarian you have established certain relationships which have aroused my emotions. This is Architecture.

Here we have a view of architecture fundamentally grounded in the idea that what makes an artifact architecture is the capacity to arouse emotion, and further that this capacity is a product of the intentions of the creator. In sharp contrast to this idea is Eisenman's (1982) philosophy of decomposition:

> Traditionally, the architect produced an initial form-image in response to a program of needs... The understanding of the final image was thought to reside in part in the capacity to register the final object back to the original concept...[Decomposition] is making by analysis...it may not be possible to trace the final object from its preceding development.

Eisenman was concerned with the making of a product, but his comments are equally relevant to its evaluation. What is important is not the intentions of the creator but the information, the meaning that can be read into and gleaned from the product. A candidate proposal may obtained by purely random means or by very directed, although possibly unconscious, thought. What is important is the capacity to evaluate the significance of that proposal.

An argument could be made that if intentions of the creator are not important, then recognition of the creativity of a product should not be a necessary condition of a creative process. This opens up the question as to when a creative process should be considered complete. A creative process is one that yields a creative product. A creative product is determined as such by judgements that are societally dependent. It would be premature to consider a creative process to be complete prior to the execution of such judgement. Thus a text is not poetry until a meaning for that text has been negotiated, as Geissner (1988) observed:

> Depending on the capability of the program, more precisely, depending on the combinatory imagination of the programmer, one can say that computers can compose poetry. For the question of what poetry is,

that can be determined only in social terms, especially through the negotiation of meaning between the listener/reader (as well as the performer) and the text.

Similarly a found object is not art until it has been accepted as such.

Some objections to Koestler's and de Bono's assumptions about the nature of normal thought and their resulting accounts of the nature of the human thought processes that make creativity possible have already been discussed. Having noted these objections it is important to point out that it is not necessary to take a position on this issue in order to see that the processes described by both Koestler and de Bono could yield candidate creative outcomes. These processes are thus potentially applicable as component processes in the overall development of a creative product but they are insufficient to be called creative processes in themselves. Furthermore techniques such as those devised by de Bono may be inappropriate in the emphasis that they place on a particular means of generating ideas rather than the all important task of evaluation.

In order to illustrate the limitations of Weisberg's claim that creative processes can be viewed as problem solving, some consideration is given to the circumstances surrounding Watson's and Crick's discovery of the structure of DNA, an example used by Weisberg himself. Watson (1968) gave the following account of the discovery:

> When I got to our still empty office the following morning, I quickly cleared away the papers from my desk so that I would have a large flat surface on which to form pairs of bases held together by hydrogen bonds. Though I initially went back to my like-with-like (the bases adenine with adenine, guanine with gaunine, thymine with thymine, cystosine with cystosine) prejudices, I saw all too well that they led nowhere. ... I... began shifting the bases in and out of various other pairing possibilities. Suddenly I became aware that an adenine-thymine pair held together by two hydrogen bonds was identical in shape to a guanine-cytosine pair held together by at least two hydrogen bonds. All the hydrogen bonds seemed to form naturally; no fudging was required to make the two types of base pairs identical in shape...

A number of points should be made in relation to this discovery. First, the problem space had been highly circumscribed prior to the event related earlier. The relevant bases were known, a tentative decision had been made to pursue a double strand helical model, and a decision to adopt the practice of working with physical models of chemical structures had been made. The appropriateness of at least some of these decisions could be confirmed only after Watson's and Crick's discovery. Thus the process of establishing the problem space was a tenuous and value laden activity. Furthermore Watson's claim that he suddenly "became aware" of a feature of a particular model indicates that a criteria for the evaluation of the model emerged only as that model developed. This violates the condition of predefined goals required of processes that may properly be classified as problem solving.

Finally, the characterization of creative processes proposed here incorporates the view that we are in the world (Murray, 1986), in that it acknowledges that our evaluation of new information must be a product of the relation of that information to the idiosyncratic and constantly developing knowledge bases of individuals. Coyne and Snodgrass (1990) characterized design activity as dialogue between the design situation and the designer. They suggested that such a process is incompatible with models of design activity based on systems of rules or induction. Although such models are clearly insufficient if their characterization holds, the use of rules and induction in the course of generating proposals should not be excluded. A rule or a system of rules, like any text, is grounded in the context in which it is developed. Similarly the choice of features and instances on which the induction of a generalization is based is also context dependent. As the designer becomes more familiar with the design situation through the course of developing a proposal and considering that proposal in the light of his current understanding of the design situation, the context will change. Coyne and Snodgrass's argument against the existence of universal systems of rules (Alexander et al., 1977; Mitchell, 1989) and universal forms gleaned by induction (Rossi, 1982) is an important one but it should not be extended to exclude the use of the techniques of formal systems to express and explore those aspects of a designer's understanding of a particular design situation that can be articulated.

4.5 The computability of creative processes

Computational investigations into the nature of creative processes have invariably focussed on the issue of originality. Consider the following definition taken from Coyne et al. (1987) which was developed specifically to capture the views that pervade definitions of creativity from a knowledge-based design perspective:

> Design is concerned with search within spaces of possible designs ...
> Creativity is concerned with exploration within a space that is only
> partially defined ... As well as the search for designs, creativity ...
> involves the search for the knowledge defining the space within which
> that search should take place.

This definition is quite possibly literally correct, but it (a) says nothing about potential sources of the knowledge that will eventually define the space and (b) implies that there is something special about the generation process, that is, that additional information must be acquired in order to generate a candidate outcome.

In the previous Section we illustrated that mechanical generation can yield outputs of sufficient originality to be candidate creative products. Why then has the question of originality been a concern? The problem arises from the way that notions of value are built into computational processes. The value of outcomes is typically ensured by building absolute notions of value into the processes used to generate proposals. Such practice is a characteristic of all programs that fall within the problem solving paradigm (Newell and Simon, 1972; Akin, 1986).

A notable exception to this rule is Lenat's AM program (Lenat, 1983a). AM was developed to explore the nature of the types of heuristics that might be useful in the development of mathematical theorems. AM starts from a base of concepts such as sets and lists, and operations such as union and composition. In addition heuristics such as the following are incorporated:

> If there is a function, f, that accepts two arguments, define a function, g, that accepts the same value for each argument. (This heuristic leads to squaring from multiplication, doubling from addition.)

> If f is a function that transforms elements of A into elements of B, then consider just those members of A that are transformed into extremal elements of B. (Leads to notions of the empty set and disjointness from one extreme of consideration of the intersection of sets, and the notion of subset from consideration of the other extreme.)

AM establishes the worth of particular concepts on the basis of derivation from more than one source, and on the basis of interestingness, as defined by heuristics such as those given earlier. Lenat stated that given a base of 115 core concepts with only a few slots filled and 243 heuristics, AM was able to discover concepts such as de Morgan's laws and the unique factorization theorem. He also suggested that AM's discovery of interesting properties of highly composite numbers have lead to the development (by hand) of dramatically shorter proofs of those properties. One of the principal criticisms of AM is that it is naive. Furthermore AM required a human to monitor its performance and establish the interest of certain conjectures.

These criticisms reveal an important characteristic of a processing system that could be deemed to be creative. Selection must be made on the basis of information of the extent and complexity that humans employ in making subjective evaluations. Acquisition and development of such information may well require a capacity to interact with the environment as humans do (Dreyfus, 1979). The problem is one of confidence. We have attempted to show that scientific theories and art works are not accepted for their correctness or their embodiment of absolute qualities but for their relationship to that which is already known to us. A system will never be able to be labelled a creative processing system unless it has a capacity to make judgements by reference to knowledge bases that are sufficiently similar to our own. This necessarily entails a capacity to manipulate these knowledge bases in the way that is sufficiently similar to the human capacity that allows us to modify and in some cases explain our judgements. A number of processes have been automated that have yielded creative outcomes. These include Lenat's EURISKO program (Lenat, 1983b) and Freudenstein and Maki's exhaustive enumeration system (Freudenstein and Maki, 1983). Often the question that is posed in judging the 'creativity' of the processes used is the degree to which the output has been anticipated in formulating the processes. The proposal here is that such questions should be replaced with queries as to the degree to which the automated process approximates societal evaluations of newly presented information. On that basis, these systems, EURISKO and Freudenstein and Maki's program, should not be regarded as particularly creative. The knowledge bases that they draw on are very circumscribed; the mechanisms that they draw on to establish the relationship of the developing proposal and these knowledge bases, overly simplistic. The all important value judgements that have created the possibility of developing creative outcomes, consisted primarily of the decision as to the information to be included in the knowledge bases, a decision made outside the systems.

The principal difficulty in judging the creativity of processes is that we know so little about the basis on which societal evaluations of newly presented information are made. Earlier in this chapter we attempted to develop a characterization of the nature of emergent value. The principal characteristics of such value were found to be consistency with previously diverse aspects of existing knowledge and possibly some degree of conflict with existing information. Furthermore it may be the case that consistency with some aspects of information, a notion of symmetry for example, may be more important than consistency with others. Such priorities are a function of the knowledge base against which the newly presented information is being evaluated and are thus subject to variation across individuals, societies, and time.

At a very coarse level it may be useful to conceive of recognition of emergent value as a product of monitoring the spreading of activations, activations initiated by the presentation of new information, throughout the

representations that define our existing knowledge. If recognition of emergent value could be operationalized as such, the following issues would need
to be addressed: the nature of the representations of existing knowledge,
including the representation of priorities; the nature of criteria for judging
patterns of activation to be significant; and the nature of the way that we
interpret newly presented information such that we are able to construct
relations to aspects of existing knowledge. All these issues remain open
questions in relation to human information processing. Although there is no
requirement that human processes should be replicated, the difficulties that
philosophers and psychologists have in explicitly setting down the criteria
on which we judge a work to be aesthetically valuable should underscore the
complexity of the task.

4.6   Conclusion

A creative product is one that is both original and valuable. The value of a
creative product is established by its having relations to aspects of existing
knowledge. The condition of originality in a creative product entails that
this set of relations is in some sense unique. We use the term *emergent value*
to refer to the original value embodied in a creative product.

Although a precise characterization of emergent value cannot be given,
some indication as to the nature of such value may be gleaned from two conflicting motivational tendencies: a tendency towards maintaining consistent
cognitive models as predicted by cognitive dissonance theory; and a tendency
to seek novel information. Perhaps the most important characteristic of
emergent value is that it is relative rather than absolute. The absolute basis
on which products are evaluated varies across individuals, societies, and
time.

A creative process is one that yields a creative product. It is impossible to
define any process that is guaranteed to yield a creative outcome. Given our
definition of creative products and the observation that potentially creative
candidate outcomes can be generated by a variety of processes, it is however
possible to state a necessary condition of creative processes: any process
that can in itself be regarded as a creative process must have the capacity
to perform selection based on recognition of emergent value.

Interest in the question of the computability of creative processes is
twofold. On the one hand there is interest in creative processes themselves.
Creativity has long been regarded as a black box process. Attempts to
develop computational models or approximations of creative processes allow
some of our assumptions about such processes to be tested. On the other
hand there is the interest generated as a product of the value associated with

creative outcomes and the desire to utilize automated techniques to facilitate the development of such outcomes. The model of creative processes proposed has important implications in relation to each of these orientations.

Where interest is in exploring the nature of creative processes a number of orientations are possible. Our principal consideration in this chapter has been to explore the possibility of the development of automated processes that can in themselves be called creative. We have suggested that the requirement of a capacity to perform selection based on recognition of emergent value in a creative process entails that any system that may properly be called creative must exhibit a self awareness of the information that it has available to the extent that the relation of novel information to this existing information can be established. Furthermore this awareness and the information base that is available must be sufficiently similar to that of experts in the domain to which the product is relevant that the evaluations made by the automated system will correspond to societal evaluations of the product. A fundamental aspect of this awareness is the ability to make aesthetic judgements. Alternatively information processing techniques may be used to articulate and explore post facto explanations of the development of a creative product. Lenat's AM program is an example of such an exercise.

Where interest is in supporting the development of creative products again a number of approaches are warranted. Information processing techniques may be used as tools for exploring the implications of value judgements made by a user. Examples of programs developed with such an objective in mind are EURISKO, Freudenstien and Maki's exhaustive enumeration program, Coyne's (1990) PDP based model for merging design schemas, and Maher and Zhao's (1987) analogically based design system. The diversity of techniques employed reflects the fact that many different types of processes may be used in the generation of candidate proposals.

Finally, given the complexity of the selection task that must be performed in the development of a creative product and the fact that our current understanding of that task is insufficient to develop appropriate computational models of it, emphasis may be placed on the construction of semiautomated design environments where the difficult act of selection is performed by a user. Such an environment may be seen as the architectural or engineering equivalent of today's business information systems. Some features of an appropriate environment may include the following: convenient and natural input and editing facilities (Kharrufa et al., 1988); simulation programs including three dimensional modeling facilities (Carrasco, 1988); routine design development processes (Wolchko, 1987; Gross et al., 1987); and the provision of richly indexed libraries of past designs with convenient browsing facilities (Smith and Weiss, 1988).

References

Akin, O. (1986). *Psychology of Architectural Design*, Pion, London.

Alexander, C, Ishikawa, S., & Silverstein, M. (1977). *A Pattern Language: Towns, Buildings, Construction*, Oxford University Press, New York.

Armsbruster, B. B. (1989). Metacognition in creativity, *in* J. A. Glover, R. R. Romming, & C. R. Reynolds (Eds), *Handbook of Creativity*, Plenum Press, New York.

Aronson (1968). Dissonance theory: progress and problems, *in* R. P. Abelson, E. Aronson, W. J. McGuire., T. M. Newcomb, M. J. Rosenberg, & P. H. Tannenbaum (Eds), *Theories of Cognitive Consistency: A Sourcebook*, Rand McNally, Chicago.

Atrens, D., & Curthoys, I. (1982). *The Neurosciences and Behaviour: An Introduction*, Academic Press, Sydney.

Bailin, S. (1988). *Achieving Extraordinary Ends: An Essay on Creativity*, Kluwer Academic Publishers, Dordrecht.

Baume, M. (1967). *The Sydney Opera House Affair*, Nelson, Sydney.

Beardsley, M. C. (1965). On the creation of art, *Journal of Aesthetics and Art Criticism*, **23**: 291–301.

Berlyne, D. E. (1971). *Aesthetics and Psychobiology*, Appleton-Century-Crofts, New York

Bexton, W. H., Heron, W., & Scott, T. H. (1954). Effects of decreased variation in the sensory environment, *Canadian Journal of Psychology*, **8**: 70–76.

Butler, R. A. (1954). Incentive conditions which influence visual exploration, *Journal of Experimental Psychology*, **154**(48): 1–23.

Bruner, J. S. (1974). *Beyond the Information Given*, Allen and Unwin, London.

Bugelski, B. R. (1983). Imagery and the thought processes, *in* A. A. Sheikh (Ed.), *Imagery: Current Theory, Research, and Applications*, Wiley, New York.

Carrasco, R. (1988). Three-dimensional modelling as part of architectural design, *Computer-Aided Design*, **20**(4).

Collingwood, R. G. (1938). *The Principles of Art*, Clarendon, Oxford.

Coyne, R. D. (1990). Modelling the emergence of design descriptions across schemas, *Working Paper*, Design Computing Unit, University of Sydney, Sydney.

Coyne, R. D., & Snodgrass, A (1990). Is designing hermeneutical?, *Working Paper*, Design Computing Unit, University of Sydney, Sydney.

Coyne, R. D., Rosenman, M. A., Radford, A. D., & Gero, J. S. (1987). Innovation and creativity in knowledge-based CAD, *in* J. S. Gero (Ed.), *Expert Systems in Computer-Aided Design*, North-Holland, Amsterdam.

Crandall, J. E. (1967). Familiarity, preference and expectancy arousal, *Journal of Experimental Psychology*, **73**: 374–381.

Darke (1979). The primary generator and the design process, *Design Studies*, **1**(1): 36–44.

de Bono, E. (1967). *The Use of Lateral Thinking*, Jonathan Cape, London.

Delago, M. M., Roberts, W. W., & Miller, N. E. (1954). Learning by electrical stimulation of the brain, *American Journal of Physiology*, **179**: 587–593.

Derry, T. K., & Williams, T. I. (1960). *A Short History of Technology*, Clarendon Press, Oxford.

Dreyfus, H. L. (1979). *What Computer's Can't Do: The Limits of Artificial*

Intelligence, Harper and Row, New York.

Ecker, D. W. (1963). The artistic process as qualitative problem solving, *The Journal of Aesthetics and Art Criticism*, **21**: 283–296.

Einstein, A. (1919). *The Fundamental Idea of General Relativity in its Original Form*, manuscript, trans. G. Holton, Einstein Archives, Institute for Advanced Study, Princeton, New Jersey.

Eisenman, P. (1982). *House X*, Rizzoli, New York.

Eliot, T. S. (1975). Hamlet *in* Kermode, F. (Ed.), *Selected Prose of T. S. Eliot*, Faber, London.

Festinger, L. (1957). *A Theory of Cognitive Dissonance*, Stanford University Press, Stanford.

Festinger, L., Riecken, H. W., & Schachter, S. (1956). *When Prophecy Fails*, University of Minnesota Press, Minneapolis.

Foz, A. (1973). Observation on designer behavior in the parti, *Design Research and Methods* **7**: 4.

Freudenstein, F., & Maki, E. R. (1983). Development of an optimum variable-stroke-internal-combustion engine mechanism from the viewpoint of kinematic structure, *ASME Journal of Mechanics, Transmissions and Automation in Design*, **105**: 259–266.

Geissner, H. (1988). Can a computer create poetry? *American Behavioral Scientist*, **32**(2): 136–46.

Ghiselin, B. (1952). *The Creative Process: A Symposium*, University of California Press, Berkeley.

Gotz, I. L. (1981). On defining creativity, *The Journal of Aesthetics and Art Criticism*, **Spring**: 297–301.

Gross, M., Ervin, S., Anderson, J., & Fleisher, A. (1987). Designing with constraints, *in* Y. E. Kalay (Ed.), *The Computability of Design*, John Wiley, New York.

Guilford, J. P. (1967). *The Nature of Human Intelligence*, McGraw-Hill, New York.

Haensley, P. A. and Reynolds, C. R. (1989). Creativity and intelligence *in* J. A. Glover, R. R. Romming, & C. R. Reynolds (Eds), *Handbook of Creativity*, Plenum Press, New York, pp. 111–134.

Hasburg, G. (1987). Creation as translation, *The Journal of Aesthetics and Art Criticism*, **46**(2): 249–258.

Hausman, C. R. (1981). Gotz on creativity, *The Journal of Aesthetics and Art Criticism*, **40**(1): 81.

Hausman, C. R. (1985). Originality as a criterion of creativity, *in* M. Mitias (Ed.), *Creativity in Art, Religion and Culture*, Konigshausen and Neuma, Wurzburg.

Hayes, J. R. (1989). Cognitive processes in creativity, *in* J. A. Glover, R. R. Romming, & C. R. Reynolds (Eds), *Handbook of Creativity*, Plenum Press, New York.

Hebb, D. O., & Donderi, D. C. (1987). *Textbook of Psychology*, Lawrence Erlbaum, Hillsdale, New Jersey.

Hebb, D. O. (1946). On the nature of fear, *Psychological Review*, **53**: 259–276.

Hershman, D. J., & Lieb, J. (1988). *The Key to Genius*, Prometheus Books, Buffalo, New York.

Isozaki, A. (1972). About my method, *Japan Architect*, **August**: 22–27

Kharrufu, S., Sutto, A., Aldabbagh, H., & Mahmood, W. (1988). Developing CAD techniques for preliminary architectural design, *Computer-Aided Design*, **20**(10): 581–588.

Khatchadourian, H. (1977). The creative process in art, *British Journal of Aesthetics*, **17**(3): 230–241.

Knight (1963). The critical moment, *The Times Literary Supplement*, July 26, p. 569.

Koestler, A. (1964). *The Act of Creation*, MacMillan, New York.

Kuhn, T. S. (1970). *The Structure of Scientific Revolutions*, University of Chicago Press, Chicago.

Le Corbusier (1923). *Vers une architecture*, Editions Cres, Paris. English translation: Towards a New Architecture (1927), trans. F. Etchells, John Rodker, England.

Lenat, D. B. (1983a). The role of heuristics in learning by discovery: three case studies, *in* R. S. Michalski, J. G. Carbonell, & T. M. Mitchell (Eds), *Machine Learning: an Artificial Intelligence Approach*, Kaufman, Los Altos.

Lenat, D. B. (1983b). The nature of heuristics III: EURISKO: a program that learns new heuristics and domain concepts, *Artificial Intelligence*, **21**: 61–98.

Maher, M. L. and Zhao, F. (1987). Using experience to plan the synthesis of new designs, *in* J. S. Gero (Ed.), *Expert Systems in Computer-Aided Design*, North-Holland, Amsterdam.

Mansfield, R. S., & Busse, T. V. (1981). *The Psychology of Creativity and Discovery*, Nelson-Hall, Chicago.

Mitias, M. H. (1978). The institutional theory of artistic creativity, *British Journal of Aesthetics*, **18**(4): 330–341.

Mitchell, W. J. (1989). *The Logic of Architecture*, MIT Press, Cambridge.

Moore, C. (1976). Hadrian's Villa: a whole world in a circle and a square *in* C. Moore and G. Allen (Eds), *Dimensions: Space, Shape and Scale in Architecture*, Architectural Record Books, New York, pp. 79–94.

Murray, E. L. (1986). *Imaginative Thinking and Human Existence*, Duquesne University Press, Pittsburgh.

Newell, A., & Simon, H. S. (1972). *Human Problem Solving*, Prentice-Hall, Englewood Cliffs, New Jersey.

Olds, J. (1977). *Drives and Reinforcement: Behavioral Studies of Hypothalmic Functions*, Raven Press.

Patrick, C. (1937). Creative thought in artists, *Journal of Psychology*, **4**: 35–73.

Patrick, C. (1935). Creative thought in poets, *Archives of Psychology*, **178**.

Petri, H. L. (1986). *Motivation: Theory and Research*, Wadsworth, Belmont.

Pfieffer, R. S. (1979). The scientific concept of creativity, *Educational Theory*, **29**(2): 129–137.

Piaget, J. (1952). The origins of intelligence in children, *International Universities Press*, New York.

Rossi, A. (1982). *The Architecture of the City*, MIT Press, Cambridge.

Rothenberg, A. (1979). *The Emerging Goddess*, University of Chicago Press, Chicago.

Schank R. C. (1982). *Dynamic Memory*, Lawrence Erlbaum, Hillsdale, New Jersey.

Schank, R. C., & Abelson, R. P. (1977). *Scripts, Plans, Goals and Understanding*,

Lawrence Erlbaum, Hillsdale, New Jersey.

Scheffler, I. (1982). In praise of the cognitive emotions, *in* I. Scheffler, *Science and Subjectivity*, Hackett, Indianapolis.

Schön, D. A. (1969). *Invention and the Evolution of Ideas*, Tavistock Publications, London.

Sheppard, A. (1987). *Aesthetics: An Introduction to the Philosophy of Art*, Oxford University Press, Oxford.

Smith, J. B., & Weiss, S. F. (1988). Hypertext, *Communications of the ACM*, **31**(7): 816–819.

Smithers, T., Doheny, J., Logan, B., & Millington, K. (1989). Design as intelligent behaviour, *in* J. S. Gero (Ed.) *Artificial Intelligence in Design*, Springer-Verlag, Berlin, pp. 293–334.

Spence, B. (1962). *Phoenix at Coventry: The Building of a Cathedral*, Geoffrey Bles Ltd, London.

Stiny, G. (1986). A new line on drafting systems, *Design Computing* **1**: 5–9.

Tomas, V. (1958). Creativity in art, *Philosophical Review*, **67**, *reprinted in* W. E. Kennick (Ed.) (1979), *Art and Philosophy*, St Martin's Press, New York, pp. 131–142.

Utzon, J. (1962). Platforms and plateaus: ideas of a Danish architect, *Zodiac*, **10**: 112-140.

Utzon, J. (1965). The Sydney Opera House, *Zodiac*, **14**: 48–56.

Wallas, G. (1970). The art of thought, *in* P. E. Vernon (Ed.), *Creativity: Selected Readings*, Penguin, Harmondsworth.

Watson, J. D. (1968). *The Double Helix*, Weidenfeld and Nicolson, London.

Weisberg, R. W. (1986). *Creativity: Genius and Other Myths*, W. H. Freeman, New York.

Wicklund, R. A., & Brehm, J. W. (1976). *Perspectives on Cognitive Dissonance*, Lawrence Erlbaum, Hillsdale, New Jersey.

Wolchko, M. J. (1987). Design by zoning code: The New Jersey office building, *in* Kalay, Y. E. (ed.), *The Computability of Design*, John Wiley, New York.

Wundt, W. M. (1874). *Grundzuge de Physiologischen Psychologie*, Engelmann, Leipzig.

Yeomans, J. (1986). *The Other Taj Mahal: What Happened to the Sydney Opera House*, Longmans, London.

Young, J. Z. (1987). *Philosophy and the Brain*, Oxford University Press, Oxford.

Ziegler, O. (Ed.) (1973). *Sydney Builds An Opera House*, Oswald Ziegler Publications, Sydney.

5 A Neuropsychologically-Based Approach to Creativity

Tapio Takala

General features of creativity are discussed, aimed at providing a clear definition. In the view of general design theory, creativity is seen as a communication process aiming at consistency between different intensional and extensional representations of design. Basic concepts of classical neuropsychology and the functional structure of the brain are reviewed, emphasizing the self-controlling role of the mid-brain. Based on these, a model of creative behavior analogous to the brain model is presented. A key concept is called view, a restricted field of attention, or the momentary collection of objects and relations considered interesting in a situation. Drawbacks of traditional knowledge bases in implementing the model are pointed out, and their development towards creative behavior is discussed. The approach aims at deriving new connections and analogs between neuropsychology, general design theory and knowledge engineering, with special emphasis in the motivating forces of creativity.

5.1 What is creativity?

Creativity is usually understood as a person's ability to produce something new and unexpected. It is considered a desirable property and characteristic of intelligent human beings. It is involved in works of art and science, but may also appear in situations of everyday life. Essential in creativity is that something recognizable is produced, and that the result is novel.

But how and why this happens is often considered unknown, even mystical. Creativity is a concept hard to define. Some people totally deny the possibility of an exact definition, because it inevitably would be too specific and restrictive.

Intelligence and extensive training are considered necessary but not sufficient conditions for creativity. In addition, specific traits of creative people are a flexible, nondefensive openness to experience, an autonomy or independence of authorities, an ability to toy with conceptual ideas, and an aesthetic sensibility—the ability to judge and desire (Maher et al., 1989).

However, it may not be possible to define creativity exactly with a list of specific static attributes of a person, because so many different, even contrary properties may be associated to creativity. Instead, a clear definition can be based on the *processes* of mind recognized as creative behavior.

5.1.1   Process models of creativity

Indeed, creativity is nothing but the ability to perform creative processes. Such processes have through the ages been investigated and modeled both introspectively and by objective observations. Problem-solving is a common paradigm to describe creativity, and is useful in the context of design. Typically we can distinguish four phases in the process (Wallas, 1926):

1. *Preparation*, the collecting of facts related to the problem, and their analysis from different points of view—also trials to solve the problem,

2. *incubation*, subconscious organizing processes while the subject is not concentrating in the problem, but doing something else (e.g., while sleeping),

3. *illumination*, sudden appearance and recognition of the solution, and

4. *verification*, deepening and detailing the solution by comparing it against various constraints and requirements of the problem.

However, creativity is not only the solving of given external problems. Strong *internal motivation* is needed in order to start a creative process. A material reward can hardly compensate the gratification and satisfaction achieved from successful comprehension.

According to Freudian theories, creative activity is often explained as sublimation of other more primitive driving forces. From the psychoanalytical point of view the motivating force of creativity is a person's need to compensate for the feeling of imperfection. The person is building solutions to a loss (death of a close person, mother envy, phallic-narcissistic wound, etc.) by recreating the lost object in a transformed form. This behavior is learned in the childhood, when parts of the mother-child relationship are transferred to 'transitional objects.' From this perspective, imagination and animation with toys are the child's first creative attitude toward the environment (Hägglund, 1976).

In neuropsychological (psycho-physiological) terms a creative process can be understood as the autonomous (i.e. independent of immediate sensory stimulation) formation of new activation patterns in the brain, recombining already existing self-activating loops. Production of something new from existing prerequisites is not restricted to a 'creative personality,' but happens all the time. There are only different grades of its appearance: a housewife finding a new way to make food may be as creative as a novel writer giving us new insights into human lives. A child imagining the doll speaking is creative, as well as a drunken man seeing hallucinations (Hebb, 1958).

A biologist may generalize that creativity is an attribute of all life. It is the mind's morphogenetic tendency to build organized structures out of chaos, a feature not peculiar to humans but appearing even in lower animals (Sinnott, 1959).

5.1.2 Defining creativity

In this chapter the term *creativity* is understood mainly the same way as by Hebb and Sinnott: a creative process forms new patterns from previously existing patterns in the human mind. The patterns are conscious and strong enough to stimulate sensory areas of the brain, thus they are potentially externalizable. But even if not observable from outside, the patterns should at least be recognized by the creative individual him/herself.

Creativity is largely identical to imagination, but not all imagination is creativity. Mednick (1962) distinguished creative thinking from original thinking by the imposition of requirements of usefulness. His definition (cited e.g., by Morris, 1982: p.333), that "creativity is the forming of associative elements into combinations which either meet specific requirements or are in some way useful," is especially suitable in design. Mednick admitted that usefulness is difficult to measure. In actual design situations it is hard to judge objectively the degree of novelty and practical value required to call a new product creative. They are a matter of cultural environment.

Instead of cultural novelty and usefulness, special emphasis in this chapter is given to the subjective motivation of creativity, that is to the requirement that a creative process should give the feeling of pleasure and gratification. The motivation for creative behavior is an explicit or subconscious problem, a dilemma or inconsistency, an initial displeasure that becomes rewarded and relieved when the problem is solved. From this point of view, creativity is not only the ability to solve problems, but includes the brain's homeostatic tendency to actively seek or autonomously produce problems, in order to get pleasure from solving them.

5.2   Design theory

In design we consciously aim at a useful concrete or abstract product. A design process typically starts with the analysis of the product's intended context. This analysis results in a heterogeneous set of loosely connected details and perhaps some insight into potential solutions.

The design problem is first structured and its solution is defined through its implicit properties. Without contradicting the context, a new construction should be made that will satisfy a given set of additional requirements. The requirements are *intentional*—their fullfillment can be tested and detected, but they don't yet directly devise a product. But what we actually want is an explicit solution, a unique *extensional* model or representation from which the product can be constructed (Takala, 1987b).

If the requirements and the context determine a unique solution, it may be derived algorithmically. Then 'designing' is simply the problem's transformation from intensional to extensional form. Such design automation can be performed by three alternative strategies or by any combination of these, depending on the formulation of the problem and the knowledge available about its solutions (Yoshikawa, 1981).

1. *Catalog model:* known standard solutions are stored in a database, from which they can be retrieved using the required properties as keys.

2. *Calculation model:* the basic form of the solution is known, but its dimensions or other explicit parameters have to be numerically calculated, based on mathematical formulas connecting them to the implicit properties.

3. *Production model:* inference rules are used to derive a solution logically from the requirements (much the same way as mathematical formulas are used in the calculation model, but in a more qualitative sense).

Often no algorithmic rules are known or the problem is underspecified, leaving space for free decisions and creativity. Then we have to search a solution by trial and error, generating and testing different proposals. Typically this is not done completely at random, but we have a paradigmatic solution, which is compared against a partial, gradually growing set of requirements, and modified if needed. This *paradigm model* describes design as the *convergent evolution* of solutions (Yoshikawa, 1981). Its gradual steps form the history of a design, which may branch and involve backtracking, but finally contains a path leading to the solution (Takala, 1987a). The end goal of design is that all the related facts, both the original requirements and the created constructions, are consistent.

5.2.1   Views to the design knowledge

The evolution is not often successful by straightforward derivation from one single direction only. Instead, the problem should be approached from various points of view. The designer's attention focuses to different aspects of the same problem, wandering around and slowly approaching it like a spiral (Zeisel, 1981).

The limited set of facts that are taken into account at a time, that is the focus of attention, will here be called a *view*. During a design process the focus is continuously fluctuating—the 'looking glass' is changing its size and location within the whole set of available knowledge (Figure 5.1). Within each view, partial solutions are constructed and tested against the respective facts.

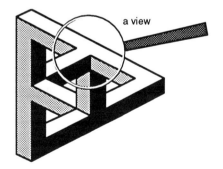

Figure 5.1. A geometrically consistent design when looked through a focused view, but globally a nonrealizable object (in the style of M. C. Escher).

The design is considered finished, when a sufficient number of views have been successfully handled this way without discrepancy (Takala and Silén,

1989). Larger design situations, that is architectural design of a building, are 'wicked problems.' They are so complex that there is no way to handle all relevant information within active views. This is why they cannot be completely designed before actually building the whole product.

Many design theories are based on a stereotypical hierarchical model of the design object or design process. However, each such model corresponds to one particular view only. No single hierarchy alone can describe all aspects of a design, but several crossing hierarchies are needed. For example, an architect has two complementary views to a room, one concerning its walls and another its enclosed space. They are not independent, and neither alone is sufficient for design.

In creative design the attention focusing, as described earlier, is essential. If all the requirements and all partial constructions made so far were taken into account at once, it would quickly lead to contradictions and a dead-end. Instead of convergent thinking, that is getting stuck in the first idea and following the most obvious logical reasoning straight-ahead, a creative mind applies divergent or lateral thinking, that is looks the problem from different points of view, "not digging the hole deeper but digging in a new place" (de Bono, 1967). In other words, creativity requires a "flat association hierarchy" Mednick (1962).   Creativity enhancing techniques, like brain-storming and synectics, intentionally do this by leaving away critics for a moment, producing many partial solutions and new associations between seemingly unrelated things. Gradually the views are then enlarged, until they finally cover all the relevant facts (see Figure 5.5 also).

5.3   Communication and creative design

The paradigmatic solutions during design evolution are usually presented in models, drawings, or other external forms, which facilitate their com-munication both to other people and to the designer himself (autocommu-nication). It is important to note that such *an external representation is always ambiguous and metaphorical*. A house doesn't consist of the ink lines representing it in a drawing, nor of the pieces of paper in its scale model nor of words used to discuss it. A message, even if described with abstract concepts, has to be coded in a physical form, and the relevant information contained in a representation has to be interpreted, in order to be comprehended (Figure 5.2).

Understanding a new message is itself a creative process. During inter-pretation we make hypotheses about the meaning, which are then verified or changed as new information is attained. All the details have to be put

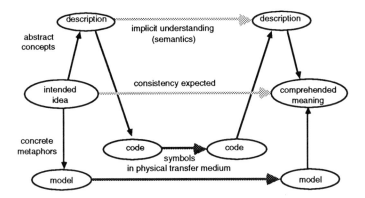

Figure 5.2. Model of metaphorical communication (Takala, 1989).

together into a coherent set. We are learning by *designing a mental model* of the world. However, in this process we also need to focus our attention to limited views, because a representation may contain too much information to be processed at once. This is especially true in auditory communication, speech, and music, where the sensory processing is strictly sequential, and memory has to be utilized to construct a holistic view.

In creative design the external models have an important communicative role. A representation may be interpreted not only in the obvious way, but it may stimulate various other associations and views also, which potentially lead to new solutions. This is why graphical sketching is so fruitful. Even an image totally unrelated to the problem at hand may give rise to innovative ideas. Particularly stimulating are incomplete and ambiguous messages, which can be understood in several alternative but logically consistent ways. Although exact communication is the act of understanding an ambiguous message in the intended way, creativity is the art of *misunderstanding in a meaningful way*.

In creative artistic design consistency within every view is even not always the goal. Surrealistic works are interesting and aesthetically pleasing for the reason that in most views they are consistent with the real world, but in some sense they are strikingly controversial. For example, if we scan Figure 5.1 with a looking glass, its small aperture gives a perfect image everywhere, but the geometric impossibility is only discovered when these are combined within a wider view. The discovery of such ambiguities is the essence of the art's appeal. Creative art is that which stimulates creative processes in its viewers!

5.4   Neuropsychological basis of thinking

In order to understand the mechanisms of mind and to find potential methods to simulate creativity, we have to take a look at the structural and functional physiology of the brain. This can be done at different levels of detail, ranging from individual cells and assemblies to functional areas of brain tissue, and finally to overall behavioral regulation. Thorough surveys are given by Kolb and Whishaw (1990) from the physiological point of view, and by Churchland (1986) with special emphasis on philosophy and computer science. A synthesis of these viewpoints may lead to a working computational model of human behavior, including creativity.

5.4.1   Microlevel neural structures

The information processing in the brain takes place in a huge number of neural cells called *neurons*, which form a network tightly cross-coupled by synaptic interconnections. Each cell itself roughly behaves like a linear summation element, taking many inputs with different weights, and producing one output that is activated by some inputs and inhibited by others.

Although the nerves transmit information as digital pulses, the signals are of analog nature: the frequency of pulses corresponds to a continuous value, and the pulses are not synchronized. Perceptrons, digitally simulated cells without these properties, have strictly limited abilities in pattern recognition and learning (Minsky and Papert, 1969).

The topology of the network is formed in childhood and remains rather fixed thereafter. However, the synaptic connections (the summation weights for each cell) are still highly adaptive, facilitating learning. The connections have the tendency to reinforce when both connected cells are activated simultaneously, and to decay otherwise. This simple principle gives the network the ability to organize itself while working. Simulations of such neural processes, on the microlevel of individual cells, are called neurocomputers or *neural networks* (Kohonen, 1984; McClelland et al., 1986; IEEE, 1988).

Groups of tightly coupled neurons that can stimulate each other, may form feedback loops where activation is reverbarated and retained for some time. Hebb (1949, 1958) called these *neural assemblies* and used them to model brain functions on a higher level than single cells (see also Kolb and Whishaw, 1990: 527-530). They can act as mediating processes, making associations between nonsimultaneous stimuli. Except for simple reflectory learning, these loops are essential for any cognitive processes. According to Hebb, the three forms of cognitive learning are (Figure 5.3):

1. *Self-organization*, the formation and reinforcement of a feedback loop
   by repeating the same sensory stimulus,

2. *conditioning*, forming associations between loops when they are activated concurrently or closely sequential, and

3. *attaining knowledge*, forming connections between loops already formed
   by a set of stimuli and by several potential ways to react.

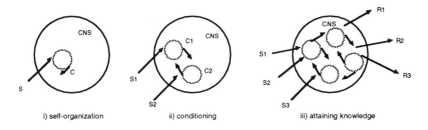

i) self-organization   ii) conditioning   iii) attaining knowledge

Figure 5.3. Hebb's three principles of learning with self-activating neural loops.
CNS = Central Nervous System, S = Stimulus, R = Response, C = self-activating
feedback loop.

The third type is considered closest to cognitive thinking, because it
can be performed purely internally, without simultaneous appearance of the
stimuli and the response reactions. Obviously it also corresponds to our
definition of creativity: New patterns of activity are autonomously formed
from existing ones.

5.4.2   Functional organization of brain

The brain as a whole is modeled by Luria (1973) with three main functional
units (see also Kolb and Whishaw, 1990: 173–176, 183–202):

1. The 'input unit,' which obtains, processes and stores arriving sensory
   information,

2. the 'output unit' for programming, regulating and verifying the performance of mental plans and motoric movements of the body, and

3. the unit regulating tone or waking (the reticular activating system).

Information in the nervous system flows inwards from sensory organs
through afferent nerves into the central nervous system (the spinal chord

and the brain), and outwards through efferent nerves to the motoric organs (muscles). In the brain cortex these input and output channels are organized and interconnected by several hierarchical layers (three by Luria, more according to some others):

1. The primary projection areas, where each organ has a well-defined corresponding location, and where primitive features of senses are analyzed and topographically organized,

2. the gnostic and premotor areas, performing modally-specific synthesis of sensory functions and preparation of motor impulses, and

3. overlapping zones, enabling groups of several modal functions to work concertedly. This third 'supramodal' layer, performs integration of external stimuli, preparation of action programs and verification that actions are carried out.

Each of the main functional units has this layered structure, with modal specificity decreasing from the projection areas to the overlapping areas.

All three units have to work in close interaction for any perception to take place. A continuous optimal tone is required by the brain to work properly, and no spatial comprehension can be formed without proper correlation between sensory information and the body movements.

Perception is an active process including search for elements of information, their comparison, creation of hypotheses concerning the meaning of information, and verification of these hypotheses by comparison with the original elements. It is heavily dependent on the overlapping zones which, according to Luria, are located mainly in the frontal lobes of brain cortex. They are well-developed in humans, and are considered the place of higher mental processes. Actually the frontal lobes are found to facilitate divergent thinking, essential in creativity (Kolb and Whishaw, 1990: 474).

5.4.3   Role of the limbic system

Luria's third functional unit (tone regulation) is located in the limbic system and the reticular formation of midbrain and brain stem. These areas are phylogenetically very old, occupying the main part of lower vertebrates' brains. Their exact function is not yet clear, but we know at least that they strongly affect our emotions and general tone, including the homeostatic control of body temperature and other physiological processes.

Because of adaptation and habituation of sensory and other neural processes, no single form of behavior can maintain a constant activation, but there has to be a continuous fluctuation of activation from one area to another in the brain. The macrolevel activity never covers the whole cortex but continuously fluctuates from one place to another, corresponding to changing focuses of our thoughts and attentions, and being concentrated only temporarily during an intellectual activity (Luria, 1973: 98). This moving pattern of high level of coherent activity among cell ensembles can reasonably be called consciousness (John, 1976).

It seems evident that a mechanism focusing conscious attention to restricted views, a process similar to that described in the previous section, actually exists in the midbrain. Findings about the behavior of thalamus as a selective switchboard and reverbarating unit suggest it acts like a moving searchlight, paying attention to one thing at a time (Crick, 1984).

In the limbic system there are other areas, the excitation of which may cause ultimate pleasure or displeasure. They have a special role as the general controller and motivator of other activities. The behavior of any animal, including humans, acts towards getting the pleasure areas activated (Campbell, 1973). With this background, the limbic system's responsibility is to generate arousal and attention to new areas over and over again. It keeps on the activity to find potential new problems, and to feel satisfaction when a problem becomes solved. Its interaction with the frontal lobe and other associative areas selects which subjects we are interested in, and which arguments we consider relevant for reasoning, ultimately determining our values of life (Bergström, 1986).

It is important to note that the real neural system in itself has such a source of activity with a higher-level homeostatic control. Despite the intensive research done on artificial neural networks, such aspects seem to be totally neglected so far (Freeman, 1988). However, in order to simulate creativity we also have to model these motivation mechanisms of mind (Takala, 1987b).

5.5   A model of creativity

A model about how the brain works in a creative process is inevitably hypothetical and subject to speculation. Also, because of the brain's enormous complexity, it hardly ever can be exactly simulated with computers. Nevertheless, we can draw some analogs and conclusions about how computers can be developed towards more intelligent and creative behavior.

5.5.1   An associative network

First of all, we need a representation, that is data structures holding the knowledge of our design problem. The importance of adequate explicit representations in any form of artificial intelligence cannot be emphasized too much (Winston, 1984).

In our model the knowledge relevant for a situation is represented as a network, whose nodes stand for self-activating neural loops, and the lines stand for mutual activating or inhibiting associations between the loops. It is a network of entities (objects) and relationships, where one can build a coherent model of the world.

The four phases of a creative process, as described in the first section (Wallas, 1926), can be explained with the associative network model (Figure 5.4).

a) In the first phase, knowledge items relevant to the problem are formed. Some associations arise between them and other possible items. They are manipulated in small, possibly overlapping groups, corresponding to different views, but are not yet organized holistically.

b) In the next phase attention is moved away from the problem's network. Then the general activity in the loops is reduced, and the established associations are not continuously reinforced, but become subject to decay and change. Such a situation models the relaxation of constraints, typical in this phase of creative work. Because of the neural network's inherent tendency to organize itself (due to more or less random activation), new associations are automatically formed. However, because of mutual inhibition, not every such network is stable and most such trials soon decay. Contradicting knowledge items tend to compensate each other.

c) Whenever a potentially stable network starts to form, it grows very rapidly due to lack of inhibition, and the corresponding view widens. Almost simultaneous mutual activation is so strong that it starts to activate other brain areas, and suddenly comes to consciousness. This is felt as the moment of discovery.

d) After the sudden illumination, attention will be focused onto the problem again, and the new network will be related and compared, part by part, to other existing knowledge in the network. If no serious conflicts are encountered, the solution will be established and considered verified.

The overall behavior of the model is like assembling a jigsaw puzzle. Some pieces are first found to fit together and to form partial images, but a breakthrough happens only after finding some key pieces connecting them. The rest is then just to mechanically fill in the remaining pieces.

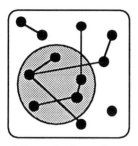

a) Preparation: items of a network have been attained, a partial network is under focus.

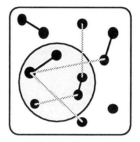

b) Incubation: established relations have been relaxed, enabling new formations.

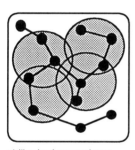

c) Illumination: consistent relations have suddenly emerged in an unexpected way.

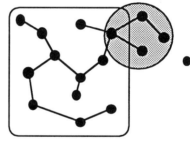

d) Verification: newly formed network is compared with more distant knowledge.

Figure 5.4. The four phases of creative process, performed on an associative network. The points stand for knowledge items (objects) and lines for relations between them. Circles are the moving foci of attention. Crossing lines symbolically represent contradictions.

5.5.2 Implications for knowledge engineering

The basic representational idea of objects and relations is similar to that in traditional knowledge bases; the objects can be understood as facts or frames, and the relations as inference rules or reference slots, respectively.

In traditional knowledge bases and expert systems all facts are considered of equal importance, available for inference all the time. Monotonic logic is applied, which restricts every assertion, whether proved by backward reasoning or generated by forward reasoning, to be within the transitive closure of original knowledge. Therefore the whole set of facts is forced to be consistent. Even a single contradiction would make anything logically inferrable with monotonic deductive logic.

In design, however, inconsistencies are a rule rather than an exception. Contrary tentative design alternatives are often kept open before final decisions. And even within one alternative discrepancies between representations may appear (e.g., a dimension may be calculated from other related measures in various ways with slightly different results; calculated results may also differ from preset nominal values). Also, the 'reasoning' in neural systems is concurrent and typically not logical. Even if we may afterwards explain and defend our findings with careful sequential inferencing, the solutions have usually not been reached that way. The order in which facts are considered is nondetermininstic, facilitating chance. Also the 'facts' handled in neural systems are not logical truth values, but continuously-valued signals with variable strength, reinforced by active usage. This means that traditional logic programming is not a sufficient tool for implementing a creative system.

The difference between logical and creative, or vertical and lateral thinking respectively, can be explained with the movement of views (Figure 5.5). It is the same as between monotonic and nonmonotonic reasoning. The former happens with a gradually increasing view where nothing once accepted cannot be discarded anymore, whereas the latter is realized by the focus of attention spontaneously jumping from place to place. This allows some facts to hold in one view and to be contradicted in another (although each view alone is consistent), as required by design practice.

A kind of nonmonotonic reasoning may be achieved using certainty factors associated with facts and rules. Actually such a knowledge base would effectively do the same as the 'connectionistic' neural network described by Rumelhart et al. (1986), later elaborated for creative design by Coyne et al. (1990). Parallel forward reasoning, using additive certainty factors, corresponds to iteratively multiplying the vector of cell activities by the network's connectivity (autocorrelation) matrix. The possible stable states of the network are then the eigenvectors of the matrix (although slightly complicated by the thresholding after summation of cell inputs). Rumelhart et al. (1986) did not analyze the situation that thoroughly, but recognized that the stable states maximize a 'non-energy' function, and that these local maxima are reached by 'hill-climbing' (i.e., optimization by the gradient method). Sejnowski and Hinton (1987) modified the system by 'heating' it with random noise, and then letting slow 'annealing' to statistically reach the global optimum.

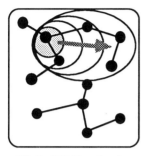 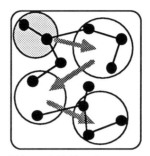

a) Vertical thinking: the view
follows most obvious routes
with monotonic movement.

b) Lateral thinking: the
spontaneously jumping view
explores more alternatives.

Figure 5.5.   The difference between strictly logical and creative thinking, illustrated with movement of views within a knowledge base.

What happens in our model within one view during the incubation phase is actually the same relaxation process as described earlier, although with the minor difference that not only cell activities but also their association strengths may vary (they are not assumed to be direct synaptic connections but mediated by other active cells).

However, a fundamental difference from usual knowledge engineering and connectionistic neural networks is that here we have a dynamically partitioned knowledge base. Each view is the selection of knowledge considered interesting. At any moment during design, only a small portion of all facts is considered and made consistent, but there always remains a possibility for contradictions with the rest of facts. The whole knowledge base may never become consistent, as actually happens with 'wicked problems.'

We also need a mechanism controlling the changes of the focus of attention. In the brain such mechanisms are on one hand the pleasure areas, determining if we enjoy a state or wish to move into another. Where to move, on the other hand, is directed by the associative areas of cortex, coordinated by the frontal lobes. They generate free associations, not necessarily following the most logical reasoning routes.

In the computer model this mechanism could be based on time-dependent feedback from a consistency detector, which continuously measures the currently active view's coherence. It would keep us in an inconsistent view, trying to solve its problem. However, if no progress is made for some time, the view will automatically be changed, that is some knowledge may be dropped and new items added, or a totally new focus may emerge.

The basic idea is that a view is stable only as long as it is enjoyable. The interest is sustained within the view as long as there are inconsistencies being resolved, but ceases when full coherence is achieved. The system would widen the view whenever consistency is reached—the faster the easier consistency is found—but ultimately, if everything became rigidly consistent, the system would disturb itself by randomly corrupting any facts, producing new motivating problems for itself. It would have a homeostatic tendency to always be active (Takala, 1987b).

5.6   Conclusions

In this chapter, a system has been sketched, which might have creative behavior. It is an associative network of knowledge, combining features from both the neural network models and the functional neuropsychological models of brain. A classical process model of creativity has been demonstrated within this model.

A fundamental concept in the system is a view—a dynamic partition of the knowledge base, containing those objects and relations that are considered relevant at a moment. It allows the knowledge base to contain partial design solutions, which during a design process are not yet consistent with each other.

The control strategy for the views is based on a consistency detector, which corresponds to the pleasure areas of brain. It keeps the system continuously active, solving problems given from outside or generated by itself. Creativity is understood as the system's inherent tendency to solve problems and to enjoy that.

The goal has been to research, how creativity could be developed within a computer system, and which basic mechanisms are needed for this. An active, creative system could serve as a more intelligent apprentice for a human designer than the current logical knowledge bases. However, still much reasearch is needed in order to make the approach practical.

A simple experimental system with the features described earlier may be constructed using hypermedia techniques. A generalized product model, consisting of objects (simple facts) and associative relations (activating or inhibiting) between them, is a network where the designer can freely move and make new constructions. The hypermedia environment makes it easy to incorporate any types of representations and to utilize the designer's associative and creative capabilities through the interactive user interface.

Acknowledgments. This work has been supported by the Technology Development Center of Finland through the ESPRIT-II project #3143, 'Factory of the Future.' I also thank the reviewers for their comments and encouragement.

References

Bergström, M. (1986). Mind-brain interaction: Consciousness as a neural macrostate, *in* M. Karjalainen et al. (Eds), *Finnish Artificial Intelligence Symposium, Vol. 1, AI and Philosophy*, Finnish Society of Information Processing Science.

Campbell, H. J. (1973). *The Pleasure Areas—A New Theory of Behaviour*, Delacorte Press, New York.

Churchland, P. S. (1986). *Neurophilosophy—Toward a Unified Science of the Mind-Brain*, MIT Press, Cambridge, Massachusetts.

Coyne, R. D., Newton, S., & Sudweeks, F. (1990). Modeling the emergence of schemas in design reasoning, *in* J. S. Gero, & M. L. Maher (Eds), *Preprints Modeling Creativity and Knowledge-Based Creative Design*, Design Computing Unit, Department of Architectural and Design Science, University of Sydney, pp. 173–205.

Crick, F. (1984). Function of the thalamic reticular complex: the searchlight hypothesis, *Proc. National Academy of Sciences of USA, Vol. 81: Neurobiology*, pp. 4586–4590.

de Bono, E. (1967). *New Think: The Use of Lateral Thinking in the Generation of New Ideas*, Basic Books, New York.

Freeman, W. J. (1988). Why neural networks don't yet fly: inquiry into the neurodynamics of biological intelligence, *Proc. of IEEE International Conference on Neural Networks*, San Diego, California, pp. II-1–7.

Hebb, D. O. (1949). *Organization of Behavior*, Wiley, New York.

Hebb, D. O. (1958, 1972). *A Textbook of Psychology*, W. B. Saunders, Toronto.

Hägglund, T. B. (1976). *Dying—A Psychoanalytical Study with Special Reference to Individual Creativity and Defensive Organization*, Monographs from the Psychiatric Clinic of the Helsinki University Central Hospital, Helsinki.

IEEE (1988). *Proc. of IEEE International Conference on Neural Networks*, San Diego, California.

John, E. R. (1976). A model of consciousness, *in* G. Schwartz, & D. Shapiro (Eds), *Consciousness and Self-Regulation: Advances in Research*, Vol. 1, Plenum Press, New York, pp. 1–50.

Kohonen, T. (1984). *Self-Organization and Associative Memory*, Springer-Verlag, Berlin.

Kolb, B., & Whishaw, I. (1990). *Fundamentals of Human Neuropsychology*, 3rd ed., W. H. Freeman, New York.

Luria, A. R. (1973). *The Working Brain—An Introduction to Neuropsychology*, Penguin, London.

Maher, M. L., Zhao, F., & Gero, J. S. (1989). Creativity in humans and computers, *in* J. S. Gero, & T. Oksala (Eds), *Knowledge-Based Systems in Architecture*, Acta Polytechnica Scandinavica, Helsinki, pp. 129–141.

McClelland, J., Rumelhart, D., & the PDP Research Group (1986). *Parallel Distributed Processing: Explorations in the Microstructure of Cognition*, Vol. 1-2, MIT Press, Cambridge, Massachusetts.

Mednick, S. A. (1962). The associative basis of the creative process, *Psychological Review*, **69**(3): 220-232.

Minsky, M., & Papert, S. (1969). *Perceptrons*, MIT Press, Cambridge, Massachusetts.

Morris, C. G. (1982). *Psychology; An Introduction*, 4th ed., Prentice-Hall, New Jersey.

Rumelhart, D. E., Smolensky, P., McClelland, J., & Hinton, G. (1986). Schemata and sequential thought processes in PDP models, *in* J. McClelland, D. Rumelhart, & the PDP Research Group, *Parallel Distributed Processing: Explorations in the Microstructure of Cognition, Vol 2: Psychological and Biological Models*, MIT Press, Cambridge, Massachusetts.

Sejnowski, T., & Hinton, G. (1987). Separating figure from ground with a Boltzmann machine, *in* M. Arbib, & A. Hanson (Eds), *Vision, Brain, and Cooperative Computation*, MIT Press, Cambridge, Massachusetts, pp. 703-724.

Sinnott, E. W. (1959). The creativeness of life, *in* H. H. Anderson (Ed.), *Creativity and its Cultivations*, Harper, New York; also in P. E. Vernon (Ed.), *Creativity—Selected Readings*, Penguin, London, pp. 107-115.

Takala, T. (1987a). Theoretical framework for computer aided innovative design, *in* H. Yoshikawa, & E. A. Warman (Eds), *Design Theory for CAD*, North-Holland, Amsterdam, pp. 323-334.

Takala, T. (1987b). Intelligence beyond expert systems: a physiological model with applications in design, *in* P. J. W. ten Hagen and T. Tomiyama (Eds), *Intelligent CAD Systems I*, Springer-Verlag, Berlin, pp. 286-294.

Takala, T. (1989). Design transactions and retrospective planning—tools for conceptual design, *in* P. J. W. ten Hagen, & P. Veerkamp (Eds), *Intelligent CAD Systems II*, Springer-Verlag, Berlin, pp. 262-272.

Takala, T., & Silén, P. (1990). Application of history mechanism in architectural design, *in* P. J. W. ten Hagen, & P. Veerkamp (Eds), *Intelligent CAD Systems III*, Springer-Verlag, Berlin.

Wallas, G. (1926). *The Art of Thought*, Jonathan Cape; also in P. E. Vernon (Ed.), *Creativity—Selected Readings*, Penguin, London, pp. 91-97.

Winston, P. H. (1984). *Artificial Intelligence*, 2nd ed., Addison-Wesley, Reading, Massachusetts.

Yoshikawa, H. (1981). General design theory and a CAD system, *in* T. Sata, & E. Warman (Eds), *Man-Machine Communication in CAD/CAM*, North-Holland, Amsterdam, pp. 35-53.

Zeisel, J. (1981). *Inquiry by Design: Tools for Environment-Behavior Research*, Cambridge University Press, Cambridge.

PART II

Knowledge-Based Models of Creative Design

Part II comprises different approaches to modeling creativity within the context of computer programs. The first chapter, "Creativity in design using a design prototype approach" by Rosenman and Gero, considers a conceptual schema called design prototypes as a basis for computational creativity. The second chapter, "Creativity and design as exploration" by Logan and Smithers, challenges the power prototypes have as a computational model without considering the role of exploration in design. The third chapter, "A connectionist view of creative design" by Coyne, Newton, and Sudweeks, questions the use of fixed boundary schemas and proposes the use of trained neural networks as a means to unusual but acceptable combinations of designs. The fourth chapter, "A genetic approach to creative design" by Woodbury, presents a genetic-based approach to producing creative designs in which design grammars provide a 'genetic code.'

6 Creativity in Design Using a Design Prototype Approach

Michael A. Rosenman and John S. Gero

Creative design is the creation of new structure in response to functional requirements. Various ways of producing creative designs are investigated and the key element in all of these is experience. A schema is needed whereby experiences are generalized and stored as concepts wherein function, behavior and structure are associated. The design prototype schema is seen as providing such a suitable structure. The use of the design prototype schema for creative design is discussed.

6.1 Introduction

There is a difference between the terms creation and creativity. *Creation* means that things that did not previously exist are brought into being, they are generated or synthesized. This, in a sense, applies to all design in that a description of a product, which did not previously exist, is created. *Creativity* has all the properties of creation plus implications that such higher level activities as ingenuity and imagination are brought to bear in creating novel products of perceived value.

The term creativity may be applied to both product and process (Coyne et al., 1990). A product may be termed creative if it exhibits the properties of

111

being novel, having value and/or having richness of interpretation. All these properties are subjective and are relative to time, place, and the observer. A process may be termed creative if it has the potential or the tendency to produce creative products. Once a process is well understood, it, however seems to no longer merit the term creative (or intelligent) and becomes in our view—mundane. It is, however, possible for creative products to be produced by processes that are well-understood, for example random syntactical mutations. Coyne et al., (1990) defined a creative process in terms of its level of entropy, a concept put forward by Shannon and Weaver (1949). The higher the level of entropy in the process, the more likely that order will be made from seemingly little organization, and the more likely that the process will be regarded as being creative. A connection is made to generality. The more that a system can deal with general concepts and abstractions the greater the capacity of the system to be creative.

There is a difference between creative thinking and creative design although design, being a cognitive activity, employs creative thinking. Design requires that the form of an artifact, or more precisely, a description of the structure of an artifact, be produced. The formation of new interpretations for existing products, that is finding new applications for existing products, is an example of creative thinking but not of creative design because no new structure is created. For example, realizing that a filing cabinet may be used as a ladder to change a light bulb involves no design activity. On the other hand, such realization involving the recognition that certain properties in an artifact are useful for some other purpose than that intended may indeed form a most important step in creative design. In this case, generalizations have to be made from the artifact and its properties and these generalizations then used to produce different specific forms in the new specific context.

Another important aspect of creative thinking in creative design is the formation of the new functional specifications for a new situation, especially in those cases where a creative design is produced by the creative configuration of known elements. The main step in such cases is the configuration of the concepts involved to satisfy the main requirements. This implies that much creative thinking needs be done before thinking about the syntactical elements that will form the design. In Navinchandra's (1989) example regarding a biomedical engineer, the main creative activity is not so much in making the analogies to catheters and balloons but the formation of the concepts of 'a non-surgical-method' and 'expansion of the tract.'

6.2 Classification of design

There seems to be some general acceptance of the classification of design into routine, innovative and creative design. However, because the boundaries between these are imprecise, it is not surprising that there are some differences in defining what is meant by these classifications (Navinchandra, 1989; Cagan and Agogino, 1989; Coyne et al., 1990). Routine design is accepted as being that design which proceeds within a well-defined state space. That is, all the design variables and their possible range are known and the problem is one of instantiation. Instantiation means the selection of the relevant design variables and the subsequent determination of values for them. Much of the design activity carried out in practice is routine design. An example of routine design is the design of an HVAC system including the selection of the type of plant, the type and layout of the ductwork, registers, and so forth, and finding values for the sizes of these items. That is not to say that routine design is necessarily always easy. The state space is usually very large and clever ways of navigating (searching) are required to arrive at desired solutions.

There is some difficulty in defining the terms innovative and creative design as it is not always clear where a design falls. There is no clear distinction between the two and, as has been stated (Coyne et al., 1990), successive innovations can lead to a sufficiently different product as to be called creative design. For our purposes, innovative design is as defined by Maher et al. (1989) as being that design in which the space of known solutions is extended by making variations or adaptations to existing designs. That is, designs that were not previously known are produced although there is no departure in kind from previous designs of the same type. The range of values of existing design variables is extended. Innovation may occur, for example, where a state space (for a given domain) is implicitly, completely defined by some set of transformations (e.g., mathematical function, shape grammar) but only some designs have been produced. When new designs are arrived at, they may be considered to be innovative (Figure 6.1).

A design grammar may be produced from induction over a set of examples taken from existing designs, as in the Palladian grammars of Stiny and Mitchell (1978) and the Federation style eaves detailing examples of Mitchell and Radford (1986). However, application of the design grammar generates new designs that were not part of the existing examples set. These new designs are innovative, rather than creative, in that they are implicitly defined by the grammar and hence part of the space of domain solutions even though not known to a designer initially. An example of innovative design is the single-pedestal chair in which the four legs of previous examples

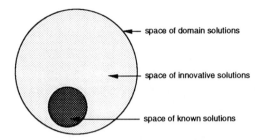

Figure 6.1. Innovative design.

are replaced by a single central pedestal with cantilever seat supports. In this example, there is no departure in kind, the new design is recognizably a chair, but at one level of description a new design variable, namely the single pedestal, has been introduced into the domain of chair design. At a higher level of description, however, it can be argued that the description of a chair merely demands a seat support, not a specific means, and that the single pedestal merely extends the range of values that this seat support can take.

Creative design incorporates innovative design but involves the creation of products that have little obvious relationships to existing products. Whereas, routine design involves the instantiation of a given type and innovative design involves the generation of new subtypes, creative design involves the generation of entirely new types. With this definition in mind designing an air-conditioner to meet certain requirements constitutes routine design, designing the first reverse-cycle air-conditioner constitutes innovative design whereas designing the first air-conditioner constitutes creative design. However, because the description of what constitutes a type and what constitutes a subtype is a matter of subjective perpsective, it is no wonder that there are difficulties in deciding into which classification to place certain design activities. For example, is the design of the first jet-propelled airplane an act of innovative design or creative design? This depends on our perspective of whether the jet plane constitutes a major type or whether it is merely a subtype of the airplane type. Is the design of the motor car an act of creative design or an act of innovative design where, as can be clearly seen in examples of early cars (Coyne et al., 1990), the horse in horse-drawn carriages was replaced by a motor. In creative design the state space has to be formulated. This may include extending the state space of possible solutions or creating a new state space (Figure 6.2).

Figure 6.2 shows the existence of a universal domain space. This could be in terms of all the atoms in the universe if we so desired. It merely

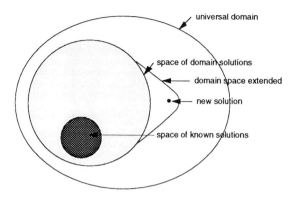

Figure 6.2. Creative design.

indicates that in some way all the means for generating entities exist. The space of solutions in some domain, not shown to scale, is greatly more restricted whereas the space of known designs within this domain is smaller still. A new design is formulated that is not within the present domain space. This general domain space is now extended to include this new design, for example, the domain space of transport facilities is extended to include heavier-than-air machines.

6.3 Structure, behavior and function

Design deals with the formulation of structure in response to functional requirement. The vocabulary elements manipulated vary with the particular discipline and particular view. In architecture the vocabulary may be, at one level, the spaces and, at another level, the building elements that serve to define or are included in the spaces; in electrical engineering, at one level, the vocabulary includes elements such as conductors, capacitors, resistors, power supplies, and so forth, whereas in computer programming design the vocabulary is the symbols of the particular language, that is, reserved words and identifiers.

Creative design deals with the formulation of new structure, that is, new vocabulary elements or new configurations of existing vocabulary elements in response to either existing or new functional requirements. In many cases, designs exist with the realization that they are not perfect and there is a continual commitment to their improvement. Many of the functional requirements that drive design are standing commitments. For example, the commitment to make our life more comfortable by making tasks easier to be carried out, to travel faster, and so forth. In domains such as fashion design, architecture, and industrial design, there is a standing commitment to variety, so that even if existing designs are adequate in terms of their utility and symbolic functions at a particular time, this commitment ensures that there is a continual search for new designs. In living organisms there is a standing commitment to survival. This is manifested in a variety of ways by different organisms. In humans it is manifested in both physical and metaphysical ways—being happy, comfortable, rich, and so forth. It may well be that we have to inculcate computers with such standing commitments in order for them to continually search for better products.

In routine design, there are views, as exemplified by shape grammars (Stiny, 1980), that systems based on structure alone can produce all the designs required. However, in a large space finding a design that meets a given set of functional requirements may not be practically possible. It is obvious that human designers reach satisfactory solutions in a much more direct manner than random search by using the functional requirements to guide the synthesis of the necessary structure. In order to do this there must be recognizable relationships between function and structure. One way to do this is to have this relationship explicitly stated,for example, in the form of abductive rules as in the RETWALL system for designing earth-retaining structures (Hutchinson et al., 1987). An abductive rule takes the form as shown in Figure 6.3.

IF   type of application OF wall IS temporary OR emergency
       OR marine   AND
       required height OF earth retaining structure =< 3000   AND
       NOT deflection at top OF wall IS critical
THEN   suitable type OF structure IS sheet pile   AND
       design OF earth retaining structure IS cantilever sheet pile

Figure 6.3. An abductive rule from RETWALL (Hutchinson et al., 1987).

However, it is obvious, that any system based on such abductive rules is too inflexible to allow for creative design. Therefore, to have the capacity to carry out creative design we require a more flexible way to encode the relationships between functional and structural descriptions of designs.

Once an object exists, it has a set of behavioral attributes and, as a result, can carry out certain functions. The behavior and possible use of an object may or may not be obvious. Glass allows light through, it is transparent and may be used for windows. It is not so obvious, however, that quartz crystals when excited oscillate at a constant rate and are therefore useful to keep time. Such relationships are found by inducing knowledge in the form of general principles, this being the task of science. What then is obvious and what is not depends greatly on the knowledge available to a designer.

There are some works concerned with deriving behavior from structure (Bobrow, 1984; DeKleer and Brown, 1984; Kuipers, 1984) but not function. This is not surprising as behavior describes what the product does whereas function is what the product is for and, as such, function is a somewhat arbitrary decision placed upon the product by humans. Behavior, however, gives clues as to what objects may be used for, that is, what functions may be decided upon. A piece of stone with a honed edge is sharp, it cuts other softer objects, it can be used as a weapon (a knife); a plane slab of wood is solid and stable (within limits), it can be used to support other objects (a table). We must also differentiate between intended function and functions that arise out of the behavioral attributes of the product. A motor car is intended to carry persons from place to place. However, because of its behavioral attributes, such as momentum and ability to be guided, it can be used as a weapon.

Although there exists a direct mapping from structure to behavior only those behaviors that are deemed interesting are derived or remembered. For example, the electrical resistance of a painting is of little interest even though this is a property of the painting. We are interested in those behavioral attributes of an object as perceived by what we see as its intended function. Of course, we have the capability of reassessing the properties of a product when required. In a computer system, indexing is done using existing indices. This leads to the 'chicken and egg' problem as noted by Navinchandra (1989). A creative design system needs to access syntactical elements through attributes that may not have been deemed interesting for that element at the time of indexing but could prove to be so. Yet we cannot afford to access every element just in case it may prove to have attributes matching those required.

Behavioral attributes are the key to matching structure to function and vice versa. We work both ways, bottom-up from structure to derived or actual behavior and top-down, from intended function to required behavior and we try to match the required and actual behaviors. A system to be useful will have to store a large set of structural elements with both syntactical and interpretive knowledge. The more efficient the system is in controlling the selection of structural elements and the more adept it is at manipulating such elements the greater the opportunity there will exist for creative design.

6.4   Design prototypes as a conceptual schema for the representation of design knowledge

Any schema for the representation of design knowledge will have to represent function, behavior and structure, and the relationships between them explicitly. Systems, such as shape grammars, which are based on structure alone are not sufficient by themselves although they can provide the means by which configurations of structural elements can be produced. Moreover such schemata will need efficient indices or triggers to allow for the retrieval of the appropriate concepts. Such indices need to be from several directions, that is, functional, behavioral, structural, and contextual.

Not all problems are foreseen by designers at the start of a design, nor are all requirements explicitly stated. Some are understood to be standing commitments, for example, structural stability, fit of one element into another, and so forth. The design process must identify and satisfy new requirements as they come up because of certain design decisions as well as all standing requirements.

A system based on design prototypes (Gero, 1987; Gero and Rosenman, 1989; Gero, 1990) as a generalization of design elements provides a framework for storing design experience incorporating the necessary functional, behavioral, and structural information. A design prototype may be accessed from functional, behavioral, structural, or contextual information. Figure 6.4 shows a design prototype schema containing functional, behavioral, and structural attributes all existing within the envelope of knowledge and context. At a higher level, knowledge exists regarding the relationship of design prototypes to other design prototypes.

The design prototype schema as described has a modular structure, a design prototype is a class of design elements. In this sense it may seem to be too strongly related to physical elements, for example, beams, doors, transistors, and so forth. However, in order to provide for more general knowledge, higher level concepts can also be formulated as design prototypes, for example, engineering structures, toys, and so forth (Figure 6.5). At this level resides the general knowledge that we carry, for example, that certain types of stresses may occur and must be taken care of, that loads must be resisted, that engineering structures must be stable, that toys must be safe, and so forth. This knowledge is inherited by an instance during the design process. So that, for example, when dealing with the case of the single column mutated into four columns, each resultant column must be recognized, that is, classified as a long column (Figure 6.6). All the requirements (buckling, equilibrium, stability, etc.) of all the relevant design

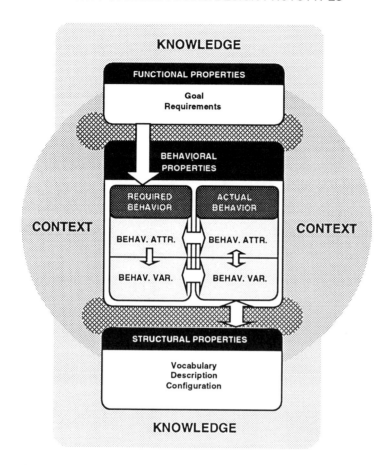

Figure 6.4. Diagram of design prototype schema.

prototype classes (from long column to action-resisting structure) must be inherited and satisfied.

In addition to a schema of design prototypes representing design elements, to provide for the integration of elements, there must be a schema of joint design prototypes ranging from general to more specific. Such knowledge will need to be brought to bear when configuring new designs and therefore specific knowledge associated with particular design prototypes may not be relevant.

However, in addition to knowledge associated with this type of object-centered design prototypes there is general knowledge that applies to processes. For example the knowledge that if trying to put something inside

```
┌──────────────────────────────────────────────────────────────┐
│            ( ACTION-RESISTING STRUCTURE )                      │
│  ┌──────────────────────────────────────────────────────────┐ │
│  │ ( TYPOLOGICAL PROPERTIES )                                │ │
│  │                                                            │ │
│  │   PARTITIONS:           [force state, spatial organization]│ │
│  └──────────────────────────────────────────────────────────┘ │
│  ┌──────────────────────────────────────────────────────────┐ │
│  │ ( FUNCTIONAL PROPERTIES )                                 │ │
│  │   PURPOSE:              [to resist external actions]       │ │
│  │   REQUIREMENTS:                                            │ │
│  │     must-be-satisfied:  [equilibrium, stability, strength, │ │
│  │                          stiffness]                        │ │
│  │     may-be-satisfied:   [safety, economy, aesthetic]       │ │
│  └──────────────────────────────────────────────────────────┘ │
│  ┌──────────────────────────────────────────────────────────┐ │
│  │ ( BEHAVIOURAL PROPERTIES )                                │ │
│  │  ┌────────────────────────────────────────────────────┐   │ │
│  │  │ ( PERFORMANCE ATTRIBUTES )                          │   │ │
│  │  │   equilibrium                                        │   │ │
│  │  │     .                                                │   │ │
│  │  │     .                                                │   │ │
│  │  │   aesthetic                                          │   │ │
│  │  └────────────────────────────────────────────────────┘   │ │
│  │  ┌────────────────────────────────────────────────────┐   │ │
│  │  │ ( PERFORMANCE VARIABLES )                           │   │ │
│  │  │   sum of forces                                      │   │ │
│  │  │   sum of moments                                     │   │ │
│  │  │     .                                                │   │ │
│  │  │   deformation                                        │   │ │
│  │  │     .                                                │   │ │
│  │  │   cost                                               │   │ │
│  │  └────────────────────────────────────────────────────┘   │ │
│  └──────────────────────────────────────────────────────────┘ │
│  ┌──────────────────────────────────────────────────────────┐ │
│  │ ( STRUCTURAL PROPERTIES )                                 │ │
│  │   PARTS:                                                   │ │
│  │     must-have:      [external actions, internal actions,   │ │
│  │                      action-resisting element n>= 1]       │ │
│  │     may-have:                                              │ │
│  │   DESCRIPTION:                                             │ │
│  │   CONFIGURATION:                                           │ │
│  └──────────────────────────────────────────────────────────┘ │
│  ┌──────────────────────────────────────────────────────────┐ │
│  │ ( KNOWLEDGE )                                             │ │
│  │   R1   IF     sum of forces = 0 and sum of moments = 0     │ │
│  │        THEN   equilibrium OF action-resisting structure    │ │
│  │               IS satisfactory                              │ │
│  │   R10  IF     exists a tendency for structure to move      │ │
│  │               from given position                          │ │
│  │        THEN   stability OF action-resisting structure      │ │
│  │               IS unsatisfactory                            │ │
│  │   R33  IF     actual deformation <= required deformation   │ │
│  │        THEN   stability OF action-resisting structure      │ │
│  │               IS satisfactory                              │ │
│  └──────────────────────────────────────────────────────────┘ │
└──────────────────────────────────────────────────────────────┘
```

Figure 6.5. An example of a design prototype at a high conceptual level.

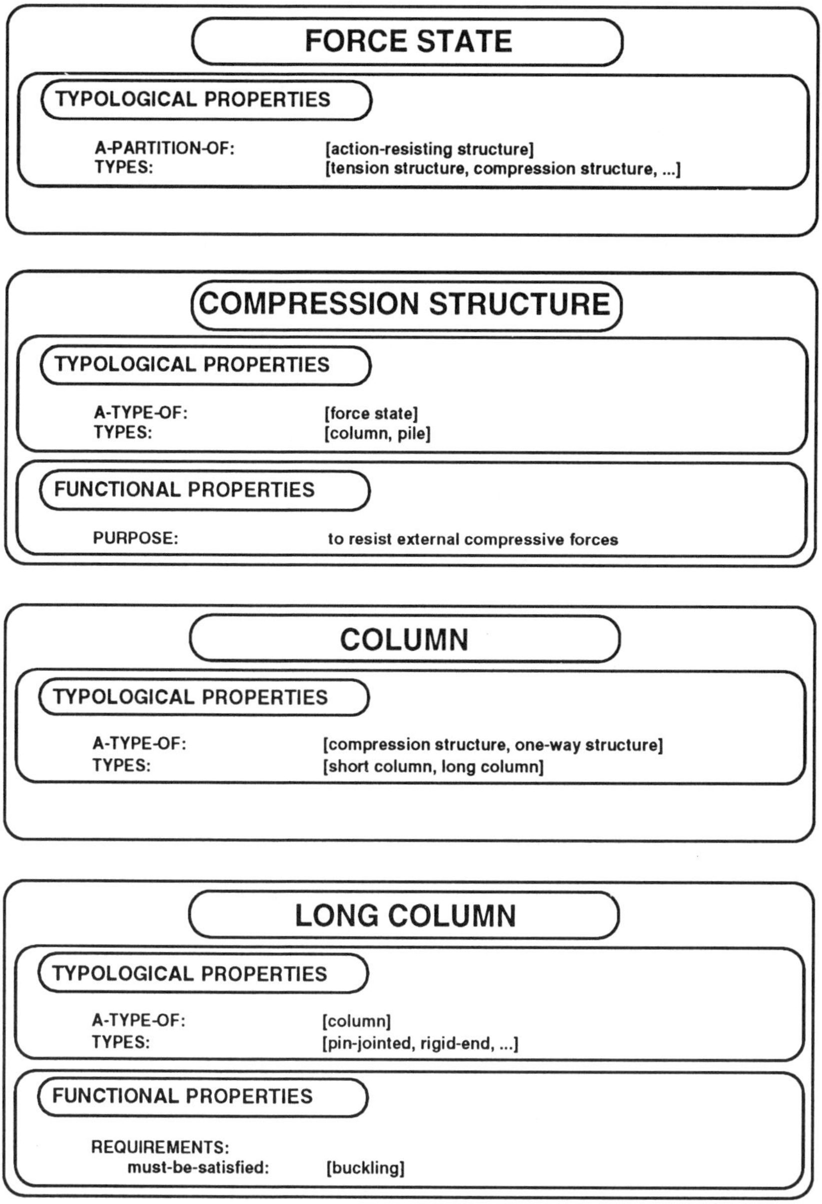

Figure 6.6. A set of design prototypes related to the design prototype of Figure 6.5 showing how more specific requirements are given.

something else then the first element must be smaller than the second. There is also general knowledge regarding the relationship of functions to each other and between functions and behaviors. In order to represent this type of knowledge it will be necessary to provide a schema based on functional terms, thus providing an inference structure for general goal decomposition and the provision of general requirements (Figure 6.7). Such a structure, as found to a degree in EDISON (Dyer et al., 1986), provides the means to relate various similar functional concepts, for example, that chopping, hewing, cutting, and slicing are related and that certain attributes, for example, sharpness and hardness are required.

6.5   Using design prototypes in creative design

6.5.1   The creation of new structure

Creative design is the production of new structural elements including both vocabulary elements and configurations of vocabulary elements, namely designs. The question is then, how can we produce new structure? If we have a defined design space how do we produce designs that are outside that space? How can we induce new structural knowledge? It is not possible to start from nothing and produce something and therefore new structure must be produced from some starting point or foundation. In order to produce anything we must have the necessary resources and the (knowledge of the) means of manipulating these resources. Similarly with design, we must have the necessary vocabulary elements and general concepts as well as the knowledge to manipulate them. Even the most fertile imagination needs seeds from which to sprout. Therefore, even though we define creative design as producing artifacts that are not obviously derived from existing ones, there must exist a store of information and knowledge, at some level, sufficient to allow the formation of new concepts and new structures to match.

There are two basic approaches in creating new structural elements. One way is to start from existing elements either in the domain or outside it and modify them to produce elements that did not exist before. The second way is to configure the new elements from basic 'building blocks.' The first approach includes combinatorial design, analogical design, and design through mutation whereas the second approach is that of design from first principles. The current emphasis seems to be on the first approach but there are many examples of designing from first principles. Design from first principles becomes mandatory when no existing elements can provide parts that are satisfactory for combination nor can analogical associations can be found nor can mutations prove themselves useful. Most probably designers employ combinations of all these methods at any given time.

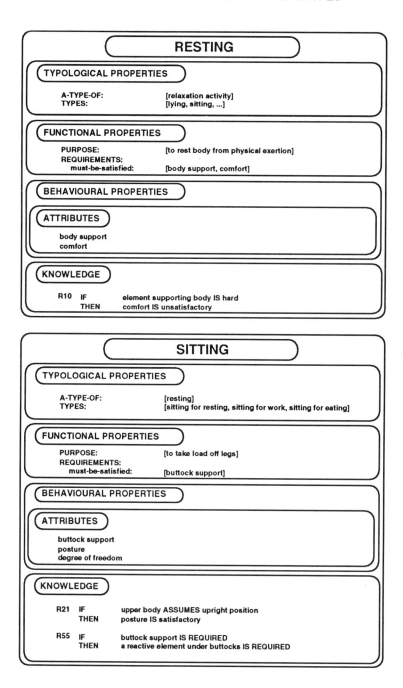

Figure 6.7. A schema for functional concepts.

The development of design prototype schemas has so far been towards routine design (Gero and Rosenman, 1989). In this case the main requirements are for design prototype selection and instantiation and for deriving values of the variables in the instance. For routine design the existence of a large number of design prototypes with their function to behavior to structure relationships will allow for different design solutions to be derived for a variety of design situations. Even at this level of design the use of direct function to structure knowledge in the form of abductive rules of the form shown in Figure 6.3 is avoided because this would mean that every different set of requirements would have to be catered for. The selection of a suitable design prototype instance is carried out through matching the actual behavioral attributes of a design prototype to that of the required behavioral attributes. However, the existence of concepts with relationships to more and more general concepts should allow for traversing the scheme and arriving at new destinations. A design prototype schema should therefore allow for design prototype adaptation to produce creative designs. There must, however, exist the ability to retrieve design prototypes based on partial matching and similarity concepts. The design prototype matches part of the requirements and thus needs some modification, if possible. In some cases several design prototypes may match some of the requirements, the relevant parts in each design prototype must be identified, duplication deleted, and the parts merged in a consistent manner. Current work being undertaken takes an evidential reasoning approach similar to that of Shastri (1989) for recognition of design prototypes. However, the approach taken is qualitative rather than quantitative using fuzzy logic. This approach seems to be mirrored well by a parallel distributed process and such a method may well form the basis for design prototype recognition based on partial matching (Coyne and Newton, 1990).

There is the danger of relying overly on the structural descriptions contained in a design prototype. A design prototype is a class of designs and as such the structural description covers all instances of that class. However, the structural description can only cover those instances that are currently known. In that sense a design prototype is frozen to current knowledge. This would seem to negate the possibility of using the design prototype schema for creative design, especially using first principles. However at more general levels, a design prototype has a rich semantic description but very little specific structure. The semantic description can be rich enough to allow for new instances to be produced. This semantic description should relate to the appropriate functional or behavioral concepts and thus allow for the formulation of the operational objectives as discussed previously. If we only concentrated on the structural description of a chair we could never have arrived at the 'balance' chair. But the functional description describing a chair as an element for sitting and prescribing certain required behavioral attributes allows for new forms to be incorporated into the structural description. The balance chair is a new design prototype, as distinct, from say a wheel chair, but it is still a chair. A creative design will be sufficiently different from previous designs to constitute a design prototype in its own right. The design prototype schema must therefore allow for change. Any creative process will mean change, as new design prototypes are formed and existing ones modified. The changes are incorporated into the schema and become part of the experience.

Figure 6.5 shows an example of a high level design prototype named 'action-resisting structure' (this is an engineering structure). There exists much information with respect to the functional and behavioral properties but not much regarding the structural properties except in a general sense. Figure 6.6 shows a more specific design prototypes within the same taxonomy. Note how the information in the design prototype named 'long column' states that a requirement that must be satisfied is buckling. When carrying out the mutation regarding the single column, as described previously, the resulting elements, that is, the four columns, would have to be recognized, that is classified, as long columns and thus the new requirement would have to be checked.

Let us have a look at how design prototypes might be used in the creative design processes of combination, mutation, analogy, and design from first principles. Figure 6.8 shows these processes and suggests that when we design we first search our experience to see if what we want exists. That is, if a suitable design (design prototype) exists and is satisfactory then all we have to do is instantiate it, that is select specific values of the variables. If a design prototype exists but is not fully satisfactory, then we try to modify it if possible. If there exist other design prototypes that may either by themselves or by some of their parts satisfy that part of the design prototype which is unsatisfactory, we may combine the various parts into a consistent entity. As an example, a shelter, such as a small hut or cabin, can be made portable (e.g. by vehicle) by adding a wheel and means of towing it. This could suggest a caravan. On the other hand, it may not be a question of importing other elements but of making a modification to some aspect of the design prototype itself. We use our requirements to guide the actual syntactical processes involved in this mutation. Figure 6.8 suggests how the classical triangular tent may be mutated into a pentagonal shaped tent when extra head height is required. If existing design prototypes are not capable of being modified to meet the requirements, we search other domains for concepts possessing those required attributes that can be applied to the problem at hand. For example, it is suggested that the inflatability and deflatability properties of balloons may lead to pneumatic structures. In designing from first principles, the given requirements have to be analyzed to determine required attributes and elements must be found or configured to produce those attributes. Figure 6.9 shows the sort of products, within the chair context, that might have been produced by the processes of combination, mutation, analogy, and design from first principles.

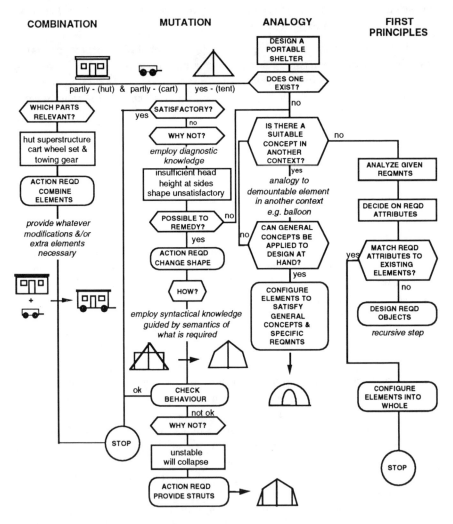

Figure 6.8. Diagram of processes involved in creative design.

COMBINATION   MUTATION   ANALOGY   FIRST PRINCIPLES

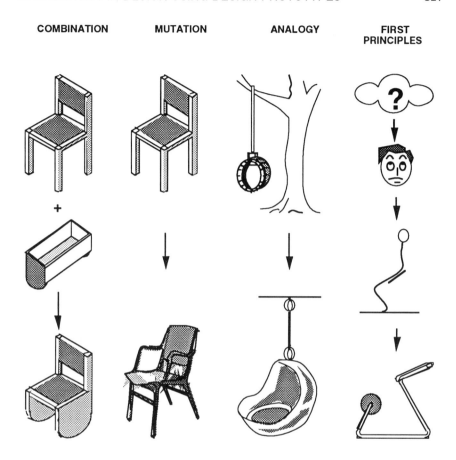

Figure 6.9. Possible results of the processes of mutation, analogy, and first principles in the chair domain.

6.5.2 Design by combination

Design by combination involves importing parts from various designs and combining them into a new design. For example replacing a manual drive with an automatic drive. Problems with this method include: selecting parts that are consistent in structure and knowing how to integrate the disparate parts into a consistent whole. This will involve finding appropriate modifications to make to each part to allow combination.

The use of design prototypes in design by combination involves the selection of relevant design prototypes which may be parts of some entities but that by themselves satisfy some of the given required attributes. These design prototypes then may have to be specialized in such a way that they can be configured together. This configuration may itself post some new requirements for the joining of the various elements and new elements may have to be incorporated to make the combination possible. Design by combination presupposes that the relevant design prototypes exist as needed by the combination. If this is not the case, then the elements themselves need be generated and are subject to the design process in general.

6.5.3   Design by mutation

Mutation involves a modification to a structural element. It differs from the process of combination in that it involves a modification to the structure of an existing element and not from importing elements from outside. For example, changing two adjacent angles of a rectangle equally leads to a trapezium. We can mutate randomly or control the mutation. Random mutation has the potential to produce structures that might have been impossible to imagine but, like random search, it is much more likely to produce meaningless products. Structural production involves an evaluation mechanism to discard useless solutions and retain meaningful ones. Dawkins (1986) made a case for random mutation and natural selection in his process of cumulative generation for evolution. He did not, however, give a satisfactory answer to the question of where is the evidence for the countless number of failed mutations that must have occurred before any successful ones. Without getting too deeply into the argument regarding the process of evolution, we argue that design is a conscious goal-directed process and therefore it should be a controlled process rather than a random one. The PROMPT system (Murthy and Addanki, 1987) is an example of controlled mutation in that the required behavior (required torsional stress resistance and low weight) guide the mutation. However, although we argue that mutation must be directed by function for meaningful design, we do not rule out the process in which a certain amount of 'playful' experimentation leads to the recognition of interesting results.

The problems facing us, when mutating are firstly: which feature of the element should be selected for mutation; secondly, what mutation operator should be selected; thirdly having carried out the mutation, how do we evaluate the result and, finally, what do we do with a new partial description. We should like to select for mutation that part of an existing design that possesses those attributes related to those we wish to achieve so that a mutation might best bring the required results. Similarly, it might be a good policy to identify those parts that negatively affect the behavior of an existing design with regards to the attributes we desire and change them in an opposite sense. Another policy that needs looking at is the merging of several parts that carry out similar functions into a single part (Ulrich and Seering, 1988). When an element is mutated the new element will possess behavioral attributes that are different to the original element. This is similar to the process of emergent shapes in the calculus of individuals put forward by Stiny (1982). These new behavioral attributes may not be recognized by the system or by the designer. For example, when a single column is mutated into four smaller columns (Maher et al., 1989) it may not be appreciated that each column, being more slender than the original, may buckle under load. We can only evaluate the new element for buckling if we are aware that a buckling problem has arisen. As designers, we may be aware, through experience, of the general structural knowledge that, when dealing with axial loading, buckling is something that must be checked (along with other properties). This seems to suggest that there exists a structure of generalized situations, some being at quite high level of abstractions. So that when working in a particular context there will exist a given set of requirements that must be satisfied even if we do not state these ourselves. If an element behaves in a manner that we are not aware of, then any shortcomings will only become apparent through subsequent experience. Explanations (for failure), in the form of knowledge, will be sought and these shortcomings will then serve as goals for improving the design. When importing a new element, it still has to be integrated into a consistent whole as its new configuration may no longer fit within the assembly as a whole.

Mutation involves the retrieval of some specific design prototype based on the closest, or at least a good, match between actual and required behavioral attributes. Diagnostic knowledge needs to be employed to determine which features of the structure part of the design prototype are causes of 'failure', that is, are causing behavior that does not meet the required behavior. Remedial knowledge is required that selects how to modify those features so that the required behavior is attained. This remedial knowledge needs to guide the appropriate syntactical transformations required.

6.5.4 Design by analogy

Design by analogy involves making associations to generalizations outside the current domain. The association is made through the required function or set of required behavioral attributes. It may be made at several levels of abstraction away from the design situation. For example, in designing a vehicle to travel over any terrain, including water, we may move to the level of abstraction of forces and friction. This may lead to the formation of the concept of providing a 'frictionless' cushion between the vehicle and the terrain and hence lead to the design of the hovercraft (Figure 6.10). The more levels of abstraction we pass through the more the design will be deemed creative. Once an analogy is made at a conceptual level we still have the problem that a structure, different to that in the analogical domain, has to be derived in the current domain. Again, a critical problem is that of integration of various parts into a consistent whole.

Analogy requires the recognition of a design prototype in another context as matching the required behavioral properties, for example the fact that umbrellas open and close matches the required behavior required of doors, as described in EDISON (Dyer et al., 1986). The generalizations involved in the structural properties of that design prototype must be brought over into the current context so that specializations can be made. A new design prototype must be created, if one does not exist, at a level higher than that of existing design prototypes so that the new generalizations can be included with other required attributes. Below this level, the actual new design prototype must be created as a specific example of the more general type using the imported knowledge as well as previously existing contextual knowledge.

6.5.5   Design from first principles

Creative design may be carried out from first principles. This will have to be done when no satisfactory association can be made to existing designs or all existing designs tend to produce the same type of unsatisfactory results. Designing from first principles appears to have the potential to create designs that could be more different from existing designs than the previously mentioned methods. Because combination, analogy, and mutation take existing structures as a starting point there is some suggestion that the resulting structure will resemble the existing structures to a greater degree than can be achieved by using first principles. Designing from first principles also gives designers the opportunity to examine the requirements divorced from structural representations (at least at that level of representation). The 'balance' chair (Figure 6.11), for example, shows very little relation to previously existing types of chairs and it would have been very difficult to arrive at this solution if locked in to existing designs. That is not to say that when designing from first principles we do not consider structure. We must at least have some elementary vocabulary elements at our disposal, that is, some building blocks, but these could be at the level of a basic material only which must be configured appropriately.

The ability to design from first principles presumes that, at some level, there is a recognizable mapping from function to behavior and from behavior

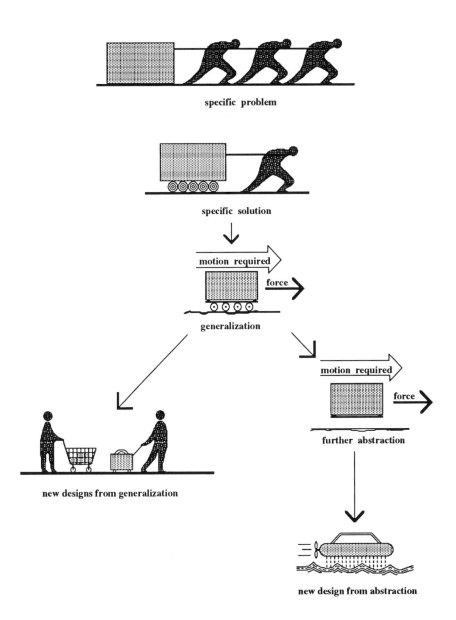

Figure 6.10. Creating new designs from abstractions of concepts.

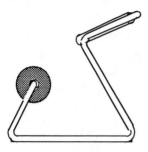

Figure 6.11. The 'balance' chair.

to structure. That is, given a required function or behavioral attribute there is a recognizable appropriate structure that will satisfy it.

Alexander (1964) put forward the idea of goal decomposition until a sufficiently primitive level was reached where the relationship between the behavioral and the structural became obvious. He postulated that, in the natural environment, structure is formed as a natural response to a pattern of forces and, hence in conscious design, if requirements could be represented by a pattern of forces it should be possible to find a matching structure in a metamorphic transition. However, no matter how 'primitive' the primitive level there is the same 'leap' from a 'pattern of forces' to a pattern of elements requiring that we have prior knowledge of this pattern of elements. The notion of formulating the design requirements into an operational set of objectives before making the transition to structure may be compared to Schank's (1986) asking the right questions in arriving at the most suitable explanation question. This is the vital part of Schank's creativity process as the transition to explanation patterns is considered to be almost automatic.

Let us have a look at the design of the balance chair as an example of designing from first principles. Previous to the balance chair, there existed chairs of various forms (four-legged, single-support, rocking chairs, etc.) but basically they had a horizontal seat at some height, a more or less vertical back supporting element and some supporting element for the seat. Even though some attention was paid to comfort it was perceived (at least by the designers of the balance chair) that the existing designs fell short of providing good posture. That is, it was recognized that no existing form was suitable. An anthropometric study of the human body when seated (Figure 6.12) revealed that the human spine can be made to assume the correct position for good posture if the seated position is such that instead of a horizontal seat support the thighs are supported at a forward angle. This is a radical realization, something that would have been difficult to arrive at from previous designs. This new functional requirement is translated into a required set of behaviors for the chair and into a new structural reality.

Figure 6.12. Going back to first principles. Good posture achieved when thighs are sloped forward.

In designing from first principles most of the creativity is achieved in formulating the operational objectives, that is in the investigation of the requirements and what is needed to satisfy them in terms of required performance. Therefore, this process of goal decomposition forms an important part of creative design.

In designing from first principles we can only start with the design prototype schema, as the design prototype, itself does not exist. We can however, fill in some of the parts of the schema,for example, the functional properties, maybe some of the required attributes and maybe even some of the structural properties in terms of possible parts and structural knowledge. However, what is needed are the concepts and the knowledge regarding these concepts required to analyze the functional requirements in order to arrive at a full set of operational objectives. Let us take, for example, the design of a 'portable shelter' if such a concept (design prototype) did not exist. What is required are the concepts of portability and shelter. These could exist as design prototype schemas, portable elements and shelter elements. The portable element design prototype would then have associated with it such required attributes as lightweight, compactness, erectability, demountability. This might involve arriving at a more specific type of portable element, defining portable as, for example, portable by a single human rather than by truck or large crane. The shelter, or perhaps temporary shelter, design prototype would have associated with it such attributes as weatherproofness, accommodation, vermin-proofness, privacy, and so forth. These attributes may be sufficient or else they themselves may be associated with schemas to further decompose the requirements. At some point the required behaviors so determined must be able to be matched with some existing design proto-types that will then serve as the building blocks for the required product.

6.6   The configuration problem

The main problem in all classes of design is the configuration problem. None of the work to date satisfactorily provides solutions to this problem. Design is seen as selecting and giving values to the parts of some product. But how do we put the parts together? If we know exactly what we are producing, that is, routine design, the configuration knowledge will exist. For example if we are designing, that is, selecting the size of members in a given truss, the configuration of the truss is given. But what of the situation when we are putting something new together for the first time? Let us say that we were creating a steel-bladed knife for the first time. The functional and required behavioral information for the blade would let us decide the size and shape of the blade whereas the information regarding the handle may, say, select a wooden handle of certain shape and size (Figure 6.13).

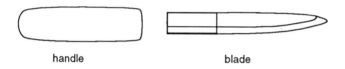

handle   blade

Figure 6.13. Selecting and designing parts.

How does a system decide that the steel blade needs a thickening at its edge, (shoulder) perhaps a protuberance (tang) and that the handle needs to have a recess to accommodate the protuberance so that the parts may be suitably joined (Figure 6.14). In other words the integration of parts into a whole is a process carried out relatively easily by humans but not as yet by systems that do not have a holistic approach. There must be knowledge that is associated with the whole and not the parts yet directs the structure of the parts. Obviously this knowledge is behavioral in nature in that certain structural requirements and/or topological requirements need be satisfied. In some cases this knowledge may decide that extra elements are necessary for integration, for example, an architrave to provide a satisfactory junction between a door jamb and a wall. It may well be that there needs to be special knowledge on junctions, treating junctions in the same way as other objects.

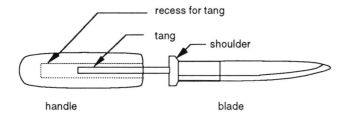

Figure 6.14. Integrating parts into a whole by making necessary modifications to the parts.

6.7   The role of experience in design

We have seen that in all the aforementioned methods put forward for creative design the role of experience is paramount. Experience includes the acquisition of knowledge as well as information. In all cases, the 'leap,' no matter at how a primitive level, from the function or behavior to the structure can only be achieved by recourse to prior experience. Schank (1986) argues that creativity is an adaptation of the new into the old and that creativity is not magical but mechanistic in principle. Whereas Schank is concerned with creativity as providing explanations to new situations, the same concepts hold for producing new designs for new requirements. In Schank's view there exists a set of standard explanation questions from which the closest matching is selected when a particular question arises. A standard explanation question is closely associated to a standard answer or explanation pattern. This standard explanation pattern is then 'tweaked' to fit the particular situation. This process is an example of analogy followed by mutation.

It has been shown (Heath, 1984) that although there is some belief that if you are a designer you can design anything, this is not generally true. For example, architects have not generally been good furniture designers. Moreover, the fact that interior designers make good livings shows that architects have not adequately satisfied that aspect of design. Designers are, generally, experts in a particular field having become familiar with that field through training and experience over time. They are familiar with the vocabulary with which they deal but once they are faced with a new domain, that is, new vocabularies, their navigation becomes uncertain.

The more extensive the experience, both in terms of knowledge and vocabulary, the greater the possibility of producing new structural configurations. A richer environment has a greater potential for cross-fertilization as noted by Stefik (1986) when pointing out the need for a knowledge medium.

Designers accumulate knowledge and experience over time. They accumulate a store of design situations each with associations to other situations. However, as well as accumulating a number of separate instances of particular situations, designers generalize their experiences into concepts. These concepts then form a framework from which particular cases may be formed. The most appropriate concept is recalled as necessary to solve a particular problem. One mark of experts is their ability to arrive at the most relevant area for solution to a problem.

6.8 Conclusion

This chapter discussed creativity in terms of creating new structural descriptions. It was pointed out that creative thinking, related to the formulation of operational objectives, forms the main part of creative design and that once creative thinking is achieved, the transition to structural form should be almost routine. It was discussed that although new structural form could be produced by modifying existing form through the processes of combination, analogy, and mutation, a great deal of creative design must be done from first principles. In all cases the role of prior experience was stressed as providing some basis from which to start. It is not suggested that each of these processes is carried out in mutual exclusion of the other. Indeed, many design problems will involve all the processes. Some parts of a product may be designed using analogy followed by mutation, whereas other parts may require design from first principles.

A design prototype schema is seen as a suitable vehicle for representing design knowledge including functional, behavioral, and structural information and the necessary relationships between them. Although most work involving design prototypes, to date, has been directed towards routine design with perhaps a view to innovative design, it is felt that this schema could be extended to provide for creative design. Such an extension should allow for creative thinking at the functional and behavioral levels before making transformations to structural descriptions. The use of a design prototype schema as a way of encapsulating design experiential knowledge needs to be treated carefully as using a store of experiences can act as a two-way sword. Although experience can provide ready answers to problems, it must not be used to lock a designer in to preconceived patterns. An important aspect is the evaluative mechanism, whereby partial matches are found to be satisfactory or not, as a basis for adaptation or analogy.

The main problem of configuration is still seen as a stumbling block to the development of design systems. Much more work is required in this area both in the sense of configuring a single element from basic material and in configuring a complex integrated product.

References

Alexander, C. (1964). *Notes on the Synthesis of Form*, Harvard University Press, Cambridge.

Bobrow, D. G. (1984). Qualitative reasoning about physical systems: an introduction, *Artificial Intelligence* **24**: 1–5.

Cagan, J., & Agogino, A. M. (1989). Why AI-researchers should distinguish between creative, innovative, and routine levels of design, *in* J. S. Gero (Ed.), *WAID: Workshop on Research Directions for Artificial Intelligence in Design*, Design Computing Unit, University of Sydney, Sydney, pp. 43–52.

Coyne, R. C., & Newton, S. (1990). Design reasoning by association, *Environment and Planning B: Planning and Design*, **17**: 39–56.

Coyne, R. C., Rosenman, M. A., Radford, A. D., Balachandran, M., & Gero, J. S. (1990). *Knowledge-Based Design Systems*, Addison-Wesley, Reading, Massachusetts.

Dawkins, R. (1986). *The Blind Watchmaker*, Penguin Books, London.

De Kleer, J., & Brown, J. S. (1984). A qualitative physics based on confluence, *Artificial Intelligence*, **24**: 7–83.

Dyer, M. G., Flower, M., & Hodges, J. (1986). EDISON: an engineering design invention system operating naively, *in* D. Sriram, & R. Adey (Eds), *Applications of Artificial Intelligence in Engineering Problems, Volume 1*, Springer-Verlag, Berlin, pp. 327–342.

Gero, J. S. (1987). Prototypes: a new schema for knowledge-based design, *Working Paper*, Architectural Computing Unit, University of Sydney, Sydney, Australia.

Gero, J. S. (1990). Design prototypes: a knowledge representation schema for design, *AI Magazine*, **11**(4): 26–36.

Gero, J. S., & Rosenman, M. A. (1989). A conceptual framework for knowledge-based design research at Sydney University's Design Computing Unit, *in* J. S. Gero (Ed.), *Artificial Intelligence in Design*, CMP/Springer-Verlag, Southampton, pp. 363–382.

Heath, T. (1984). *Method in Architecture*, Wiley, Chichester.

Hutchinson, P. J., Rosenman M. A., & Gero, J. S. (1987). RETWALL: an expert system for the selection and preliminary design of earth retaining structures, *Knowledge-Based Systems*, 1(1): 11–23.

Kuipers, B. (1984). Commonsense reasoning about causality: Deriving behavior from structure, *Artificial Intelligence*, **24**: 169–203.

Maher, M. L., Zhao, F., & Gero, J. S. (1989). An approach to knowledge-based creative design, *Preprints of NSF Engineering Design Research Conference*, College of Engineering, University of Massachussetts, Amherst, pp. 333–346.

Mitchell, J. R., & Radford, A. D. (1986). Adding knowledge to computer-aided detailing, *AUSGRAPH-86*, Australasian Computer Graphics Association, Sydney, NSW, Australia, pp. 31–35.

Murthy, S. S., & Addanki, S. (1987). PROMPT: an innovative design tool, *in* J. S. Gero (Ed.), *Expert Systems in Computer-Aided Design*, North-Holland,

Amsterdam, pp. 323–348.

Navinchandra, D. (1989). Research directions for AI in design, *in* J. S Gero (Ed.), *WAID: Workshop on Research Directions for Artificial Intelligence in Design*, Design Computing Unit, University of Sydney, Sydney, pp. 69–76.

Schank, R. C. (1986). *Explanation Patterns: Understanding Mechanically and Creatively*, Lawrence Erlbaum, Hillsdale, New Jersey.

Shannon, C., & Weaver W. (1949). *The Mathematical Theory of Communication*, University of Illinois Press, Urbana, Illinois.

Shastri, L. (1989). Default reasoning in semantic networks: a formalization of recognition and inheritance, *Artificial Intelligence*, **3**(3): 283–355.

Stefik, M. (1986). The next knowledge medium, *AI Magazine*, **7**: 34–46.

Stiny, G. (1980). Introduction to shape and shape grammars, *Environment and Planning B*, **7**: 343–351.

Stiny, G. (1982). Shapes are individuals, *Environment and Planning B*, **9**: 359–367.

Stiny, G., & Mitchell, W. J. (1978). The Palladian grammar, *Environment and Planning B*, **5**: 5–18.

Ulrich, K. T., & Seering, W. P. (1988). Function sharing in mechanical design, *AAAI-88*, pp. 342–346.

7 Creativity and Design as Exploration

Brian Logan and Tim Smithers

This chapter considers the problem of creative design, and in particular the role of *a priori* knowledge or 'prototypes' in the design process. A design problem is characterized as one in which both the objectives and the means available for achieving these objectives are (of necessity) initially only poorly defined. Some observations concerning the nature of design process based on this characterization are presented, and a model of the design process as a knowledge-based exploration task is described. The role of prototypes in organizing this knowledge is examined, and the widely accepted view that prototypes can form the principal source of knowledge for creativity in design is challenged. In a final section we outline the structural principles of a representation scheme that aims to overcome some of these difficulties and describe a design support system that uses this scheme to support the design process.

7.1 Introduction

There have been a number of attempts to define 'creative' design. Several authors have identified creativity with different kinds of design processes associated with different levels of problem difficulty or the novelty of the resulting solution (Brown and Chandrasekaran, 1984; Gero and Rosenman,

139

1989; Westerberg et al., 1989). For example, Gero and Rosenman (1989) identify three different types of design: *routine* design, in which the design variables and their ranges are known and the problem is one of instantiation of variable values; *innovative* design, in which the space of known solutions is extended by making variations or adaptions to existing designs; and *creative* design, in which the state space of possible solutions is extended or a new state space created. Other authors have argued that any such categorization must be based on the nature of the designed artifact irrespective of how it was produced (Cagan and Agogino, 1989; Coyne and Subrahmanian, 1989; Woodbury, 1989). For example, Cagan and Agogino (1989) emphasize the characteristics of the product rather than the process used to produce it, reserving the term *creative* for those artifacts so judged by the designer's (human) peers and leaving open the possibility of creative designs produced by 'mundane' means. These two approaches appear to be irreconcilable. The first, process-oriented view, characterises creativity as an absolute, inhering in the nature of particular kinds of processes, whereas the latter, product-oriented view is essentially relativistic in emphasizing that creativity is recognizable only within a particular context. Either these definitions are equivalent, or one (or both) of them must be wrong. However assuming their equivalence involves making a number of very strong assumptions.

If this claim is to be taken seriously, it must mean that the application of a given set of operators to a particular body of design knowledge always results in designs that are judged to be creative by the designer's human peers. The body of knowledge and/or operators are presumably specified relative to some (current) context, as different designs will be judged creative in different contexts. (The alternative involves a set of operators and/or prototypes that produce creative designs in all contexts, which violates the second definition.) Note that the relevant design knowledge doesn't have to correspond to the current design practice against which creativity is judged, although this would be the most obvious interpretation. There may be other bodies of knowledge (and sets of operators) which inevitably produce creative results. We could, for example, imagine a stock of 'creative solution' prototypes to which the identity operator is applied to produce a creative solution. Such a set would, however, still be defined relative to the current design context. Clearly, this must be a *sufficient* condition, otherwise it would rule out the production of creative designs by other means.

However, this is a very strong claim. Presumably what you want to say if you take the process-oriented view is (something like) the production of creative designs involves the use of certain operators, that is, that the use of such operators is a *necessary* condition for creativity. But this is just what the equivalence of definitions rules out. The operators must be sufficient for the production of creative designs if they are to constitute any sort of a definition of creativity. (The only other interpretation, that the operators may produce creative designs hardly amounts to a claim at all; it would be strange indeed if no creative designs could be produced by the application of such operators, whatever they are.) There have been several attempts to define such a set of operators in the literature: as some transformation of one or more class variables of a prototype (Oxman and Gero, 1988); as mutations of existing designs (Murthy and Addanki, 1987); in terms of reasoning by analogy (Maher et al., 1989); or as design from first principles (Rosenman and Gero, 1989). However for the definition to be complete requires a characterization of the corresponding context for which these operators will produce creative designs. As far as we are aware, no such characterization has been proposed. Nor has any adequate metric for the determination of creative designs been developed (Cagan and Agogino, 1989). All this seems to suggest that our intuitions about creativity are problematic.

In this chapter we adopt a different approach based on distinguishing between different kinds of problems. We define a design problem as one in which either the objective to be achieved or the means of achieving it (or both) are initially only poorly defined. Design in this sense is explicitly not a search process in which the task is essentially one of selection or optimization over a completely defined space. To qualify as a search problem, a problem must be well-defined; that is, it must be possible to specify completely both the goal to be achieved, and the means available (in terms of legal moves or operators) to achieve it. More precisely a search problem is defined by a triple consisting of: an initial problem description; a set of operators for transforming problems into subproblems; and a set of primitive problem descriptions (Barr and Feigenbaum, 1981). A solution to a given problem consists of a sequence of operators that successively transform the initial problem description into a set of primitive problems whose solution is immediate. Search problems have been extensively studied in the artificial intelligence literature, and a wide range of computational techniques have been developed for solving them. This type of problem solving corresponds approximately to the "routine design" identified by Gero and Rosenman (1989).

In our view then, design is the activity of 'solving' design problems. Design is a much less well understood activity than search, involving the modification of both the problem goals (the design requirements) and the means available to achieve these goals (the design knowledge). In fact one might almost say that the defining characteristic of design problems is that they are not amenable to purely search-based problem solving techniques.

This is not to deny that problem solving forms part of the design process. However, it is not what characterizes design as a distinct kind of intelligent behavior. Neither should it be interpreted as claiming that all design problems are in some sense equivalent. Within the class of design problems there are wide variations in complexity and scope. Clearly design problems do differ in terms of the skill and effort required to solve them; some problems will require considerably more creativity or ingenuity on the part of the designer than others. However, even in the simplest of design tasks, the fundamental problem of how a solution is *generated* (as opposed to selected) remains. Our use of the term 'design' is similar to the "nonroutine" design identified by Gero (1989).

This approach has the advantage of classifying different kinds of design processes in terms of the kinds of problems they attempt to solve, thereby avoiding *a priori* decisions about the nature of design processes or the character of designed artifacts. We believe it offers a fruitful perspective on nonroutine design in general and serves to highlight some of the problems of attempting to extend the concept of problem solving to nonroutine design.

In the next section we develop our characterization of design problems in more detail. We then present some observations concerning the nature of design process based on this characterization, and develop a model of the design activity as a knowledge-based exploration task. The role of 'prototypes' in organizing this knowledge is examined, and we challenge the widely accepted view that prototypes can form the principal source of knowledge for creativity in design. In a final section we outline the structural principles of a representation scheme which aims to overcome some of these difficulties and describe a design support system that uses this scheme to support the design process.

7.2   The nature of design problems

We begin by presenting our characterization of design problems in more detail. At its most general level, a design problem is concerned with the production of a description of an artifact or process that meets a given set of objectives or requirements. These requirements are often initially ill-defined and may be in conflict. In general they will not all be equally important; legislative controls are often value free, whereas user requirements may be modified during discussions with the client, and constraints generated by the designer may be extensively revised, or even abandoned altogether during the design process (Lawson, 1980). However, the real difficulty is that these objectives cannot easily be related to one another. Lawson (1980) stated: "the relative importance of the various requirements change constantly during the design process as the designer's value system is itself affected by the exploration of objectives and what he finds to be possible." The value judgments regarding 'trade-offs' between criteria are therefore context dependent, and the balance of satisfaction for such requirements may not be clear until the designer explores the various possibilities in appropriate detail. Such value judgments apply not only to the 'qualitative' criteria such as aesthetics, but also to the relative importance of quantitative criteria, which themselves may be susceptible to objective measurement. Questions about which are the most important problems and what kinds of solution most successfully solve these problems are also value laden. The answers given by designers to these questions are therefore frequently subjective and highly context dependent.

The nature of the 'real' problem is thus often not apparent but must be discovered; problems may suggest certain features of solutions, but these solutions in turn create new and different problems. The initial expression of the problem is often misleading, and designers must typically expend considerable effort in identifying the actual nature of the problem that confronts them. Design problems have no obvious or natural boundaries, but rather seem to be organized roughly hierarchically. Many elements of the problem cannot be expected to emerge until some attempt has been made at generating solutions. Given the essentially subjective nature of design, it is inevitable that some aspects of the problem will remain either unrecognized or undeveloped for much of the design process. As a result design problems are full of uncertainties both about objectives and their relative priorities, and both priorities and objectives are likely to change as solutions emerge. Simon (1973) called such problems 'ill-structured' and argued that any problem with a large base of potentially relevant knowledge falls into this category. The design task is ill-structured in this sense in a number of respects. There is initially no definite criteria to test a solution, much less a formal process to apply the criteria. In addition, the problem space cannot be completely defined due to a radical lack of knowledge. Also, although the set of alternative solutions may be given in a certain abstract sense, it is not given in the only sense that is practically relevant. As a result there can never be an exhaustive list of all the possible solutions to such problems.

Design problems are therefore often multidimensional and highly interdependent. It is rare for any part of a design to serve only one purpose, and it is frequently necessary to devise a solution that satisfies a whole range of requirements. Design decisions may have results other than those intended, which highlight previously unrecognized criteria and relationships.

In many cases the stated objectives are in direct conflict with one another and the designer cannot simply optimize one requirement without suffering losses elsewhere. For example, although enlarging a window may well let in more light and give a better view, it will also result in greater heat loss and may create greater problems of privacy. Different trade-offs between the criteria result in a whole range of acceptable solutions, each likely to prove more or less satisfactory in different ways to different clients and users. It is the very interrelatedness of these factors that is the essence of design problems rather than the isolated factors themselves, and it is the structuring of relationships between these criteria that forms the basis for the design process (Lawson, 1980). The fundamental objective thus becomes one of understanding the structure of the problem (rather than the solution), and analyzing the interrelationships between criteria to gain some insight into the relationships between each individual design decision and all of the other decisions that together define the solution.

7.3   The nature of the design process

The designer's exploration of this structure begins with the initial formulation of the problem. To a large extent, a design problem has no inherent structure; it acquires structure as solutions are proposed and problems are reduced to subproblems. In a very real sense the relationships between criteria can be seen as a function of the approach to design embodied in the proposed solution rather than as inherent in the problem itself. This initial formulation forms the basis of subsequent exploration of the problem.

Consider, for example, the problem of providing a particular view from the living room in designing a house. (This example is based on one given by Bazjanac (1974).) Such a requirement may have been specified in the original problem description or it may have been generated during the design process. In either case, an architect might choose to formulate the associated design problem in terms of some standard solution, as a problem of the arrangement of the living room and the placement of a window in a way that will provide the desired view from the relevant areas of the room. Through such a formulation of the design problem the designer has also formulated the general form of the solution; any particular design solution is determined by a specific placement of the window and a specific disposition of the living room. The designer then proceeds to explore the implications of this particular design decision. In doing so he or she may make further design decisions and consider a number of design alternatives. This process of exploration may lead to the discovery that in providing the desired view it becomes impossible to maintain the relationship between the living area and the entrance to the house, or that the basic structural system of the house will not allow the positioning of a window of the required size in the desired location. As a result the designer comes to realize that the problem of providing a view from the living room has other aspects and its solution may involve finding a more appropriate layout for the house on the site, or the redesign of the structural system in a way that will accommodate the desired window. The formulation of both the problem and the solution may therefore change as a consequence of an attempt to solve a particular problem.

It might be argued that in this case the original formulation of the problem was unrealistic and that an experienced designer would approach the problem at a more appropriate level. However such an argument misses the point. In trying to develop a solution to a particular design problem even the most experienced designer will gain new insights which necessitate the redefinition of the problem and suggest alternative solutions. The need to understand (at whatever level) the details of a particular case and how they interact are in a sense what makes a design problem a design problem.

As a solution develops it provides an increasingly detailed context against which to test the designer's hypotheses, and the evaluation of a proposal can result in the discovery of previously unrecognized relationships and criteria. In a sense later decisions are constrained by earlier decisions in that they are taken within the context of an existing partial solution, and each decision further limits the range of possible alternatives. Solutions to particular subproblems are apt to be disturbed or undone at a later stage when new aspects are attended to and the considerations leading to the original solution are forgotten or not noticed. Such side effects accompany all complex design processes. As a result, although the final solution may satisfy all the requirements that are evoked when it is tested, it may violate some of the requirements that were imposed (and temporarily satisfied) at an earlier stage in the design. The designer may or may not be aware of these violations. Other appropriate design criteria may simply remain dormant, never having been evoked during the design process. The development of a design is thus constrained by what best fits the knowledge the designer has at that time.

The formulation of the problem at any stage is not final; rather it reflects the designer's current understanding of the problem. As the design progresses, the designer learns more about possible problem and solution structures as new aspects of the situation become apparent and the inconsistencies inherent in the formulation of the problem are revealed. As a result, designers gain new insights into the problem (and the solution) which ultimately result in the formation of a new view; the problem and the solution are redefined. This process of exploration and redefinition continues until one or more of the following conditions is met (Bazjanac, 1974):

1. The incremental gain in knowledge has become insignificant and the understanding of the problem (and the solution) cannot change enough to warrant further redefinition. (i.e., the designer has reached the limits of his or her understanding).

2. The incremental gain in knowledge has become too costly.

3. The available resources (primarily time) have become exhausted.

There is no meaningful distinction between *analysis* and *synthesis* in this process; problems and solutions are seen as emerging together rather than one logically following from the other. The problem is explored through a series of attempts to create solutions and understand their implications in terms of other criteria. The designer comes to understand the critical relationships and possible forms as a solution evolves. Between generic solutions planning is less a search for the best solution than an exploration of the compromises that give sufficient solutions. These explorations help the designer appreciate which requirements may be most readily achieved. As part of this process, the designer learns which criterion values will achieve the design requirements and how much variation of these values can be tolerated while still achieving acceptable performance, the implications of achieving the current goal, and any other decisions required to make the attainment of these goals consistent with the existing solution.

Discovering more is the most important part of this process. The fundamental objective becomes one of understanding the structure of the problem, with a major part of the effort in design being directed towards structuring problems and only a fraction of it devoted to solving them once they have been structured (Simon, 1970). The design process can be viewed more generally as a process of discovering information about problem structures that will ultimately be valuable in developing possible solutions.

7.4 Knowledge in design

In this section we describe a model of the design process that has been developed as part of the AI in Design research program at the Department of Artificial Intelligence, Edinburgh University. In this model design is viewed as a knowledge-based exploration task (Smithers et al., 1990) (Figure 7.1). According to this exploration-based model, a design task starts with the construction of an initial requirement description R_i. R_i is usually a weak statement; it is typically incomplete in the sense that it fails to identify some necessary aspect of a possible solution, and it may be inconsistent in the sense that it may specify two or more mutually exclusive properties of a solution or conditions that must be met.

It is not possible to say in what way R_i is incomplete and inconsistent as it requires knowledge of the structure of the space of possible designs (SPD) to identify any omissions or inconsistencies. The initial requirement description cannot therefore serve as a specification for a search problem—because if it is incomplete and inconsistent it cannot define a goal-state in a SPD. The design process, E_d, is one of exploring the space of possible designs. This process draws on the designer's experience of previous designs together with information gained within the context of the current problem. The problem is analyzed through a series of attempts to create solutions and understand their implications in terms of design requirements. As part of this process, the designer discovers those sets of design decisions (if any) that jointly achieve the design goals and their implications in terms of design criteria. The designer acquires knowledge about the nature and structure of parts of the SPD, and thus of possible design specifications that perhaps partially meet the current requirement description, or which indicate why aspects of it cannot be satisfied. As a result, incompletenesses and inconsistencies in R_i are discovered. The requirement description is then modified in a way that resolves identified incompletenesses and inconsistencies, and the exploration is continued until a point in the design space is found that fully specifies a design that satisfies the evolved requirement description. The result is a final, complete, and consistent, requirement description, R_f, and an associated design specification, D_s, which is consistent with it.

The requirement description thus evolves from an initial statement that only incompletely defines a region in the SPD (and may not even do that) to a final requirement description that completely and consistently defines a region of the SPD. The design specification represents a subregion of the region of the SPD defined by R_f, or, in the case of more than one design specification they represent subregions of the region of the SPD defined by R_f. The record of the designer's exploration of the SPD constitutes a history, H_d, of the design process. It is a description of the nature and structure of the space surveyed—in other words the paths taken, the reasons for doing so, and what it looked like on the way.

To start the exploration process both knowledge of the domain, K_{dm}, and knowledge about how to design in the domain, K_{dn} is required. Domain knowledge is knowledge about the characteristics of the domain: the nature of the underlying physical reality, the materials and techniques available to the designer, legislative controls, codes of practice and other norms and

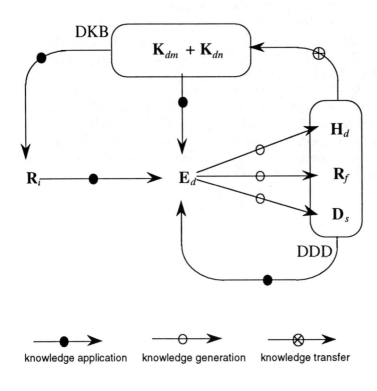

knowledge application   knowledge generation   knowledge transfer

DKB — Domain Knowledge-Base
$\mathbf{K}_{dm}$ — domain knowledge
$\mathbf{K}_{dn}$ — design knowledge
$\mathbf{R}_i$ — initial design requirement description
$\mathbf{E}_d$ — design exploration process
$\mathbf{H}_d$ — design exploration history
$\mathbf{R}_f$ — final design requirement description
$\mathbf{D}_s$ — final design specification
DDD — Design Description Document

Figure 7.1. An exploration-based model of design.

standards that are largely invariant across designs (and designers) within the domain. For example, when designing the structural frame of a building, a decision to use steel rather than reinforced concrete requires the application of domain knowledge about such things as the maximum economic span possible in steel, the availability of standard steel sections and the legislative controls governing the use of exposed steelwork in loadbearing structures. This knowledge ultimately constrains the form of any solution by defining the boundaries of the space of possible designs. It gives structure to the exploration space, and thus the problem, and identifies and locates interesting regions and important discontinuities.

Design knowledge is knowledge about how the space can be explored. This consists of design methods and strategies, and might include, for example, knowledge of different structural layouts or how the system of forces set up by the wind and imposed loads is best solved to determine the size of the structural members. This knowledge indicates paths through the terrain of the design space. K_{dm} and K_{dn} are not orthogonal kinds of knowledge, there is often an important dependency relationship between domain knowledge and design knowledge which means that one cannot sensibly be expressed without reference to the other. This is why they are not indicated as being two separate, and thus independent, inputs to the exploration process in Figure 7.1.

In the following sections we consider the form of this design knowledge and its role in the generation of solutions in more detail.

7.5 Prototypes in design

The generation of solutions draws on an extensive knowledge of design methods, strategies, and solutions to previous problems. Design proposals are not produced blindly but result from a general understanding of the kinds of solutions that may be appropriate in a given situation, and how these solutions may be pursued. An important component of this knowledge is what might be termed 'compiled experience.' The role of a priori knowledge derived either from a familiarity with related problems or, in the form of published guides and standards, has been widely recognized in studies of design. Akin (1978) discussed the use of 'problem transformations', which "make the current solution more specific, such as a precompiled solution, an analogous solution, a generic solution etc. ... if explicit transformations are not possible at the time, use previous experience to assume that certain aspects of the current solution can be further specified." Foz (1972) has shown how exploration of the problem evokes previously known solutions from memory. These examples are used as 'guides' or 'templates' for analyzing or developing possible solutions in terms of the problem requirements. More recently, Gero et al., (Gero, 1987; Gero et al., 1988; Oxman and Gero, 1988) have proposed that design knowledge is stored and retrieved in a series of abstract schemata called 'prototypes'—"generalized groupings of elements in a design domain ... from which instances of elements can be derived."

These approaches to design may be broadly characterized as 'knowledge-based,' in viewing the design process as a series of problem transformations governed by 'rules' or 'codes' linking design solutions and abstract requirements. There are clear parallels between, for example, Akin's 'problem transformations,' Foz's 'templates,' and Gero et al.'s concept of 'prototypes.' Common to all these approaches is the idea that design proceeds through the utilization of an organized body of *a priori* knowledge, which is used both to structure and understand the design problem and which forms the basis of design hypotheses.

Steadman (1979) has argued that in architectural design this body of general or collective knowledge is perpetuated through architectural education, architectural journals and publications, and the study of existing buildings. However it is not, with certain exceptions, of an organized, explicit, or scientific nature. Rather, empirical experience of a range of related designs provides a body of knowledge and understanding on the basis of which it is possible to build a generalized theory (or theories) of a class of artifacts, which is used to extrapolate, beyond the tried cases, to hypothetical but related designs yet to be constructed. It is this body of knowledge, concerning, for example, the relation of physical performance to shape, which informs the creation of solutions.

However, when we turn to the application of this knowledge in the design process, a major difficulty immediately becomes apparent. A design problem is by definition unique. (If an artifact already exists that is recognized as satisfactorily meeting all the design requirements, there is by definition no design problem). The question then arises: How can an infinite number of designs be generated from a presumably finite set of schemata? A complete answer to this question is impossible given our current understanding of the design process, however we attempt to develop a small part of such an answer in the remainder of this chapter. Briefly, we argue that, in general, design can only proceed through the development of new schemata and strategies within the context presented by the current design problem. In this view the primary function of *a priori* knowledge or cases is to structure the problem space, not to instantiate a solution or act as an initial starting point for one. These ideas form the basis of a simple model of discovery in design.

To the extent that the role of schemata in design has been made computationally explicit, they have tended to be seen as as 'parameterized design descriptions' or 'parameterized design description generators' generic groupings of design elements with associated variables and methods representing a class of possible designs within the context of a 'routine' or 'variant' design task. The most developed of these treatments is probably the work on prototypes (see, for example, Gero (1987), Oxman and Gero (1988)). For example, Gero (1987) identified four components of a prototype: a parameterized design description; a set of goals or requirements expressing the functions provided by the prototype; a vocabulary of design elements; and knowledge relating vocabulary, requirements and design description. In this view design involves a search for a prototype (or set of prototypes) that potentially satisfy the design requirements. Once a suitable prototype has been found, an instance in the form of a parameterized design description is generated using the knowledge and the vocabulary associated with the prototype. This involves reasoning from function or behavior to structure using knowledge of the relationships between function, structure, and behavior which forms part of the prototype. This in turn may involve the selection of a value from a range of specified values, or searching for a 'lower-level' prototype that satisfies the design requirements associated with a particular design parameter. In the PRODS system (Oxman and Gero, 1988), this knowledge is encapsulated in the form of procedures or 'methods' attached to the prototype. The 'instantiation' of a prototype ultimately results in a set of assignments to design variables that further specify the design description. This process is complicated by the requirement that the resulting values and/or prototypes be 'globally' consistent, that is, consistent with the rest of the emerging design solution.

Whereas the resulting problem is a search problem, it is not a trivial one, and there is no guarantee that even if a solution exists it will be found. One of the difficulties of much of the published work on routine design is a failure to be explicit about the kinds of control strategy required to find a consistent set of assignments to design variables. However, in principle, such problems should be amenable to conventional goal-directed problem solving techniques. A more fundamental problem is that there appears to be nowhere within such a prototype-based model that control information can be expressed. This omission becomes more problematic when we turn to nonroutine design and the problem of control comes to assume a major role.

In more recent work, Rosenman and Gero (1989) have attempted to extend their prototype-based model to include creative design. This has involved the introduction of two new classes of prototypes: 'joint prototypes' which "allow the configuration of new designs"; and 'functional prototypes' which represent the relationship of functions to each other and to behaviors to provide "an inference structure for general goal decomposition and the provision of general requirements." In addition, the relationship between function, behavior and structure is now explicitly represented, and forms the basis of the generation of new prototypes. New prototypes can be produced in a number of ways including combination, analogy, mutation, and design from first principles. However we are given no computational interpretation of these processes. Furthermore, although the problem of 'configuring' prototype instances representing partial solutions to form an overall solution is identified, there is no attempt to address the problem of what happens when a prototype fails to meet its local or global goals. Presumably this becomes a new design problem to which the same processes apply.

However, whereas such an approach may be adequate for routine design problems, a moment's reflection shows that it cannot work in general. Even assuming that a prototype, as an abstraction from known cases or previous solutions, is capable by definition of achieving its own 'local' goals (a very strong assumption—much of the knowledge linking function to structure is abductive or heuristic in nature), it is incapable of resolving interactions between criteria. When an irreducible conflict between two or more criteria arises then either: a) a solution exists but the search strategy is incapable of finding it; or b) no solution exists within the solution space defined by the prototypes. This happens when no way can be found of achieving a particular requirement or set of requirements within the constraints imposed by the rest of the solution context. This may either be because although the available prototypes are capable of achieving their immediate goals, the resulting 'local' solutions have unacceptable consequences elsewhere (solutions can be found for each of the subproblems considered in isolation, but these partial solutions are mutually inconsistent), or because no way can be found of achieving a particular goal even in the absence of other constraints (the problem lies outwith the scope of any known prototype). Such conflicts are common in design, indeed we have identified the existence of conflicts between criteria as one of the characteristics of design problems.

In such a situation the designer must either modify the problem, that is, relax one or more constraints until the current solution meets the revised design requirements, or modify the means available to solve the problem by modifying an existing prototype or creating a new prototype. (In many situations, it will be necessary to modify both the requirements description and the available problem solving strategies to achieve a consistent solution.) However neither of these strategies appears to be available within a prototype framework. We cannot modify the problem as prototypes contain no explicit representation of the current problem requirements (as distinct from the functional properties of the prototype). Requirements are represented implicitly in the initial problem definition and are elaborated and refined as the instantiation of prototypes implicitly creates new goals to be achieved by lower-level prototypes. If instead we decide to modify the solution, there are two problems to be solved: a) deciding which part of the current inconsistent solution is to be modified; and b) deciding how to modify it to achieve the design requirements. In the prototype model, this corresponds to: a) deciding which prototype to modify (or to create a new prototype); and b) determining how it is to be modified (or created). Although Rosenman and Gero identify a number of ways in which new prototypes can be produced, we are given no formal definition of the individual operators. More importantly, the control of this process—which operators to use and to which part of the solution they should be applied—is not made explicit. Control information does not form part of the definition of a prototype and in Rosenman and Gero's model there appears to be nowhere else to put it, as the prototype model itself contains no explicit meta-level or control strategy. In the terminology of Section 7.4, prototypes contain only domain knowledge, they have no design knowledge.

Prototypes are only a representational framework and as such are provably equivalent to many others in terms of expressive power. Ultimately the question is not one of how the knowledge is organized (although this is important), but what knowledge is represented. Until we address the problem of what should be represented we will not have a model of creative or any other sort of design.

These difficulties are a result of a series of mistaken assumptions about the role of a priori knowledge in design. Viewing prototypes as 'parameterized design descriptions,' or 'design description generators' results in an emphasis on local problem solving. Design problems are solved piecemeal, but this is often the easiest part of a design task—the hard part is integrating the solutions to the various subproblems to form an overall solution.

Underlying this model of design are the assumptions that:

1. The design problem can be broken down into a series of independent subproblems, that is, that there are no, or only weak, interactions between the prototypes; and

2. each of the resulting subproblems can be solved by search.

In dealing with design problems, neither of these assumptions is valid.

The defining characteristic of design problems is that they are highly inter-dependent. Attempting to solve one problem will, in general, produce new problems elsewhere. The designer must explore the space of possible designs. However, a prototype seen as simply a 'parameterized design description' or a 'parameterized design description generator' is incapable of support-ing such exploration. Note that the designer cannot simply select another prototype—the problem is not solvable by search by definition. Even if this were possible, the designer would still require knowledge about which of the possible alternatives to choose, which can only be obtained from knowledge about the relationship between the prototype and the solution context, that is, the structure of the space in which they are embedded.

A prototype is more usefully characterized as a tentative hypothesis about how to proceed with the design. The evocation of a prototype from memory provides the designer with two types of information: it tells the designer what is possible within a given set of constraints, that is, that an artifact or class of artifacts with a given set of attributes is *feasible*, and, more importantly, it contains information about the structure of the space of possible designs—a way of looking at the current problem that proved successful in dealing with similar problems in the past. In other words, it is knowledge of what previous explorations were carried out and how that is important, not what the specific results were. In effect a prototype can be seen as a rule that states: 'given a situation in which you are trying to achieve A, use B,' where B can be seen as a tag or a pointer to a set of relationships, strategies, problem decompositions, standard or generic solutions, default values, and so forth. The evocation of the prototype makes these strategies and relationships available for use in achieving the current goal. However, the fact that the prototype may subsequently be used to infer some aspect of the design from the design requirements (in the form of a default value or through the application of some procedure or algorithm), should not obscure the fact that the prototype itself must be modified in the event that the solution attempt is unsuccessful. Similarly, in the event that it becomes necessary to modify the current requirement description, this structural information is essential in identifying the goal(s) to be abandoned.

Design therefore becomes a process of modification or refinement of the designer's general strategies and prototypes within the context of the current problem. More generally we can see the problem of design as one of discovering how to develop and represent these basic prototypes to solve a particular problem. Starting from a set of prototypes or models representing, for example, a previous solution to a similar problem or the underlying physical reality of the problem domain, certain relationships are emphasized while others become less important or are ignored as the design process progresses. New relationships may be introduced, either empirically or through the introduction of facts or relations that had previously been suppressed.

Hillier and Leaman (1974, 1976) have characterized this process as one of the elaboration and modification of cultural stereotypes or 'templates.' They argue that the designer is situated in "a richly connected universe whose connections are those dissimilar domains that must be related in design; activity and space, psychology and climate and so on". These structures are embedded in the language the designer uses and in the instrumental set—the technologies or kits of parts (concepts) and typical design solutions (prototypes or 'prestructures') to which his systems of representation refer (Hillier and Leaman, 1974). Even to name an architectural problem—say, 'design a school'—implies a whole range of solutions that will be more or less immediately activated by the designer's prestructures. These structures form an evolving typology of standard solutions to recurring problems in design, modified by the designer's experience, ideology, and the physical, social, and cultural environments that form the context of design.

Such deep cultural structures may be transmitted unchanged through several generations yet produce great variety at the observable level. Hillier argued that such underlying stable structures or 'manifolds' correspond to what biologists call 'genotypes' as opposed to the 'phenotypes' (or variably developed observable forms) that constitute individual solutions. The cultural genotypes of architectural and urban form mutate gradually or are suddenly altered to reflect much more profound mutations in the relations between changes in society and changes in its spatial form. This evolutionary process is concerned with "the gradual unfolding of a socio-spatial morphology, which includes the development and stabilization of technologies, social processes of environmental control, and all constructions of the mapping from social form into spatial form" (Hillier and Leaman, 1974). Over a much shorter timescale the genotype is, in turn, elaborated into a phenotype appropriate to a particular set of local conditions, through the activity of designers, users, and others.

In this view design is seen as the process of discovering "the appropriate transformation or 'unfolding' of prestructures (genotypes) in relation to the constraints imposed by the environment of the problem" (Hillier and Leaman, 1974). Both the transmission and transformation of prestructures form a process of elaboration and discovery, which underlies the active formation of relationships and within which every solution may be unique. The development of individual designs is, in general, of less significance in the overall design of the artificial environment than events that take place less obviously in evolutionary time. These changes have the effect of altering the general form of the prestructures, which designers bring to bear on individual problems of phenotype production, effectively acting as a framework of autonomic assumptions within which they operate (Hillier & Leaman, 1974).

7.6   Representing design knowledge

The problems identified with prototypes in the previous section suggest that another approach is required. In this section we outline an attempt to develop a declarative representation scheme for domain and design knowledge, and describe how this representation is used by a design support system to assist the designer in exploring the space of possible designs. We use the terminology introduced in Figure 7.1.

Both the DKB (Domain Knowledge-Base) and the DDD (Design Description Document) constitute knowledge about a particular SPD (space of possible designs), but each represents knowledge of a different kind.

The DKB partially defines a SPD (for a particular domain) is terms of domain knowledge, K_{dm}, and design knowledge, K_{dn}. The domain knowledge expresses facts about the domain, such as the heat conduction properties of different building materials, and the properties and attributes of basic objects and processes associated with the domain—its ontology—such as walls, windows, doors, and so forth. It also reflects scientific, technological, sociological and statutory knowledge, and constraints relevant to the domain. This knowledge must be represented declaratively so that it can be freely used in general inferencing, not encapsulated in procedures that are only applicable in certain circumstances. It is this domain knowledge that determines the basic structure of the space of possible designs. In our representation scheme domain knowledge is organized hierarchically using *specialization* relationships between representation objects.

Design knowledge derives from previous designs and is concerned with how domain knowledge is used to define and solve design problems; how the space of possible designs is explored and how a developing design problem structure is created, modified, and refined. Design knowledge includes useful decomposition criteria and strategies, synthesis and analysis methods and techniques, and required validation, documentation, and presentation procedures, for example. Whereas domain knowledge governs the underlying behavior of a design problem, design knowledge is used in deciding how it is to be configured—what priority to put on requirements and constraints, what is to be ignored, and what is to be included and so forth. Because, during the design process, this problem structure is often modified and revised as its nature is explored and understood, design knowledge must also be represented declaratively. It must not be wrapped up in preconceived and fixed approaches to design problems, as a 'parameterized design description' and its associated 'methods.' As more designs are carried out so more ways of approaching, structuring, and solving the problems that occur in a particular domain will be discovered. It therefore needs to be related to the domain knowledge. In our representation scheme an *aggregation* relationship is used to 'chunk' design knowledge expressed in terms of domain knowledge.

Using the specialization and aggregation relationships the representational objects used to declaratively define domain and design knowledge are organized in a way that can support design tasks. In general this means that the DKB partially defines a SPD in terms of 'regions of interest' and the relationships between them. These regions of interest represent regions in the space of possible designs that have been explored as a result of doing previous designs, and in which design knowledge has been embedded in the domain knowledge—regions in which the relationships between the structure of the space of possible designs and possible design problem structures and their development and exploration have been previously worked out, and which can therefore be used to start and subsequently support new exploration processes.

The DDD resulting from a particular design task defines a region of interest in the SPD. It typically represents an elaboration and/or extension of the region defined by the DKB. Its structure and content directly reflects the nature and results of a particular design task; its exploration history, evolved requirement description, and final design specification, or specifications if more than one design results. The structure and content of a DDD is thus particular to each design task undertaken, but each DDD represents an important source of knowledge for extending and modifying the DKB.

The relationship between a DKB and the DDDs resulting from a series of design tasks is one of abstraction and generalization. Carrying out individual design tasks does not just result in solutions to particular design problems, it also results in greater knowledge and understanding of a class, or type, of design problem. Initially some of this additional knowledge is expressed in the DDDs of particular designs. In order to make it available for use during other design tasks it needs to be transferred to the DKB built to support the class of problems concerned. This transfer process represents a kind of design problem in itself; new domain and design knowledge structures and relationships need to be designed and incorporated within an existing DKB so that it can be used to advantage in future design problems. As design is practiced today this process of abstraction and generalization of knowledge from particular design tasks is largely implicit in the practice of designers—it is part of becoming an experienced designer; of becoming an expert. Because the abstraction and generalization process of transferring knowledge from DDDs to a DKB is described as a design problem, it should also be characterized by our exploration-based model described in Section 4. The details of this await elaboration and are currently the subject of research.

In the remainder of this section we briefly outline how this declarative knowledge representation scheme can be used to support the exploration process described in Section 7.3. We describe the architecture and operation of the Edinburgh Designer System (EDS), a design support system for mechanical engineering design developed as part of the Alvey large scale demonstrator 'Design to Product' (Smithers, 1987), which uses this knowledge representation scheme. A *design support system*, unlike a CAD system, attempts to actively assist the designer throughout the design process. EDS doesn't actually design anything—rather it attempts to support the designer in exploring the space of possible designs. This support is manifest at two distinct levels:

1. Support for the overall control of the design process; and

2. support for the production of alternative design solutions.

These might loosely be described as strategic and tactical support. Strategic support is primarily concerned with the overall organization of design process: the generation and maintenance of alternatives or solutions to particular subproblems; and the selection of the most promising candidates for further development. Tactical support is concerned with the solution of particular problems, the assignment of values to design parameters, and the evaluation of the resulting partial design solutions. To the extent that the exploration of the space of possible designs is carried out through the development of possible solutions, the overall control of the design process is dependent on the production of alternative solutions. For example, the comparison of alternative proposals relies on there being some means of generating and evaluating alternative solutions.

The process of analysis-through-synthesis outlined earlier typically results in the generation of a large number of alternative designs or variants. These alternatives may embody radically different approaches to the problem or they may be variations on a common theme or both. Alternatively a problem may be broken down into a set of simpler subproblems (for example, the design of an assembly may be reduced to the design of its constituent components), together with the problem of integrating the resulting part solutions, or it may be broken down into a set of associated functions. A major task of any design support system will therefore be one of complexity management—keeping track of the various alternative design proposals and the information required to solve particular problems, both as a record of the design process (which alternatives have been tried and what was learned) and to allow the designer to partition the problem appropriately (Logan, 1989).

At the level of individual design problems the designer requires both information about the consequences of design decisions and assistance with the solution of problems. Of particular concern are inconsistencies that arise in attempting to satisfy multiple goals. The system should therefore provide support for context specific inference based on design decisions, constraints, and the requirements defining the design problem, together with physical laws, heuristics, and other domain knowledge relating the parameters of the design. In addition the system should, where possible, provide assistance in solving particular design problems, drawing on the large amounts of knowledge encoded in design handbooks, codes of practice and in the expertise of individual designers.

EDS consists of four main functional elements that together embody the model of design support outlined earlier:

1. Consistency Maintenance

2. Context Management

3. Knowledge Representation

4. Inference

In EDS, the context management and consistency maintenance subsystems provide strategic support, and the knowledge representation and inference subsystems provide tactical support. In what follows we concentrate primarily on the consistency maintenance and inference subsystems of EDS that are implemented as an assumption-based truth maintained blackboard system. The user interface and the overall design of the system are discussed in more detail elsewhere (Smithers et al., 1990).

The production of a large number of alternative design solutions results in a major consistency maintenance problem. If the system is to effectively aid the designer at the strategic level, the various incompatible design alternatives must be considered in isolation. This, together with the need to retain alternatives for comparison and/or possible later development, led to the adoption of an assumption-based truth maintenance system (ATMS) as the basis of EDS (de Kleer, 1984). The ATMS forms the core of the system and all of the other system components are implemented using the facilities it provides. The ATMS builds and maintains the Design Description Document and provides an interface between the contents of the DDD and the other subsystems, passing out relevant pieces of information to them as required and incorporating new information, which it receives from them, into the dependency structure. Its central role in the system architecture has resulted in a number of extensions to the 'conventional' ATMS model which are discussed in more detail later.

At the tactical level a number of particular tasks within the overall exploration process can be identified for which partial support is possible. In our work on mechanical design, for example, we have identified algebraic equation solving, constraint manipulation, reasoning about spatial relationships, shape and space occupancy, and reasoning about relational information as common to several different activities in the design process. Support for particular design tasks is provided by a series of general purpose support systems—forward chaining or data-driven inference engines which attempt to infer by means of constraint satisfaction the consequences of the designer's decisions. In general the inferences engines derive necessary consequences of what is currently known about the design and can be allowed to proceed relatively unhampered by the designer, with the sole constraint that they should refrain from rederiving information that is already present in the DDD.

Control of the interactions between these inference engines is in the style of a blackboard system (Hayes-Roth, 1985), with the inference engines acting as knowledge sources. The system maintains an agenda of Knowledge Source Activation Records (KSARs), which mark an intent to perform some particular task. The ATMS truth maintains the KSARs within the DDD on an equal footing with existing data and its justifications. This benefits the system by automatically removing flawed bids as they come to light as a result of other inferences and the operation of the ATMS. The agenda control mechanism therefore does not need to be vigilant on this matter. A similar arrangement can be found in Jones and Millington (1986). Blackboard systems are usually designed and implemented as 'single context' problem solving systems in which the knowledge sources work together to construct one consistent solution. Truth maintaining the blackboard has therefore resulted in a number of departures from the conventional practice in blackboard systems, notably the absence of deletions (except for KSARs) or amendments as it is unclear how these fit into an assumption-based truth maintenance scheme.

EDS represents domain knowledge in a Domain Knowledge Base containing definitions of domain objects, called *module classes*, related by *kind_of* (specialization) and *part_of* (aggregation) relations. Each module class declares a set of parameters, variables, and constraints that define a particular class or type of object. The creation of an instance of a module class results in datum nodes being created in the ATMS for each of the module's parameters, variables and constraints. *Justifications* link new data introduced into the DDD as a consequence of applying a knowledge source to some particular set of domain data already present in the DDD. This existing data is also pointed to by the justification. Note that a particular datum can be supported by more than one justification—for example if it can be derived in different ways or from different sets of assumptions.

Design proceeds by creating instances of module classes and assigning values to their parameters to define one or more possible solutions. (This is something of an oversimplification—the user can also define new parameters and constraints and assemble novel designs from existing modules.) When the user makes an assumption one (or more) datum nodes are created in the DDD to hold the new information. As new information becomes available, it is examined by the knowledge sources to see if it, together with any information already in the DDD, can be used to make further inferences. If a knowledge source indicates that it can make an inference, it generates a bid in the form of a Knowledge Source Activation Record, which is scored and merged into the agenda. When a KSAR reaches the front of the agenda, it is executed and the results are claimed into the ATMS. This information may in turn form the basis for a new round of bids and this cycle continues until no executable KSARs remain in the agenda. As new values for parameters or bounds on them are assumed or derived, consistency checks are performed between constraints and values by the *valueConflict* KS. Conflicts result in the creation of a justification for the distinguished node ⟨false⟩ recording the fact that the assumptions involved are mutually inconsistent and causes the ATMS to partition the assumptions into mutually consistent sets. If there is no conflict, EDS marks this by justifying the datum ⟨consistent⟩ and proceeds as usual. The user is viewed as a knowledge source whose 'bids' are always processed first. This allows the system to follow several lines of reasoning as it attempts to infer the consequences of the user's design decisions, while still giving priority to user input.

To conclude this section, we present a simple example to illustrate the operation of the system. This is not intended to explain in detail all of what the system does, but to indicate how the various subsystems described earlier work together to support the exploration of the space of possible designs. The example we have chosen is the design of a beam supporting a precast concrete floor in a small office development. The beam spans

7.4m, the total dead load is 292.7kN, and the imposed load is 362.3kN, both uniformly distributed. It is assumed that the beam is simply supported and is adequately restrained against lateral buckling.

The design process begins with the designer searching the DKB to see if it contains anything relating to the problem in hand. If a complete design closely satisfying the requirements exists in the DKB, the designer may decide to use it and modify it by changing the existing values of various parameters. Alternatively, and more usually, an object representing a class of some useful kind of functional mechanism is used and an instance of it is assumed, and named. This results in instances of all the constraint expressions represented by the chosen object class, and all that it inherits from its parents (if any) being passed to the ATMS, which builds them into the Design Description Document. Having loaded all the instances of object classes thought to be required, at least for the moment, the DDD will effectively represent a particular part of the space of possible designs selected to be explored in more detail. The designer might then start exploring the possible solutions to the particular problem in hand by choosing values to assign to parameters appearing in the instances of constraint expressions, to see what the consequences of such values, or combinations of values, are.

In this case we assume that the DKB contains an appropriate module class representing a simply supported beam with uniformly distributed load, UB001 (see Appendix). (It should be emphasised that this is a rather unrealistic example in that it presupposes the existence of a module class appropriate to the problem. In reality, such a problem would probably be solved by combining instances of a number of simpler and/or more general modules relating to particular beam types and loading conditions. The standard 'beam set' consists of about 10 module classes covering various beam types, end support and loading conditions. However, it serves to illustrate the operation of the system and highlights the differences between the approach taken here and that taken in, for example, Gero et al. (1988).) The module class definition consists of three main sections: the module class header; parameter, variable, and constant declarations; and constraints, each of which in turn consists of one or more subsections.

The module class header contains information relating to the creation of the module and its modification history, its place in the *kind-of* and *part-of* hierarchies, and the names of any diagrams or figures relevant to the module class that should be displayed by the DKB browser. The declaration [B] : universalBeam declares the *typical name variable* of the module, B, which is used to refer to the module relative to its parts or in describing its position relative to other objects and is similar in many respects to the notion of 'self' in object oriented programming languages. The next section declares the module's parameters, variables, and constants. *Parameters* describe some property of the designed artifact such as its size, shape, or the material of which it is made. The set of parameters can be viewed as properties of the object for which values need to be determined in order to form a description of the object that is sufficient to consider this part of the design complete. *Variables* are properties of the design that relate the parameters of its description, and may change during the operation of the designed object, such as its speed or power output. *Constants* are symbols that will appear in the constraints and for which no substitution of numerical values will be performed. Examples of these are symbols denoting things like 'aluminium' or 'pi.' Each subsection consists of zero or more entries declaring a parameter, variable or constant, one per line. Each declaration consists of the name of the parameter, variable or constant followed by its type, dimension, and an identifier consisting of a '#' and an integer (used by the system to uniquely identify the parameter variable or constant). The remainder of the line, up to the 'double hash' (##) symbol, is treated as a comment and ignored by the system for the purposes of inferencing. The '$' symbol is an operator used to create references to the parameters or variables of a particular named instance of a module class from the instance name and the declared name of the parameter or variable.

The format of the constraint declarations is similar to that for parameters, variables, and constants. Each constraint consists of an expression containing parameters, variables or constants, followed by a relational operator, an expression (involving other parameters, variables or constants) or value, followed by a constraint number and a comment. Tables are viewed as a special kind of constraint, relating a 'dependent variable' (a parameter or variable) to one or more 'independent variables.' Each table is introduced by the `functionTable` or `catalogueTable` keyword, followed by the name of the table, its dimension, the type of interpolation to be used by the table engine and the independent and dependent variables in order. The system contains a syntax checker and translator that converts this human-readable form of the module class definition into an internal form used by EDS.

We assume that the designer begins by creating a named instance of the module class UB001. This results in EDS constructing, in the DDD, a uniquely identified instance of UB001 using the knowledge declared in the module class definition. This is done using the following user instruction:

```
USER: assume [b1] : universalBeam
```

which says create in the DDD an instance of the module class UB001 called b1. The inner workings of the system can be viewed in one of the EDS output windows, and looks like the following:

```
EDS: NEW > N    1: [b1] : universalBeam
     NEW > J    0: assumption
     NEW > K    0: findSuperClass (125)
     NEW > K    1: findDirectParts (122)
     NEW > K    2: findDirectConstraints (121)
     NEW > K    3: declareLabels (124)
     NEW > K    4: declareDirectAttributes (123)
     NEW > J    1: findSuperClass
     RIP > K    0: findSuperClass (125)
     NEW > N    2: Declaration of b1 as a label
     NEW > J    2: declareLabels
     RIP > K    3: declareLabels (124)
     NEW > N    3: Declaration of g$b1 as a parameter
     NEW > N    4: Declaration of py$b1 as a parameter

                   .

                   .

                   .

     NEW > N   26: Declaration of e$b1 as a constant
     NEW > J    3: declareDirectAttributes
     RIP > K    4: declareDirectAttributes (123)
     NEW > J    4: findDirectParts
     RIP > K    1: findDirectParts (122)
     NEW > N   27: wif$b1  =  1.6 * wi$b1
     NEW > N   28: wdf$b1  =  1.4 * wd$b1

                   .

                   .

                   .

     NEW > N   41: functionTable(~, 2, 0, ~)
     NEW > N   42: catalogueTable(~, 2, 0, ~)
     NEW > J    5: findDirectConstraints
     RIP > K    2: findDirectConstraints (121)
     NEW > K    5: bbTermination (50)
     RIP > K    5: bbTermination (50) yes
```

Here **NEW** means a item has been created in the DDD, **N** means that it is a datum node, that is, a piece of information, **J** means that it is a justification, the method by which the information was introduced into the DDD (used by the consistency maintenance system to record dependencies), and **K** means it is a Knowledge Source Activation Record, which marks the intent to perform some particular piece of work (used by the agenda control mechanism to schedule the work done by EDS). (The "~", in "**NEW >**

N 41: functionTable(˜, 2, 1, ˜)" indicates that a structure has been compressed to allow the output to fit on a single line. In this example the first "˜" stands for a table.) RIP indicates that the work associated with a particular KSAR has been carried out. The numbers following these type identifiers are the tags that the system uses to identify the corresponding nodes in the ATMS. RIP > K 5: bbTermination (50) (the last line in the EDS output listed earlier) indicates that the EDS blackboard system has terminated, EDS has done all the work it can, and that it is awaiting further user interaction. At this stage there are no inferences that the system can make, other than to simplify the constraints into an internal 'canonical' form.

As the design proceeds the consequences of the designer's assumptions are derived by the support systems. Such derived information typically relates to the predicted performance of the designed artifact (including any constraints violated by the proposed design) and any parameter values that can be inferred from the designer's assumptions or their consequences and the constraints linking these values.

For example, if the designer makes further assumptions about the the yield stress and the self weight of the beam:

```
USER: assume py$b1  = 275
      assume wbf$b1 = 0
```

and the problem requirements (the imposed load, dead load, and the span):

```
USER: assume wi$b1  = 326.2
      assume wd$b1  = 292.7
      assume l$b1   = 7.4
```

the system can infer values for the maximum bending moment, shear force, and plastic modulus:

```
EDS: NEW > N  48: w$b1  = 654.9
     NEW > N  49: mc$b1 = 605.8
     NEW > N  50: s$b1  = 2202.9
     NEW > N  51: fv$b1 = 327.5
```

This information can be used to assist in selecting a beam size from the standard sections represented in the catalog table in the module class UB001. For example, if the designer decides that a 457 × 191 × 98 beam of type 43 steel would be suitable:

```
USER:  assume g$b1  = 43
       assume sd$b1 = 457
       assume sb$b1 = 191
       assume wb$b1 = 98
```

EDS will rederive the values for self weight and yield stress assumed earlier and, using information from the catalog table in the module class, can check the proposed design for consistency against the other constraints:

```
EDS: NEW > N  67: s$b1      = 2320.8
     NEW > K  27: valueConflict (150)

     !!! > New nogood set: [[1 45 46 47 52 53 54 55]]
     !!! > J  49: valueConflict

     OUT > J  49# valueConflict
     OUT > K  27# valueConflict (150)
     IN  > N   0: <false>
     RIP > K  27# valueConflict (150)
     NEW > N  68: pv$b1     = 847.2
     NEW > N  69: defx$b1   = 12.7
```

The beam is satisfactory in shear and deflection, but fails in bending (constraint 7 is violated) as the required plastic modulus, s$b1, is greater than that of the selected section. Conflicts are noted by creating a justification for a distinguished datum ⟨false⟩, which results in the ATMS partitioning the assumptions made so far into sets that are mutually consistent. If there is no conflict then EDS marks this by justifying the datum ⟨consistent⟩ and proceeds as usual. A inconsistent set of assumptions is called a *nogood*. In the aforementioned example, the nogood set consists of the constraints declared in the module class and loaded when the instance **b1** was created (assumption 1), which are jointly inconsistent with the assumed problem description (assumptions 45, 46 and 47) and the chosen section (assumptions 52, 53, 54 and 55).

When an inconsistency arises or the design is found to be unsatisfactory (as is typically the case), the designer can attempt to modify the offending parameter values using information on which assumptions are jointly inconsistent provided by the ATMS. To assist the designer in understanding the dependencies between assumptions and derived results, EDS provides various utilities that allow the user to examine the contents of the DDD. For example, using the graphical explanation facility, the user can display a graphical representation of how a parameter was inferred by viewing its justification, environment, and inferencing method. In particular the user can discover the reason for the inconsistency signaled before by requesting that the system display the mutually inconsistent assumptions (and their consequences) which led to the derivation of ⟨false⟩. Alternatively, the designer can ignore the inconsistency and continue to pursue the development of the inconsistent design based on what can be coherently derived. The opportunistic nature of the blackboard control strategy means that whatever can be consistently derived from a set of assumptions will be derived. This approach may be appropriate when, for example, the inconsistency is considered minor or peripheral and the main interest lies with the consequences of some (consistent) set of assumptions that are considered central to the proposed solution. Even if the design fails to violate any constraints the designer may elect to pursue several different designs in parallel in an attempt to determine which gives the best overall performance, or to determine the sensitivity of the derived performance to the values of the design parameters. This will typically involve trying several alternative values for parameters until the constraints are satisfied or the relative performance of the various alternatives is understood. Multiple assignments to parameters (giving rise to multiple alternative solutions) and their interactions are handled automatically by the ATMS as are inconsistencies between parameter values and any assumed constraints.

In this case we assume that the designer elects to continue with the current approach and selects a larger beam with an appropriate plastic modulus, for example a 533 × 210 × 92 beam with a plastic modulus of 2366 cm^3:

```
USER: assume sd$b1 = 533
      assume sb$b1 = 210
      assume wb$b1 = 92
```

EDS again derives the consequences of the decision and this time the constraints are satisfied; the section meets the design requirements (although it is not necessarily optimal). However, the chosen section is over half a meter deep and although it solves the 'structures problem' a beam of this size may be unacceptable for other reasons, for example the cost of the structure may be too great or the size of the structural zone may add unacceptably to the total building volume, which must be air-conditioned. (This is when the 'real' design problem begins to emerge. Unfortunately, we can do little more than indicate the nature of the problem here. For more details, see Logan and Newton (1989).) If the size of the structure is deemed to be unacceptable, there are several options open to the designer: the designer can change the bay size, reducing the span and hence the size of the structure; alternatively the designer could change the structural system, perhaps to reinforced concrete or a loadbearing masonry construction drawing on knowledge about these structural systems represented in the hierarchy of module classes. However, to avoid complicating the example, we shall assume that the designer decides to explore the possibility of using a higher stress steel (type 55):

```
USER: assume g$b1 = 55
```

The system rederives the parameter and variable values for the current 533 × 210 × 92 beam size using data about the yield stress of type 55 steel obtained from the *function Table* in the module UB001. (Note that the system derives this information for both the 457 × 191 × 98 beam and the 533 × 210 × 92 beam. If this is undesirable, the designer can create a new instance for each alternative design. However this is unnecessary as the ATMS maintains consistency of the information and can be cumbersome when we wish to exploit information that has already been derived for an existing design.) The maximum bending moment is unchanged, but the higher yield stress of type 55 steel means that the plastic modulus is reduced to 1365.5 cm³. From the table of beam properties, the smallest section with an adequate plastic modulus is a 406 × 178 × 74. However if we check this section by assuming new values for the beam depth, width, and self weight, we discover that although satisfactory in bending and sheer the beam fails in deflection:

```
EDS: NEW > N 104: defx$b1 = 21.3
     NEW > K  87: valueConflict (150)

     !!! > New nogood set: [[1 45 46 47 93 94 95 96]]
     !!! > J  91: valueConflict
```

This difficulty can be overcome by using a deeper beam. For example, a 457 × 152 × 67 beam meets the deflection criterion. (Another option would be to relax the deflection criterion.) However, the decision to use a larger section results in a corresponding increase in the depth of the structure and offsets one of the principal advantages of the more expensive, high stress steel. Whether the reduction in depth achievable with the high stress steel is worth the increased cost will depend on a number of factors: the relative cost of the various grades of steel; the implications of a smaller structural bay for the flexibility of the building in use; the consequences of the increased construction time associated with a reinforced concrete structure for the financial viability of a speculative development and so forth.

The example could be further elaborated by introducing additional criteria, or utilizing modules representing different components (such as a reinforced concrete beam), or the analysis of complete structural systems consisting of a number of modules. However, whereas the example described earlier presents an oversimplified view of the design process, it serves to illustrate the use of the system. The designer can pursue the development of the design without worrying about inconsistencies except insofar as they indicate the shortcomings of a proposed solution. The ATMS ensures that only valid inferences are drawn from the current design description by automatically detecting inconsistent sets of assumptions and violated constraints and partitioning the design description to restore consistency. One of the advantages of the exploration based model of design and the truth maintained blackboard system control structure used in EDS is that it is easy to make different assumptions corresponding either to design choices available within one module class definition or to choices between module class definitions. By choosing different types of structure, that is, loading different module class definitions and assigning values to their parameters, the implications of different approaches to the structures problem become apparent. The investigation of design alternatives leads to a better understanding of the design problem. These explorations help the designer appreciate which requirements may be most readily achieved and those that may be neglected without loss. As part of this process the designer learns which criterion values will achieve the design goals and how much variation in these values can be tolerated while still achieving acceptable performance. The designer also discovers the implications of achieving the current goal and any other decisions required to make the attainment of the goal consistent with the current solution.

We believe this provides a flexible environment for the exploration of the structure of design problems. However, making the best use of the exploration based model of design and control structure of EDS does rely heavily on the designer's understanding the problem and knowledge of the contents of the module class definition files.

7.7 Conclusion

We have argued that the design process can be seen as one of exploring the space of possible designs to discover its structure, and hence the nature of possible designs. The designer proceeds by proposing solutions and evaluating their implications in terms of solution criteria. Decisions regarding any single criterion often have widespread implications, highlighting previously unrecognized criteria and relationships. These interactions between one requirement and another define what we have termed the 'structure' of a design problem. It is the pattern of constraints defining the problem space and the relationships between them and the basic structure of the space of possible designs that forms the essence of design problems, and the discovery of appropriate relationships between these criteria that forms the basis for the design activity. The fundamental objective in design is therefore to understand the structure of the problem, with a major part of the effort in design directed at structuring problems, and only a fraction of this effort directed at 'solving' them once they are structured. The technique of 'analysis-through-synthesis' discussed in the preceding sections can be viewed more generally as a process for gathering information about problem structure that will ultimately be valuable in discovering a solution.

An appreciation of these relationships is fundamental to the design process and necessary for the production of new designs. The adaption of prototypes within the framework of the exploration based model of design presented earlier can be viewed as a simple model of this (in reality, complex) process. The modification of a prototype within the context of the current problem can be seen as a very crude model of, or perhaps a metaphor for, what happens when a designer begins to 'understand' the structure of a problem, and its relationship to the space of possible designs. It is at this level that the problem of creativity in design—or simply design—must be addressed.

The most important limitation of our exploration-based model is its failure to say anything about this process of prototype adaption and in particular how it is controlled—the problem of deciding which prototype to modify and determining how it is to be modified. This limitation is reflected in the kinds of support EDS is capable of providing. EDS attempts to support the designer's exploration of problem structure by automatically deriving the necessary consequences of the designer's decisions, detecting inconsistencies in the requirements or the problem description and maintaining the justification structure which expresses the dependencies between the designer's assumptions and their consequences. This strategy has two main advantages: it allows us to tackle more complex (although still not very complex) problems; and it allows us to concentrate on those parts of the problem we think we do understand for example, knowledge representation and a few limited forms of inference while offloading the rest onto the human designer. However, although it is possible to modify a module class by introducing *ad hoc* assumptions into the DDD or by creating a new module class in the DKB, the system offers little or no support in this area beyond tools to assist in the creation of new modules. This lack of understanding also limits the effectiveness of the kinds of support that the system can provide. Because it has no understanding of what the user is trying to do or the information relevant to a particular design task and consequently of where it should concentrate its efforts, the system is capable of providing only weakly directed support unless the user exercises close control. We are currently working on an extension to this framework which is intended to help better understand this aspect of design (Logan et al., 1990).

Acknowledgements. We are grateful to Nils Tomes who read an earlier draft of this chapter and made a number of helpful comments, and to her and the other members of the AI in Design research program at Edinburgh for many discussions during the development of these ideas. The AI in Design research program being conducted at the Department of Artificial Intelligence, Edinburgh University, is partially funded by the UK Science and Engineering Research Council under grant number GR/F/6200.1.

References

Akin, O. (1978). How do architects design, *in* J.-C. Latombe (Ed.), *Artificial Intelligence and Pattern Recognition in Computer Aided Design*, North-Holland, Amsterdam, pp. 65–98.

Barr, A., & Feigenbaum, E. A. (Eds) (1981). *The Handbook of Artificial Intelligence, Volume 1*, Pitman, London.

Bazjanac, V. (1974). Architectural design theory: models of design process, *in* W. R. Spillers (Ed.), *Basic Questions of Design Theory*, North-Holland, Amsterdam, pp. 2–19.

Brown, D. C., & Chandrasekaran, B. (1984). Expert systems for a class of mechanical design activity, *in* J. S. Gero (Ed.), *Knowledge Engineering in Computer-Aided Design*, North-Holland, Amsterdam pp. 259–276.

Cagan, J., & Agogino, A. M. (1989). Why AI-design researchers should distinguish between creative, innovative and routine levels of design, *Working Paper 89-0202-0*, Intelligent Systems Research Group, Department of Mechanical Engineering, University of California at Berkeley.

Coyne, R. F., & Subrahmanian, E. (1989). Computer supported creative design: a pragmatic approach, *Preprints Modeling Creativity and Knowledge-Based Creative Design*, Design Computing Unit, Department of Architectural and Design Science, University of Sydney, pp. 35–68.

Foz, A. T. K. (1972). *Some Observations on Designer Behavior in the Parti*, MA Thesis, MIT Press, Cambridge, Massachusetts.

Gero, J. S. (1987). Prototypes: a new schema for knowledge-based design, *Working Paper*, Architectural Computing Unit, University of Sydney, Sydney.

Gero, J. S. (1989). Routine and nonroutine design: A prototype-based approach, *International Conference on Expert Systems in Engineering Applications*, Huazhong University of Science and Technology Press, Wuhan, China, pp 369–371.

Gero, J. S., Maher, M. L., & Zhang, W. (1988). Chunking structural design knowledge as prototypes, *in* J. S. Gero (Ed.), *Artificial Intelligence in*

Engineering: Design, Elsevier, Amsterdam, pp. 3–21.

Gero, J. S., & Rosenman, M. A. (1989). A conceptual framework for knowledge-based design research at Sydney University's Design Computing Unit, *in* J. S. Gero (Ed.), *Artificial Intelligence in Engineering Design*, CMP/Springer-Verlag, Southampton and Berlin, pp 363–382.

Hayes-Roth, B. (1985). Blackboard architectures for control, *Artificial Intelligence*, **26**: 251–321.

Hillier, W., & Leaman, A. (1974). How is design possible, *Journal of Architectural Research*, **3**: 4–11.

Hillier, W., & Leaman, A. (1976). Architecture as a discipline, *Journal of Architectural Research*, **5**: 28–32.

Jones, J., & Millington, M. (1986). An Edinburgh Prolog BlackBoard Shell, *DAI Research Paper No. 281*, Department of Artificial Intelligence, University of Edinburgh, Edinburgh.

de Kleer, J. (1984). Choices without backtracking, *Proceedings of the National Conference on Artificial Intelligence*, Austin, Texas, pp. 79–85.

Lawson, B. (1980). *How Designers Think*, Architectural Press, London.

Logan, B. S. (1989). Conceptualizing design knowledge, *Design Studies*, **10**: 188–195.

Logan, B. S., Millington, K., & Smithers, T. (1990). Assumption-based context management in the Edinburgh Designer System, *DAI Research Paper No. 494*, Department of Artificial Intelligence, University of Edinburgh, Edinburgh.

Maher, M. L., Zhao, F., & Gero, J. S. (1989). An approach to knowledge-based creative design, *Preprints of the NSF Engineering Design Research Conference*, University of Massachusetts, Amherst, pp. 333–346.

Murthy, S. S., & Addanki, S. (1987). PROMPT: an innovative design tool, *Proceedings of AAAI Sixth National Conference on Artificial Intelligence*, Seattle, pp. 637–642.

Oxman, R., & Gero, J. S. (1988). Designing by prototype refinement in architecture, *in* J. S. Gero (Ed.), *Artificial Intelligence in Engineering: Design*, Elsevier, Amsterdam, pp. 395–412.

Rosenman, M. A., & Gero, J. S. (1989). Creativity in design using a prototype approach, *Preprints Modeling Creativity and Knowledge-Based Creative Design*, Department of Architectural and Design Science, University of Sydney, Sydney, pp. 207–232.

Simon, H. A. (1970). *The Sciences of the Artificial*, MIT Press, Cambridge, Mass.

Simon, H. A. (1973). The structure of ill-structured problems, *Artificial Intelligence* **4**: 181–201.

Smithers, T. (1987). The Alvey Large Scale Demonstrator Project Design to Product, *in* T. Bernhold (Ed.), *Artificial Intelligence in Manufacturing, Key to Integration*, North-Holland, Amsterdam, pp. 251–261.

Smithers, T., Conkie, A., Doheny, J., Logan, B., Millington, K., & Tang, M. X. (1990). Design as intelligent behavior: an AI in design research program, *Artificial Intelligence in Engineering*, **5**: 78–109.

Steadman, P. (1979). The history and science of the artificial, *Design Studies*, **1**: 49–58.

Westerberg, A., Grossmann, I., Talukdar, S., Prinz, F., Fenves, S., & Maher, M. L. (1989). Applications of AI in design research at Carnegie Mellon University's

EDRC, *in* J. S. Gero (Ed.), *Artificial Intelligence in Design*, CMP/Springer-Verlag, Berlin, pp. 335–361.

Woodbury, R. F. (1989). Design genes, *Preprints Modeling Creativity and Knowledge-Based Creative Design*, Department of Architectural and Design Science, University of Sydney, Sydney, pp. 133–154.

Appendix: The UB001 Module Class Definition File

```
beginSection: moduleClassHeader

    beginClassName
      class name [B]  : universalBeam
      created :         November 1990
      created by :      bsl
    endClassName

    beginModification
      modified:    none
      modified by: none
      reason:      none
    endModification

    beginIsAkindOf
      none
    endIsAkindOf

    beginHasAsParts
      none
    endHasAsParts

    beginFigureReferences
      none
    endFigureReferences

endSection: moduleClassHeader

beginSection: parametersVariablesConstants

    beginParameters

      g$B     integer   -     #1   steel grade                   ##
      py$B    real  N/mm**2   #2   minimum yield stress          ##

      sd$B    integer   mm    #3   nominal depth of beam         ##
```

```
    sb$B     integer   mm     #4   nominal width of beam                ##
    wb$B     integer   kg/m   #5   beam weight (linear)                 ##
    d$B      real      mm     #6   beam depth                           ##
    b$B      real      mm     #7   beam width                           ##
    tw$B     real      mm     #8   web thickness                        ##
    tf$B     real      mm     #9   flange thickness                     ##
    i$B      integer   m**4   #10  moment of inertia (x-x axis)         ##
    s0$B     integer   m**3   #11  plastic modulus (x-x axis)           ##

endParameters

beginVariables

    wi$B     real      N      #1   imposed load                         ##
    wd$B     real      N      #2   dead load                            ##
    wif$B    real      N      #3   imposed load (factored)              ##
    wdf$B    real      N      #4   dead load (factored)                 ##
    wbf$B    real      N      #5   self weight (factored)               ##
    l$B      real      m      #6   beam length                          ##

    mc$B     real      N m    #7   maximum bending moment (mid-span) ##
    s$B      real      m**3   #8   plastic modulus                      ##
    fv$B     real      N      #9   shear force                          ##
    pv$B     real      N      #10  shear capacity                       ##
    def$B    real      mm     #11  maximum permissible deflection       ##
    defx$B   real      mm     #12  beam deflection                      ##

endVariables

beginConstants

    e$B      real   N/mm**2   #1   young's modulus                      ##

endConstants

endSection: parametersVariablesConstants

beginSection: constraints

    wif$B    = 1.6 * wi$B                                    #1      ##
    wdf$B    = 1.4 * wd$B                                    #2      ##
    wbf$B    = 1.4 * l$B * wb$B * 9.81 * 10 ** (3)           #3      ##
    w$B      = wif$B + wdf$B + wbf$B                         #4      ##

    mc$B     = w$B * l$B / 8                                 #5      ##
    s$B      = mc$B / py$B                                   #6      ##
    s$B      < s0$B                                          #7      ##
```

```
fv$B    = w$B / 2                                           #8     ##
pv$B    = 0.6 * py$B * a$B                                  #9     ##
a$B     = d$B * t$B                                         #10    ##
fv$B    < pv$B                                              #11    ##
fv$B    < 0.6 * pv$B                                        #12    ##
def$B   = l$B / 360                                         #13    ##
defx$B  = (5 / 384) * (wi$B * l$B * 10 ** (12)) /
                      (e$B * i$B * 10 ** (4))               #14    ##

functionTable   yieldStress                                       ##
dimension: 2
interpolation: match

g$B      tf$B     py$B

         0        17       41       64       100
43     275      265      255      245      245
50     355      345      340      325      325
55     450      430      415      undef    undef              #1 ##



catalogueTable  sectionProperties                                 ##

sd$B  sb$B  wb$B   d$B     b$B    tw$B  tf$B   i$B     s0$B

914   419   388   920.5   420.5   21.5  36.6  718742  17675
914   419   343   911.4   418.5   19.4  32.0  625282  15474

914   305   289   926.6   307.8   19.6  32.0  504594  12583
914   305   253   918.5   305.5   17.3  27.9  436610  10947
914   305   224   910.3   304.1   15.9  23.9  375924   9522

                          .
                          .
                          .

254   102    28   260.4   102.1    6.4  10.0    4008   353.4
254   102    25   275.0   101.9    6.1   8.4    3408   305.6
254   102    22   254.0   101.6    5.8   6.8    2867   261.9

203   133    30   206.8   133.8    6.3   9.6    2887   313.3
203   133    25   203.2   133.4    5.8   7.8    2356   259.8 #1 ##

endSection: constraints
```

8

A Connectionist View of Creative Design Reasoning

Richard D. Coyne, Sidney Newton, and Fay Sudweeks

Connectionist models can be used to model important aspects of design reasoning: the way design involves memory; and a 'holistic' kind of reasoning by which designs appear to emerge from that memory. A simple connectionist model is constructed to demonstrate how information about schemas (in this case, room types) is stored implicitly after exposure to a number of examples of specific rooms. Using connectionist models as a basis for reasoning, new room types can emerge from this information.

8.1 Introduction

The study of design cannot readily be separated from the study of the agents of design. We would therefore expect models of cognition to occupy an important place in the development of computer systems that are to be of assistance to designers. There are several important models of cognition currently under scrutiny within cognitive science and artificial intelligence, each with its own fervent advocates and each withstanding its own burden of criticism. The controversies will not be entered into in this chapter. The model followed in this chapter is that afforded by *connectionism*, a body of theory based on parallel distributed processes.

Connectionist models are simple mathematical models that shadow the microstructure of the brain. One of the most remarkable claims being made about these models is that, in spite of their simplicity, they exhibit properties that could be considered essential features of human cognition: the idiosyncratic way they 'learn,' their reliance on 'memory,' their abilities to deal with partial information, and even their pathologies. A further claim is that they exhibit a propensity to behave in a way that captures the essence of creativity and design. They appear to synthesize, to innovate. In a way, it is difficult to prevent them from doing this.

In general, enormous effort needs to be expended in contriving automated reasoning systems to work against their natural propensity to do deductive logic, and thereby perform the designerly task of *abduction*. Yet it is possible to construct a simple connectionist model that manifests a kind of abduction in a nontrivial way. The example we present is simple, and if it were to form the basis of a computer system it would be of only limited usefulness. However the example is compelling. On the one hand it suggests that designing appears to inhere within the connectionist model of human cognition. Of more interest from the point of view of computer applications, it persuades us of the value of connectionist models in computer systems that assist in design reasoning.

The example we follow is our reworked version of a seminal experiment by Rumelhart, Smolensky, McClelland, and Hinton (1987). As it is so well suited to a discussion of design we have also kept to the same domain, pertaining to descriptions of rooms in houses. Other major sources include the collections of papers by Rumelhart and McClelland (1987a), and McClelland and Rumelhart (1987a) which at present constitutes the major source for connectionists, much of which has been critically interpreted by Clark (1989) and others. The interpretation of the story in terms of design is our own.

8.2   A connectionist approach to modeling cognition

Connectionist models are reasoning devices based on the uniform distribution of information across networks of relatively simple elements (weighted arcs and units). Units have numerical parameters. At the level of the arc and unit, the behavior of the system is generally opaque to human interpretation and is best understood quantitatively or numerically. Yet there are important properties of the overall system that lead cognitive scientists to identify significant parallels with human reasoning. Needless to say, connectionist models have been proposed by some as the basis of useful models of human cognition (Dreyfus, 1981; Rumelhart and McClelland, 1987a; Clark, 1989).

Arguments for basing automated reasoning systems (such as expert systems and computer programs generally) on connectionist models are compelling. There are problems with the models, and these are well known. As they do not provide significant barriers to theoretical exploration it is worth calling attention to the major problems before proceeding, and thereby dispensing with them. First, there are considerable implementation problems in applying connectionist modeling techniques. Connectionist models involve the simulation of parallel processes, entropy calculations, and the optimization of parameters within nonlinear systems. Simplifications are generally made, but the processes are still computationally expensive. Much hinges on expectations of faster and cheaper computational power if the techniques are to be practical. Although fraught with combinatorial expense the numerical processing is relatively well understood. The second problem is that the theories that lead to predictions of behavior are not well understood. The approach to research is generally empirical, and the properties of connectionist models are determined and supported by experimentation rather than proof. (A notable exception is the influential proofs presented by Minsky and Papert (1969) that established the apparent limitations of simple neural networks.)

Third, controversies surrounding connectionist models generally relate to the psychological reality or otherwise of the approach. In opposition to connectionism there are the advocates of the symbolically-oriented, rule-based models of 'classical cognitivism' (Putnam, 1960; Fodor, 1968). These controversies are of less concern to those interested primarily in applications. Fourth, within the applications field, potential controversy centers on the extent to which explicit structures such as procedures, rules, semantic networks, frames, and scripts should be abandoned in favor of connectionist models that are essentially black boxes. The knowledge they contain is not open to scrutiny with the same clarity, for example, as rules in an expert system. Clark (1989) advocated an 'ecumenical approach' within endeavors to model cognition. Within the eclectic world of computer applications there is certainly scope for hybrid approaches.

We now turn to the compelling arguments in favor of a connectionist approach. This is a very brief summary. Detailed discussion is presented by McClelland et al. (1987), and Clark (1989). There are several categories of argument. The first category derives from research on the microstructure and micro-organization of the nervous system and relates to biological plausibility: the similarity between the components of the brain and mathematically-based connectionist models. Persuasive arguments have also been presented as to why evolution should favor the development of sophisticated cognitive faculties that are built upon relatively basic mechanisms (that is, connectionist models) for responding quickly to patterns of input from the environment (Churchland, 1987; Clark, 1989). The second category of argument: There are properties of these simple systems (connectionist models) that accord well with observations of human cognition. The models accord with some important strengths and also supposed weaknesses of human cognitive behavior. Some of the positive aspects are discussed subsequently. Many of the limitations of neural network approaches are also limitations of human reasoning, such as poor serial processing. Neural networks can also appear to simulate certain human pathologies such as amnesic syndromes, interference phenomena, cross talk, and blending errors (McClelland and Rumelhart, 1987a; Clark, 1989). Certain learning behaviors, such as generalizing and 'overregularalizing' can also be observed (Rumelhart and McClelland, 1987b).

Of course, even if there is a strong case for biological and psychological plausibility, this is not sufficient reason to embrace connectionist models for applications. The third category of compelling argument is that artificial connectionist models can be made to work at a simple level to perform certain tasks, sufficient to enhance our confidence and to persuade us of their usefulness. The main tasks are pattern recognition, pattern completion, fuzzy reasoning, and the emergence of schemas (this chapter). Applications include computer vision, image enhancement, process control and design.

8.3   Modeling design

The quest for theories about design ranges far and wide. Some recent accounts are provided by Rowe (1987), Coyne (1988), Mitchell (1989), and Coyne et al., (1990). An interest in computer applications generally propels us towards formal models. There is considerable agreement about the following: the extent to which design is problem solving, design is ill-structured; the extent to which design involves search, the search space is being defined while exploration is in progress; if logical *deduction* has a role to play in design, then it is to be set against logical *abduction*, an apparent reversal of formal reasoning operations; to the extent that design involves goal satisfaction, the goals are poorly understood at the outset. It is difficult to extract principles of design from the 'properties' of designers. There are properties that inhere within the design agent that are inseparable from the task. The following properties of design would appear to be crucial, irrespective of whether we are referring to properties of the world, of designers of artifacts or of design in the abstract.

1. *Precedence in design*

   Design takes place within a rich context that includes, amongst other things, worlds of other designs, partial designs, unrealized designs, as well as abstractions of designs in the form of defined design categories (types). It also takes place within the context of design experiences, some immediate to the designer, others vicarious. This could be extended to the idea of a 'memory,' not just of designs and design experiences but of things generally. From this rich repository come associations. The idea that one particular event can trigger the recollection of other specific events from the past is well established (Collins and Loftus, 1975). Design reasoning systems that acknowledge the role of past experience or episodic memory have been developed and discussed by Dyer et al., (1986), Maher and Zhao (1987), and McLaughlan and Gero (1989).

2. *The emergent nature of design*

Design appears to be linked with a range of processes. Terms such as **search**, **dialogue** and **exploration** come to mind as descriptors of processes that can be externalized. These are among the processes we may attempt to simulate in computerized knowledge-based systems. Yet there appear to be other operations that are not amenable to externalization, that cannot be made explicit in the same way. There are aspects of the design process by which designs or partial designs appear simply to emerge. In popular language we may talk of designs arising from the subconscious, or being the products of intuition.

There is reason to suspect that this facility has everything to do with experience and memory. In some way the more experienced designer is able to recognize and associate new design situations with old. In a process probably similar to that of how the chess master can instantly recognize the 'pattern' of a game play, the experienced designer may 'see' a potential design solution, without recourse to serial or logical introspection. The existence of such ability is thought to arise from the refined capacity such experience provides in linking between the past, learned events, and the potentially novel. So the capacity to associate between instances of events, concepts, descriptions, data, and every other level of design abstraction, has a criticality in design that demands attention.

3. *The 'holistic' nature of design*

A third property of design tasks involves coming to terms with the crucial interrelation of parts. This interrelatedness is one of the many plagues that beset attempts to formalize design. The idea of decomposing a design problem into subproblems has great appeal. At some stage it becomes necessary to decide on forms (subparts) that address the subproblems and then assemble the subparts to produce a whole—the approach both championed and criticized by Alexander (1964, 1972). As an informal strategy this operation has merit (especially when combined with other strategies). However, in attempts to formalize this operation in computer programs a consideration of the interrelationships of subparts can so overwhelm the endeavor that it overrides most of the benefits of decomposition. Subparts interact, they exhibit emergent properties and there can be incompatibilities. This applies equally to the subparts of problems as to the subparts of solutions.

Set operations to achieve decomposition and synthesis are insufficient. In computerized knowledge-based systems the knowledge required to resolve clashes between constraints and incompatibilities between parts is formidable. Design appears to involve an appreciation of the whole—arguably an important property of human cognition.

Significant aspects of these three properties of design—precedence, emergence and holism—are partly addressed by connectionist models. Before explaining how, it is necessary to describe the idea of schemas.

8.4   Design schemas

People have a liking for breaking the world into compartments. 'When studying the world, we especially attend to edges and boundaries. We see shapes in a heavy mist; we put edges on clouds' (Katz, 1984). To 'know' something is to have a package for that 'thing' or 'item' by which it can be related to, and distinguished from, other things. It appears that people accumulate knowledge by using various strategies to group related things into concepts or categories (Bruner et al., 1956). These categories, or rather the classifications that govern each category, provide the necessary schemas through which the world is perceived. Two ways of describing schemas are current within the study of cognition. Schemas can be regarded as explicit entities, or they can be hidden, so that the apparent presence of schemas is only detected by the behavior of the system. The latter approach is that favored by connectionism, and will be pursued here.

Learning would appear to involve the processing of schemas. Learning however is not just a process of accumulating schemas. It involves a continuous transformation of the schemas as new instances are experienced, new boundaries are established, new associations between things are made. It has been posited that schemas, and the associations between them, are fundamental to an understanding of cognition (Rumelhart et al., 1987).

This notion of schemas helps in an understanding of the design process (Lansdown, 1987; Gero, 1988). From such a perspective design appears as an evolving attempt to develop an appropriate structure for the design problem at hand (Newton and Logan, 1988). ('Structure' in this sense refers to the way in which the various relationships linking design variables interact.) Designers tend to analyse their problems through the generation of solutions. Their main effort is directed at the structuring of problems. Only a fraction of it is spent in specifically studying the problem itself, or in solving problems once they have been structured (Eastman, 1970). Such problems cannot be fully addressed through purely serial or logical thought processes. For design to occur at all, there must be some recourse to the emergent or implicative order. The idea of emergence becomes central to the design activity. In seeking to address design problems through the medium of computer-aided design, it seems prudent to focus some attention on how emergence might best be supported. The support must come through an improved understanding of how both explicit and implicit associations are made between individual schemas.

8.5   Schemas and cognition

The idea of schemas has received considerable attention within the study of the psychology of language (psycholinguistics). It is worth digressing to acknowledge the major source of current thinking about schemas and to add weight to the centrality of schemas in an understanding of cognition generally.

Most people have experienced the confusion of understanding individual sentences but failing entirely to make some sense of what the writer or speaker had been trying to convey. In the process of comprehension, not only do individual sentences need to be understood, but information from topically related sentences must be integrated to form a coherent theme. In order to understand the following text, for example, much information must be inferred.

> I went into the kitchen. The fridge was empty. I was hungry but dinner would have to wait.

Although it has not been stated explicitly that the fridge was in the kitchen, the fridge door was opened, or that there was no food, our cognitive faculties enable us to apply bridging inferences to the task. Cohesive connections are established between sentences by using, for example, knowledge of objects usually found in kitchens. When 'kitchen' is explicitly mentioned, various parts of it, such as fridge, sink, and cupboards, are brought into implicit focus (Sanford and Garrod, 1981).

The 'knowledge about the world' that is used in comprehension has been described as an organized framework of knowledge, referred to variously as scripts (Schank and Abelson, 1977), frames (Minsky, 1975) or schemas (Rumelhart and Ortony, 1977). The idea of such schemas is useful when devising automated reasoning systems and in the development of theories of information processing generally. Schemas can be represented as propositional networks incorporating both knowledge about the world generally and episodic information of particular events.

Paradoxically, one of the major sources of support for schemas comes from the observation of minor foibles in human perception. Using the notion of schemas as a theory of information processing, and building on the ideas of Bartlett's (1932) early work on memory, recent research has concentrated on the effect of world knowledge on apparently simple linguistic tasks. When hearing separate sentences such as 'The ants ate the jelly,' and 'The ants were in the kitchen,' for example, most people report having heard 'The ants in the kitchen ate the jelly' or similar combinations (Bransford and Franks, 1971). Episodic information is integrated and inferences are made by activating existing knowledge structures. Events in existing schemas that are not in the sentences are inferred to have taken place; they are imposed on the sentences obviating the need for a full syntactic analysis.

Another source of support for schemas comes from recent developments in computational models of word recognition. In their NETtalk model, Sejnowski and Rosenberg (1987) have represented the mapping of orthography (spelling) and phonology (the sound of words) in a parallel distributed network. Using a backward error propagation, NETtalk learns to pronounce English words. The network does not have an initial organization for grapheme-phoneme correspondence but, during the training period, an organization emerges and the phonological features are fed into a speech synthesizer. Expanding on the scope of NETtalk, Seidenberg and McClelland (1988) have developed a model that handles a broad range of performance tasks including visual word recognition and pronunciation, and the acquisition of these skills.

8.6   Reasoning with schemas in design

There are several major applications of the schema idea in design. We argue for an understanding of schemas where they are not represented explicitly. However, it is worth considering the utility of the explicit representation of schemas first.

There are aspects of the design process that appear to constitute a process of instantiation. Consider a kitchen schema for example. This schema may contain information about all the things that could be expected in a kitchen: workbench, stove, fridge, and so on. It would also contain information about possible configurations of benches (island bench, U-shaped plan, walk-through) and possible sizes. Initially, design involves the selection of the kitchen schema or one of its variants, and second, the instantiation of various elements. This instantiation will involve a refinement within the scope allowed by the schema and in response to the nuances of the particular context. An argument can be presented that much of design activity accords nicely with this kind of process (Moneo, 1978). We would expect that there are hierarchies of schemas and subschemas (kitchen types) such as L-shaped kitchens, country kitchens, and canteen kitchens that inherit the properties of kitchens in general. There may be schemas within schemas. So that workbenches and stoves have their own schemas. The field is very rich for representing this kind of information in computerized knowledge-based systems. (In fact, one argument against this approach is that there are no limits in setting up useful schemas.)

Of particular interest is the creation of new schemas, or rather the creation of entities that appear to cross over the boundaries between schemas. This appears to be pivotal in an understanding of design, as designers are adept at proposing artifacts that violate well-established schemas, such as combination kitchen/laundries, outside kitchens, and kitchens in space capsules. Codifying the knowledge for this kind of instantiation where schemas are predefined is extremely difficult.

Consider the example of instantiating between the kitchen and laundry schema. One approach is to unite the two schemas; simply take all the elements of a laundry and combine them with those of a kitchen. Inevitably there will be a clash between descriptors in one with the other. There are some descriptors that cannot logically coexist. For example, the kitchen/laundry cannot be both medium and small in size. The size descriptor of the kitchen would be at odds with that of the laundry. There are certain elements that are acceptable in a laundry, like the provision of storage for toxic substances and garden tools, that may be considered incompatible with the food preparation facilities like stoves, sinks, and work tops within a kitchen.

A second approach is to find the 'intersection' between the two schemas. This would involve looking for elements in common as the basis of a kind of synthesis. So the essential ingredients of a kitchen/laundry may be impervious floor finish, water supply, and storage. These may constitute a useful starting state from which to explore the inclusion of other elements.

The third, and most fruitful approach, is to consider hierarchical abstractions of the schemas, subschemas, and schemas within schemas. This may involve looking at abstractions of the descriptors or contents of kitchens and laundries. So a stove is a kind of food preparation facility, and a lawn mower is a kind of garden tool. In order to resolve the problem of conflict between these two items it may argued thus: food preparation facilities process food and garden tools process things in the garden; food needs to be kept from undue contamination and things from the garden are a potential source of contamination. So the reasoning may continue until the conflict is detected and its resolution inferred: exclude the lawn mower storage or at least keep it away from the stove.

An alternative approach might be to look at the design requirements. Perhaps a space is needed to wash clothes and prepare food on a limited budget. It may become apparent that not every feature we normally associate with a laundry is required. A kitchen with a washing machine will suffice. There are several variants of these approaches we could consider (Gero and Rosenman, 1989).

In the development of automated reasoning systems based on the explicit representations of schemas attention focuses heavily on two issues: formulating the most concise set of schemas that will facilitate the reasoning task; and providing the knowledge and reasoning mechanisms that allow for the instantiation of designs that fall across schemas. An alternative approach to design reasoning inspired by connectionism neatly skirts around these issues.

The approach is this: first develop a simple connectionist model on a computer. Then present the system with a series of examples of kitchens, laundries, bathrooms, and living rooms. The examples are presented in terms of descriptors, that is, what the rooms contain and some of their obvious features. The system is denied two important pieces of information: a) what constitutes a typical kitchen, laundry, or bathroom, and b) the 'kitchen,' 'laundry,' and 'bathroom' labels. In other words it is up to the system to establish its own linkages between descriptors and work out which ones are significant.

8.7   Schemas and connectionist models

The connectionist approach has been lightheartedly described as a 'kludge' (Clark, 1989). From the point of view of nature and of computation there are aspects of connectionist models that appear messy and inefficient. Nonetheless they get the job done (at least within nature). The approach to representing and reasoning with schemas that inhere within connectionist models that have been correctly 'schooled,' accepts the expedient that not everything needs to be known before we can start reasoning. Connectionist models operate by storing many instances. So reasoning is memory-based. Connectionist models develop their own schemas, established on the basis of familiar patterns. There is no deep knowledge of functions and relationships, nor of naive physics (Hayes, 1979), nor of class or goal hierarchies. This is contrary to the products of rule-based machine learning systems (Michalski, 1983; Quinlan, 1979) as rules or decision trees, the generalizations made by connectionist models are not open to scrutiny. They only become apparent in the behavior of the system.

The approach is introduced through a simple example. Figure 8.1 shows a set of unconnected units—a network with very weak or non-existent arcs. The units have labels. The units indicate the presence or absence of certain room descriptors. If a unit is colored black then it is present as a descriptor of a particular example. White means it is not present. It is not necessary or usual that the units in connectionist models map so conveniently onto entities we can understand, like stoves and beds. We could have represented the presence of descriptors by some combination of units, constituting a kind of binary code. The labeled units are better for explanation however.

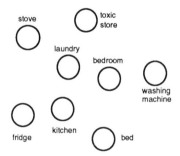

Figure 8.1. A set of unconnected units relating to room descriptors.

The task is now to expose the network to a number of examples. Each example is described in terms of combinations of descriptors. Figure 8.2 indicates what happens when the network is taught the pattern: 'stove,' 'fridge,' and 'kitchen,' once. The information may be supplied from a database of rooms. The 'stove,' 'fridge,' and 'kitchen' units are activated by the example, and a learning algorithm is brought into play to strengthen the linkages between the units. Figure 8.3 shows the linkages established by another example. Figure 8.4 shows what happens when a further example is introduced that has features in common with a previously learned pattern. Each new example presented to the system serves to strengthen the linkages between clusters of the relevant units. In parallel with this operation, units that fail to be associated are establishing negatively weighted links between each other. The final result of the learning process, perhaps after at least 12 examples, is something like the network of Figure 8.5. The black lines indicate a positive association, and the grey lines indicate an inhibitory effect. The thickness of the line indicates the strength of the excitatory or inhibitory link. Figure 8.5 is a network 'schooled' in a subdomain of domestic room specification.

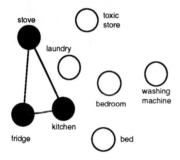

Figure 8.2. 'Teaching' the system to associate stove, fridge, and kitchen.

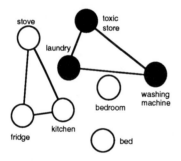

Figure 8.3. An example associating washing machine, toxic store, and laundry.

The network can now be used in a simulation exercise. It should answer the question: 'what would we expect to find associated with a kitchen?' If we activate the kitchen unit (if this were a graphic system we would 'click' on the kitchen unit) and clamp it so that its 'on status' is not altered by the surrounding weights, then we would expect the fridge and stove units to be activated. These are indicated grey in Figure 8.6. In essence the mechanism for doing this is simple. It involves the multiplication of weights

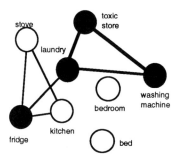

Figure 8.4. A further example that strengthens existing weights.

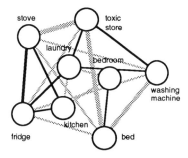

Figure 8.5. A weighted network. The grey arcs have negative weights.

and activation values of units ('on' or 'off' are represented by 1 and 0) between pairs of units. Intuitively we can see that because there is a strong link between 'kitchen' and 'stove,' 'stove' is likely to be active. This brings in 'fridge' because of its strong linkages. The 'fridge' might have brought in the 'laundry' unit, but because of the inhibitory link between 'kitchen' and 'laundry,' the activation of the 'laundry' will receive little support.

Implementations of this mechanism are usually stochastic. Units are activated at random to see if they have sufficient support to stay on. Cliques of units form and disappear as the network settles down to a stable cluster of mutually excitatory units. With graphical connectionist systems such as MacBrain (Chait and Jensen, 1987) this process can be observed as a satisfying resolution of disorder into order under the influence of a few (in this case one, 'kitchen') intransigent units.

Figure 8.7 shows the result of clamping and activating 'fridge' and 'washing machine.' There is an inevitable response from 'laundry,' and the 'toxic store' is brought in by virtue of its strong associations with 'laundry' and 'washing machine.' This is in spite of the inhibitory effect of the 'fridge.' This

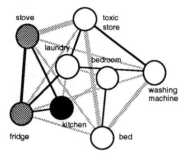

Figure 8.6. When the kitchen is 'clamped' on during simulation, stove and fridge become active.

would accord with the intuition that generally fridges and toxic substances should be kept away from each other, but there are exceptions where fridges are kept in laundries. Of course, at no stage has the system been presented with that rule. The extent to which the rule exists, it has been derived from the examples, and is now implicit in the performance of the network.

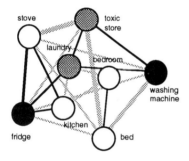

Figure 8.7. When the washing machine and fridge are 'clamped' on during simulation, laundry and toxic store become active.

Figure 8.8 indicates the most interesting property of the system from the point of view of design. Here we have clamped and activated two units that are unlikely to have occurred together in any of the examples, 'stove' and 'washing machine.' The resultant pattern suggests a 'new' entity, a 'kitchen/laundry'. Leaving aside the unspectacular nature of this toy example we can see that something very interesting has occurred. The system has resolved not to incorporate 'toxic store' into the arrangement, presumably due to its strong inhibitory connection with 'stove.' If we imagine a much extended network then the resolution of subtle excitatory and inhibitory connections in order to produce plausible mergers between schemas presents a powerful computational model of the emergence of new artifact descriptions.

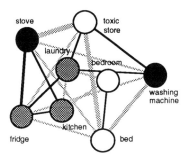

Figure 8.8. Clamping stove and washing machine produces a description of a room not present among the initial examples but the new type of space is consistent with the constraints established through the examples.

The final step is to consider the removal of the 'laundry,' 'bedroom' and 'kitchen' units from the network. This is shown in Figure 8.9. These three nodes are in fact unnecessary schema labels. They tend to pre-empt, and in a way inhibit, the emergence of instantiations from the many schemas implicit within the network. In the worked example that follows in Section 8.9 there has been no attempt to preemptively label combinations of descriptors. A more formal description of the implementation of connectionist models now follows.

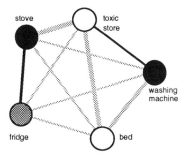

Figure 8.9. The network exhibits the same performance when the room type nodes are removed.

8.8 Connectionist models

In summary, the key features of a connectionist model relate to the uniform distribution of information, the mechanism of excitation and inhibition, and the incremental nature of its learning that is dependent on the current state of the system. Each of these features will be described in detail.

8.8.1 Uniform distribution

The connectionist approach is a kind of representation based loosely on the old management structure of delegation on a 'need to know basis.' No single aspect of the connectionist network is sufficiently sophisticated to represent the complexity of a complete, large scale data structure (schema). Instead, each individual aspect is a rather simplistic entity (termed a 'unit'), capable only of processing local information. There is an intended parallel here with the human brain, where each of the billions of neurons acts only on the local information they receive from connecting neurons. Similar to the worker in a 'need to know' management structure, no one individual—and no one neuron—has an overall picture. The 'picture' is said to be distributed—hence connectionist systems are often termed parallel distributed processing (PDP) systems.

8.8.2 Excitation and inhibition

Each 'unit' in a connectionist model is mechanically simple (Figure 8.10). It has only a single piece of memory, termed the unit's **activation value**. The activation value is a measure (applicable only to that particular unit) of how strongly activated the unit has become. The activation of a particular unit is determined (through some function, termed the **activation function**) by the inputs it receives from other units, and it in turn determines (again through some function, termed the **output function**) the output that the unit conveys to other units.

Individual units are linked to form a network (Figure 8.11). Each link is a directional connection from one unit to another. The links can be in any direction, and between any pair of units. The link between a pair of units is termed a **weight**. The weight determines the relative effect of each unit on another.

The inputs to a unit can determine the activation value in a variety of ways. There are various activation functions. At its simplest, the activation value will equal the net input value. Again at its simplest, the net input

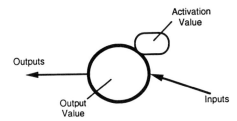

Figure 8.10. A connectionist unit and its parameters.

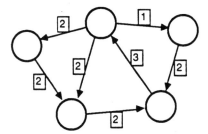

Figure 8.11. A simple connectionist model with weighted arcs.

value is the sum of the output values for each connected unit, multiplied by the weights of each corresponding link.

The value output from a unit can also be determined in a variety of ways. There are various output functions. Typically, the output value will be a fixed value that 'fires' whenever the activation value reaches a particular threshold.

Consider, for example, each of the units illustrated in Figure 8.11 to be identical. The weights are as illustrated, and each activation value is equal to the sum of the output values for each connected unit, multiplied by the weights of each corresponding weight. The value output from each unit will equal 1 whenever the activation value reaches a threshold value of 2. A resolved network (termed its **relaxed** state or **output pattern**) is illustrated in Figure 8.12. In fact the particular network illustrated will always adopt one of only two possible output patterns depending on the starting conditions. The starting conditions describe the initial activation value, or 'input pattern,' of each unit.

Finally, there is a need for some mechanism that controls how the individual activation values are propagated through the network of connections in order for the system to 'learn.' This mechanism is termed the propagation rule. As the name PDP suggests, the **propagation rule** is intended to be parallel. A simple technique to overcome the problems of implementing a PDP system on a serial computer, is to consider time steps. At each time step

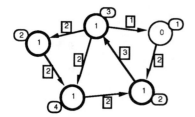

Figure 8.12. A resolved network with activations.

the activation value for each unit is updated, based on the input values for the previous time step. Figure 8.13 illustrates the three time steps involved as the network of weights, activation functions, and output functions used in Figure 8.12 are 'relaxed' from a given set of starting conditions.

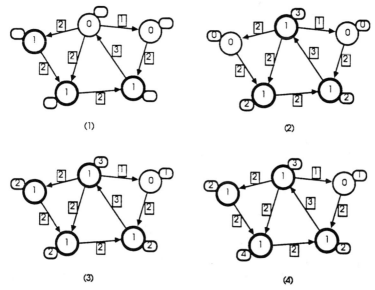

Figure 8.13. A network as it 'relaxes' from the starting condition.

So far, six major aspects of a connectionist model have been introduced:

- the idea of a unit, or set of processing units

- an activation function for each unit

- an output function for each unit

- a set of weights, or pattern of connectivity among units

- a state of activation—in particular the input pattern (starting conditions) and the output pattern (relaxed state)

- a propagation rule

Rumelhart et al., (1987, p.46) summarize these aspects more formally as:

> There is a set of processing units ...; at each point in time, each unit u_i has an activation value, ... $a_i(t)$; this activation value is passed through a function f_i to produce an output value $o_i(t)$. This output value can be seen as passing through a set of unidirectional connections ... to other units in the system. There is associated with each connection a real number, usually called the weight or strength of the connection designated w_{ij} which determines the amount of effect that the first unit has on the second. All of the inputs must then be combined by some operator (usually addition)—and the combined inputs to a unit, along with its current activation value, determine, via a function F, its new activation value.

8.8.3 Incremental learning

These aspects describe the basic form of a connectionist model, but take no account of the way in which an appropriate pattern of connectivity might first be produced (or 'learned'), or how such a system might then be applied in some useful way.

Learning involves presenting a series of paired input and output patterns. The set of weights and each activation function are automatically adjusted (using some 'learning rule') to reproduce the appropriate output pattern when presented with any one of the input patterns. For example, a simple learning rule can be applied as follows:

1. Calculate the relaxed state output value of each unit (j) produced from the given input pattern.

2. Inspect each of the connections between units (w_{ij}) in turn.

    If   the value input to unit i is X, the predicted output value for unit j is Y but if the required output value for unit j is $< Y$

    then subtract from the weight of the connection w_{ij} and add to the threshold of the output function for unit j.

> If   the input value to unit i is X, the predicted output value for
> unit j is Y but if the required output value for unit j is $> Y$
> then   add to the weight of the connection w_{ij} and subtract from the
> threshold of the output function for unit j.

By decreasing the weights and raising the threshold, it is making it 'harder' for a predicted output value to exceed that required. (Note: negative weights are also legal, and act to inhibit the activation of two units in cohort.) Of course, there is no change to weights and thresholds if the predicted and teaching outputs are the same. Once again a variety of learning rules are possible. However, virtually all can be considered a variant of the simple example presented earlier.

So there are two operations in the use of a neural network system: that in which the system is taught various input and output patterns, and the simulation or matching operation where the system is presented with the input only and it generates an output. The teaching operation involves cycling through the set of given input-ouput patterns. The length of time this takes to compute obviously increases with the number of examples presented. Simulation is a much simpler operation and computation time is independent of the numbers of teaching examples.

In fact, there are two very distinct classes of connectionist model:

1. *The Input/Output Model, or 'pattern associator.'*   This is a basic structure with two distinct groups of units—a set of input units and a set of output units. All weights between the input units themselves and all weights between the output units themselves are fixed at zero. (Effectively, this means that the only connections are those between the input units and the output units, and not within each set.) During training, patterns are presented to both the input and output units. The weights connecting these units, and their corresponding thresholds are then modified accordingly. During simulation, a pattern is presented to the input units only and the response on the ouput units is observed.

2. *The Pattern Completion Model, or 'auto-associator.'*   All units are both input and output units. All units can be connected to all other units, including the special case where each unit feeds back on itself as well as on each of its neighbors. During training, patterns are presented over all units. The weights and thresholds are modified to associate the input pattern with itself. During simulation, a portion of a pattern is presented which the system then seeks to complete.

Finally, these two classes of a connectionist model are actually subcases of a particular learning paradigm, termed **associative learning'**. Associative learning admits an arbitrary pattern on one set of units to produce an arbitrary pattern on another set (potentially the entire set) of units. The focus is simply on storing patterns that can be recalled at some future instance.

An alternative learning paradigm is termed **regularity discovery**. In this case the focus is on producing an internal representation to augment the input pattern. The internal representation units (termed **hidden units**) receive no direct input from outside the system, and produce no direct output. Information coming to the input units is recoded into an internal representation and the outputs are generated based on the internal representation rather than by the original input pattern.

The need for hidden units, and multilayered systems generally, was first noted by Minsky and Papert (1969). They showed that in a large number of interesting cases, the two layer system of an associative learning approach is incapable of solving the problems. A classic example of this case is the 'exclusive-or' problem, where a {true, true} or {false, false} input pattern should produce a {false} output pattern and a {true, false} or {false, true} input pattern should produce a {true} output pattern. This problem, and many others like it, cannot be solved without hidden units. (Note: had the input patterns contained a third input taking the value 'true' whenever the first two had value 'true,' a two-layer system would still have been adequate.)

The two learning paradigms can be summarized thus (Rumelhart et al., 1987, p.55):

> Associative learning is employed whenever we are concerned with storing patterns so that they can be re-evoked in the future. These rules are primarily concerned with storing the relationships between subpatterns. Regularity detectors are concerned with the meaning of a single units response. These kinds of rules are used when feature discovery is the essential task at hand.

8.9 Simulating the emergence of schemas

Some applications of connectionist models to design have been discussed and demonstrated by Coyne and Postmus (1990) and Coyne and Newton (1990). Here we explore, in some detail, how the emergence of schemas can be modeled. In this example, a set of room descriptors and their interrelation constitutes the schema for a particular room type. The connectionist approach has the unique and significant advantage that the schema for each room type is not 'hard-wired' into some prescribed set of features. Room schemas are certainly evident. The 'bedroom' schema it produces can be distinguished from the 'living room' schema. However these schemas are only apparent. There is no firm partitioning between the description of a bedroom and that of, say, a living room or bathroom. To predetermine and fix the partitioning between schemas, as in script or frame-based approaches, tends to deny the possibility of generating novel room types. A novel room type might include a bed-sitting room or an en-suite bathroom. These are rooms that did not appear in the input data.

The connectionist model is taught 10 house plans. (Note: this example application is loosely based on one reported by Rumelhart et al., (1987).) Several rooms from different house floor plans are described to the system in terms of contents. There are 40 possible features (Table 8.1).

1	Bath	2	Blinds	3	Bookcase	4	Carpet
5	Coffee table	6	Comfy chair (a)	7	Comfy chair (b)	8	Cupboards
9	Desk and chair	10	Dining chairs	11	Dining table	12	Doorways
13	Double bed	14	Double sink	15	Drapes	16	Dresser
17	Ferns	18	Fridge	19	Lamp	20	Large floor
21	Lounge suite	22	Medium floor	23	Open plan	24	Rug
25	Shower	26	Single bed	27	Sink	28	Small floor
29	Small table (a)	30	Small table (b)	31	Sofa bed	32	Stove
33	Tiled/timber floor	34	Television	35	Very large floor	36	Wardrobe (a)
37	Wardrobe (b)	38	WC	39	Window	40	Work tops

Table 8.1. List of the 40 features used to describe the contents of each room.

The system is an auto-associator, incorporating 40 units. Each example is taught using a learning rule very similar to the basic algorithm already described earlier. The weights between the units are symmetrical. So the weight w_{ij} is equal to the weight w_{ji}. The activation function simply computes the sum of the output values for each incoming unit multiplied by the weight of the corresponding link. The output function maps the difference ($Diff$) between the input to a unit and its threshold, onto a probability value (p) depending on a constant (T). The constant T is known as the 'temperature,' and it determines the slope of the function curve. (A simple explanation of this mechanism is given by Coyne and Postmus (1990)).

A total of 50 room descriptions are taught to the system, at a temperature of 0.005. During simulation (after the learning phase), as each feature is added to the description of a room, it becomes part of the starting conditions from which the connectionist model undertakes pattern completion. Pattern completion is achieved by asynchronous updating of the unit activation values over several cycles, or time periods. Asynchronous updating involves selecting units at random, and computing their new activation and output values based on the output values current during the previous time cycle. The activation and output functions are the same as for learning. But the temperature is 0.5. (Note: the selection of suitable parameters is based largely on experimentation.) In this case however, when the network has fully relaxed, the output function is used to produce a 'shaded' output of nonbinary values from 0 to 9. These measures give some indication of the degree of confidence, or strength of association between the partial pattern and the pattern when fully completed by the system. The additional features being associated with the current partial description can then be ranked as to their likelihood of forming part of the intended room description.

As a further elaboration to the connectionist model, the output values for each feature in the partial description are clamped 'on.' That is to say, the output values for each feature in the partial description are set at their highest possible value, regardless of the output values computed using the activation and output functions for those units. The effect of this is to remove any possibility of features already included in the description being turned 'off' (that is, not forming part of the description) during the pattern completion phase.

Consider for example, the room in Figure 8.14. If its current description (small floor and window) are input to the connectionist model, the prediction 'PREDICT 1' in Table 8.2 is made. If we then included some blinds over the window, the prediction is modified to 'PREDICT 2'. Table 8.2 charts the progression of a predicted room description from one based on only two features (PREDICT 1), to one based on six features (PREDICT 5). At this stage, the predicted room is fairly well recognizable as a small bedroom (Figure 8.15).

Figure 8.14. Graphical representation of the initial descriptors of PREDICT 1 in Table 8.2.

In the fifth example (PREDICT 5) the prediction settles into a 'small bedroom' schema, despite the fact that the initial prediction (PREDICT 1)

DRAWING CONTENTS / INPUTS					
Small Floor Window	Small Floor Window Blinds	Small Floor Window Blinds Carpet	Small Floor Window Blinds Carpet Dresser	Small Floor Window Blinds Carpet Dresser Single Bed	Small Floor Window Drapes
PREDICT 1	PREDICT 2	PREDICT 3	PREDICT 4	PREDICT 5	PREDICT 6
Blinds 9	Carpet 9	Cupboards 9	Cupboards 9	Cupboards 9	Blinds 9
Carpet 9	Cupboards 9	Door Ways 9	Door Ways 9	Door Ways 9	Bookcase 9
Cupboards 9	Door Ways 9	Drapes 9	Drapes 9	Drapes 9	Cupboards 9
Door Ways 9	Drapes 9	Dresser 9	Single Bed 9	Lamp 9	Door Ways 9
Drapes 9	Dresser 9	Single Bed 9	Wardrobe 9	Small Table 9	Double Sink 9
Sink 9	Single Bed 9	Wardrobe 9	Coffee Table 8	Wardrobe 9	Fridge 9
Bath 8	Wardrobe 9	Coffee Table 8	Fridge 1		Lamp 9
Coffee Table 8	Coffee Table 8	Fridge 1			Rug 9
Sofa Bed 1	Fridge 1				Stove 9
WC 1					TV 9
					Sofa Bed 2

Table 8.2. Predicted contents of rooms, based on existing contents.

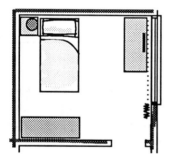

Figure 8.15. The final state depicted in PREDICT 5 in Table 8.2.

clearly favors a more 'bathroom-like' schema. Indeed had we elected to include some drapes over the window, rather than blinds, the system would have produced an entirely different response, actually more in keeping with a 'kitchen' (Figure 8.16). PREDICT 6 indicates the extent of this variation in prediction given what amounts to an otherwise superficial change in the input features.

Figures 8.17 to 8.21 show the steps leading to PREDICT 1 using a different graphical representation. The nodes representing descriptors have been clustered to give some indication of the extent to which they each contribute towards readily recognizable schemas (such as kitchens, bathrooms, and bedrooms). Figure 8.17 shows the initial state of the system with the small floor and window units clamped. Subsequent figures indicate how units become activated and are either strengthened, because of 'support' from units with which they are strongly related, or they fade out, due to inhibitions or lack of support. The network settles into an optimal set of activations. Figure 8.21 is effectively a peak in a hyperspace of 40 dimensions. Similar sets of diagrams could be generated for each of the examples given in Table 8.2.

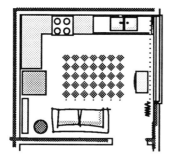

Figure 8.16. The final state depicted in PREDICT 5 in Table 8.2.

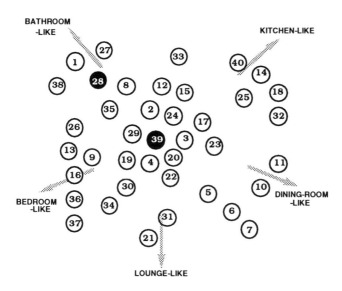

Figure 8.17. The room descriptors clustered according to their contribution to well-known room schemas. Units 28 (small floor) and 39 (window) are clamped on. This is the initial state of the network prior to 'relaxing' on PREDICT 1 (Table 8.2).

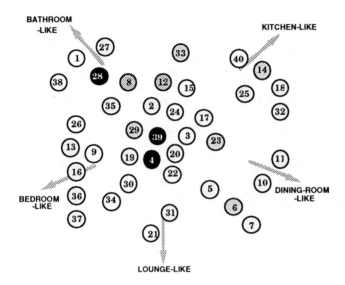

Figure 8.18. The state of the network after 1 cycle.

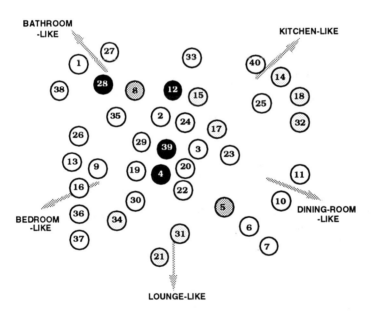

Figure 8.19. The state of the network after 3 cycles.

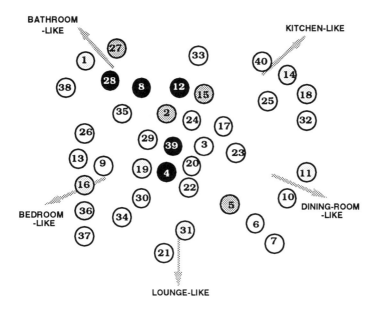

Figure 8.20. The state of the network after 5 cycles.

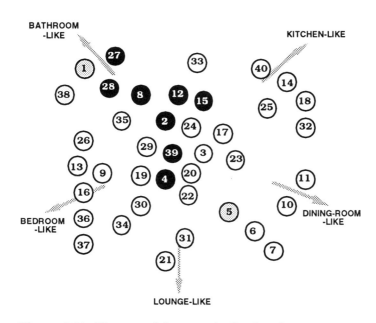

Figure 8.21. The state of the network after 8 cycles.

It is worth considering just how sensitive the prediction is to what would otherwise appear minimal changes to input. Blinds and drapes appear together in all six predictions. Why should they have such distinctive effects individually? The answer lies in the mechanics of how connectionist models attempt to complete the input patterns. Essentially, pattern completion involves an iterative process which seeks to maximize the overall value of what Rumelhart et al., (1987) call the 'goodness-of-fit.' (This measure is equivalent to the 'energy'considered by Hopfield (1982) and Hinton and Sejnowski (1986), and the 'harmony'considered by Smolensky (1986).) Goodness-of-fit, loosely stated, is a measure of the potential contribution of the units as a function of their actual contribution. The connectionist model moves towards a state that maximizes the actual contribution, and thereby the overall goodness-of-fit for the system. Figure 8.22 shows the 'goodness of fit landscape' when one descriptor is held constant (that is, clamping on the small room descriptor unit). The vertical axis is goodness of fit, and the peaks form 13 clearly delineated room examples (prototypes). The highest peak forms at a kitchen-like description. Clamping on other descriptors, individually or in combination, produces very different topographies.

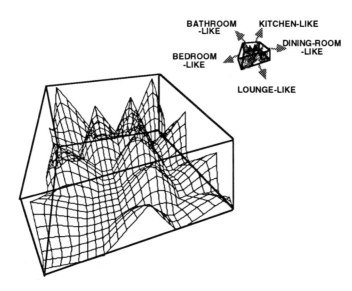

Figure 8.22. A 'goodness of fit landscape'.

The critical factor in what is otherwise a standard hill-climbing technique, is actually the subtle interplay of values across all connections (weights). For example, the blinds and the drapes are probably strongly attracted to one another. They occurred together often in the learning patterns. The two are said to act in cohort. However, the effect of this cohesion (that is, the choice of which other features will be drawn into the active group) will depend on the overall attraction of each feature to the group of currently activated features, and their current activation values. Thus the attraction between blinds and drapes will have an effect that is very much dependent on the context. For this reason they act very differently as individuals. In fact they act very differently again if the small room is changed to a large room, or the window is replaced by a door, and so on.

The mechanics of this interplay is conceptually simple. If the blinds occur strongly before the drapes appear, they will tend to attract (in the context of a small floor with window) more bedroom-like features (PREDICT 2). By the time drapes become more activated (attracted at least in part by the blinds), many of the bedroom-like features are already acting to inhibit the kitchen-like features that the drapes might otherwise attract. Similarly, when the order of activation is reversed so too is the effect (PREDICT 6). When both features are activated more or less together, their combined effect is different again, and results in the bathroom-like features of PREDICT 1.

The pattern of interrelationships is intricate and is not amenable to neat decomposition. The type of reasoning demonstrated defies representation using media such as frames and rules. Only some of the many schemas implicit within the network have been explored here.

Even though the paradigm presented here is different to other formal ways of looking at design we can see certain similarities with our intuitions about design. The idea of 'search' can be recast in terms of traversal across an 'energy landscape.' However, this is carried out without recourse to operators (as design rules) and the representation of discrete states. The usual definitions of creativity in terms of moving outside the space defined by operators does not apply. Here we see creativity as arising 'naturally' out of a thorough grounding in experience and history.

8.10   Conclusion

This example has served to demonstrate how it is possible to simulate a simple kind of memory-based reasoning with connectionist models. An interesting feature of this approach is that the system is able to determine its own categories, or types, and that these categorizations have fuzzy and highly interrelated boundaries. This accords with our intuitions about design objects, such as rooms in buildings. What is the definitive description of a bedroom? Is a room automatically a bedroom because it contains a bed? What if you put a bed in the living room? Is it still a living room? These conundrums cause very little trouble in daily discourse about buildings, but they are extremely problematic when we attempt to construct automated reasoning systems that make use of design knowledge. But the issue goes further. Hard-wiring categories into formal systems actually inhibits the creation of new categories. The creative, innovative component of design would appear to surface where we are able to produce descriptions of objects that cross over commonly accepted boundaries: hence our demonstration of the emergence of artifact descriptions across schemas.

Connectionist models are ideally implemented on machines with parallel architectures. The iterative nature of the demonstrations given here is deceptive. As with biological systems, we would expect emergence to involve something close to a single step reasoning process. We have demonstrated that there are computational mechanisms by which it is possible to simulate nonserial and nonrule-based reasoning mechanisms. Of course, design involves much more than this. However, the connectionist approach provides a necessary supplement to approaches based on explicit knowledge and reasoning with the aid of external media.

Acknowledgments. This work is supported by a University of Sydney Special Project Grant.

References

Alexander, C. (1964). *Notes on the Synthesis of Form*, Harvard University Press, Cambridge, Massachusetts.

Alexander, C. (1972). The city is not a tree, *in* G. Bell, & J. Tyrwhitt (Eds), *Human Identity in the Urban Environment*, Pelican, Harmondsworth, Middlesex, pp. 401–428.

Bartlett, F. C. (1932). *Remembering*, Cambridge University Press, Cambridge.

Bransford, J. D., & Franks, J. J. (1971). The abstraction of linguistic ideas, *Cognitive Psychology*, **3**: 331–50.

Bruner, J. S., Goodnow, J., & Austin, G. (1956). *A Study of Thinking*, Wiley, New York.

Chait, D., & Jensen, M. (1987). *MacBrain 2.0 User's Manual*, Neuronics, Cambridge, Massachusetts.

Churchland, P. S. (1987). Epistemology in the age of neuroscience, *Journal of Philosophy*, **84**(10): 544–555.

Clark, A. (1989). *Microcognition: Philosophy, Cognitive Science and Parallel Distributed Processing*, MIT Press, Cambridge, Massachusetts.

Collins, A. M., & Loftus, E. F. (1975). A spreading-activation theory of semantic processing, *Psychological Review*, **82**: 407–28.

Coyne, R. D. (1988). *Logic Models of Design*, Pitman, London.

Coyne, R. D., & Newton, S. (1990). Design reasoning by association, *Environment and Planning B*, **17**: 39–56.

Coyne, R. D., & Postmus, A. (1990). Spatial applications of neural networks in computer-aided design, *Artificial Intelligence in Engineering*, **5**(1): 9–22.

Coyne, R. D., Rosenman, M. A., Radford, A. D., Balachandran, M., & Gero, J. S. (1990). *Knowledge-Based Design Systems*, Addison-Wesley, Reading.

Dreyfus, H. (1981). Misrepresenting human intelligence, *in* R. Born (Ed.), *Artificial Intelligence: The Case Against*, Croom Helm, London, pp. 41–54.

Dyer, M. G., Flowers, M. and Hodges, J. (1986). EDISON: an engineering design invention system operating naively, *Artificial Intelligence in Engineering*, **1**(1): 36–44.

Eastman, C. M. (1970). On the analysis of intuitive design processes, *in* G. T. Moore (Ed.), *Emerging Methods in Environmental Design and Planning*, MIT Press, Cambridge, Massachusetts.

Fodor, J. (1968). The appeal to tacit knowledge in psychological explanation, *Journal of Philosophy*, **65**: 627–640.

Gero, J. S. (1988). Prototypes: a basis for knowledge-based design, *in* J. S. Gero, & T. Oksala (Eds), *Symposium on Knowledge-Based Design in Architecture*, Helsinki University of Technology, Helsinki, pp. 3–8.

Gero, J. S., & Rosenman, M. A. (1989). A conceptual framework for knowledge-based design research at Sydney University's Design Computing Unit, *in* J. S. Gero (Ed.), *Artificial Intelligence in Design*, CMP/Springer-Verlag, Southampton and Berlin, pp. 361–380.

Hayes, P. (1979). The naive physics manifesto, *in* D. Michie (Ed.), *Expert Systems in the Micro-Electronic Age*, Edinburgh University Press, Edinburgh.

Hinton, G. E., & Sejnowski, T. J. (1986). Learning and relearning in Boltzmann machines, *in* D. E. Rumelhart, & J. L. McClelland (Eds), *Parallel Distributed Processing: Explorations in the Microstructure of Cognition, Vol. 1, Foundations*, MIT Press, Cambridge, Massachusetts, pp. 282–314.

Hopfield, J. J. (1982). Neural networks and physical systems with emergent collective computational abilities, *Proceedings of the National Academy of Sciences, USA*, **79**: 2554–2558.

Katz, M. J. (1984). *Templets and the Explanation of Complex Patterns*, University Press, Cambridge.

Lansdown, J. (1987). The creative aspects of CAD: a possible approach, *Design Studies*, **8**(2): 76–81.

Maher, M. L., & Zhao, F. (1987). Using experience to plan the synthesis of new designs, *in* J. S. Gero (Ed.), *Expert Systems in Computer-Aided Design*, North-Holland, Amsterdam, pp. 349–369.

McClelland, J. L., & Rumelhart, D. E. (Eds) (1987a). *Parallel Distributed Processing: Explorations in the Microstructure of Cognition, Vol. 2: Psychological and Biological Models*, MIT Press, Cambridge, Massachusetts.

McClelland, J. L., Rumelhart, D. E., & Hinton, G. E. (1987). The appeal of parallel distributed processing, *in* D. E. Rumelhart, & J. L. McClelland (Eds), *Parallel Distributed Processing: Explorations in the Microstructure of Cognition, Vol. 1, Foundations*, MIT Press, Cambridge, Massachusetts, pp. 3–44.

McLaughlan, S., & Gero, J. S. (1989). Requirements of a reasoning system to support innovative and creative design activity, *Knowledge-Based Systems*, **2**(1): 62–71.

Michalski, R. S. (1983). A theory and methodology of inductive learning, *Artificial Intelligence*, **20**: 111–161.

Minsky, M. (1975). A framework for representing knowledge, *in* P. H. Winston (Ed.), *The Psychology of Computer Vision*, McGraw-Hill, New York, pp. 211–277.

Minsky, M., & Papert, S. (1969). *Perceptrons*, MIT Press, Cambridge, Massachusetts.

Mitchell, W. J. (1989). *The Logic of Architecture*, MIT Press, Cambridge, Massachusetts.

Moneo, R. (1978). On typology, *Oppositions*, **13**: 23–45.

Newton, S., & Logan, B. S. (1988). Causation and its effect: the blackguard in CAD's clothing, *Design Studies*, **9**(4): 196–201.

Putnam, H. (1960). Minds and machines, *in* S. Hook (Ed.), *Dimensions of Mind*, New York University Press, New York.

Quinlan, J. R. (1979). Discovering rules by induction from large collections of examples, *in* D. Michie (Ed.), *Expert Systems in the Micro-Electronic Age*, Edinburgh University Press, Edinburgh, pp. 168–201.

Rowe, P. (1987). *Design Thinking*, MIT Press, Cambridge, Massachusetts

Rumelhart, D. E., & McClelland, J. L. (Eds) (1987a). *Parallel Distributed Processing: Explorations in the Microstructure of Cognition, Vol. 1, Foundations*, MIT Press, Cambridge, Massachusetts.

Rumelhart, D. E., & McClelland, J. L. (1987b). On learning the past tense of English verbs, *in* J. L. McClelland, & D. E. Rumelhart (Eds), *Parallel Distributed Processing: Explorations in the Microstructure of Cognition, Volume 2, Psychological and Biological Models*, MIT Press, Cambridge, Massachusetts, pp. 216–271.

Rumelhart, D. E., & Ortony, A. (1977). The representation of knowledge in memory, *in* R. C. Anderson, R. J. Spiro, & W. E. Montague (Eds), *Schooling and the Acquisition of Knowledge*, Lawrence Erlbaum, Hillsdale, New Jersey.

Rumelhart, D. E., Hinton, G.E. and McClelland, G. E. (1987). A general framework for parallel distributed processing, *in* D. E. Rumelhart, & J. L. McClelland (Eds), *Parallel Distributed Processing: Explorations in the Microstructure of Cognition, Vol. 1, Foundations*, MIT Press, Cambridge, Massachusetts, pp. 45–76.

Rumelhart, D. E., Smolensky, P., McClelland, J. L., & Hinton, G. E. (1987). Schemata and sequential thought processes in PDP models, *in* D. E. Rumelhart, & J. L. McClelland (Eds), *Parallel Distributed Processing: Explorations in the Microstructure of Cognition, Vol. 1, Foundations*, MIT Press, Cambridge, Massachusetts, pp. 7–57.

Sanford, A. J., & Garrod, S. C. (1981). *Understanding Written Language: Explorations in Comprehension beyond the Sentence*, Wiley, Chichester.

Schank. R. C., & Abelson, R. P. (1977). *Scripts, Plans, Goals, and Understanding: An Inquiry into Human Knowledge Structures*, Lawrence Erlbaum, Hillsdale, New Jersey.

Seidenberg, M. S. and McClelland, J. L. (1988). A distributed, developmental model of word recognition and naming, *Technical Report 8801*, McGill University.

Sejnowski, T. J., & Rosenberg, C. R. (1987). Parallel networks that learn to pronounce English text, *Complex Systems*, **1**: 145–168.

Smolensky, P. (1986). Information processing in dynamical systems: foundations of harmony theory, *in* J. L. McClelland, & D. E. Rumelhart (Eds), *Parallel Distributed Processing: Explorations in the Microstructure of Cognition, Vol. 2, Psychological and Biological Models*, MIT Press, Cambridge, Massachusetts, pp. 194–281.

9 A Genetic Approach to Creative Design

Robert F. Woodbury

It would be instructive to have implementable mechanisms that exhibit creative properties. This chapter proposes an organization for such a mechanism, a *genetic design system* (GDS), that is derived from two sources: (a) the search paradigm in computer-aided design, (b) the structure of natural evolution. Both sources are presented in an abstract form that exposes their mechanism. The components of the search mechanism are related to those of natural evolution, and a system design based on this correspondence is advanced. A critical discussion of the design and a proposed research program are presented.

9.1 Introduction

Two distinctly different research programs coexist in computer-aided design (at least in architecture). I shall call these respectively: *cognitive modeling* and *design mechanics*. The former takes as its goal the explanation of human designing in information processing terms. The latter seeks computable mechanisms for making designs, and is indifferent to their source. To be sure, these strands of research overlap and enrich each other. For example, cognitive models of design are extremely useful if one proposes to build an effective human computer interface. Conversely, computational mechanisms provide the substrate upon which cognitive simulations are built. The results

211

of both are necessary in building 'symbiotic' human computer systems in which labor is divided between humans and computers according to their respective capabilities. A problem arises when the two emphases are confused and particularly when an attempt to simultaneously advance both of them is made. Put bluntly, human cognition is a poor sole basis upon which to build automatic design systems. Humans and computers have fundamentally different information processing architectures, the latter much more malleable than the former. Blindly adopting a human model only hamstrings the search for mechanisms that take full advantage of computation.

With this opening blast, I reveal my initial bias to the question of creativity in computer based design. I am baldly interested in mechanisms that create, irrespective of their source. I will judge a mechanism interesting by its invention of the unexpected, by its computational clarity, and by the absence of heuristics at its core. From these three criteria I argue for several constraints on any mechanism that might be proposed:

1. The first constraint is that of the use of constructive rules. In this constraint lies my sole use of human cognitive models of design. Two arguments support the constraint:

   - Appreciation of computational clarity is a function (however partial) of human cognitive structure. A clear model for creativity is likely to be used over a murky one. The rule-like behavior of human problem solvers seems to me to be a crucial constraint to be respected in searching for clear mechanisms.

   - Human cognitive models have been a rich source of analogy for design mechanics in its search for new computer-aided design approaches. As design mechanics has matured, it has become more discriminating. Some parts of the analogy have been adopted and transformed, and have become a part of the foundations of design mechanics. Other parts have been (or should be) discarded as the need for the crutch of analogy has diminished. A principal retained concept from the analogy to human cognition is that of rule-like behavior. Rules appear to have distinct advantages when compared with other means of organizing generative knowledge. (a) Rules support the incremental build-up of knowledge. (b) Rules can be applied in unexpected circumstances. (Serendipity seems to be important to creativity.) (c) Rules act locally, yet their consequences may be global. Thus they can potentially create the unexpected.

2. Using rules would appear to imply that a form of *search* is the main mechanism for design. Rules specify allowable moves, and these moves

form a *derivation tree*. Moving through the derivation tree to find designs requires search. In architectural design, the enormity of the derivation tree for any significant problem would appear to eliminate any search procedure that depends solely on exhaustive search, however discriminating its pruning rules might be. Obvious extensions to exhaustive search, for example, hierarchical decomposition, seem to me to embody heuristics that are too intertwined with the method. I prefer a heuristic free mechanism, therefore I must adopt a different form of search.

3. Architecture is concerned with the creation of spatial compositions, so geometry must be a main preoccupation of any search. Representations for geometry are thus needed, and such representations appropriate to search remain rare in the literature. It seems to me that any representation of geometry must have a certain 'richness' (about which I shall be more precise later) if it is to be used at the core of a creative system. It must be capable of representing many if not all configurations that might be of interest in a particular problem. Especially, it must be able to model the appropriate spatial coincidences that seem so pervasive in architecture. This last point appears to require less abstract representations than are usual, for example, in layout problems.

4. A form of generate-and-test search mechanism seems inevitable, for the following reasons:

   - Designs are composed in terms of their spatial (and other physical) properties, but are evaluated according to a range of criteria, that rely on (but are not defined by) these properties. It is beyond the range of current theory (at the least) to devise synthesis procedures that simultaneously create form directly from a variety of performance criteria.

   - Serendipity seems to be an important aspect of creative design. Finding a concept by accident is only likely to happen when a wide variety of 'accidents' are floating about.

Together, constructive rules, search, geometric richness, spatial coincidences, and generate-and-test present a tall order for a mechanism for design. However, I believe that just such a mechanism can be proposed by analogy to evolution and genetics. Evolution has produced astounding variation in the natural world, and much of this variation would be called creative were it the construction of humans. Yet evolution is an absolutely blind process that proceeds mechanically, with neither guidance nor goal.

In outline, I suggest that an object called a *design space* constitutes the genotype, development process, and selection environment of designs. Genes are captured by grammars; development by search strategies. Selection of genotype occurs on the phenotype; selection of grammars occurs by testing members of their language in simulated environments. Designs are evolved by introducing mutative changes to either the search space operators, the development process, or the simulated environment and by selection on the resulting developed designs. The product of an evolutionary design process is a design space that can be 'turned on' to create a set of designed objects.

Before building an analogy to biological evolution, I present a brief sketch of the mechanics of evolution (largely following the popular book by Dawkins, 1987).

9.2   Natural evolution

Evolution occurs by cumulative selection; new structures in organisms emerge through a process of many small changes over generations of reproduction. Each change must be *spontaneously plausible*. Successful changes will be *reproductively effective*. For cumulative selection to work three things must simultaneously exist. (a) There must be entities (*replicators*) that are capable of producing replicas of themselves. (b) There must be a source of error (essentially random in accounts of biological evolution) in the replication process. These errors must be passed on to the replicas, so that they are reproduced when the replica replicates. (c) Entities must be able to exert influence over their likelihood of being replicated. The new entities that are produced by the replication process will be different from their progenitors. Some differences will have no effect on entities' ability to reproduce. Other differences will have a positive or negative effect. Entities *inheriting* changes that have a positive effect will, over generations of replication, become prevalent over entities that inherit changes having a neutral or negative effect.

Living things (at least the multicellular ones) realize these requirements via a process that employs a genetic code (the genotype, stored in genes) and a process of embryonic development governed by that code. The genetic code in these systems is akin to a program for creating individuals. This program governs a process of cell division, growth, and death that creates an actual living thing (the phenotype). Replication is accomplished by parent(s) providing a seed (or its egg) that contains a genetic code and an appropriate development environment for its growth into another living thing (a child). Errors in replication can occur either in the seed where they are called mutations, or in the development process, where (at least in mammals) they are called congenital defects. Only the former are transmitted through the replication process from one generation to the next. Individuals inheriting changed genetic information are more or less likely to reproduce in the environment in which they live. The successful ones are said to be selected to reproduce; the unsuccessful ones produce no descendents. Over time the result is a population of individuals that are increasingly adapted to the environment in which they live. Thus the genetic errors that 'improve' the individual are retained from generation to generation. Genotypes are recipes rather than blueprints; they specify a set of directions, not a miniature model for an individual. Through the development process specified (in part) by the recipe in the genotype, a living thing that bears no physical resemblance to the recipe emerges. *Sexual reproduction*, or crossover, is a combining of part of the genetic code from each of two parent individuals to produce a seed, different from that of either parent, that, through development, becomes an individual in its own right. Crossover allows a small population of actual individuals to effectively store a very large population of possible individuals through the combinatorial possibilities of genetic composition.

A group of genetically sufficiently similar living things constitutes a species. Over time (and space) species bifurcate, to create new species; this process is called speciation. If the speciation process is considered as a mathematical graph (the phylogeny of species), its properties are those of a tree; it branches, and branches never merge.

The process of natural evolution is goalless in that it has no final arrival point. It is a continuous process of adapting to an environment, that in itself may also be continually changing. Once started, it requires no guidance, and it depends on no vision of its future. It produces astonishing variations and marvellous levels of adaption. It does, however, require a certain stability in the environment in which it operates. The environment must not change so quickly or drastically that many individuals fail to survive and replicate. Such changes lead to a collapse, from which diversity must emerge anew, if at all.

Before proceeding any further with the analogy I present a summary of the notion of *design spaces* and arguments for its relevancy. I use (and italicize) terms that have a precise meaning with respect to design spaces, definitions for which may be found in the Appendix.

9.3   Design spaces

Informally, a design space is all the machinery required to computationally search for designs. It consists of a *search space* and a *search strategy*. A search space is a way of describing the possible configurations that might be considered as solutions to a design problem. A search strategy is a policy for making the decisions required in search as well as a problem context in which that policy applies.

There are three main reasons for using design spaces as the basis for a genetically inspired design system: preservation of meaning under mutation and crossover, leveraging of change through rules, and explicit description of a search process.

In a design space, the *representation space* is defined by a grammar (or algebra), but is searched by a (possibly) separate set of *search operators*. The representation space itself can be much larger than the set of objects that can be reached by the operators, yet under certain restrictions (those of the *representation scheme*), all of its members retain the ability to actually *represent* a design. If the search operators are defined in terms of the representation space grammar, and if mutations are similarly defined, the operators can be mutated without fear that the objects they produce will become malformed in an essential way. This is in contrast to prototype based approaches to representation in which the meaning of the component symbols is internally arbitrary.

Search spaces do not define designs directly; they rather specify *derivation sequences* by which designs can be developed. Simple changes to rules can create complex and far-reaching changes to the designs that they imply. Thus mutations can be small (randomly plausible), but can have large effect. Search space specification by rules parallels the biological development process governed by genes; both can magnify the effect of small changes.

Search spaces define not a single design, but a *design collection*. A search strategy must control rule applications to guide the way to an individual design or a set of designs that are only a tiny fraction of the entire representation space. A strategy is explicitly part of a design space, and its presence as data means that it too can be subject to change, both mutative and crossover, in the genetic search process.

In the next part of the chapter I build an analogy between biological evolution and a proposed mechanism for generating creative designs. As the analogy emerges in the discussion, so will a number of constructs that, in addition to design spaces, constitute the organization of a proposed *genetic design system*, GDS. My construction uses biology more as a point of departure than as a target for complete analogy. Wherever computational capabilities suggest changes I freely make them, subject to the constraint of maintaining a capability that provides for replication, error, and power.

9.4   The genetic analogy

In building my analogy between biological evolution and a proposed design mechanism, my first step is to posit two representations for any design, one implicit and one explicit.

- The implicit representation is a design space, and corresponds to the biological genotype. Several of the entities in a design space carry genotypic information. The search space operators are the closest analog to biological genes. These describe the allowable mechanisms for synthesizing various parts of a design. They operate locally, but produce global or emergent form. Three other design space components: the search strategy, the goals, and the evaluation devices, can all be considered to carry genotypic information (a departure from strict analogy to biological genetics). The search strategy of a design space is closely analogous to the embryonic development process of biology, in that it is an implicit specification of the process by which a design space is translated into a design. However, it is genotypic as well, in that changes to it can be preserved in a copy and can therefore be transmitted between generations. Goals guide the search strategy and questions concerning them are answered by the evaluation devices in a design space. Like operators and search strategies, these can be freely copied, but at the expense of changing the environment for which a design is intended.

- The explicit representation is the result of 'executing' a design space, it is a representation of some design or set of designs, and it corresponds to the biological phenotype. Design space 'execution' is thus an analogy to the process of embryonic development. Designs are members of the representation space of a design space, and they correspond (in a mathematical sense) to some possible artifacts. They are generated, through a search strategy, with the intention of meeting the goals in a design space, and this is the second departure from strict analogy with biology. Biological systems have no goals; embryos develop quite independently (modulo environmental poisons, etc.) of the outside environment that they will eventually inhabit. Goal constructs in design are added here to provide: (a) a means of reducing the language of possibilities implicit in the search space to a manageable set, and (b) a mechanism for direct intervention into a genetic design system.

The next part of the analogy equates heredity with copying, not of designs or artifacts (Steadman, 1979), but of design spaces. Any design space can be copied to create a new space that is identical with the original. The requisite copying errors are introduced through 'mutation operators' that can act on any (or all) of search space operators, search strategies, goals, and evaluation devices. These mutation operators may be purely random with respect to the selection process, as in they are in biology. More interestingly, and without disturbing the overall organization of the system, they might themselves be knowledge based. This is another departure from strict analogy. Knowledge based mutations are to GDS as an intrusive God would be to natural evolution. When search space operators are mutated, they imply a different language of designs in which the eventual design phenotypes exist. See March and Stiny (1985) and Knight (1981, 1983a, 1983b, 1983c, 1988) for a formal discussion of related ideas in shape grammar systems.

Finally, selection is equated with testing designs against their goals (and using the evaluation devices in the process). The goals and evaluation devices form a *simulated environment* in which designs either 'live' or 'die.' Those that 'live' are selected for the next generation; those that 'die' are simply discarded. Actually, it is not the explicit representation of a design that is selected, it is the design space (the implicit specification). Complexities would likely be introduced if the design goals themselves are subject to mutation. The potential for such changes should be included to allow for the well known phenomenon of gradual goal discovery in design.

The entire process is captured in a single infinite loop that respectively:

- Copies and mutates each element of a set A of design spaces. Includes all copies in A.

- Develops the spaces into individual designs.

- Tests these designs against the design space goals.

- Selects a subset of designs and places their corresponding design spaces in A.

As shown in Figure 9.1, GDS thus consists, in the abstract, of a collection of design spaces, mechanisms for mutation, development, and selection (the latter largely accomplished by design space goals and evaluators), and an infinite loop that implements the overall evolutionary process. In more concrete terms, I would expect an implementation of GDS to use a particular kind of design space that may be characterized as a spatial grammar. Spatial grammars allow the capture, in a set of rules, of knowledge that is explicit and particular about its manipulation of spatial form. They provide, in

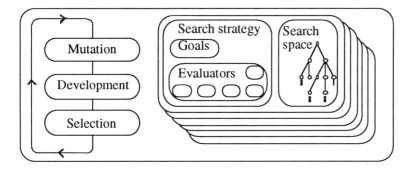

Figure 9.1. The organization of GDS.

essence, a programming language for constructive rules and an interpreter for their application. Such rules can be modified (mutated) into other rules. Also, as I argue later, spatial grammar systems seem to be the best candidates for capturing the property of *emergent form*.

9.5 Relation to other work

The biological analogy in architecture is not new; it has a history that is far older than Darwinian theories of evolution. One book length (Steadman, 1979) and numerous shorter works have been published in the area. To my knowledge, none of these builds an analogy to evolution in the manner that I do here. In particular, the works I have encountered do not take a computational view of the evolutionary analogy.

There has been much work in genetically inspired methods for optimization and search; Goldberg (1989) presented an overview, a historical survey, and an extensive bibliography. The work and applications that he reported only encounter design tangentially, but provide what appears to be a rich source for insight into mechanisms within the genetic analogy. The basic material on genetic algorithms treats the coding of representations quite informally; as a point of departure, I maintain that the coding should be as formally represented as possible, so that the units of genetic code that are manipulated might be, to the greatest extent possible, semantically relevant to a design domain.

Lenat and Brown (1984) built a series of programs that learn by discovery. The earliest of these, AM, combines a frame-like data structure (with inheritance) and a set of constructive rules, indexed to their locations of applicability, that operate on the frame. The frame-like structures represent mathematical concepts and the rules: (a) refine these or transform (mutate) them to form other concepts, and (b) propose new tasks to be performed. Control of the rules is accomplished by a scheduler that acts upon priority ratings of tasks. AM was able to discover interesting mathematical knowledge, beginning from basic definitions of set theory. A later program, EURISKO, developed similar capabilities for non-mathematical domains (including 3-D VLSI design) by developing frame structures and mutations whose form closely mimicked knowledge of heuristics. A main lesson from Lenat and Brown's (1984, p. 276) work is that:

> ... it's important to find a representation in which the form↔content mapping is as natural (i.e., efficient) as possible, a representation that mimics (analogically) the conceptual underpinnings of the task domain being theorized about.

Within design research, there have been several forays into a "discovery" approach to design, in which mutation operators are introduced into what are essentially prototype based design representations and processes. Murthy and Addanki (1987) reported modifications to prototypes by moving between nodes in a *graph of models*. They use *modification operators* that capture heuristics for (a) recognizing applicability, (b) calling appropriate analysis procedures, and (c) direct changes to the prototype. Maher et al. (1989) proposed *analogy* and *mutation* on search space operators as mechanisms for enlarging the design space of a prototype based design system. They noted that their mutation operators tend to be domain specific. Both of these works appear to gain much of their capability from the structure of the prototypes and operators that are available to the system, neither of which are addressed formally. To me, this is a crucial question in the search for a clear design mechanism; if much of the mystery is buried in a structure of knowledge that can be critiqued only by example, then how much insight is really gained? In this chapter I attempt to set some "ground rules" for more explicit capture of meaning.

9.6   Implications of the analogy

It appears to me that the organization of GDS presents a possible mechanism for the generation of designs that could be judged creative. In this section I present, in no particular order, a number of observations and arguments that support my contention, as well as some of the problems that I see.

At the beginning of this chapter I set out three criteria for a proposed creative design system: invention of the unexpected, computational clarity, and absence of heuristics. The organization of GDS is, I believe, remarkable in its achievement of the latter two. The mechanism I propose is, at its highest level, simple. It consists of nothing more than an infinite loop, and a small set of conceptually simple mechanisms for mutation, development, and selection. It does require design space machinery, but several exemplars of this have, to greater or lesser degrees, been created, for example shape, structure, and solid grammars, and rectangular layout systems. The mechanism, by itself, contains no heuristics, although there is ample opportunity to introduce them, and to imagine hybrid human-computer systems, without disturbing the organization in any essential way. Search space operators, search strategies, mutation operators, goals, and evaluators are the chief vehicles for such insertions.

Whether GDS can meet my first criterion, creation of the unexpected, can only be determined experimentally. However, natural evolution provides a strong existence demonstration of the potentials of the GDS organization.

Rules appear to have a magnification effect on designs. As demonstrated in Knight (1983a, 1983b, 1983c), changes to rules lead to substantial changes in the corpora of designs specified by those rules. As a specific example consider Figure 9.2. The initial rule (a) simply rotates a square about its centroid by 45 degrees. Some of its (well-known) derivations are shown. A simple mutation of this rule involves adding a translation of less than $\sqrt{2}/8$ times the side length of the square along the vector $(1, 1)$. When combined with the original rule, the mutated rule produces a new sequence of derivations whose geometry is very different from that of the first derivation set. Such magnification gives me hope that insights into creative acts in terms of simple rule changes could be a welcome serendipitous result of an implementation of the GDS organization.

Other researchers (Coyne et al., 1987) have drawn distinctions of creativity in designs by the method of design generation employed. These methods appear to me to be based on the behavior of human designers, and to provide plausible and interesting explanations of such behavior. To me they do not prescribe how creation by computer might best be accomplished, but do introduce a lot of machinery in the process. GDS is more parsimonious in this regard; it uses a single method for all design generation.

The GDS organization is not guaranteed to produce creative designs, nor are tests of completion or exhaustion likely to be easy (or possible) to find. In this matter it is very much like human designers, who also can provide no guarantees of creativity. I suspect that an implementation would be a tool, qualitatively different from any that exist, for exploring vast design spaces, and would be quite likely to find creative solutions.

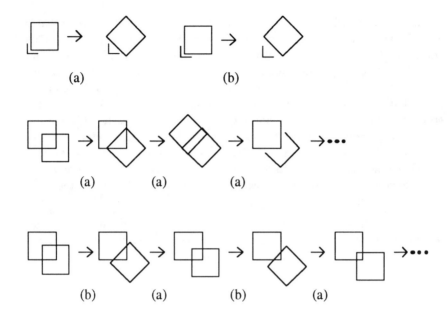

Figure 9.2. A mutation of a single rule can have a large effect on the derivations it might generate.

GDS provide opportunities for experimentation with knowledge based approaches to increasing its capabilities. Through changes to search space operators, search strategies, mutation operators, goals and evaluation devices, heuristics can be introduced, without in any way changing the overall structure of GDS. I would contend that this distinguishes GDS from current proposals for extending systems based on exhaustive enumeration (Coyne, 1989).

Formal extensions to GDS in terms of grammars that act on mutations seem plausible.

Different types of reproduction can be imagined within GDS. Design spaces for different designs can be merged, resulting in 'genotypes' that are widely different from their parents. For these, the criteria for survival can be relaxed, in contrast to the situation in natural evolution, for several generations, until new successful adaptations emerge. An implication of merging of design spaces is that the 'phylogeny' of designs can be reticulated and need not be limited to the tree that must occur naturally. This would bring the behavior of GDS in accord with observed 'cultural evolution' of designs (Steadman, 1979, p.101).

New technologies can be introduced as new rule sets for forming and combining parts. Thus the GDS organization can be responsive to technological change in a manner uniform with its basic mechanisms.

The process requires mimimal bootstrapping. As long as designs that can be evaluated are produced, then the process starts and is thereafter self-sustaining.

GDS presents a goalless process in the sense that it wanders wherever 'fitness for survival' takes it. The goals and evaluation devices of design only provide a simulated environment. The larger process has no goals; and is utterly mechanistic.

With correct technical formulation, the process will work. There is in biological evolution an existence demonstration (if not proof) for it. The vast spans of time required for biological evolution can be greatly reduced because: (a) designs (at least in architecture) are much simpler than living things, (b) the generation cycle can be greatly shortened, and (c) the mutation rate can be increased.

Several properties of design spaces seem to be required by the GDS. *The 'genotype' of designs must be potentially expressive.* It is important to be able to represent a wide range of variations (if not all of them). Thus the representation scheme of the design space needs to be highly expressive. For realistic systems this would seem to preclude simple attribute selection schemes that are obvious when naively using frames. *The search space operators must be semantically relevant.* If the behavior of GDS is to be transparent to humans, then the search space operators in a design space should specify plausible 'design moves.' Of all current formal approaches, that of spatial grammars seem to best fit this requirement. A consequence of using rules of this type is that properties of the phenotype cannot in general be predicted, but I do not see this as a problem, in that 'genotypes' will change constantly as 'evolution' in GDS progresses. *A representation scheme appears to be a necessity.* The representations manipulated by GDS must have a correspondence with real designs. If they did not, the necessary evaluation mechanisms could not be built and the loop at the heart of GDS could not be closed. This requirement appears to pose certain problems for drawing based representations (but see Stiny, 1981). *The search space operators should be based on a grammar (or algebra) that makes a strong sense of emergent form possible.* The stronger the sense of surprise in the process of generating the 'phenotype' from the 'genotype,' the more leverage the 'embryonic development process' will have. Shapes from shape grammars (being individuals) and the algebra of r-sets (being based on point sets) are two extant examples. *The mutation operators must be highly redundant.* It must be possible to mutate one form into a large variety of others by a series of small mutations. In other words, the transitive closure of the mutation relation between design spaces must be as dense as possible.

A problem with the evolutionary analogy is its absolute requirement for some mutations that present survival enhancement (or at least neutrality) at every step. Without this, the mechanism breaks down. Thus, in its most naive form, GDS would display some of the shortcomings of hill-climbing search strategies, although the pertubations introduced by random mutation should partially surmount this problem.

9.7   Conclusions and Research Directions

To my knowledge, only toy genetically inspired design systems have been implemented (see Maher et al., 1989; Lenat and Brown, 1984), and few direct theoretical results have been achieved (see Goldberg, 1989). However, much of the requisite formal machinery, especially that related to design spaces, does exist in some form. A research program on genetic design systems would be constrained by this state of affairs.

I see two somewhat conflicting issues that should be addressed in a research program on genetic design systems. The first is a requirement for further formalization. It would be very useful to precisely describe the structure of a GDS in some mathematical form. Having definitions for each class of computational object and precise abstract descriptions of the over-all process would greatly aid both understanding of the known theoretical problems and implementation of prototype systems. The second issue is the importance of having an experimental laboratory for GDS research. It is through a working implementation that insights to the crucial research questions will arise. An implementation would also provide measures of the performance of the idea, and these would not easily be found in another way. Therefore the implementation would need to achieve an entire mechanism; it would be important to have a base case of purely automatic behavior. Genetic design systems essentially perform search in a space of rule-sets, and are sufficiently abstract that insights, at least in the beginning, will come most easily through empirical (in contrast to analytic) means.

I propose then a research program with two parallel (but interconnecting) threads. The first (*theory*) would aim at mathematical description, and would meet its major milestone with the production of a set of precise definitions of all of the components in a GDS. The second (*application*) would aim initially to produce a minimal GDS, containing all components of the architecture, and making the necessary technical compromises to quickly achieve an operational system. Care would be taken to make this initial application as modular as possible, so parts of it could be independently replaced. At this point the two threads would hopefully begin to inform each other. From the implementation, theory would learn what questions are important and what theories should be formulated and proved; these would be the second major task for theory. From the theoretical results, application would fine-tune its implementation, rewriting some modules and replacing others, but this would not be its major second task. Application would embark on a series of experiments in design, posing problems, observing results, and gaining insight into the operation of the genetic system. At some point, all of the implementation of application would be discarded, and the two parts of the research program would come together with the goal of creating and using a theoretically sound implementation.

The research of each thread would have different criteria against which success would be measured. For theory the criteria are the relevance and quality of its formal results. For application, the criteria must be more vague; a partial list is: performance in terms of example generated designs, discovery of new mechanisms and effects, and the quality of the system design.

References

Coyne, R. D., Rosenman, M. A., Radford, A. D., & Gero, J. S. (1987). Innovation and creativity in knowledge-based CAD, *in* J. S. Gero (Ed.), *Expert Systems in Computer-Aided Design*, North-Holland, Amsterdam, pp. 435–465.

Coyne, R. F. (1989). Planning in design synthesis: Abstraction-based LOOS (ABLOOS), *Technical Report*, Engineering Design Research Center, Carnegie Mellon University, Pittsburgh.

Dawkins, R. (1987). *The Blind Watchmaker*, W.W. Norton and Company, New York.

Flemming, U., Coyne, R. F., Glavin, T., Hsi, H. and Rychener, M. D. (1989). A generative expert system for the design of building layouts, *EDRC-1989 Report Series*, Engineering Design Research Center, Carnegie Mellon University, Pittsburgh.

Goldberg, D. (1989). *Genetic Algorithms in Search, Optimization and Machine Learning*, Addison-Wesley, Reading, Massachusetts.

Knight, T. W. (1981). Languages of designs: From known to new, *Environment and Planning B* 8: 212–238.

Knight, T. W. (1983a). Transformations of languages of designs: Part 1, *Environment and Planning B* 10: 125–128.

Knight, T. W. (1983b). Transformations of languages of designs: Part 2, *Environment and Planning B* 10: 129–154.

Knight, T. W. (1983c). Transformations of languages of designs: Part 3, *Environment and Planning B* 10: 155-177.

Knight, T. W. (1988). Comparing designs, *Planning and Design* **15**(1): 73–110.

Lenat, D. B., & Brown, J. S. (1984). Why AM and EURISKO appear to work, *Artificial Intelligence* **23**(3): 269–294.

Maher, M. L., Zhao, F., & Gero, J. S. (1989). An approach to knowledge-based creative design, *Preprints NSF Engineering Design Research Conference*, University of Massachusetts, Amherst, pp. 333–346.

March, L. (1976). The logic of design and the question of value, *The Architecture of Form*, Cambridge University Press, Cambridge, UK, pp. 1–40.

March, L., & Stiny, G. (1985). Spatial systems in architecture and design: Some history and logic, *Environment and Planning B* **12**(1): 31–53.

Murthy, S. S., & Addanki, S. (1987). PROMPT: An innovative design tool, *Sixth National Conference on Artificial Intelligence*, AAAI'87, Morgan Kaufmann, pp. 637–642.

Newell, A. and Simon, H. A. (1972). *Human Problem Solving*, Prentice-Hall, Englewood.

Radford, A. D. and Gero, J. S. (1988). *Design by Optimization in Architecture, Building and Construction*, Van Nostrand Reinhold, New York, NY.

Requicha, A. G. (1980). Representation for rigid solids: theory, methods and systems, *Computing Surveys* **12**(4): 437–464.

Steadman, P. (1979). *Cambridge Urban and Architectural Studies. Volume 5: The Evolution of Designs*, Cambridge University Press, Cambridge, UK.

Stiny, G. (1981). A note on the description of designs, *Environment and Planning B* **8**(3): 257–268.

Woodbury, R. (1990). Searching for designs: paradigm and practice, *Building and Environment*.

Appendix: The design space formalism

In this chapter, a genetically based variant of *search* is proposed as a fundamental mechanism for creative design. The discussion makes use of terms with precise intended meanings; these require grounding. This Appendix presents, defines, and discusses these terms, structuring their meanings around a set-theoretical conception of design as search. A more lengthy account may be found in Woodbury (1990). Two more fundamental sources are Requicha (1980) for representation schemes, and Newell and Simon (1972) for search.

Whether done by human or machine, design search operates on *symbol structures*, that is, organized collections of *symbols*. The collection of all symbol structures that might be considered in a design task constitutes a *representation space R* and each member $r \in R$ is called a *representation*. Each $r \in R$ may have interpretations as one or more actual designs. If these interpretations are to be precise, a crisp characterization of designs must be made, and for this, the concept of a mathematical *modeling space M* is employed. *M* is usually described by predicates, universally quantified over

M, that describe properties (of all $m \in M$). These predicates capture only certain properties of physical objects, leaving others undescribed. For example, the well-known oriented 2-manifold conditions describe the idealized geometry of physical solids, but do not describe materials, surface textures, reflectance, or a host of other properties. The *semantics* of representations are defined by building a relation $\Theta : M \rightarrow R$ on the sets M and R that associates elements of R with elements of M. If $(m \in M, r \in R) \in \Theta$ then r is said to *model* or *represent m*. Θ itself is called a *representation scheme*.

In interesting design problems, the set R cannot be directly enumerated; its size is typically huge (or infinite). Various techniques of indirect specification, for example, algebra and grammar notations, are typically used instead. All members of R are generated by these indirect syntactical methods and are therefore *syntactically correct*. Members of the set M are not directly generated at all; they are only known by the existence of members of R that can be shown to represent them.

Since only members of R are directly available to any computational process it is convenient to define Θ in terms of its inverse relation Θ^{-1}, for mapping members of R to members of M, and this is shown in Figure 9.3. It is useful to describe Θ^{-1} as a *characteristic predicate*:

$$P(r) = \begin{cases} 1 & \text{if } \Theta^{-1}(r) \in M \\ 0 & \text{otherwise} \end{cases}$$

that determines if a symbol structure in R represents an element of M. This predicate can be thought of as a test that can be implemented as a computer program. Θ is defined as $\Theta^{-1^{-1}}$. The domain of Θ, denoted by D, is the set of all elements of M that have corresponding elements in R. The codomain of Θ is R. The range of Θ, denoted by V, is the set of all members of R (by definition syntactically correct), that correspond to elements in D.

With these preliminaries in place it is possible to more formally describe certain properties of a representation scheme, namely: *extent of domain (expressiveness), syntactic validity, well-formedness, completeness (unambiguousness), uniqueness,* and *abstractness*.

When compared to the entire modeling space M, the size of the domain D of a representation scheme is a measure of the descriptive power of the scheme. D is that part of the modeling space that is accessible by construction of representations in R. If $D = M$ the representation scheme is *semantically exhaustive*.

Every element of V (the range of the representation scheme) is considered to be *valid*, as it is both syntactically and semantically correct (i.e. it can be constructed by the rules that define R and has corresponding elements in

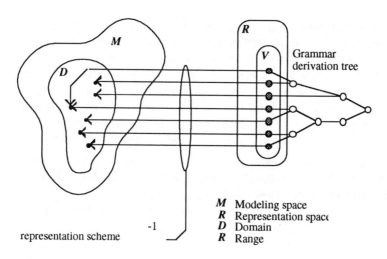

Figure 9.3. An abstract depiction of a representation scheme

D). If $V = R$ then the representation scheme is *syntactically valid*, as every syntactically correct representation corresponds to an element of D.

If, in addition to syntactic validity, a representation scheme is semantically exhaustive, then the scheme is *well-formed*. A consequence of well-formedness is that the characteristic predicate of Θ^{-1} is always TRUE. With a well-formed scheme, it is theoretically possible to generate a representation that corresponds to an arbitrary member of the modeling space, using only the syntax rules that define the representation space. Well-formedness is an essential quality for exhaustive search strategies.

A representation $r \in V$ is *unambiguous*, or *complete*, if it corresponds to a single element in D. It is *unique* if its corresponding objects in D have no other representations in V. Intuitively a valid representation is ambiguous if it models several objects in D, and an object in D has non-unique representations if it corresponds to more than one element of V. A representation scheme is unambiguous, or complete, if all members of its range are unambiguous. Similarly, a representation scheme is unique if all members of its range are unique.

Related to unambiguousness is the property of *abstractness*. In constructing representation schemes for design it is very useful to keep the size of either or both of the representation space R or the range V of the representation scheme as small as possible. This implies a smaller space to search. Given a particular modeling space M, a common way of achieving this is to introduce a kind of controlled ambiguity into the representation scheme. Figure 9.4 provides an example, the LOOS system (Flemming et al., 1989), in which the modeling space is the set of all arrangements of loosely packed, non-overlapping, orthogonally oriented rectangles in two dimensional euclidean space $\Re^2$. The representation space consists of a set of graphs, where the nodes of the graph denote rectangles and the arcs denote the spatial relations *to-the-right-of*, *to-the-left-of*, *above*, and *below*. Each graph in the representation space represents an entire class of rectangular layouts in the modeling space that differ in the dimensions and locations of the constituent rectangles but are the same with respect to the spatial relations specified in the graph. Thus the representation scheme for LOOS is decidely ambiguous, as every representation corresponds to an infinite set of rectangles, yet the ambiguity is precisely controlled, since specific spatial relationships are faithfully modeled.

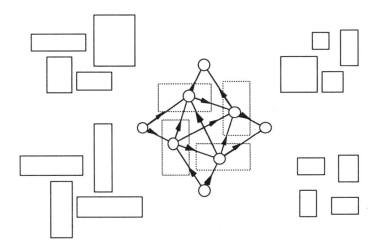

Figure 9.4. Ambiguity in the representation scheme of LOOS.

Another, less formal, way of looking at the concepts of abstractness and unambiguousness is to employ the ideas of *instance* and *class*. An instance is a single object and an unambiguous representation scheme can be said to model instances in modeling space. A class is a group of objects and an abstract scheme models classes, where all instances in a class have some (hopefully relevant) common properties. With the ideas of instance and class, another relation, the *same-class* relation $\Upsilon : M \rightarrow M$, can be constructed between elements of the modeling space. Two objects are in Υ if both correspond to the same representation in V. If Υ is an equivalence relation then all representations in V unambiguously denote *blocks* (alternatively *pieces*) of a *partition* of M.

The formal properties of a representation scheme can be used to describe properties of the search operators that act in a representation space, but another formal construct, the *search space*, is also required. A *search space S* is comprised of a modeling space M, a representation space R, a representation scheme Θ, a set of operators O, and a set of initial representations $I \subset R$. An *operator application* within S consists of an operator from O applied to a representation from R. More formally, when an operator from O is applied to a representation $r \in R$ to yield another representation $r' \in R$, then r is said to *directly derive* r' in O, or symbolically $r \underset{O}{\Rightarrow} r'$. If there exists a sequence of direct derivations using operators from O, such that $r_0 \underset{O}{\Rightarrow} r_1 \underset{O}{\Rightarrow} \cdots \underset{O}{\Rightarrow} r_{n-1} \underset{O}{\Rightarrow} r_n$ then r_0 *derives* r_n in O, $r_0 \underset{O}{\overset{*}{\Rightarrow}} r_n$. The *design collection* of a search space is all representations $r \in R$ such that $i \underset{O}{\overset{*}{\Rightarrow}} r, i \in I$.

Operators in a search space may individually or as a set have the properties of *closure* and *monotonicity*. Other properties of search space operators, *completeness* and *non-redundancy*, are defined only on the search space itself. An operator is *closed* in V if its application to any member of V can never result in a representation not in V. A search space is closed in V if all of its operators are closed in V. If operators are closed, and begin from elements in V, then the characteristic predicate of the representation scheme, $P(r)$, need never be applied to test for representational validity.

An operator can be *monotonic* with respect to both properties in M (*modeling space monotonicity*) and to the symbol structures in R (*representational monotonicity*). If a set of properties P_M of any $m \in M$ cannot be altered by the application of an operator, then the operator is monotonic with respect to P_M. If an operator can only add to, but otherwise never alter, the symbol structures of R, then it is monotonic with respect to R. A search space is monotonic in either sense if all of its operators are monotonic in that sense. These two types of monotonicity are quite different and do not imply each other.

A search space S is *complete* in the domain of its representation scheme Θ if, by application of any combination of operators from O starting from any elements of I, representations in V sufficient to model all of D can be reached. If Θ is semantically exhaustive and the operator set is complete in D, then the operator set is complete in M. Informally, completeness in M means that every conceivable solution can be reached by some sequence of operator applications from O. A search space S is *non-redundant* in R (or V) if there is at most one sequence of operator applications beginning from $i \in I$ that can generate any $r \in R$ (or V).

A search space exists in the absence of any specific design context; it is simply a description of possibilities. By applying operators beginning at initial states it is theoretically conceivable that one might eventually *visit* any design within the space. But such unguided wandering is unlikely to be interesting. To pursue design requires more: a way to choose operator applications, a sense of where in the space one wishes to go, and a means of knowing when one has arrived at a goal. These are accomplished by a *search strategy*.

A search strategy is a policy; a way of making decisions. Under its guidance it is possible to move through a search space purposefully, visiting new states and remembering or forgetting them; that is, making them active or inactive until an appropriate design is found (or is not found). Each visitation of a state is called a *step* and typically occasions four types of decisions.

1. Is the design problem solved?

2. Which from among the active designs will be selected next?

3. Which search space operator will be applied to the selected design?

4. Which of the active designs will remain active? (Which will be made inactive?)

To make these decisions requires two additional components in a search strategy: *design goals* and *evaluation devices*. Design goals are statements of intent; they describe in some way the characteristics possessed by a successful solution. Design problems typically have multiple and conflicting goals. Designs are compared against goals as they are reached by search space operators and these comparisons are used in making the decisions at each step in design. The separation of generation, goals, and evaluation devices in the search paradigm is more than a formal nicety; given the current understanding of designing physical artifacts, it appears to be a necessity. Deriving form from its behavior has proven to be extremely difficult, even in single performance design problems. The alternative is to consider the behavior of forms that are generated in some other terms, and to use the knowledge of behavior to guide the generation process.

To understand performance, a design is tested (according to various criteria) against its predicted context. A set of such tests, one for each criterion, together with a means for understanding their collected results constitutes the evaluation devices of a search strategy. The tests alone are not enough, for designs perform according to many different criteria, and these cannot be treated separately. It is commonly the case that one performance measure conflicts with another, for example, that it is impossible to improve a view without increasing heat loss. Making decisions in the face of these conflicts requires an understanding of possible tradeoffs and ultimately judgments of relative value (March, 1976; Radford and Gero, 1988).

With search strategies our portrait of the search paradigm is complete. To search requires a space and a strategy. A search space is composed of a representation scheme, a set of search operators and a starting point. It provides an implicit specification of a world of possibilities. A search strategy is a decision making policy and its associated machinery. It provides a means to move purposefully through a search space. A *design space* consists of a search space and a strategy.

It is only with the concept of a design space in place that a crucial idea can be introduced. A set of operators in a design space is *semantically relevant* if its members correspond to meaningful moves in design. For example, if one is doing preliminary design for an airport, it is useful to have operators for placing runways, organizing pedestrian and vehicular traffic flow, developing spatial signage conventions, etc. A set of operators that describes the actual construction of runways and hangars would be much less semantically relevant.

PART III

Computer Supported Creative Design

Part III includes accounts of implementations that support creative design. The first chapter, "Creativity enhancing design environments" by Fischer, presents a system in which the user interaction style promotes and supports creativity. The second chapter, "Knowledge-based systems and new paradigms for creativity" by Edmonds, shows by example how rule-based systems can produce creative designs through search leaving the evaluation to the human. The third chapter, "Inducing optimally directed non-routine designs" by Cagan and Agogino, presents a mathematical approach to finding creative solutions in which variables are split to change the formulation of the optimization. The fourth chapter, "Computer supported creative design: A pragmatic approach" by Coyne and Subrahmanian, considers how a specific generate-and-test approach to layout design can potentially produce creative designs. The fifth chapter, "Dynamic associations for creative engineering design" by Maher and Zhao, considers how indexing and associations during problem specification can be automated to direct a designer towards more creative solutions.

10 Creativity Enhancing Design Environments

Gerhard Fischer

Computers have the potential to be tools that enhance creativity. But most of the current systems have not lived up to these expectations— they have restricted rather than enhanced creativity. Designers were forced to express their goals, ideas, and (partial) solutions at levels that were too remote from the problem domains they were dealing with. To overcome these limitations, conceptual framework and proto-typical systems that allow designers to work with personal meaningful operations have been developed. Beyond providing domain-specific abstractions, these knowledge-based design environments can evaluate and criticize an evolving design and provide feedback to the designer. They integrate constructive and argumentative components. Support for end-user modifiability allows designers to extend the environments themselves. Knowledge-based design environments turn the computer into an invisible instrument and support cooperative problem solving between the human designer and the computer.

10.1 Introduction

Tools (either conceptual or physical ones) have played a major role for human beings in scientific discoveries, problem solving capabilities and in the power to design and create. Good tools provide only the necessary requirements and although they are not sufficient by themselves, without them creativity is severely limited. The computer has been seen by many as the ultimate tool to support creativity. But the achievements so far have fallen short of these expectations.

In this chapter I first discuss a conceptual framework for creativity and enumerate a set of requirements for enabling creativity. Then I explore why there are so few computational environments for enabling and supporting creativity. Innovative system building efforts (construction kits and design environments) as steps towards creativity enhancing environments are described and evaluated against the conceptual framework.

10.2   Creativity and computers

10.2.1   Creativity

Creativity can be informally defined (Hayes, 1978) as consisting of acts that have some valuable consequence and that are novel or surprising. It is a special kind of problem solving thinking requiring high motivation and persistence. The problem itself (as initially posed) is vague and ill-defined, so that part of the task is to formulate the problem itself. Creativity is often associated with divergent production abilities (i.e., doing tasks in which many different responses to the same situation must be generated) and less with convergent production abilities (i.e., tasks in which a person is expected to generate a single correct answer).

Design (Simon, 1981) is one of the most promising activities in which to study creativity, based on the following attributes of design problems: designers who tackle the same problem are likely to come up with different solutions (Jacob, 1977), good designers break rules all the time, design deals with ill-structured (Simon, 1973) and wicked problems (Rittel, 1972) (i.e., problems that are intrinsically open-ended, situation specific, and controversial), and in design there are no optimal solutions, only trade-offs.

10.2.2   How can creativity be enhanced?

Hayes (1978) stated the obvious that "there is no procedure which will guarantee that a person will invent something important or initiate a new artistic movement." The advice "Be more creative!" is about as helpful for a problem solver as saying to a software engineer "Think more clearly!" But software engineers in the 1980s are writing more complex and more interesting programs than their predecessors in the 1960s. High school children write programs today that would have earned them a PhD twenty years ago. New technologies (e.g., better hardware, powerful programming environments) and new methodologies (e.g., structured programming, object-oriented programming, reuse, and redesign) have enhanced the problem solving power of the programmer. Can creativity be enhanced in similar ways in other computer-supported design tasks with the right tools and environments?

In the following I enumerate requirements and techniques that have the potential to increase our chances of being more creative:

- **Developing a knowledge base.** Having relevant knowledge does not guarantee creativity, but it is one important condition for it. Experts (uniformly across different domains, e.g., in chess, physics, painting, composing, etc.) have at least 50,000 chunks about the relevant knowledge in their domain (Simon, 1981).

- **Create the right environment for creativity.** Instead of putting all of our knowledge "into the head," some of this knowledge can be put "into the world" (Norman, 1988). Ideas generation benefits from being reminded of the right thing at the right time, or being forced to argue for a position.

- **Look for analogies and the impact of representation on problem difficulty.** Seeing a problem from a different perspective often helps to turn a difficult problem into an easy one. The mutilated checker board problem[1] becomes trivial when it is seen as the matchmaking problem[2]. The crucial point is the switch from searching within a problem space to searching for a problem space.

- **Supporting the incremental unfolding of design spaces.** In most design tasks, the design space only unfolds as designers work in it. Many requirements emerge only in the course of the design process, when partial design solutions provide enough context to realize which

---

[1] *The Mutilated Checker Board Problem.* A checkerboard with 64 squares and a set of 32 rectangular dominoes are given. Each of the dominoes covers exactly 2 checkerboard squares. Obviously, the 32 dominoes can be arranged to cover the board completely. Now suppose that two (black) squares were cut from the opposite corners of the board. Can the remaining 62 squares of the board be covered using exactly 31 dominoes (Hayes, 1978; Newell and Simon, 1975; Kaplan and Simon, 1989; Boecker et al., 1986)?

[2] *The Matchmaker Problem.* In a small village in the Midwest, there were 32 bachelors and 32 unmarried women. Through tireless efforts, the village matchmaker succeeded in arranging 32 highly satisfactory marriages. Then one Saturday night, two drunken bachelors fatally stabbed each other. Can the matchmaker, through some quick arrangements, come up with 31 satisfactory marriages among the 62 survivors?

issues are really important. This situation is aptly characterized by Simon (1981):

> Architecture can almost be taken as a prototype for the process of design in a semantically rich task domain. The emerging design is itself incorporated in a set of external memory structures: sketches, floor plans, drawings of utility systems, and so on. At each stage in the design process, the partial design reflected in these documents serves as a major stimulus for suggesting to the designer what he would attend to next. This direction to new subgoals permits in turn new information to be extracted from memory and reference sources and another step to be taken toward the development of the design.

In our work we have demonstrated the relevance of supporting incremental approaches to design and problem solving with a system that allows users to incrementally formulate and reformulate a query in an information retrieval task (Fischer and Nieper-Lemke, 1989).

- **Reuse and redesign.** If computational media live up to their name, namely that software is truly "soft," then they offer unique possibilities for reuse and redesign. Future developments should be directed towards the goal that programmability and end-user modifiability will allow professionally produced items to become changeable, adaptable, fragmentable, and quotable in ways that present software is not. Not only would professionals be able to construct grand images, but others would be able to reconstruct personalized versions of these same images (diSessa and Abelson, 1986). Another important argument for reuse and redesign is that complex systems evolve faster if there are stable subsystems.

- **Exploiting what people already know.** A crucial element for increasing the competence and the independence of designers is to build environments that exploit what designers already know or that allow them to build natural bridges to their existing knowledge. For example, to support a spatial metaphor is so important, because we all know how to move around in space. Our concept of *human problem domain communication* (see section 10.3.1) is relevant for this goal, because it allows designers to work with abstractions of their own domain of expertise.

- **Explanation and argumentation.** If knowledge with respect to the problem to be solved is "in the world," and partial designs serve as stimulus for further action, then we have to understand these partial designs and their rationale. If the partial designs are embedded in design environments, then these environments should provide explanations and argumentation for them. Explanations and argumentation assist us in understanding someone else's rationale. They have the potential to enhance creativity, because they allow us to increase our knowledge base and to reason against another opinion. They can stimulate critical thinking, because every reason given is ammunition for the different people involved to argue about. Both help us to rethink our own implicit assumptions, enabling us to notice flaws in our own thoughts or to discover alternative ways to think about a problem.

- **Taking care of low-level clerical details.** Environments are needed that allow designers to think and work on the important parts of problems. Designers should not worry about low-level details that are far removed from their actual objectives. The UNIX writer's workbench tools (Cherry, 1981) allow writers to focus on their ideas and not spend most of the time with spelling and style issues. Our LISP-CRITIC (Fischer, 1987a) frees LISP programmers from worrying about details of the coding activity, giving them more time to concentrate on their problem solving activity.

- **Affection and appropriation.** Papert (1986) convincingly argued that one of the most important aspects of engaging people in creative acts is that they must "fall in love with what they are doing." They must make activities their own and they must be able to care about their work, a principle that he calls "appropriation." To achieve affection and appropriation is more likely if designers can engage in activities in which they are truly interested and if they learn and do something that is of immediate benefit to them. People learn things best if they can use them—not sometimes in the future, but to solve a problem that they face right at this moment.

With this informal characterization of creativity, I investigate the question of why there have been so few creative solutions in computational media and then discuss knowledge-based design environments in the next section as steps towards creativity enhancing environments.

10.2.3 Why have there been so few creative solutions in computational media?

The summary answer to this question is that current computer systems inadequately support the issues enumerated in the previous section. In certain cases computational media of the past were just too impoverished to support creative expression. As long as:

COMPUTER OUTPUT LOOKED LIKE THIS

there was little room for creativity. Over the last few years, first daisy wheel printers started producing output that was called "typewriter-quality;" nowadays laser printers allow *italic*, **bold**, and other typographic niceties, such as $sub_{scripting}$ and $super^{scripting}$. These technological capabilities gave people control over features with which they had no experience. Because few support tools and heuristics were provided, the set of new features led to the problem (Bentley, 1986) that:

"Powerful

tools can SOMETIMES be powerfully **abused!!**

Creativity is more than using any existing feature. High functionality computer systems (with tens of thousands of tools embedded in them) have to provide guidance to the creative use of their features (Fischer and Lemke, 1989). The situation changed from having weak generators (e.g., providing only uppercase letters) for problem solutions that gave no room for creativity to having powerful generators without support for selectivity and critiquing.

Another major reason for limiting creativity is that to do anything interesting, computers often require too much time and too much effort. Imagine the task of designing a pinball machine on your computer by writing statements in a programming language. The transformation distance between the goal state (the pinball machine) and the start state (a programming language) is too large. This prevents designers from thinking about the right kind of problems (e.g., how to locate bumpers, how to create a scoring scheme, etc.), and from getting something interesting done in a reasonable time.

The music and pinball construction kits (two interesting programs for the Apple MacIntosh from Electronic Arts; see Figures 10.1 and 10.2) provide domain-level building blocks (e.g., notes, sharps, flats, bumpers, flippers, etc.) to build artifacts in the domains of music and pinball machines. Designers can interact with the system in terms drawn from the problem domain; they need not learn abstractions peculiar to a computer system.

Our empirical investigations have shown that users familiar with the problem domain but inexperienced with computers had few problems using this system, whereas computer experts unfamiliar with the problem domain were unable to exploit its power. Most people considered it a difficult (if not impossible) task to achieve the same results using only the basic Macintosh system without the construction kit. Using the construction kit, our

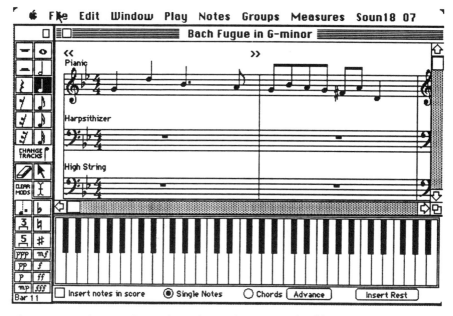

Figure 10.1. A screen image from the music construction kit.

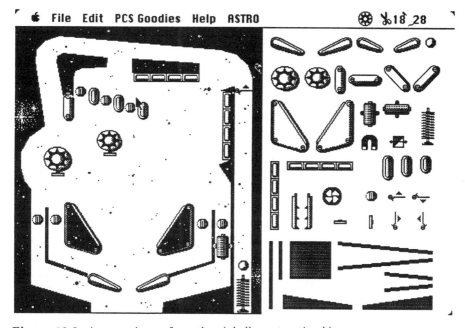

Figure 10.2. A screen image from the pinball construction kit.

subjects experienced a sense of accomplishment, because they were creating their own impressive version of something that works (at least to a certain extent), yet is not difficult to make. By reducing the transformation distance between problem domain and system space, people were able to spend most of their time on interesting problems. They produced an interesting artifact quickly and were able to change it with little effort, supporting an additional requirement for creativity: "To come up with a great idea, one must have and explore *many* ideas."

As long as computational environments require substantial knowledge of computers, domain experts will be limited in using the computer as a creative medium. Another possibility would be that software engineers become the creative designers. This also has its limitations, because computer systems model more and more real world domains requiring a substantial amount of domain-oriented knowledge. This was revealed in a recent empirical study (Curtis et al., 1988), which showed that a major limitation in software engineering is *the thin spread of application knowledge among software engineers.* In the long run it seems a more promising approach to let the domain experts work within domain-specific environments than educating software engineers to become experts in a variety of different disciplines. The role of the software engineer in the future should be to build domain-oriented environments in an interdisciplinary effort together with domain experts.

10.3   Knowledge-based design environments

In this section an evolving framework and a number of system building efforts are discussed that try to instantiate our ideas about creativity enhancing environments.

10.3.1   Human problem-domain communication and construction kits

To do anything in this world, it is not good enough to have weak methods, that is, to be smart in selective search and means-ends analysis (Simon, 1986). In addition to that, we have to have knowledge about the task domain. Designers (e.g., architects, composers, user interface designers, database experts, knowledge engineers, etc.) are experts in their problem domain. The computer, because of its generality, can be a support tool for all knowledge workers. But domain specialists are not interested in learning the "languages of the computer;" they simply want to use the computer to solve problems and accomplish tasks. To shape the computer into a truly usable and useful medium, we have to make low-level primitives invisible and let users work directly on their problems and tasks. We must "teach" the computer the languages of experts by endowing it with the abstractions of application domains. This reduces the transformation distance between the domain expert's description of the task and its representation as a computer program. *Human problem-domain communication* (Fischer and Lemke, 1988) provides a new level of quality in human-computer communication by building important abstract operations and objects of a given area directly into the computing environment. In these systems, the designer can operate with personally meaningful abstractions, and the cognitive transformation distance between problem-oriented and system-oriented descriptions is reduced.

Many current knowledge-based systems use knowledge representations at a too low level of abstraction. This makes both system design and explanation difficult, because system designers have to transform the problem into a low-level implementation language and explanations require translating back to the problem level.

Construction kits are tools that foster human problem-domain communication by providing a set of building blocks that model a problem domain. The building blocks define a design space (the set of all possible designs that can be created by combining these blocks) and a design vocabulary. A construction kit makes the elements of a domain-oriented substrate readily available by displaying them in a menu or graphical palette (see Figure 10.3). This kind of system eliminates the need for prerequisite, low-level skills such as knowing the names of software components and the formal syntax for combining them.

Human problem-domain communication allows us to redraw the borderline between the amount of knowledge coming from computer systems versus coming from the application domain. Systems built to support human problem-domain communication establish an "application-oriented" vocabulary that is essential for effective reasoning and communication. They eliminate some of the opaqueness of computational systems by restricting them to specific application domains.

Construction kits are not good enough. Evaluating the pinball construction kit as a prototypical example against our objective to support human problem-domain communication, we have identified some shortcomings. The system helps to construct an artifact quickly, but it does not assist the designer in constructing *interesting and useful* artifacts. The pinball construction kit allows designers to build pinball machines in which balls get stuck in corners and in which devices may not be reachable. To assist designers in constructing truly interesting objects, design environments are needed.

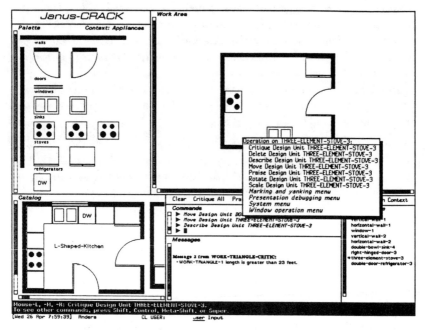

Figure 10.3. JANUS construction interface. JANUS is a knowledge-based system to support kitchen designers. The interface of JANUS' construction component is based on the world model (Hutchins et al., 1986). Design units are selected from the Palette, and moved into the work area. Operations on design units are available through menus. The screen image shown displays a message from the WORK-TRIANGLE-CRITIC.

10.3.2   Design environments

Design environments give support that is not offered by simple construction kits. In addition to presenting the designer with the available parts and the operations to put them together, they incorporate knowledge about which components fit together and how they do so, and they contain cooperative critics that recognize suboptimal design choices and inefficient or useless structures. They support multiple specification techniques in creating a new system and understanding an existing one. They link internal objects and the external behavior and appearance, they provide animated examples and guided tours—techniques supporting the incremental development of a system. In the following, two design environments are described that we have constructed over the last few years:

1. JANUS (Fischer et al., 1989; McCall et al., 1989), which supports architectural design; and

2. FRAMER (Lemke, 1989; Fischer and Lemke, 1989), which supports window-based user interface design.

JANUS: A cooperative system for kitchen design

JANUS allows designers to construct artifacts in the domain of architectural design and at the same time informs them about principles of design and their underlying rationale by integrating two design activities: construction and argumentation. *Construction* is supported by a knowledge-based graphical design environment (see Figure 10.3) and *argumentation* is supported by a hypertext system (see Figure 10.4).

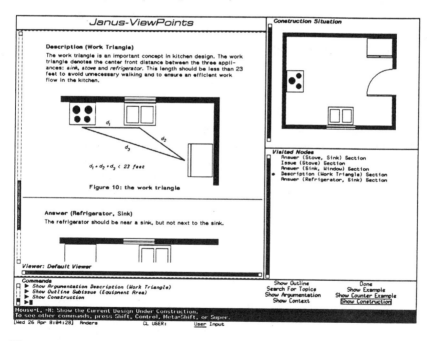

Figure 10.4. JANUS argumentation interface. JANUS' argumentation component uses the Symbolics Document Examiner as a delivery interface. The construction situation can be displayed in one of the panes to allow users to inspect the constructive and argumentative context simultaneously.

JANUS provides a set of domain-specific building blocks and has knowledge about properties and constraints of useful designs. With this knowledge it "looks over the shoulder" of users carrying out a specific design. If it discovers a shortcoming in the users' designs, it provides a critique, suggestions, and explanations, and assists users in improving their designs. JANUS is not an expert system that dominates the process by generating new designs from high-level goals or resolving design conflicts automatically. Designers control the behavior of the system at all times (e.g., the critiquing can be "turned on and off"), and if they disagree with JANUS, they can modify its knowledge base.

Critics (Fischer and Mastaglio, 1989) in JANUS are procedures for detecting non-satisficing partial designs. JANUS' concept for integrating the constructive and argumentative component originated from the observation that a critique is a limited type of argumentation. The construction actions can be seen as attempts to resolve design issues. For example, when a designer is positioning the sink in the kitchen, the issue being resolved is "Where should the sink be located?"

The knowledge-based critiquing mechanism in JANUS bridges the gap between construction and argumentation. This means that critiquing and argumentation can be coupled by using JANUS' critics to provide the designer with immediate entry into the place in the hypertext network containing the argumentation relevant to the current construction task. Such a combined system provides argumentative information for construction effectively, efficiently, and designers do not have to realize beforehand that information will be required, anticipate what information is in the system, or know how to retrieve it.

JANUS' *Construction Component.* The constructive part of JANUS supports building an artifact either from scratch or by modifying an existing design. To construct from scratch, the designer chooses building blocks from a design units PALETTE and positions them in the WORK-AREA (see Figure 10.3).

To construct by modifying an existing design, the designer uses the CATALOG (lower left in Figure 10.3), which contains several example designs. The designer can browse through this catalog of examples until an interesting one is found. This design can then be selected and brought into the WORK-AREA, where it can be modified.

The CATALOG contains both good designs and poor designs. The former satisfies all the rules of kitchen design and will not generate a critique. People who want to design without having to bother with knowing the underlying principles, might want to select one of these, because minor modifications of them will probably result in few or no suggestions from the critics. The poor designs in the CATALOG support learning the design principles. By bringing these into the WORK-AREA, users can subject them to critiquing and thereby illustrate those principles of kitchen design that are known to the system.

The *good designs* in the CATALOG can also be used to learn design principles and explore their argumentative background. This can be done by bringing them into the WORK-AREA then using the "Praise all" command. This command causes the system to generate positive feedback by displaying messages from all of the rules that the selected example satisfies. The messages also provide entry points into the hypertext argumentation.

JANUS' *Argumentation Component.* The hypertext component of JANUS is implemented using Symbolics Concordia and Document Examiner software. The issue base is implemented using Concordia, a hypertext editor (Walker, 1988). The Document Examiner (Walker, 1987) provides functionality for on-line presentation and browsing of the issue base by users.

When users enter the argumentative part of JANUS, they are brought into a section of the issue base relevant to their current construction situation. Their point of entry into the hypertext network contains the information required to understand the issue of interest. But argumentation on an issue can be large and complex so they can use this initial display of relevant information as a starting place for a navigational journey through the issue base, following links that will lead them to additional information. After examining the argumentative information, the designer can return to construction and complete the current task.

Critics as Hypertext Activation Agents. JANUS' knowledge-based critics serve as the mechanisms to link construction with argumentation. They "watch over the shoulders" of designers, displaying their critique in the MESSAGES pane (center bottom in Figure 10.3) when design principles are violated. In doing so they also identify the argumentative context that is appropriate to the current construction situation.

For example, when a designer has designed the kitchen shown in Figure 10.3, the "WORK-TRIANGLE-CRITIC" fires and detects that the work triangle is too large. To see the arguments surrounding this issue, the designer has only to click on the text of this criticism with the mouse. The argumentative context shown in Figure 10.4 is then displayed.

FRAMER: **A design environment for window-based user interfaces**

FRAMER (Lemke, 1989) is a design environment for window-based user interfaces. The overall design support provided by FRAMER is similar to JANUS. The system supports software design in multiple ways: making components readily available in a direct-manipulation interface, taking care of interdependencies of design characteristics by knowing about necessary design issues, and assessing designs by highlighting good aspects and suggesting improvements to eliminate the shortcomings of poor designs.

FRAMER promotes reuse and redesign (Fischer, 1987b): the first step in the design is the selection of a framework from the library of reusable designs. Design with FRAMER always involves reuse. Figure 10.5 shows an intermediate design state. The system's knowledge about the design task is represented as a check list in the top left window. The check list describes the steps that a designer has to go through in designing a functioning interface. The "What you can do" window lists all design options related to the currently selected check list item. For each option the possible choices and an explanation of the significance of the option is given. The descriptive aspects of the design are specified directly in this window, which functions as a dynamic, electronic form.

The "Things to take care of" window, below, continuously displays the related messages from the critics. Critics are classified as either mandatory or recommended. Mandatory critics describe conditions necessary for the interface to function, recommended critics suggest typical decisions according to criteria such as consistency and usefulness. Each type of critic message is associated with a prestored WHY and HOW explanation. Recommended critics can be overruled by clicking the reject button. For some critic suggestions, the system knows how to fix the problem. If so, an execute button appears near the suggestion (remedy feature).

The work area contains a representation of the visual aspects of the design. It displays the window layout with the types and names of the windows. The window layout is generated and modified in a direct manipulation style using primitive elements from the palette on the right.

When all items in the check list are completed, the corresponding code can be generated. FRAMER can translate both ways between the representation used in FRAMER and executable code.

Experiences with FRAMER. The framework supported by FRAMER makes possible a major shift in the design process. In traditional environments the emphasis is on writing algorithms, whereas with high functionality computer systems supported by knowledge-based design environments, the emphasis is on finding, understanding, and applying existing tools. Designing applications in these environments means that few algorithms are created and that the descriptive part of software design grows correspondingly large.

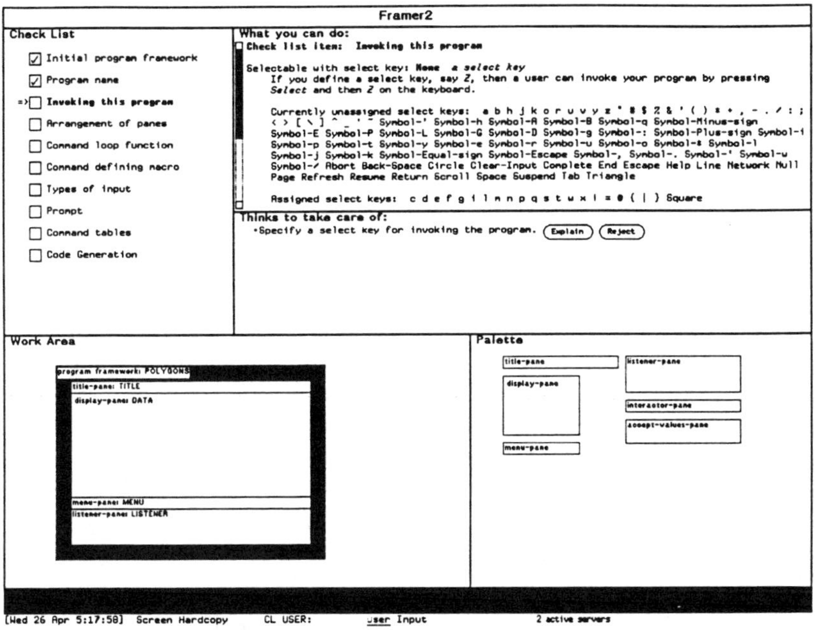

Figure 10.5. FRAMER—a design environment for window-based user interfaces. The check list item "invoking the program" is currently selected. The "What you can do" window shows the issue what the select key (short cut) for invoking the program should be. the critic window shows a message recommending that a select key be defined. The designer can find out why this is recommended by pressing the Explain button, and then reject the critic if desired.

FRAMER has turned out to be a powerful tool for rapid prototyping, which is of crucial importance for an ill-defined domain such as user interface design. FRAMER supports the coevolution of specification and implementation in a natural way. The critics, the explanation component, and the remedy feature allow the designers to use the environment to get some feedback about the quality of their designs.

As an artifact, FRAMER transforms a task by replacing a specification in terms of implementation concepts with an environment based on the "world model" metaphor (Hutchins et al., 1986). It changes the cognitive requirements for bridging the gap between the designer's intentions and actions on the system's interface. The direct manipulation metaphor for the graphical layout reduces the transformation distance from conceptual to executable representation. The continuous visualization allows the designer to directly monitor the characteristics of the artifact being created. With a system based on this metaphor, the designer can operate with a representation much more closely related to the designed artifact. FRAMER thus brings the task of designing a user interface much closer to the conceptual level at which the human interface designer operates.

10.3.3   End-user modifiability

To enhance creativity in knowledge-based design environments, end-user modifiability (Fischer and Girgensohn, 1990) is of crucial importance, because these systems (instead of serving as general purpose programming environments) provide support for specific tasks. In cases where designers of these environments did not anticipate specific activities, users must be able to modify the design environment itself. There must be enough support structures to extend the environment at the conceptual level of the task domain—requiring only to descend as few layers as possible in the layered architecture (see Figure 10.7)

In JANUS, situations arise in which users want to design a kitchen with appliances that are not provided by the design environment (e.g., a microwave). Property sheets (see Figure 10.6) help users define new design unit classes or modify existing ones by eliminating the need to remember names of attributes. The modification process is supported with context-sensitive help (e.g., showing users constraints for the value of a field). The system supports finding an appropriate place for the new class in the class hierarchy by displaying the current hierarchy. Users can display the definition of every class in the hierarchy with a mouse click. In addition, the applicable critic rules for a class can be listed and the definition of each of these rules can be be displayed.

10.4   Evaluation of our system building efforts

In this section I briefly describe what we have learned from designing and evaluating our knowledge-based design environments (for more details see Lemke (1989)).

The contribution of different system components. The contribution of the individual components of JANUS and FRAMER can be characterized as follows:

- *Palette:* Without the palette (i.e., starting with a general purpose programming language) the probability that a designer will construct a good kitchen, a good user interface, or a good pinball machine is

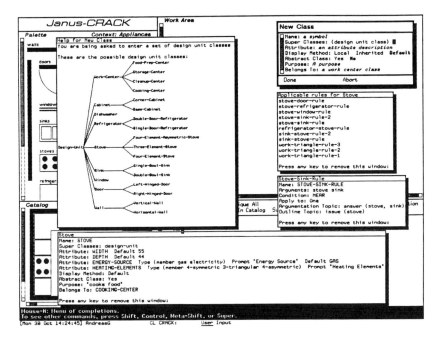

Figure 10.6. End-user modifiability in JANUS: introducing a microwave. Users are supported in the modification of the design environment itself in a variety of ways: the property sheet with the title "New Class" guides the definition of a new class, the property sheet "Stove" shows the definition of a related class which can be modified, the "help" window visualizes the inheritance hierarchy of the objects known to JANUS, the "Applicable Rules for Stove" window shows the set of rules defining the critiquing knowledge for stove, and the "Stove-Sink-Rule" window shows a specific rule in detail.

basically zero. The domain-oriented abstractions contained in the palette enable the designer to think about the problems at the right level of abstraction.

- *Catalog:* Developing a rich knowledge base and supporting reuse and redesign were discussed as important enabling conditions for creativity in section 10.2.2. These are the functions served by the catalog. It characterizes the space of possible designs and gives designers a feel for what kinds of artifacts can be constructed. In the current systems the catalog consists only of a set of drawings—the system has no "understanding" of the objects contained in the catalog. This lack of knowledge implies that an intelligent information retrieval system (Fischer and Nieper-Lemke, 1989) cannot be constructed to assist designers in finding the design that comes closest to their goals.

- *Interaction style:* The direct manipulation style (Hutchins et al., 1986) supported by the design environments allows designers to operate in "world model." They can deal with the objects in the way that they think about them, thereby avoiding the need for manipulating textual descriptions of the objects. Carrying out the construction activities within the JANUS system allows the system to become aware of what the human is doing without requiring additional elaborate procedures to map an external world into the world of the system.

- *Checklist:* The checklist in FRAMER (see Figure 10.5) provides some guidance for designers in carrying out a task. Components of this kind should remain optional, reminding designers of the things they should consider, without imposing a specific way of doing things.

- *Critics:* Critics are a major step for extending construction kits to design environments. They provide the important knowledge-based component that can analyze a specific design and provide feedback (criticism and praise) to the designer. For nontrivial design tasks, they are of crucial importance.

- *Explanation:* Comments and advice provided by the critics are not necessarily understood and an explanation component provides a rationale for the critic's world view.

- *Argumentation:* In design there are no best solutions. Therefore, design environments must acknowledge and support the judgmental nature of design. The goals of our design environments are to inform the designer and to evoke alternative understandings, not authoritarian judgment and decision making.

Further empirical research is needed to determine the precise conditions (with respect to the goals and knowledge of individual designers) under which these environments enhance or hinder creativity.

Let the situation talk back.   Design environments enhance prototyping and allow the "situation to talk back" (Schön, 1983) supporting the incremental construction of models. The critics give designers an opportunity to learn on demand. The argumentative component makes models open, discussable, and defendable. The problem domain level of the interaction illustrates the important relationships and supports not only finding a solution, but allows the designers to convince themselves with less effort that the solution is what they had in mind, to retain solutions with less cognitive effort and to explain it and discuss it with others.

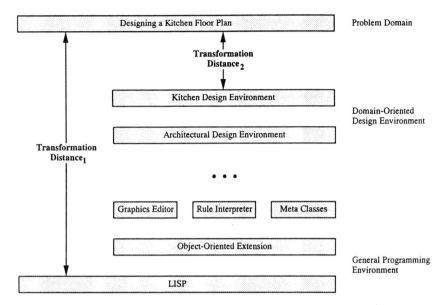

Figure 10.7. Layers of abstraction to reduce the transformation distance between problem domain and system space.

Breakdowns as a source for creativity. The critics indicate to designers that they have violated a design principle. This "breakdown" in construction provides the "knowledge in the world" that serves as the activation pattern for "knowledge in the head" and in the argumentation part of the design environment. Without an integrated system, this synergy cannot be exploited. In many other system building efforts, the development of computer support for construction and argumentation has proceeded in parallel with little or no interaction between them. The former is associated with computer-aided design (CAD), the latter with hypertext—in particular what is known as IBIS hypertext (Conklin, 1987). The major advantage offered by this integration is that designers can work towards the construction of an intelligible entity rather than on the acquisition of knowledge and facts without a context in which they can be immediately used and understood. The integrated design environment presents relevant argumentation when it still makes a difference to the decision taken on the issue. This architecture supports "reflection-in-action" (Schön, 1983; McCall et al., 1989), in which the designer acts and the situation talks back. Without such an environment, designers may not see the unintended consequences of their constructive actions. Schön pointed out that such unintended consequences—pleasant or unpleasant—are the crucial stimulus to reflection. Many problem situations do not speak for themselves, they need a spokesman such as a critic.

Layered architectures. Human problem-domain communication (see Section 10.3.1) turns the computer into an invisible instrument allowing knowledgeable, task-oriented scientists and designers to work with the abstractions and concepts of their domains. To achieve this goal, environments with an underlying layered architecture are needed. Figure 10.7 shows the layered architecture underlying the JANUS system.

Layered architectures support end-user modifiability, because users can change the behavior of the system in the layers near the top allowing them to remain in the context of the problem space. If a change extends beyond the functionality provided by any given layer, users are not immediately thrown back to the system space but can descend one layer at a time.

Augment the skill of designers—do not "de-skill" them. Our design environments are prototypical instances of a class of systems called cooperative problem solving systems (Fischer et al., 1990). These systems are fundamentally different from traditional expert systems (such as MYCIN (Buchanan and Shortliffe, 1984)). Expert systems automate designers' tasks and confront them with solutions, whereas cooperative problem solving systems augment the designers' capabilities and negotiate solutions with them. Systems such as JANUS and FRAMER aim to inform and support the judgment of designers, they do not "de-skill" them by judging or designing for them (Bodker et al., 1988). The designer working with these systems is free to ignore, turn off, or alter the criticism displayed.

Cooperation requires more from a system than having a nice user interface or supporting natural language dialogs. One needs a richer theory of problem solving, which analyzes the functions of shared representations (i.e., models of the communication partner, models of the task), mixed-initiative dialogues, argumentation, and management of trouble. In a cooperative problem solving system, the designer and the system share the problem solving and decision making and different role distributions may be chosen depending on the user's knowledge, the user's goals and the task domain. A cooperative system requires much richer communication facilities than the ones that were offered by traditional expert systems. Any cooperative system raises the important questions regarding which part of the responsibility has to be exercised by human beings and which part by the system and how things should be organized so that the intelligent part of the automatic system can communicate effectively with the human part of the intelligent system.

10.5 Conclusion

Creativity enhancing environments need to be different from traditional computer systems. Architectures must be developed that will put the domain experts into the driver's seat and that will allow them to make major contributions to the development of domain-specific design environments (Gero, 1989). Many intellectual disciplines (such as architectural design, programming, composing, writing, etc.) should not remain primarily "spectator sports" done by a few and observed by many. Convivial tools (Illich, 1973) are needed to break down the boundary between programming and using programs. Our design environments are a step in this direction. We are convinced that the texture of the computer tools of the future will depend on the people who design and use them. To the extent that domain experts from different disciplines (e.g., artistic, musical, and literary people) will find it worthwhile to become computer-literate and make use of the new medium, the medium itself will reflect the wide range of human experience. Computer systems will lack those qualities if we isolate such people from computers.

Acknowledgments. The author would like to thank Andreas Lemke, who developed the FRAMER system, Anders Morch, who developed the JANUS system, Andreas Girgensohn, who extended JANUS to be modifiable by end-users, and Raymond McCall, who provided invaluable insights in architectural design issues and their support through hypertext systems. Hal Eden and Christian Rathke provided valuable comments on an earlier draft of the chapter. The research was partially supported by grant No. IRI-8722792 from the National Science Foundation, grant No. MDA903-86-C0143 from the Army Research Institute, grants from the Intelligent Systems Group at NYNEX and from Software Research Associates (SRA), Tokyo, and support from Artur Fischer.

References

Bentley, J. L. (1986). Document design, *Communications of the ACM* **29**(9): 832–839.

Bodker, S., Knudsen, J. L., Kyng, M., Ehn, P., & Madsen, K. H. (1988). Computer support for cooperative design, *Proceedings of the Conference on Computer-Supported Cooperative Work* (CSCW'88), ACM, New York, pp. 377–394.

Boecker, H.-D., Fischer, G., & Nieper, H. (1986). The enhancement of understanding through visual representations, *Human Factors in Computing Systems*, CHI'86 Conference Proceedings (Boston, MA), ACM, New York, pp. 44–50.

Buchanan, B. G., & Shortliffe, E. H. (1984). Human engineering of medical expert systems, *in* B. G. Buchanan, & E. H. Shortliffe (Eds), *Rule-Based Expert*

Systems: The MYCIN Experiments of the Stanford Heuristic Programming Project, Addison-Wesley Publishing Company, Reading, Massachusetts, pp. 599-612.

Cherry, L. (1981). *Computer Aids for Writers*, Proceedings of the ACM SIGPLAN SIGOA Symposion on Text Manipulation, Portland, Oregon, pp. 61-67.

Conklin, J. (1987). Hypertext: An introduction and survey, *IEEE Computer* **20**(9): 17-41.

Curtis, B., Krasner, N., & Iscoe, N. (1988). A field study of the software design process for large systems, *CACM* **31**(11): 1268-1287.

di Sessa, A., & Abelson, H. (1986). Boxer: A reconstructible computational medium, *CACM* **29**(9): 859-868.

Fischer, G. (1987a). A critic for LISP, *in* J. McDermott (Ed.), *Proceedings of the 10th International Joint Conference on Artificial Intelligence* (Milan, Italy), Morgan Kaufmann, Los Altos, California, pp. 177-184.

Fischer, G. (1987b). Cognitive view of reuse and redesign, *IEEE Software*, Special Issue on Reusability, **4**(4): 60-72.

Fischer, G., Lemke, A. C., Mastaglio, T., & Morch, A. (1990). Critics: An emerging approach to knowledge-based human computer interaction, *Human Factors in Computing Systems*, CHI'90 Conference Proceedings (Seattle, WA), ACM, New York (forthcoming).

Fischer G., & Girgensohn, A. (1990). End-user modifiability in design environments, *Human Factors in Computing Systems*, CHI'90 Conference Proceedings (Seattle, WA), ACM, New York (forthcoming).

Fischer, G., & Lemke, A. C. (1988). Construction kits and design environments: Steps toward human problem-domain communication, *Human-Computer Interaction* **3**(3): 179-222.

Fischer, G., & Lemke, A. C. (1989). Knowledge-based design environments for user interface design, Submitted to the *12th International Conference on Software Engineering*.

Fischer, G., & Mastaglio, T. (1989). Computer-based critics, *Proceedings of the 22nd Annual Hawaii Conference on System Sciences, Volume III: Decision Support and Knowledge Based Systems Track*, IEEE Computer Society, pp. 427-436.

Fischer, G., McCall, R., & Morch, A. (1989). Design environments for constructive and argumentative design, *Human Factors in Computing Systems*, CHI'89 Conference Proceedings (Austin, TX), ACM, New York, pp. 269-275.

Fischer, G., & Nieper-Lemke, H. (1989). HELGON: extending the retrieval by reformulation paradigm, *Human Factors in Computing Systems*, CHI'89 Conference Proceedings (Austin, TX), ACM, New York, pp. 357-362.

Gero, J. S. (1989). A locus for knowledge-based systems in CAAD Education, *in* M. McCullough, W. Mitchell, & P. Purcell (Eds), *CAAD Futures '89*, Harvard University, Cambridge, unnumbered.

Hayes, J. R. (1978). *Cognitive Psychology—Thinking and Creating*, Dorsey Press, Homewood, Illinois.

Hutchins, E. L., Hollan, J. D., & Norman, D. A. (1986). Direct manipulation interfaces, *in* D. A. Norman, & S. W. Draper (Eds), *User Centered System Design, New Perspectives on Human-Computer Interaction*, Lawrence Erlbaum Associates, Hillsdale, New Jersey, pp. 87-124.

Illich, I. (1973). *Tools for Conviviality*, Harper and Row, New York.

Jacob, (1977). Evolution and tinkering, *Science*, pp. 1161–1166.

Kaplan, C. A., & Simon, H. A. (1989). In search of insight, *Technical Report*, Carnegie-Mellon University, Pittsburgh.

Lemke, A. C. (1989). *Design Environments for High-Functionality Computer Systems*, Unpublished Ph.D. Dissertation, Department of Computer Science, University of Colorado.

McCall, R., Fischer, G., & Morch, A. (1989). Supporting reflection-in-action in the JANUS design environment, *in*, M. McCullough, W. Mitchell, & P. Purcell (Eds), *CAAD Futures '89*, Havard University, Cambridge, unnumbered.

Newell, A., & Simon, H. A. (1975). Computer science as empirical inquiry: Symbols and search, *Communications of the ACM* **19**(3): 113–126.

Norman, D. A. (1988). *The Psychology of Everyday Things*, Basic Books, New York.

Papert, S. (1986). Constructionism: A new opportunity for elementary science education, *Proposal to the National Science Foundation*, MIT—The Media Laboratory, Cambridge, Massachusetts.

Rittel, H. W. J. (1972). On the planning crisis: Systems analysis of the first and second generations, *Bedriftsokonomen* **8**: 390–396.

Schön, D. A. (1983). *The Reflective Practitioner: How Professionals Think in Action*, Basic Books, New York.

Simon, H. A. (1973). The structure of ill-structured problems, *Artificial Intelligence*, No. 4.

Simon, H. A. (1981). *The Sciences of the Artificial*, MIT Press, Cambridge, Massachusetts.

Simon, H. A. (1986). Whether software engineering needs to be artificially intelligent, *IEEE Transactions on Software Engineering* **SE-12**(7): 726–732.

Walker, J. H. (1987). Document examiner: Delivery interface for Hypertext documents, *Hypertext'87 Papers*, University of North Carolina, Chapel Hill, NC, pp. 307–323.

Walker, J. H. (1988). Supporting document development with Concordia, *IEEE Computer* **21**(1): 48–59.

11 Knowledge-Based Systems for Creativity

Ernest Edmonds

Knowledge-based systems have introduced a new mechanism for the support of creativity. Where experts interact with a knowledge base in order to externalize and refine their knowledge they are involved in a process of coming to new understandings. It is that process that is a significant trigger for creative thought. The creative processes that can result from this approach can exist in a wide variety of fields. Two examples have been studied. One is a case study of a scientist accelerating the generation of new ideas and the other, which is reported here, is the development of a new form of computer-generated video using precisely the same knowledge-based system approach.

11.1 Introduction

The advent of knowledge-based systems has introduced a new mechanism for the support of creativity. Where experts interact with a knowledge base in order to externalize and refine their knowledge, or one might say their understanding of the problem in hand, they are involved in a process that is rather different to any that has preceded it. The very activity of expressing that knowledge in machine usable form, of running the system and so instantly seeing the consequences of revising the knowledge, and, hence, coming to new understandings, are significant triggers of creative thought. These activities also provide new ways of thinking about problems

259

and thereby may lead to new classes of solution to the problems tackled. The creative processes that can result from this approach can exist in a wide variety of fields. Two examples have been studied by way of illustration of the power and the breadth of the possibilities. One is a case study of a scientist accelerating her creative advances and the other, which is reported here, is the development of a new form of computer-generated video using precisely the same knowledge-based system approach.

The invention of the computer was clearly a very important step for our society, but understanding just what that importance amounts to is rather difficult. Our conception of what a computer actually is can be confused and its name does not help. 'Computer' sounds like a machine for computation but, although it is true that it can compute, it has no special relationship to arithmetic. The computer is a general purpose logical machine that in principle, given clever enough programming, can perform any formally describable symbol manipulation task. We know, of course, that we can connect all manner of devices to these machines, relating the symbols to the devices so that actions can automatically be generated in the devices. For example, we are continually confronted by images on screens that computers have constructed and very often we can use keyboards, joysticks, 'mice,' and so on to manipulate them. The provision of these facilities to us is the concern of the computer-human interface, that is, that part of the system that we can observe and handle, together with the methods that enable us to use it.

Research into human-computer interaction can have a variety of aims but a major one, and one that is relevant to this discussion, is to give people access to the full power of the computer; that is, to enable noncomputing specialists to use the full range of its possibilities for their particular purposes.

Human-computer interaction research is very much concerned with designing and design method. From this point of view alone it clearly links with the general activity of design but even more significantly it is specially placed to offer advances to both art and design. Some, such as three dimensional visualization, are well known but the possibilities go beyond these current influences; in particular the developments in knowledge-based systems have profound implications. Much of the work is exploratory and creative and a basic premise is that systems must be constructed to demonstrate the ideas and results and make use of whichever method is appropriate for a particular task, be it brainstorming or a highly controlled experiment. In that sense, the underlying philosophy is that the artifact itself embodies ideas and theories. This raises issues, not only about the methods employed but the nature of such scientific inquiry itself (Carroll and Campbell, 1989). The relationships between artifacts, ideas and theories is, of course, a familiar topic of debate in art and in design.

A careful study of the activities of design and of the theories used to explain it shows much in common with certain scientific activities (Coyne, 1988). Computer-based support systems for the creative design process are, however, much more familiar than such systems for the creative scientific process. The use of knowledge-based systems and the process of knowledge externalization and refinement would seem to offer a possibility of bringing these theoretically similar activities closer in practice.

11.2 Human-computer interaction and knowledge

It is interesting to notice that whenever people have used computers to help them with something that they had done before without such an aid, they tend to reflect on and change their practice. In large organizations it is common for people to suggest that the process of computerizing some function is more beneficial because of this reflection than because of the direct improvements that the computer brings. This effect has normally been noticed in relation to rather low level procedures but there is every reason to believe that it is much more important than that.

In one view, we perceive and know the world around us in terms of what we are able to construct within the language that we have available to us (Bruner, 1986). Language is meant here, of course, in the broadest sense and the very concept of the computer adds to it. Thus, it may not simply be that introducing a computer causes us to look more carefully at what we do, it could also be that it causes us to see our world differently. In particular, the use of computers in art and design may change the nature of those creative processes or extend their scope. Partly, this point must be made about any new tool but the computer is rather special. Its impact is likely to be much less on the way we handle materials and perceive our physical world and much more on our thinking processes and how we conceive that world (Edmonds, 1987).

Some of the most interesting research into computer-human interaction that is taking place at this time is concerned with enabling the computer user to express, review, and develop explicit descriptions of their understanding of whatever subject they are concerned with (Candy and O'Brien, 1989). In our case, the subject could be, for example, the principles of design in buildings for energy saving, the constraints of a particular site on a proposed building, or the underlying structure of a film that is being made. A key point about such descriptions is that they can be used by the computer to search for their implications, to interpret data, or to produce solutions, that is, construct work. For the most part, these uses of the descriptions can be put into effect in seconds. Thus, the designer or artist can use the computer to explore their understanding just as they can explore the appearance of three dimensional objects using the computer graphics system mentioned earlier. Although this research does not provide us with a computational model of creativity, it provides evidence, about what supports creativity, that can assist us in creating such a model. Moreover, it shows that employing a computational model of a problem can benefit the creative process.

As this aspect of computing advances and becomes more sophisticated, we are likely to modify our approach to art and design. These developments encourage an explicit concern for underlying structures and their relationship to form in addition to the surface level issues that many traditional tools support. We can expect to come to new understandings of the relationships between artifacts, ideas, and theories because of these increased concerns.

In what follows, two examples are discussed. The first is in the domain of science and is concerned with the exploration of theory against evidence and with the creative process that leads to new or revised theory. The second, which is covered more fully, is in fine art and is concerned with the development of a new style of computer generated video. In both cases a computer support system is used in which knowledge, or understandings, can be expressed and can then be used to explore the implications against evidence, be it collected empirical data or the resulting artifact.

A specific case of knowledge-based support for creativity in science has been studied in some detail (Edmonds, 1989c). The problem lies outside the domain of design but is easily seen to illustrate the scenario indicated in the introduction and the conclusions clearly apply on a fairly wide front.

The case studied was where a highly expert phonetician was attempting to externalize and extend her knowledge concerning the interpretation of a representation of sound signals known to have been caused by human speech, but where the speaker is unknown. In effect, she was trying to encode into the system her own knowledge about speech events that can be detected by inspecting the speech signal. The interpretation of the signal is complex and even a matter of dispute amongst experts. Thus, a most significant aspect of this process was the confirmation, development, and correction of that knowledge (Connolly et al., 1986). This is a creative process, of course, with much in common with design in terms of both its attractive nature and the unpredictability of the outcome.

The results of this study demonstrated that the scientist's performance, as a creative person, was improved by using the knowledge-based support system but also identified requirements that must be met in order to achieve such a result. One important and relevant requirement was that the user needed fast and reliable access to full descriptions of the relevant information and proposed solutions. It was the case that the same point arose in the fine art example discussed later.

11.3 An example from fine art

The author has been concerned for some time with work in an art medium that has become known as 'Video Constructs' (Edmonds, 1989a, 1989b). These pieces are time-based, that is, they exist in time just as music and film do. The concrete and final destination of the images is on a video monitor and they are synthesized by a specially constructed computer system called VICOM, which is described later. In no sense whatever are the images seen on the screen a view of some other reality. They do not represent paintings or drawings any more than they relate to images seen in television news programs. The work is concerned with precisely what exists on the monitor. However, the fact that it is generated through a computer system allows considerable attention to be paid to the structures that underlie the images, and their movement in time. In contrast to much of the geometric-based work, the image is not a view of an abstract world. In video constructs, the logic in the computer provides the underlying structure that leads to the form of the work (Edmonds, 1988). The image on the screen is the concrete reality.

To take a specific example, the video construct 'Jasper' (Edmonds, first shown at the International Conference on Electronic Art, Utrecht, 1988) is based on a number of overlapping squares of reducing dimensions, each of a different grey tone. The work starts with the grey levels stepping evenly from black to white, starting with the largest square and ending with the smallest. This order is disrupted at the beginning and the work proceeds in a search for a new resolution and it is the search itself that is the basis of the work. The image pulsates as the tones shift between the static squares in a way that is, perhaps, closer to the so-called minimalist music than normal video material (Figure 11.1).

In a more recent example, 'fragments ver.5' (Edmonds, first shown in *Reviews: Contemporary Systematic and Constructive Arts*, Small Mansion Arts Center, London, 1989), a matrix of squares is explored in a similar way, except in color. Here, the piece moves through a portion of the color space. Although the local rate of change can be fast, with some specific images only lasting for a fraction of a second, the general shift of color is slow enough for

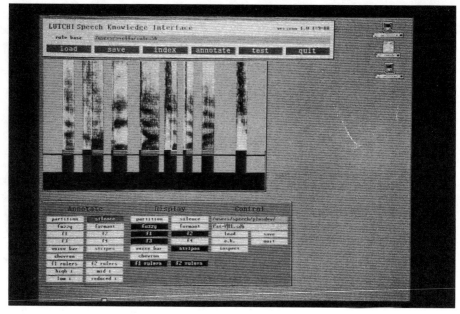

Figure 11.1. The video construct 'Jasper'.

the work to be quite different in the midafternoon to midmorning. This work, therefore, cannot be seen very satisfactorily in the context of, for example, film. Rather, it is a changing exhibit having, perhaps, more in common with light dappling on water as the sun slowly rises and eventually sets than with the simple geometry that is, at first sight, its basis (Figure 11.2). A work such as this can be transformed into a miniature exhibit by use of a small screen, as was done using a 7.5 cm color monitor for the exhibition 'Avant Garde 90' held in the Manège, Moscow, 1990.

A third example is 'Rotterdam' (Edmonds, first shown at the 3rd PRO Conference, Constructivism: Man versus Environment, held at the World Trade Centre, Rotterdam, 1989). This is a short piece intended for continuous viewing. Here, four matrices are seen together, each one changing in a different way. The effect is something like that of having four instruments playing together in music (Figures 11.3 and 11.4). In all of these works, as was mentioned earlier, the logic of descriptions held in a computer provides the underlying structure that leads to the form of the work. These descriptions use a rule-based representation of the fundamental features of the relevant work and constitute an unambiguous definition of it. However, despite the fact that the works progress in time, the description is not procedural. In fact it constitutes a declarative definition of the structure of the work. It might be thought to be closer to the ideas that underlie the

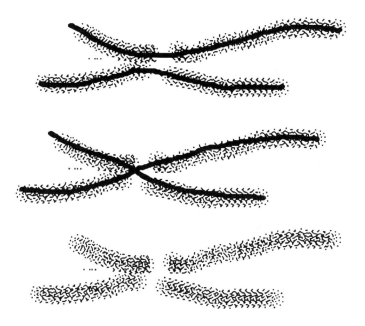

Figure 11.2. 'Fragments ver.5'.

video construct than to its realization; although very concrete issues, such as the precise colors to be used, are included in the structural description. The relationship between the descriptions and the works are discussed in the next section.

The use of a complete and concise description of the structure of the work is fundamental to the approach to supporting creativity described here. It is a question of making new possibilities available in terms of the language that can be used to describe the works and hence in which to think about them. The computer is not used just to provide more computational power in order to accelerate an existing process. It enables a new language to be used and hence a new structuring of the search space. It is in this sense that a new paradigm for creativity is introduced, because the computer support involved offers the user new ways of thinking about the problem rather than simply a faster or more accurate process. More concise representations than were available before enable new thinking to take place. Naturally, a key factor in bringing this advance into practical use is the rapid feedback from idea to concrete implication that the computer system described later offers.

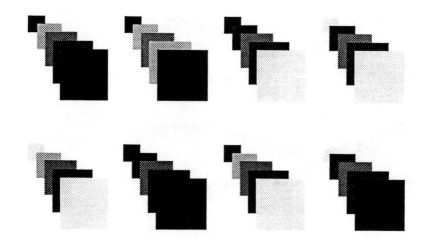

Figure 11.3. 'Rotterdam'.

11.4   A computer support system for video art

The VICOM system is based on a MacII computer with an IO research computer graphics subsystem and a Roland D-110 sound system. The IO research system consists of a frame buffer and palette with a full set of raster operations that are made available as PROLOG predicates in the MacII. Transformations have been implemented between the Munsell color system (ASTM, 1980) and the RGB values that drive the calibrated monitor. A key element in the system is the use of controlled backtracking to produce extended pieces based on structures that can be specified declaratively in the extended PROLOG.

The high level and terse descriptions of the underlying structures of the work are very important in enabling the artist to pay considerable attention to deeper aspects of the work videos. The rapid feedback available, in the instant generation of videos or video segments from the descriptions, enables extensive exploration by the user of the implications of the descriptions against the evidence of the resulting artifact. Thus an interesting relationship exists between the computer-based system and the artist. The artist proposes structures that might satisfy the artistic goals which, at their highest level, may not be stated or, possibly, even able to be stated. These structures can contain any explicit declarations that are appropriate including, for example, constraints that must be placed on any solution. The VICOM system then provides the solution implied by this description for evaluation by the user. The artist, however, does not simply rate the

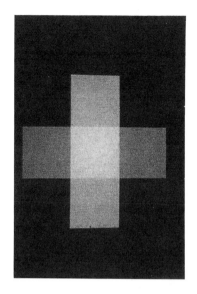
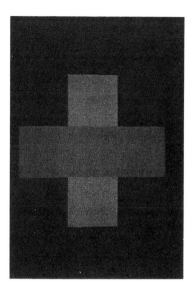
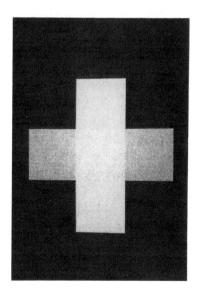

Figure 11.4. 'Rotterdam'.

solution good or bad, but reflects on the proposed structure in relation to that solution. In other words, the explicit nature of the specification of the structure, and the rapid feedback of its implications in terms of solutions, enables the artist to think in a new way, that might be thought of as at a 'higher level.' This is precisely the same process observed in the case of the scientist discussed earlier. Implicit views can become explicit, and hence available, for consideration and evaluation. For example, the speech scientist said of the structural aspect of her thinking:

> I am not conscious of a personal hierarchy of cues, but my reaction to the inappropriate identification of some phonemes [... by the system, using her rules ...] has made me aware that I have an implicit hierarchy. I had previously considered the order of actions in my annotation procedure to be partially driven by the needs of the system ... and subsequently to have become formalized as a routine to ensure that all of the appropriate annotations were made and none forgotten. ... [I]t became apparent that the annotation routine displayed a logical progression and was not an ad hoc series of steps.

Enabling the formalization of thoughts held implicitly offers the scientist, as much as the artist, the opportunity to explore his/her thinking in ways not available before.

11.5   Reflections on the creative process

It is interesting to reflect on the creative process of designing video constructs in more detail. Although the case described is only a single example, it is, nevertheless, illuminating as a model for new paradigms for creativity that arise from the provision of computer support.

No drawings or images are directly used in the creation of a video construct. Instead, rules about images are expressed in an extension of PROLOG. These rules are of a number of types. Those employed so far, in the works mentioned earlier, determine the combination of picture elements to be employed, the relationships between them, the set of colors to be used and their deployment over the picture elements. Clearly, the notion of these rules draws on Gips and Stiny's work on what they termed 'shape grammars' (Stiny and Gips, 1972; Stiny, 1975). The rules can be thought of as generative specifications of sets of images. Thus, for example, given that the image is specified in terms of the elements of a specific grid, a rule of the second type might specify which elements in the grid might coexist in a single image or, equally, which ones may not coexist at the same moment. The key point here is that the artist must state the underlying structures and rules being employed precisely. The process of stating this information is, itself, a creative act, as is demonstrated.

Now, when the system has been provided with the rules that define the structures to be employed it can run those rules, of course, and so explore the possible consequences of them. The most significant issue, here, is the instant realization of the concrete implications of the underlying structure; it is possible to create or modify the structure and then directly view the implied video construct. When compared to conventional methods for making film, for example, or even paintings, the process of moving between abstract ideas and their concrete realization is changed by a factor that is large enough to affect the nature of the process. The issue here is the very rapid process of the realization of the actual visual images.

It is necessary, at this point, to consider the time-based aspect of the video construct in more detail because it is not possible to explain the artist's creative process without reference to it. The dynamics of the video can be seen as a representation of the search for a particular image through the search space of a set of images. Thus, in this view, the rules specify the search space which could be, for example, images composed of colored squares on a four by four grid in which a particular subset of squares are always the same color and where the color space is some given subset of all possible colors. Added to the rules are then the goal image, which will become the last frame of the video, and the starting point of the search, the first frame of the video. The inference strategy then determines the search path through the space and the video construct consists of a representation of that search. In the works completed so far, the standard PROLOG inference engine has been employed, although some experimentation is underway using alternatives. However, the search strategy is determined in detail in PROLOG, of course, by the ordering of the rules and by their hierarchical structure. Therefore, the fundamental structures that define the works are expressed in terms of all of these factors.

It is clear that the methods used here for formulating the underlying structures of the works in question differ from traditional ones and so offer a new way of formulating the artist's goals. An entirely traditional aspect of this process, however, is that the artist acts as evaluator. A simple view of the process is as follows:

1. Artist defines the underlying structure for a work,

2. computer system realizes the implied work,

3. artist evaluates the result,

4. the work is complete, or

5. artist modifies structure and returns to 2.

The evaluation process is not, of course, a simple matter of producing a yes/no result. An understanding of the relationships between the structures and their concrete implications is built up through the act of evaluation. Thus the evaluation amounts to a reconsideration of the artist's goals as expressed in the system. In practice it is quite easy to predict the nature of individual frames of the video; indeed these are typically worked on through drawing, in the traditional way, before coming to the system. The much more difficult part is dealing with the dynamic behavior of the piece. Thus, the normal result of evaluation is a modification to the search strategy, that is, a change to the order or structure of the rules.

It is interesting to consider the relationship between the refinement of the artist's goals, as expressed in the system, and the more general development of artistic ideas. As was indicated in the previous section, implicit ideas are made explicit by this process. Thus, ideas that the artist might be said to have, by being made explicit, become available for inspection and reflection. The evaluation and refinement process can be looked on, therefore, as one in which the artist is able to reflect on issues previously hidden from view. It is in this respect in particular that the approach of using knowledge-based system support for creativity enables something new. Perhaps the most appropriate way of characterizing this innovation is to say that it enables the artist to manipulate the work at a higher level. The abstract structures that underpin the work are brought closer to the visual reality that they imply in terms of the artist's understanding. That understanding comprises a set of responses including expression, emotion, perception, and formal understanding in the full aesthetic sense.

11.6   Conclusion

What has become clear, through the experience described earlier, is that a very detailed technical control of the computer system is as important in producing video constructs as control over oil paint is when producing oil paintings. Having control is largely a matter of the availability of descriptions that are clear and brief enough to be understood. The most exciting element of the constructive video is the careful and very terse way in which a specification of what occurs in time is possible. The brevity of the specification is extremely important in the development of ideas. The inevitable exploration is so strongly supported by this aspect of the use of the computer that new ways of thinking about work emerge in their very construction.

The exploration of speech science and of constructive video work enabled by modern computer technology is more than a way of doing those things. The conceptual development that goes along with the science and art practice is something new itself and that has implications far beyond these two instances. The new understandings will inevitably influence art science and design in ways that have yet to be realized.

Acknowledgments. The construction of the VICOM system was greatly assisted by André Schappo and Ronnier Luo. The work has been partly funded by the UK's Alvey Program under contract MMI/062.

References

ASTM (1980). *D1535-80*, Annual Book of ASTM Standards, ASTM.

Bruner, J. (1986). *Actual Minds, Possible Worlds*, Harvard University Press, Massachusetts.

Candy, L., & O'Brien, S. (1989). The speech exemplar case study, *Internal Report*, LUTCHI Research Centre, Loughborough University of Technology.

Carroll, J. M., & Campbell, R. L. (1989). Artifacts as psychological theories: The case of human-computer interaction, *Behavior and Information Technology* **8**: 247–252.

Connolly, J. H., Edmonds, E. A., Guzy, J. J., Johnson, S. R., & Woodcock, A. (1986). Automatic speech recognition based on spectrogram reading, *International Journal of Man-Machine Studies* **24**: 611–622.

Coyne, R. (1988). *Logic Models of Design*, Pitman, London.

Edmonds, E. A. (1987). Beyond Computable Numbers: An Inaugural Lecture, Loughborough University of Technology, Loughborough.

Edmonds, E. A. (1988). Logic and time-based art practice, *Leonardo*, Supplementary Issue on Electronic Art, pp. 19–20.

Edmonds, E. A. (1989a). Vers vidó constructs, *Mesures Art International, No. 3*, Liège.

Edmonds, E. A. (1989b). Constructing with computers, *Art Monthly* **129**: 12–13.

Edmonds, E. A. (1989c). Intelligent measurement and sensing systems: Speech knowledge externalization, *Proceedings of Advances in the Science, Technology and Engineering of Instrumentation*, Australasian Instrumentation and Measurement Conference, Adelaide.

Stiny, G. (1975). *Pictorial and Formal Aspects of Shape and Shape Grammars*, Birkhäuser and Verlag, Basel.

Stiny, G., & Gips, J. (1972). Shape grammars and the generative specification of painting and sculpture, *in* C. V. Freiman (Ed.), *Information Processing 71*, North-Holland, Amsterdam, pp. 125–135.

12 Inducing Optimally Directed Non-Routine Designs

Jonathan Cagan and Alice M. Agogino

Non-routine designs are characterized by the creation of new variables and thus an expansion of the design space. These differ from routine designs in that the latter are restricted to a fixed set of variables and thus a predefined design space. In previous works, we have described the 1^{st}PRINCE non-routine design methodology that expands the design space in such a way that optimal trends dictate the direction and form of this expansion. In this chapter, we examine how inductive techniques can determine these optimal trends. The induction techniques in 1^{st}PRINCE utilize constraint information from monotonicity analysis to determine how to mutate the design space. The process observes the constraint information of mutated designs and induces trends from those constraints. Those trends and the creation of new variables may potentially demonstrate creative designs. An interesting application of the 1^{st}PRINCE concepts to determine the optimally directed shape of a spinning square block, such that resistance to spinning is minimized, leads to the discovery of a circular wheel.

12.1 Introduction

Non-routine designs differ from routine designs in that the latter are based on features from a previous design whereas the former are characterized by an expanded set of features. Non-routine designs can be viewed as innovative

273

or creative, depending on the relationship of the expanded knowledge to the original design space. We define innovative designs as designs that are original but related to some previous prototype, perhaps by mutation operators or other techniques to manipulate and expand the design space. Creative designs are not obviously based on existing prototypes, perhaps requiring outside knowledge to create an entirely new prototype.

Our definitions of design levels are based on artifact rather than process, the latter utilized in the definitions of Coyne, Rosenman, Radford, and Gero (1987) and Brown and Chandrasekaran (1983).[1] Innovative design processes may produce designs that can be interpreted as creative or routine, as can creative design processes produce innovative or routine designs. Thus to classify a design process as non-routine does not guarantee that the resulting design will be non-routine. However, if the artifact itself is classified then we know (given our opinion of non-routine designs) whether the artifact already exists or whether it is based on some existing artifact or altogether different artifact. Certain types of processes may lend themselves to produce designs of a certain class: parametric variation often leads to routine designs (Choy and Agogino, 1986); manipulation of prototypes can lead to innovative designs (Cagan and Agogino, 1987, 1988); expansion of the design space by incorporating outside information (Gero et al., 1988) and perturbation of design variables (Freudenstein and Maki, 1983) may lead to creative artifacts. However, there is no guarantee that they will produce such designs.

In this chapter we demonstrate how inductive techniques can aid in producing non-routine designs. The 1stPRINCE (FIRST PRINciple Computational Evaluator) (Cagan and Agogino, 1987, 1988; Cagan, 1990) process has been presented for use in discovering innovative designs. Competitive designs should be optimally directed (Agogino et. al., 1989) and thus 1stPRINCE uses optimization information to make decisions on how to manipulate the design space. Although parametric optimization is traditionally used for routine design when the set of variables defining the problem is fixed, 1stPRINCE utilizes optimization techniques to direct the expansion of the design space and create new variables. During the 1stPRINCE analysis much can be learned about the design itself. The inductive technique we present in this chapter observes a sequence of improved designs and recognizes the trend of a final optimally directed design. For example, in Cagan and Agogino (1988), 1stPRINCE derives a stepped beam to resist a flexural load. In the limit the optimally directed solution is a tapered beam rather than a stepped beam. Our inductive mechanism can recognize these trends and induce the

---

[1] Note that although Coyne et al. defined design based on process, they are concerned with processes which lead to designs of a certain class which is similar to our interpretation; whereas Brown and Chandrasekaran classified design via the novelty of the actual process.

tapered beam result (Cagan, 1990).

Pursuing the beam example further, because the knowledge base initially has no knowledge about tapered beams, but rather only about a solid cylindrical beam, the tapered result is a non-routine product from the method with new radial and longitudinal variables created. Creativity is based on the knowledge of the system, and thus the resulting designs may potentially be considered creative.

This chapter reviews the 1stPRINCE methodology and discusses the importance of constraint activity. Next the concept of induction is discussed and we show how non-routine design methodologies such as 1stPRINCE can utilize inductive techniques on constraint activity to induce optimally directed trends. An interesting and important example of how the 1stPRINCE methodology, by utilizing inductive techniques, can create a wheel from a square block of material is demonstrated. Finally we discuss how inductive techniques can be further examined to aid in creative design.

12.2   1stPRINCE

1stPRINCE (Cagan and Agogino, 1987, 1988; Cagan, 1990) innovates structural designs by reasoning from first principle knowledge to discover new design prototypes. Design problems are formulated as optimization problems and qualitative optimization techniques are utilized to search the design space. If resulting artifacts are not satisfactory, then 1stPRINCE manipulates the design space by techniques such as division of critical integrals, in an optimally directed manner. New variables are introduced to expand the design space and the problem is reformulated to search for improved designs.

Design knowledge is input to 1stPRINCE in the form of engineering equations (engineering first principles), as a symbolic optimization problem, which represents a good initial design we call a primitive-prototype. This primitive prototype includes, in equation form, the objective function and all equality and inequality constraints that define and limit the proposed solution and are expressed in terms of the variables relevant to its geometry. The process then utilizes the qualitative techniques of monotonicity analysis, as derived from the Karush-Kuhn-Tucker (KKT) conditions of optimality by Papalambros and Wilde (1988) and implemented for AI applications by Choy and Agogino (1986), and symbolic optimization, as implemented by Agogino and Almgren (1987), in the SYMON/SYMFUNE programs. Given the following definitions, we introduce the rules of monotonicity analysis as utilized by the 1stPRINCE methodology:

- The *monotonicity* of a continuously differentiable function $f(x)$ with respect to variable x_k is the algebraic sign of $\partial f/\partial x_k$. (Note: the problem need not be formulated with equations for monotonicity analysis; only the relative increase or decrease of one variable with changes in another need be specified. Thus the monotonicity concept can be applied equally well to noncontinuous functions.)

- A constraint $g_i(x) \leq (\geq)0$ is *active* at x_0 if $g_i(x_0) = 0$. A constraint $g_i(x) \leq (\geq)0$ is *inactive* at x_0 if $g_i(x_0) < (>)0$.

- A positive variable x_k is said to be *bounded above* by a constraint $g_i(x) \leq 0$ if it achieves its maximum value at strict equality, that is, when the constraint is active. A positive variable x_k is *bounded below* by $g_i(x) \leq 0$ if it achieves its minimum value at strict equality.

Three rules of monotonicity analysis that define well-constrained optimization problems without overconstrained cases (Papalambros and Wilde, 1988) are given as:

- *Rule One.* If the objective function is monotonic with respect to a variable, then there exists at least one active constraint which bounds the variable in the direction opposite of the objective. A constraint is active if it acts at its lower or upper bound.

- *Rule Two.* If a variable is not contained in the objective function then it must be either bounded from both above and below by active constraints or not actively bounded at all (i.e., any constraints monotonic with respect to that variable must be inactive or irrelevant.)

- *Rule Three* (The Maximum Activity Principle). The number of non-redundant active constraints cannot exceed the total number of variables.

Figure 12.1 shows a qualitative description of the meaning of the first two rules. The weight of a solid round beam under flexural load is minimized as a function of radius (r) given constraints on minimum radius (r_{min}) and maximum bending stress (σ_{max}). To minimize the weight the radius tends to 0 (Figure 12.1a). However, as radius approaches 0 it reaches a lower bound at r_{min}, preventing the solution from becoming degenerate, as dictated by the first rule. Figure 12.1b demonstrates the second rule; as radius goes to 0, the maximum bending stress increases toward infinity. The stress is blocked by the yield stress (σ_y), which is not in the objective function, to prevent the problem from becoming unbounded.

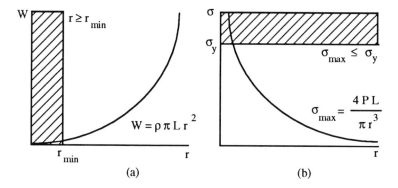

Figure 12.1. Qualitative representation of the first (a) and second (b) rules of monotonicity.

A *candidate solution* from a monotonicity analysis is defined as the objective function, relevant equality constraints, and active inequality constraints. A *prototype* is defined as a candidate solution from the analysis on a primitive-prototype which can be instantiated to at least one artifact.

1^{st}PRINCE includes a set of very general heuristics to manipulate mathematical quantities that mutate the design space. If solutions do not satisfy design criteria or the designer is not satisfied with the resulting artifact, then 1^{st}PRINCE applies these heuristics to expand the design space and direct the process of innovating new designs. The main manipulation in 1^{st}PRINCE is a technique called Dimensional Variable Expansion (DVE) (Cagan, 1990). DVE creates new variables that can expand the design space directed toward improving the objective. Intuitively, DVE can be understood as *integral division*; a continuous integral of a function of variables c and w can be divided into a series of continuous integrals over smaller ranges as:

$$\int_{z_0}^{z_n} f_i(\chi, w)dw = \int_{z_0}^{z_n} f_i(\chi^1, w)dw + \int_{z_1}^{z_2} f_i(\chi^m, w)dw$$
$$+ \cdots + \int_{z_{n-1}}^{z_n} f_i(\chi^m, w)dw \qquad (12.1)$$

where m is the number of divisions. If the objective function for an optimization formulation of a design problem is in integral form as described by the left-hand-side of equation (12.1), then it can be divided into a summation of integrals as demonstrated in the right-hand-side of equation (12.1). By permitting the properties of the integrals to be independent, new regions are formed in a body and new design variables $\chi^1, \chi^2, \ldots, \chi^m, z_1, z_2, \ldots, z_{n-1}$, are introduced. This new set of variables may have an improving effect on the objective function and designs from this expanded space of variables may be superior in the objective to designs from the previous, reduced design space.

Cagan (1990) showed that during this expansion, the degree-of-freedom (DOF) of the design prototypes of dominant constraint activity and of the feasible space of designs will be maintained or increased under certain restrictions; the *feasible design space* is the design space of feasible candidate solutions to the optimization problem. Increase in DOF is an indication of the potential for discovering innovative or creative designs.

1^{st}PRINCE can be applied to a design problem that can be formulated in the form of an optimization problem; that is, has an objective function and constraints. Further, the problem must be formulated such that manipulation of some variable will have an analogous physical manipulation that would potentially improve the objective function. In order for the fundamental heuristic of integral division to be applicable, some equation must appear in integral form as either the objective or a constraint. In practically all structures problems, some quantity appears as an integral (such as volume, weight, load distribution, stress distribution); thus this is not a limitation in the structures domain.

When applied to a solid round beam under torsion load 1^{st}PRINCE discovers a hollow tube and a composite rod, both solutions given in closed form (Cagan and Agogino, 1987). Application of 1^{st}PRINCE to a beam under flexural load leads to a stepped beam (Cagan and Agogino, 1988) when dividing the integral over the length of the beam. 1^{st}PRINCE has also been applied to a beam under flexural load dividing integrals across the face of the beam and an I-beam was discovered (Cagan, 1990).

Because 1^{st}PRINCE is a discovery program in that the expanded design space is searched for non-routine designs, it is appropriate to discuss the program EURISKO (Lenat, 1982, 1983a, 1983b; Lenat and Brown, 1983). EURISKO is a frame-based program written in LISP, which incorporates a theory of heuristics to mutate lisp and frame structures and the heuristics themselves to discover new problem solutions. In the domain of VLSI design, EURISKO discovered a Mobius strip cell. When given the rules for the Trillion Credits Squadron game, EURISKO designed a fleet of ships that won the national tournament. EURISKO utilizes no form of optimization and does not consider physical relationships and coupling between parts, which are important design considerations for mechanical/ structural design. Rather, EURISKO mutates its design space based on heuristics to find new problem solutions.

PROMPT (Murthy and Addanki, 1987) is a program that performs innovative design of mechanical structures. It, too, is able to discover a hollow tube from a solid rod, but its search mechanism is based on domain heuristics. It can efficiently perform mutations such as round sharp corners to reduce stress concentrations. However, PROMPT finds only feasible designs and not optimally directed designs. Further, the program does not reason about the problem symbolically and does not provide closed-form solutions where possible. Also, PROMPT does not reason about material and so does not permit composite solutions. 1stPRINCE could mutate a sharp corner to a rounded corner if appropriate, but it would be less efficient than PROMPT's heuristic approach. However, 1stPRINCE is domain independent and reasons from first principles when heuristics fail.

12.3   Constraint activity

Monotonicity analysis gives sets of constraints which are candidate solutions to the design problem. Given a particular binding to the set of variables, one of the solution sets will lead to a superior design. The advantage of monotonicity analysis is that the complexity of the problem is considerably reduced given that a subset of the inequality constraints is known to be active. In some situations the problem may be constraint-bound and the solution is the globally optimal solution for the given design space.

The strength of monotonicity analysis is three-fold. It is symbolic; for constraint-bound sets the design solution can be given in closed-form when symbolic algebra is feasible, for other sets of constraints the reduced set is still in parametric form. It is optimally directed; because monotonicity analysis is derived from the Karush-Kuhn-Tucker (KKT) conditions of optimality, the analysis itself is a form of optimization that satisfies the KKT conditions. It demonstrates activity of inequality constraints; it is the activity of inequality constraints that influence the solution of an optimization problem, rather than the relevance of equality constraints.

In Figure 12.1a, the inequality constraint $r \geq r_{min}$ is inactive until optimization forces $r = r_{min}$. For feasible solutions where $r > r_{min}$, the constraint could be removed altogether without affecting the results. When optimization drives the constraint to be active the constraint behaves as an equality constraint, $r = r_{min}$, reducing the complexity of the problem. Activity of inequality constraints provides important information about the design solution, whereas relevance of equality constraints adds no new information about the minimum. Constraint propagation (Serrano, 1987) is not able to perform similar analyses because it propagates inequality constraints only for constraint satisfaction, rather than reasoning directly about their activity and optimally directing the solution accordingly.

Constraint activity is a powerful tool in engineering design. By utilizing information from sets of active inequality constraints, variables and parameters associated with those constraints can be viewed as candidates to affect the objective function. Thus, from active constraints, variables to modify can be identified and trends can be observed that determine optimal behavior. In this work we induce these trends of constraint activity and utilize them to discover new design prototypes.

12.4   Inducing constraint activity

Inductive learning is presented as descriptive generalization for learning from examples to discover patterns in observational data (Michalski, 1983). Our algorithm utilizes a heuristic concept of induction whereby if some set of facts $\prod$ is true for a sequence of n steps, then $\prod$ is induced to be true for all steps greater than n. As n approaches infinity, $\prod$ is continuously true. As a program generates data, patterns can be observed. If the patterns are valid for n consecutive iterations then they can be induced to be continuously valid.

1stPRINCE performs inductive inference by observing patterns on constraint activity. Monotonicity analysis derives sets of active constraints. Each time 1stPRINCE performs a mathematical manipulation, a new analysis is performed. Constraints of each generation are mapped back to the constraints from which they were derived in regions of previous generations. A prototype is considered the next generation of a different prototype if the former prototype was derived from the latter by one level of mathematical manipulation by 1stPRINCE. Patterns are observed in constraint activity for each generation. In the implementation of 1stPRINCE, the number of steps (n) observed by the process can be chosen by the user but is defaulted to be three. We define the following:

- *Inductively active:* If a constraint is active for n consecutive generations, then it is induced to be active across the entire continuum. As with unconditionally active constraints, variable backsubstitution can be performed.

- *Inductively inactive:* If a constraint is inactive for n consecutive generations, then it is induced to be inactive across the entire continuum. As with unconditionally inactive constraints, the constraint can be removed from the constraint set.

The induction process described earlier is good for inducing trends, but even though 1stPRINCE can give a closed-form equation of the continuum solution, it may violate some constraint. This is a fundamental problem with heuristic-based induction techniques in general. Some constraint may become violated in the limit of the trend induced which may not have been active for a smaller number of regions. Thus if one constraint is induced to be active across the continuum, then all constraints must also be checked across the continuum to guarantee that no constraint is violated by the inductive leap.

A constraint will be continuously active if the constraint is dominant in all generations of prototypes. A prototype that maintains the same activity as a prototype of a previous generation is called a *generation-dominant* prototype; 1stPRINCE induces trends on sequences of generation-dominant prototypes. If different constraints can be dominant then different paths may be generated and pursued by 1stPRINCE. If each constraint remains dominant within the path, then different prototypes will be induced. When 1stPRINCE induces a set of constraints to be continuously active or inactive over a sequence of generation-dominant prototypes, it forms a *dominant prototype* of the inductively active and inactive constraints.

We propose that manipulation of dominant prototypes can derive important design solutions. For example, union of dominant prototypes can be performed, where a union of two prototypes is the combination of the prototypes such that each prototype is utilized in that portion of the body where it dominates. Union of dominant prototypes is not done arbitrarily; rather optimization requires that each prototype is dominant over a part of the solution. By inducing the sets of dominant prototypes and performing a union on these sets as appropriate, the problem of verifying that no constraints are violated in induced solutions, as just discussed, can be addressed because the trend of dominant activity can be recognized. This concept is pursued further in Cagan (1990) where the inductive mechanism is applied to a flexural beam. Over most of the beam the bending stress is dominant; however, near the tip of the beam the bending stress approaches zero and the shear stress becomes dominant.

12.5   Inventing the wheel

In this section we apply the 1stPRINCE methodology to an interesting dynamics problem that we call "inventing the wheel." We use this example to demonstrate the concepts introduced in this chapter. Note that there are many possible solution paths; we choose only the path that leads to the

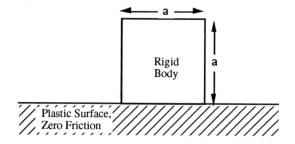

Figure 12.2. A rigid square body on a plastic surface of zero friction.

optimally directed solution.

As a body is raised and lowered from a reference point (called the datum), its potential energy increases and decreases accordingly to its height times its weight and its kinetic energy is decreased and increased by the analogous amount, assuming no loss of energy. If the potential energy is lost as the body is lowered, then the kinetic energy does not increase in value and the total energy in the system is decreased. If a body falls on a plastic surface then its energy is lost during the impact.

Utilizing these concepts, a square, rigid body (of side length a) in rectangular coordinates rests on a plastic surface of zero friction (Figure 12.2). We wish to find the optimal shape that will minimize the resistance to spinning. In particular we wish to minimize the change in energy over the perimeter distance traveled. We formulate this problem in terms of potential energy; we input just enough rotational (kinetic) energy to flip the block in Figure 12.2 onto its side. Because the body's surface contact is not point-wise continuous, it will fall onto its side and energy will be lost. Figure 12.3 shows the potential energy of the block in its initial position (Figure 12.3a) and at its maximum potential on its corner at 45° (Figure 12.3b). The necessary energy to input into the system is the difference between the two energies of the two configurations. Because energy (E) is the weight (W) times the height (h), the inputted energy ($E*$) is given as:

$$E* = Wh + W\left(\frac{\sqrt{2}}{2} - \frac{1}{2}\right)a \qquad (12.2)$$

The weight is given as the material density (ρ) times the area of the body,

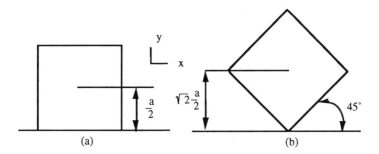

Figure 12.3. As the body rotates on its side its potential energy changes.

$$W = \int \rho dA \qquad (12.3)$$

Thus the total inputted energy to the system is $E* = .2071\rho ta^3$. Note that weight is in integral form in equation (12.3), which helps insure that this design problem will be amenable to 1^{st}PRINCE.

We wish to minimize the resistance to spinning over distance traveled given an input of energy, $E*$. As the body in its present configuration flips onto its side (traveling a distance a) it will lose all of its $E*$ energy and stop. If it lost less energy then it could continue to flip until all of the energy was lost. Thus in order to minimize the resistance to spinning, we must minimize the loss in energy as the body flips around. We maintain symmetry of the body in the x- and y-directions so that the body can assume any stable point as its starting point and at 45° so that energy can be inputted in both positive and negative directions. If symmetry is maintained, then we can assume that any change in energy is lost due to impact with the plastic surface. Therefore we wish to minimize the total change in energy over distance traveled (p), where p is called the *envelope perimeter.*

$$min : \int \frac{|de|}{p} = \int W \frac{|dh|}{p} = \sum W \frac{|\Delta h|}{p} \qquad (12.4)$$

subject to constraints:

(a) $W = \rho t A$

(b) $W \geq W_{min}$ (implying $A \geq A_{min}$ for constant t and ρ)

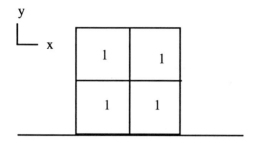

Figure 12.4. The body during its first iteration by 1^{st}PRINCE, maintaining symmetry in the x- and y-directions and at $45°$.

(c) $A \;= \sum A_j$ (for all regions j)

(d) $\Delta h \;= \sum |d_i - h_i|$ (for each region i that is an edge region)

(e) $d_i \;= [x_i^2 + y_i^2]^{\frac{1}{2}}$ (for each region i that is an edge region)

(f) h_i = perpendicular distance from surface to parallel line to
            surface through center of mass of body of each edge surface
            (found from intersection of edge and perpendicular line
            through origin for each surface i that is an edge surface)

(g) $\rho \;\geq 0,$

(h) $p \;= \sum(x_{e1} - x_{e2})^2 + (y_{e1} - y_{e2})^2]^{\frac{1}{2}}$
            (for edge vertex $e1$ next to edge vertex $e2$ along the
            perimeter envelope of the body, summed over all
            edge vertices)

(i) $z_i \;\geq z_{min}$ (for z_i the region dimensions)   (12.5)

where material density can either equal ρ or 0. All dimensions can be represented in terms of region dimensions, z_i. Calculation of h_i comes from intersecting a line through two edge vertices that form a surface edge and a line of negative, inverted slope passing through the origin; this leads to the distance from the surface to the center of mass height. Variable d_i is the distance from the center of mass to the edge vertex. Variable lengths h_i and d_i are shown in Figure 12.5b.

We maintain symmetry and initially divide the block into quarters (Figure 12.4). In this iteration all energy ($E*$) is lost. A monotonicity analysis demonstrates that dominance again affects the solution. Either the area must be at its minimum (constraints (12.5b, 12.6c) active), or the area is

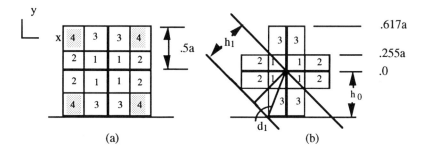

Figure 12.5. Second iteration of 1^{st}PRINCE: Region 4 is removed (a) and the optimized shape appears in (b). (b) also demonstrates the h_i and d_i variables.

not at its minimum with constraint (12.5c) still active. In the latter case, constraints (12.5i) may also be active. Numerical calculation for the case where constraint (12.5b) is inactive reveals that for reasonable values of the minimum dimensions and area, constraints (12.5i) are active in some regions (in the first iteration constraint (12.5i) is active for the single dimensional variable). It turns out that beyond the second iteration the minimum dimensional constraint is active only for part of the regions for reasonable numerical values. The resulting design problem is highly constrained in these latter cases whereas the cases with constraint (12.5b) active have many degrees-of-freedom and for reasonable minimum weight constraint (5b) will dominate over the cases of constraint (12.5c) without constraint (12.5b) and possibly with constraints (12.5i). Thus for the remainder of this discussion we consider only those cases where minimum weight dominates.

In this example, 1^{st}PRINCE considers a minimum area of $.25a^2$ for one quarter of the body of side length a (giving a minimum area of a^2 for the entire body). In the first iteration, with minimum weight dominant, the objective function takes on a value of $.0518\rho t a^2$ (the objective function is considered for one quarter rotation of the body). In the first iteration the solution is constraint-bound. The feasible design space has 2 DOF by considering dimensions and material in regions for equality and unconditionally active inequality constraints.

1^{st}PRINCE now divides the body in the x- and y-dimensions and removes material from region 4 because constraint (12.5g) is considered active in that region (Figure 12.5a). Again, constraint (12.5b) is active and a numerical optimization leads to an objective function of value $.0249\rho t a^2$. Figure 12.5b shows the optimized body. Note that new dimensional variables are created by 1^{st}PRINCE, a requirement for non-routine design. The prototype found in Figure 12.5b has 1 DOF, whereas the feasible design space has 5 DOF by considering dimensional variables and material existence in regions.

We removed region 4 from the body of Figure 12.5. From constraint (12.5g), there are many combinations of regions (2^n factorial, where n is the number of regions), which can be removed from the body (regions 1, 2, 3, 4, and any combination thereof). We pursue the path that leads to solutions that best minimize the objective. When determining design space DOF, both dimensional variables and material density for each region are considered. Via constraint (12.5g), material in each region can go to 0 or exist. In this problem, the DOF in the design space is equal to the number of dimensional variables and material densities for each region while maintaining symmetry in the $x-$ and $y-$dimensions and at 45°. We are only concerned with edge regions because modification of the interior regions does not lead to an improved solution.

We can determine the number of times the body can rotate by dividing the energy expended per perimeter distance traveled in one quarter turn into the total input energy expended per distance of the first iteration, divided by four because in the first iteration the body traveled one quarter of a turn:

$$\frac{E*}{4E} = \frac{.0518\rho t a^2}{4(.0249\rho t a^2)} = .52 \tag{12.6}$$

Thus the body can rotate one half turn before losing all of its energy.

We now divide the body again as shown in Figure 12.6a. Figure 12.6b shows one quarter of the body, maintaining symmetry. Constraint (5g) is active for regions 8 and 12 and thus the material in those regions is removed. Constraint (5b) is again active, so the dimensions can be found that optimally direct the solution as shown in Figure 12.6c, giving an objective of $.0123\rho t a^2$. The number of times the body can rotate through quarter turns is given by:

$$\frac{E*}{4E} = \frac{.0518\rho t a^2}{4(.0123\rho t a^2)} = 1.05 \tag{12.7}$$

Thus the body can spin one time on the frictionless surface and is improving the objective of minimizing the resistance to spinning. In this third iteration the prototype now has 3 DOF whereas the feasible design space has 11 DOF.

This is the third iteration. We need not continue dividing the body but choose to iterate one more time. Figure 12.7a shows one quarter of the body

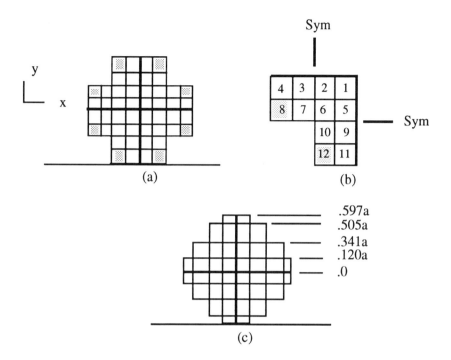

(a)

(b)

(c)

Figure 12.6. Third iteration of 1^{st}PRINCE: Regions 8 and 12 are removed (a,b) and the optimized shape appears in (c).

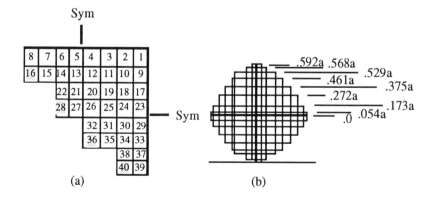

(a)

(b)

Figure 12.7. Fourth iteration of 1^{st}PRINCE: Regions 16, 28, 36 and 40 are removed (a) and the optimized shape appears in (b).

and Figure 12.7b shows the optimized body. The objective function now has a value of $.0064\rho t a^2$, once again improving the previous iteration. The number of times the body can rotate is 2.04. The prototype has 7 DOF whereas the feasible design space has 30 DOF.

Observing the constraint activity on each iteration, inequality constraint (12.5b) is active and equality constraints (12.5a, 12.5c, 12.5d, 12.5e, 12.5f, 12.5h) are relevant. 1^{st}PRINCE now induces that these constraints should be *inductively active* and thus active across the continuum. In the limit we observe that the objective function approaches zero and thus Δh approaches zero, assuming finite envelope perimeter. Setting $\Delta h = 0$ in the inductively active constraint (12.5d) implies:

$$\sum |d_i - h_i| = 0, \forall i \tag{12.8}$$

Thus,

$$|d_i - h_i| = 0, \forall i \tag{12.9}$$

For equation (12.9) to be valid,

$$d_i = h_i = 0, \forall i \tag{12.10}$$

Due to symmetry, equation (12.10) is valid along with

$$d_i = h_{i-1}, \forall i \geq 1 \qquad \text{along the edge} \tag{12.11}$$

Since

$$d_i = h_i = h_{i-1}, \forall i \geq 1 \qquad \text{along the edge} \tag{12.12}$$

we can infer that equation (12.12) can only be valid if $d_i = h_i = h_{i-1} =$ constant (called h). Thus, substituting inductively active constraint (12.5e) into equation (12.10) gives:

$$[x_i^2 + y_i^2]^{\frac{1}{2}} = h \quad \text{(continuously across the body perimeter)} \tag{12.13}$$

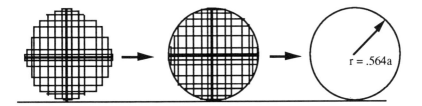

Figure 12.8. At the fourth iteration, 1stPRINCE induces that the optimally directed shape should actually be that of a circle, thereby inventing the wheel.

Equation (12.13) designates the equation for a circle of radius h. Thus in the limit, the optimal shape to minimize the change in energy over distance traveled is a circle. Since $A = .25a^2, h = .564a$. Thus the optimal shape of the edge of the body is:

$$[x_i^2 + y_i^2]^{\frac{1}{2}} = .564a \quad \text{(continuously across the body perimeter)} \quad (12.14)$$

Figure 12.8 shows the optimally directed shape of the body, a circle of radius .564a.

Starting with a square block in rectangular coordinates, the 1stPRINCE methodology derived a circular body as the optimally directed shape, and thus has "invented the wheel." Because we initially knew only of a solid rectangular block, the wheel is a non-routine design that could be interpreted as creative.

12.6   Implementation issues

Much of 1stPRINCE is implemented in Allegro CommonLISP and Flavors on a MacII. The inductive program is implemented in FranzLISP on Vax series computers running under Unix. Monotonicity analysis and symbolic algebra are implemented by Choy and Agogino (1986) and Agogino and Almgren (1987) in the SYMON/SYMFUNE systems written in VAXIMA, a symbolic algebra environment implemented in FranzLISP. Each part of the process is run independently by the user.

In the spinning block problem, much of the geometric derivations were done manually utilizing the 1stPRINCE design methodology. This example was not derived from the computer programs described earlier because of the complexity of the equations involved and in order to follow a single path that would illustrate the underlying concepts. The programs have been applied to other examples described in Cagan and Agogino (1987, 1988) and Cagan (1990). Solving the inductively active constraints is currently an interactive process that allows the user to interpret any additional traits not dictated by constraint activity. For example, in the spinning wheel problem, 1^{st}PRINCE would not have recognized that the objective function approaches zero, although such extensions pose interesting research challenges.

12.7   Heuristics and induction: Future research

We believe induction and learning in general will play an important role in creative design. Further, concepts from optimization are an important aid in directing inductive mechanisms, as demonstrated with 1^{st}PRINCE for mechanical/ structural designs. Thus constraint activity should be a fundamental source of knowledge for use in a design system. Other induction-based heuristics such as those discussed in this chapter, which we are exploring for inclusion in 1^{st}PRINCE include:

1. As each region is broken apart, the new regions each have the same set of constraints. Analysis on one region may hold for all regions.

2. If a constraint is unconditionally active (inactive) in a rejected design but never has the same activity in a good one, make the constraint unconditionally inactive (active) (i.e., change the extremum of activity).

The first heuristic may reduce the complexity of the analysis considerably. Constraint sets proposed by monotonicity analysis can be combinatorially explosive as the number of regions increases. In those cases an intelligent pruning mechanism must be utilized to control the design space search. This heuristic may be one approach to controlling the explosion. The second heuristic emphasizes that we learn from our mistakes as well as our successes. In this situation if some constraint is the driving force toward a poor design, then never let that constraint be active. This drives the discovery mechanism away from areas that are known to contain poor designs. Of course there may be other such heuristics that can be utilized by 1^{st}PRINCE to control the design space, but the important point is that the essential manipulation information is found from constraint activity.

In design systems, in general, and learning systems specifically, language bias is of fundamental importance. In order for 1^{st}PRINCE to find any optimally behaved designs, a proper set of variables must be selected and utilized in important design constraints. Inductive techniques (Michalski,

1983) may be helpful in deriving an optimal vocabulary for different design domains.

Finally, a form of case-based reasoning is important in non-routine design. Once new designs are discovered they should be investigated, indexed, and stored in a manner such that future design problems can utilize them as a basis to start a new design process. The investigation and indexing of the design is quite important. In the spinning block problem, the initial primitive was chosen in rectangular coordinates; the final artifact was a circular geometry best represented in polar coordinates. A pattern matcher could easily search through a database of fundamental mathematical representations and recognize that the geometry is circular. The final artifact could then be stored in both rectangular and polar coordinates such that when a design requires such an initial primitive, the design system could choose the appropriate representation to utilize.

12.8   Conclusions

1stPRINCE is an interactive methodology by which the human user gains insight about a design problem and creates new design prototypes. By demonstrating which variables and constraints are important for optimization and manipulating the design space by processes such as dividing integrals, the 1stPRINCE design methodology discovers optimally directed novel designs. Modifications are obtained by manipulation of the design space and not from new, exterior knowledge.

Induction is an important manipulation that aids in concept discovery. In this chapter we show that inductive techniques can be optimally directed for mechanical/structural design; constraint activity determining which bounds to put on the search space may directly lead to the optimally directed solution. Monotonicity analysis performs a form of qualitative optimization to determine candidate sets of active constraints. After a number of mutations by 1stPRINCE, inductive techniques observe trends from the constraint activity information that may lead to new prototypes.

In the case of the spinning block, 1stPRINCE induces a circular wheel; this design has little resemblance to the original artifact and could be considered a creative design. Either way, the designs derived from 1stPRINCE are non-routine. Inductive techniques play an important role in the derivation of these final artifact configurations; as the process derives better designs to satisfy the objective, 1stPRINCE learns from the examples and recognizes what trends the artifact is demonstrating toward optimality. Research into inductive techniques and applications have a promising future in aiding non-routine design.

Acknowledgments. This research is supported by the National Science Foundation under grant #DMC-8451622. The authors would like to thank Stuart Russell for his discussion on this work and suggestions to "reinvent the wheel."

References

Agogino, A. M., Bradley, S. R., Cagan, J., Jain, P., & Michelena, N. (1989). AI/OR computational model for integrating qualitative and quantitative design methods, *Proceedings of NSF Engineering Design Research Conference*, Amherst, MA, pp. 97–112.

Agogino, A. M., & Almgren, A. S. (1987). Techniques for integrating qualitative reasoning and symbolic computation in engineering optimization, *Engineering Optimization* 12(2): 117–135.

Brown, D. C., & Chandrasekaran, B. (1983). An approach to expert systems for mechanical design, *IEEE Computer Society Trends and Applications*, NBS, Gaithersburg, MD, pp. 173–180.

Cagan, J. (1990). *Innovative Design of Mechanical Structures from First Principles*, PhD Dissertation, University of California, Berkeley, CA.

Cagan, J., & Agogino, A. M. (1987). Innovative design of mechanical structures from first principles, *AI EDAM* 1(3): 169–189.

Cagan, J., & Agogino, A. M. (1988). 1st PRINCE: Innovative design from first principles, *Proceedings of AAAI-88 Workshop on AI in Design*, St. Paul.

Choy, J. K., & Agogino, A. M. (1986). SYMON: Automated SYMbolic MONotonicity Analysis System for qualitative design optimization, *Proceedings of the ASME 1986 International Computers in Engineering Conference*, Chicago, pp. 305–310.

Coyne, R. D., Rosenman, M. A., Radford, A. D., & Gero, J. S. (1987). Innovation and creativity in knowledge-based CAD, *in* J. S. Gero (Ed.), *Expert Systems in Computer-Aided Design*, North-Holland, Amsterdam, pp. 435–465.

Freudenstein, F., & Maki, E. F. (1983). Development of an optimum variable-stroke internal-combustion engine mechanism from the viewpoint of kinematic structure, *ASME Journal of Mechanisms, Transmissions and Automation in Design* 105: 259–266.

Gero, J. S., Maher, M. L., & Zhao, F. (1988). A model for knowledge-based creative design, *Proceedings of AAAI-88 Workshop on AI in Design*, St. Paul.

Lenat, D. B. (1982). The nature of heuristics, *Artificial Intelligence* 19: 189–249.

Lenat, D. B. (1983a). The nature of heuristics II: Theory formulation by heuristic search, *Artificial Intelligence* 21: 31–59.

Lenat, D. B. (1983b). The nature of heuristics III: EURISKO: A program that learns new heuristics and domain concepts, *Artificial Intelligence* 21: 61–98.

Lenat, D. B., & Brown, J. S. (1983). Why AM and EURISKO appear to work, *Proceedings of AAAI-83*, Washington, DC, pp. 236–240.

Michalski, R. S. (1983). A theory and methodology of inductive learning, *in* R. S. Michalski, J. Carbonell, & T Mitchell (Eds), *Machine Learning: An Artificial Intelligence Approach*, Morgan Kaufman, pp. 83–134.

Murthy, S. S., & Addanki, S. (1987). PROMPT: An innovative design tool, *Proceedings of AAAI-87*, Vol. 2, Seattle, WA, pp. 637–642.

Papalambros, P., & Wilde, D. J. (1988). *Principles of Optimal Design: Modeling and Computation*, Cambridge University Press, Cambridge.

Serrano, D. (1987). *Constraint Management in Conceptual Design*, ScD Thesis, Massachusetts Institute of Technology, Cambridge, MA.

13 Computer Supported Creative Design: A Pragmatic Approach

Robert F. Coyne and Eswaran Subrahmanian

Creativity is recognizable only in a given context thereby making its definition elusive. In design, creativity in a domain may depend on characteristics of the process or the product, or both. In this chapter, we argue that a better understanding of creativity can occur by focusing on the conditions that allow for creative acts. With respect to design research, we believe that it would be most productive to create *computer supported design environments* that stress the complementary nature of human and computer design capabilities. These capabilities and their relationships are reviewed to identify some of the critical issues in designing and building such environments. We argue for building such integrated design environments in order to empirically test and evaluate hypotheses about design processes and creativity in the context of real design tasks. In this regard we discuss LOOS: a partially automated approach for the design of layouts that illustrates some of the features desired for a computational design support environment.

13.1   Introduction

The idea that computers will actively aid design processes in various disciplines (or perhaps transform those processes) has been around for at least a couple of decades. Unfortunately, up to now reality has fallen far short of this promise. Each successive revolution in computing power and new paradigm for symbolic processing has been heralded by some as the needed potential that would allow computer-aided design (CAD) to fulfill its promise. Along these lines at least three successive waves of development of CAD can be crudely identified (see also Rychener, 1988).

In the first wave, CAD tools were limited to the role of mechanizing the production and duplication of drawings and to some basic analysis programs. In the second wave, more sophisticated modeling and analysis tools and systems that use design grammars, logic and production systems were developed. These approaches can be roughly characterized as attempts to computationally apply mathematical formalisms and AI knowledge-based technology directly to design as problem solving. These capabilities, although important, have so far only captured routine or repetitive design and do not support the average complex design process in a fundamental way. The third wave of CAD recognizes that design processes have unique and significant aspects that are distinctly different from other types of problem solving. A promising agenda for current design research is to gain clearer insight into the requirements of design processes and to combine this understanding with a more sophisticated application of evolving computational technologies such as knowledge-based systems and object-oriented modeling.

Perhaps the two most important aspects of design that distinguish it from other types of problem solving activity are the number and complexity of the representations required and the open-ended and exploratory nature of design processes. Our understanding of these as critical research issues is the key to building more effective design systems. Further, we believe that these issues have a fundamental connection to the nature of, and possibilities for creativity in design. We argue that a pragmatic and productive approach that design research can take right now is to build *computational design support environments*, which combine human and computer design capabilities in a complementary, integrated manner. In this chapter, we propose a conjecture that addresses design creativity in this context.

This approach to creativity in design is illustrated in the context of a partially automated design system for 'generic' layout tasks. The system, LOOS, overcomes some of the limitations of former approaches to layout design specifically and knowledge-based design in general. The generative capability of the system is formally modeled as systematic enumeration of structural design descriptions. This is combined with a human-guided evaluative capability that is built-up incrementally, evolves and can be customized. This division of labor within an overall integrated design process is crucially supported by a representation that captures appropriate levels of abstraction. The observation and evaluation of partial designs in context stimulates the designer to explore the layout task by reformulating it in terms of performance requirements and their relative weights. Further opportunities for exploration and knowledge-acquisition will be afforded by a framework now under development for the flexible decomposition of layout tasks. We argue that the computational design model incorporated in LOOS begins to satisfy some of the key features required of an evolutionary computer supported design environment that will support the achievement of creative results.

13.2 Computer supported design and creativity

Design and creativity go hand in hand in the sense that a designed artifact or a process of design is termed creative by its relative newness to the user, the domain, or period in history. Creativity is recognizable only in a given context, thereby making its definition elusive. The context specific (individual, temporal, and spatial) nature of what is considered creative is inescapable; thus the inevitability of sometimes 'reinventing the wheel.' However, even if access to the long term memory of human (design) history were available, it is not clear that searching for relevant insights for a current design would be tractable in the typical case. In this chapter, we view humans and computers as information processing systems and argue that with our current limited understanding of processes of creativity and current theories of design the most pragmatic question to ask is, 'How can we enhance the potential for design creativity within a human-computer design environment?'

Within an information processing perspective, the objective of enhancing creativity leads us to the following conjecture:

> Creative solutions to a design task occur either when a new formulation of the task is generated providing new solutions, or when a solution is found within a given formulation in a region of the space of design solutions never examined before.

Given this conjecture, the ability to be creative can be enhanced when either or both of the aforementioned processes are systematically supported. We believe that currently, computational systems can play the most effective role in enhancing creativity within human-machine design systems where the division of labor between the two participants supports exploration of problem formulations and solution spaces. We argue that this motivates investigating the *grounds* (environment) for the occurrence of a creative act from which the *figure* of creativity itself may emerge.

We first examine cognitive and computational models of design (largely implicit in systems that have been built) to summarize our current understanding of the participants, the human, and the computer, in solving design problems. We then identify an initial basis for integrating human and computational design strengths. We assert that the task of designing a human-machine environment for design is a design problem in itself that should be viewed from an evolutionary perspective. Further, such environments are needed to serve as an empirical testbed for testing conjectures about design and creativity. Design research structured around such environments will produce not only cumulative results, but also new goals for enhancing the occurrence of creativity in design.

13.2.1   Cognitive models

Cognitive modeling has its origin in information processing theories of human problem solving (Newell and Simon, 1972). Modeling process behavior is the underlying objective of cognitive science. Use of methods from cognitive science, such as protocol analysis, is relatively new in engineering design. Architects were the first to explore these possibilities (Eastman, 1969; Akin, 1986); software design is another discipline that has used protocol analysis (Adelson and Soloway, 1984). More recently, it has been applied in mechanical engineering and civil engineering (Ullman et al., 1988; Baker and Fenves, 1987). Research in cognitive models of design encompasses two levels. Most common is the construction of fine grained models of problem solving in terms of design operators, heuristics and the design problem space; the granularity of analysis and models vary. A second approach attempts to characterize the 'generic' aspects of design tasks that belong to the core of those tasks commonly understood to be design (such as mechanical design, architectural design, software design) (Goel and Pirolli, 1989). This model is coarse grained and complements the fine grained models. Further research in these areas has to be undertaken before complete cognitive theories of design are proposed. We present later a summary of assumptions common to cognitive models, the characterization of the design process that emerges from such studies, and the implications of these studies for understanding the abilities and limitations of the human problem solver performing (creative) design.

Assumptions
The following are the basic structural assumptions underlying cognitive models within an information processing theory of human problem solving

(including design) (Newell and Simon, 1972; Simon, 1973; Goel and Pirolli, 1989):

1. The structure of the information processor consists of a short-term memory, a long-term memory, and a processor for manipulating symbols; there exists a bottleneck in the transfer of information between short-term memory and long-term memory.

2. The design problem-solving environment consists of a design problem space, design task environment, and the information processing mechanism (human).

3. The design task must be solvable within reasonable time constraints and limits on resources.

The level of detail at which the design task environment is described or circumscribed for each study varies; this leads to the difference in granularity of the models proposed.

Process of design
Design tasks are prime examples of ill-structured problems where a large part of the problem appears to deal with the discovery of the very constraints or requirements that will be brought to bear on proposed solutions. This *exploratory* progression of a design task is captured nicely by Rychener in the following description of Simon's observations on the nature of ill-structured problems (Rychener, 1988; Simon, 1973):

> Architects [designers] were observed to formulate many items of information of importance to their designs only by recognizing their applicability while working out the details of a solution. They could not start out by making a list of criteria that they were seeking to satisfy with the newly-created layout [design]. Thus the search for a good solution is also a search for proper information with which to evaluate it.

Conclusions about the cognitive process(es) of design that emerge from cognitive studies support and elaborate on the exploratory characterization of the design process (Adelson and Soloway, 1984; Ullman et al., 1988; Goel and Pirolli, 1989; Baker and Fenves, 1987):

1. Design activity falls into three categories: generative, evaluative and patching. These permeate design processes in multiple ways, but some prominent examples are the generation of partial solutions, evaluation

of proposed solutions (partial and complete), and patching incompatibilities in solutions that arise when synthesizing partially dependent decomposition modules.

2. Control of design processes by human designers is dynamic, flexible, and not easily characterizable as algorithms. The decision making mode is largely one of tentative design commitments intertwined with nested cycles of generate and evaluate.

3. Human designers use a variety of symbol structures to achieve their problem objectives, and they use external memory aids.

4. Abstraction hierarchies are extensively used and appear to function coherently in the context of a problem; however, there exist no formal theories of abstractions yet.

5. Extensive problem restructuring occurs in non-routine design, and the problem structuring task and problem solving tasks are inseparable. More design time seems to be spent on structuring than on solving.

We use these conclusions about the nature of human design processes as a basis for comparison with the nature of design processes currently captured in computational models. But first, we examine how this characterization of the design process reflects both the strengths and weaknesses of the human designer.

Limitations and capabilities of the human designer
The following limitations in the human designer's behavior are a natural consequence of the cognitive limits imposed by the structure of the human information processor:

1. The human often fails to adequately manage the complexity of the design problem space due to inadequate retrieval of relevant and useful design knowledge from memory. Here, memory may consist of design material from the current design session, such as partial alternatives generated, from previous experience, or from design histories available to the designer. This failure is due to a limitation in the transfer of information between short-term memory and long-term memory (Ullman et al., 1988; Goel and Pirolli, 1989). External memory aids are used to some extent to overcome this limitation.

2. Human designers tend to make the first generated solution work or attempt to take a depth first approach to solving a design problem.

How the generative process of human designers works is not discernible in the protocol studies of single designers (Ullman et al., 1988).

Current external memory aids help to mitigate these limitations but are inadequate in overcoming the many problems of bookkeeping required in a complex design task. The impact of this failure is acute in that it restricts the extent of the design problem space that is explored, and, even in problems with known structure, it restricts the extent of the solution space searched.

Apparently, human designers overcome these limitations to deal with the complexity of design tasks through a variety of cognitive devices such as abstraction mechanisms for generalization and task decomposition, heuristics, analogies, and metaphors to provide alternate formulations, and learning and knowledge compilation to evolve and improve the quality and efficiency of the design process. The skilled use of these types of cognitive devices has come to be associated with what is typically identified as expertise and 'creativity' in human design practice. Thus, in a definitional sense, human designers employ 'creative' processes to achieve better results *because* of their cognitive limitations, not *despite* them. Emphasizing this point, Alan Turing once wrote to a colleague who suggested that a very typical property of the brain is to think in analogies (Hodges, 1985, p. 388):

> To a large extent I agree with you about 'thinking in analogies', but I do not think of the brain as 'searching for analogies' so much as having analogies forced upon it by its own limitations...

So the use of a 'creative' process, corresponding to any of the aforementioned cognitive devices, may not be a necessary or sufficient condition for producing a creative result (in the sense of a distinctly different or superior result; in other chapters in this book Cagan and Fischer also adopt similar viewpoints).

When we assess the potential that computers have for aiding the design process a more important concern is the achievement of 'creative' results, not whether the means employed are creative in the same sense as human design processes. In spite of the cognitive mechanisms that human designers employ, the complexity of design tasks and the time constraints involved often restrict exploration and synthesis of 'creative' (the best) solutions. Historically, creative solutions appear to have been proposed either by systematic study or by 'stumbling upon a solution.' As was pointed out, the solution generation process of human designers is still poorly understood in the context of their limitations.

13.2.2 Computational models

The arrival of electronic computers led to the widespread belief that they constitute a revolutionary tool that ultimately will enhance and transform the design process. However, our understanding of the strengths and limitations of computers and the relationship of these to creating an effective computational design environment has been progressing relatively slowly. As symbol processors, speed of processing information and an enormous capacity for memory were immediately recognized as the obvious strengths of computers. Perhaps not obvious at first, it has been slowly recognized that a very significant limitation of computers performing design is their lack of capacity for evaluative judgment and selection, and their lack of what has been called 'commonsense' knowledge. Without this broader and incisive knowledge it appears to be very hard for computers to employ strategies akin to the mechanisms for abstraction, analogy, and so forth, that appear to be key abilities of human performing design. On the other hand, because the proper goal of computer-aided design is to produce superior designs regardless of the process employed, then the expectation that computers imitate or duplicate human processes may be mistaken; entirely new processes for producing better designs may emerge that depend on utilizing the strengths of computers in ways that complement (or surpass) human designers abilities but bear little resemblance to human design processes (Flemming, 1989). No doubt, for the aforementioned reasons and because investigation of computers as design agents is in its infancy, few explicit computational models of design exist, except those concerned with human cognitive models of design.

The early CAD systems that were used for detailing designs from a geometric point of view were based only on implicit and primitive computational models of design. Following these there have been numerous experiments in combining algorithmic and heuristic methods in design systems yielding more explicit and/or slightly less primitive computational models. For instance, automated design systems have approached design from a top-down model of refinement (Steinberg, 1987). In this approach, the design problem is structured as a fixed top-down decomposition (a well-understood problem) in which the computational system manages complexity by synthesizing solutions from a set of alternatives available for each of the subproblems in the decomposition. This approach, and that of using constraint representations and processing, have primarily yielded a series of design systems with much more explicit models, but ones largely limited to capturing routine design, as acknowledged by the developers of these design systems

More recently design research has been directed toward using AI technologies, particularly in the form of knowledge-based systems. These systems succeed, after a period of knowledge engineering, in giving the computer some (impressive) narrow design expertise and evaluative power. However, they still suffer from limitations of rigidity and brittleness articulated as general criticisms of the 'expert system' approach to problem solving (Doyle, 1984; Rich, 1984). To counter this, another round of knowledge acquisition and refinement can always take place in principle, but this is not usually planned as a continual and well-integrated part of mature systems as would be required for design tasks of even minimal complexity. To give these systems some range, flexibility, and greater efficiency, various strategies for employing layered knowledge bases of meta-knowledge and meta-level reasoning and control have been incorporated with some success (Orelup et al., 1987; Takewaki et al., 1985; Genesereth, 1983; Stefik, 1981).

With meta-level structuring, the computational system may perform in a less primitive and more sophisticated way, but the underlying model tends to be less clear, especially when dependent on domain specific meta-level concerns. Implicitly these systems are based on the hope, as yet unfulfilled, that a limited number of domain independent meta-levels with corresponding inferencing strategies and knowledge will be discovered. Also, meta-level inferencing often seems to require guidance from knowledge at yet another successive meta-meta-level and so on. As a serious concern with these meta-level models, it must be noted that effective computational models of a complex task will have to cope with the problem of organizing and effectively applying large amounts of knowledge without requiring more knowledge at ever higher levels to be applied (Levesque, 1986). Therefore, problems of knowledge acquisition, representation, and retrieval in knowledge-based systems still pose major challenges if computational systems are to obtain an autonomous capability for design and creativity as we know it in humans.

Some recent design research is concerned with modeling computational techniques that focus on flexibility and innovation as more central issues. In attempting to overcome the limitations of predefined solution spaces and knowledge bases however elaborate, some researchers propose mechanisms that produce alternative formulations and sets of solutions. These include techniques proposed and implemented for 'creative' design such as generation of analogies (Zhao and Maher, 1988), prototype modification (Gero et al., 1988), and modification operators (Addanki and Murthy, 1987). These proposals approach the problem of design and creativity by defining and modeling computational techniques for cognitive design devices such as analogy with the hope of understanding and generalizing them over a collection of tasks. Through these generalizations computational theories of creative design are expected to emerge from the 'bottom up.'

Computational models of analogy, metaphor, and other learning techniques can aid the designer with alternative problem formulation. However, postulating generative models alone of cognitive devices such as analogy is insufficient as their use may result in a combinatorial explosion (of analogies produced for instance). Any mechanism that generates a set of solutions has to be governed by means for selecting the useful instances out of the set; this selection mechanism depends on the performance criteria derived by trading-off problem objectives. This behavior has been observed in an empirical study (Kalagnanam and Subrahmanian, 1989), and has also been articulated in a critique of domain independent learning techniques by Doyle (1988). He argued that the domain independent learning methods are devoid of rational objectives thereby generating generalizations that are not useful. This point is well described for analogies by Simon in his essay on the architecture of complexity:

> Metaphor and analogy can be helpful, or they can be misleading. All depends on whether the similarities the metaphor captures are significant or superficial.

The discrimination of the significant from the superficial depends on evaluative criteria corresponding to the objectives of the problem being solved. Precisely for this reason, purely generative approaches to design innovation or creativity implicitly still require the human to participate in the process. Although requiring the integration of human evaluative and behavioral design knowledge, these approaches have not (yet) delimited appropriate roles for the human designer and for the the machine; further, they lack a comprehensive perspective for integrating these techniques into a complete design process.

From our review of computational models, we identify two crucial points that we believe are necessary in developing computer-based models for creative design. *The first point is to explicitly acknowledge and provide for a partial dependence on human design expertise and the careful integration of it with currently understood computer capabilities.* Therefore, for the creation of design environments we adopt a design research strategy similar to what Rich (1984) proposed as the gradual expansion of artificial intelligence. In describing the role AI-based systems play currently, she pointed out that even though part of the responsibility has been assumed by machines in solving problems they do not eliminate the need for the human in the system. Along these lines there are other significant approaches to understanding and aiding design based on the premise that design is an *exploratory* process and that the role of the computer is to aid the designer (Flemming, 1988; Smithers et al., 1989). Flemming, in identifying the role of rule-based computer systems stated:

> ... for tasks that are not well understood a rule-based system can serve as an effective vehicle to deepen our understanding and can thus lead to regularities, to generalizations and to the formation of theories that do not exist at the outset.

The model of Smithers et al. goes beyond rule based systems and argues for designing systems based on a prototheory (design as exploration) to understand and formulate theories of design. This is a well thought-out, ambitious undertaking with the potential disadvantage, as the developers point out, that it requires large amounts of resources and time. Achieving a useful degree of intelligent support involves a greater range and capability than is typically required of approaches adopting automated design. We have more to say concerning the relationship of such models to our conjecture in the next section.

The second point, as articulated by Doyle (1984), emphasizes the need for understanding the nature of apprenticeship versus that of constructing journeymen. He referred to expert and knowledge-based systems as instant journeymen who do not have a model of the apprenticeship process and hence do not have the capability to become masters; that is, they sometimes display impressive expertise but have no inherent structure or agenda for evolving and learning. Therefore they cannot bootstrap their knowledge through experience into more knowledge and better skills; nor, for similar reasons, can they act in flexible and innovative ways. Even though his proposal is to study the apprenticeship process without computers, we believe (as the editors of his essay also note) that computers can play a role in understanding the apprenticeship process. In order to achieve this objective, we believe we have to endow computers with the facility to generalize, observe, and experiment with problem solving theories in a domain. We view this process of transferring the nature of apprenticeship to computers as requiring a symbiotic human-machine system where there is a continual update of the division of labor between the human and computer design agents. Thus the role that each agent plays in the design process is not statically defined but may gradually change as the computer grows in knowledge and capabilities. We characterize such human/computer integrated design environments as evolutionary in the sense that they will develop and continue to improve in their overall sophistication in slow stages, guided by experience and theoretical insights gained in using these environments.

13.2.3   An evolving design environment for enhancing creativity

Design of any system that is based on the premise that it display evolutionary behavior does not have an explicit final design goal. In articulating this point in the context of social planning (a not so well structured task), as an example of the design of evolving systems, Simon (1981) asserted:

> A paradoxical, but perhaps a realistic view of design goals is that their function is to motivate activity which in turn will generate new goals.

We view the task of building a human-machine environment for creative design from a similar perspective. This view is motivated by the limited understanding we have of the activity of design in information processing terms (both cognitive and computational) and the difficulty of identifying objective evaluative criteria for creative acts. This leads us to set minimal goals for the task of designing a *computer supported design environment* (CSDE) to experiment with creativity in design. By adopting this approach we aim to encompass the issues that we believe are currently the most important in order to support design and creativity while not prescribing or restricting what concepts, mechanisms, structures, knowledge, and so forth, may have a place in such environments. We believe that this can be accomplished by building evolving human-computer systems that support the conditions in our conjecture and provide means for continually attenuating the limitations and expanding on the strengths of the participants in the design environment.

A computer supported design environment, with a single human and computer(s) as participants, is constrained by the capabilities and limitations of these two types of symbol processing systems. We have reviewed the conclusions of cognitive studies regarding human designers. And we have summarized the current state of computationally based design research which indicates that there are certain persistent and serious limitations of computers as design agents. However, we believe that these observed limitations are partially due to the restricted viewpoint, prevalent in computational models, for utilizing and instructing computers in design. This is a viewpoint that implicitly assumes autonomous behavior for the computational agent and does not explicitly address opportunities for the symbiotic interaction of human and computational design agents in an integrated model. With these points in mind, we wish to focus on the potential for CSDEs, still characterized by the strengths and weaknesses of the two participants, but with a different perspective on the initial roles of the computer (and the human designer).

In particular, their cooperative integration opens new possibilities for expanding the strengths of the computer when balanced by context sensitive human design knowledge that can be elicited, stored, refined, and structured for dynamic application. Earlier, we mentioned that the generative processes of human designers are not easily discernible from protocols, and hence present a rich area for research into formal generative languages (Ullman et al., 1988). Within a cooperative evolving environment, with an intelligent division of labor and an appropriate set of representations (of which we give an illustration later), these can take the form of purely syntactic languages. Such languages can be postulated, developed, and tested for completeness, and systematically applied using the main strengths of computers. Definition of complete designs through such languages must be balanced by the encoding of task specific performance or behavioral requirements by the human designer. These performance requirements are discovered by a process of exploration driven by the need to make a large space of solution possibilities converge and express the desired properties.

Similarly, with appropriate representations and architectures for modeling, design processes computers can provide multiple abstractions and decompositions for managing and exploring partial design descriptions, and relevant design knowledge from compiled design histories at the appropriate time and level of abstraction. These representations, languages, memory structures, and the design knowledge that they capture, interwoven with computers speed and memory capacity, will result in much more powerful models for computational design agents. With this perspective, the space of possibilities for the design of such evolving design environments is indeed large. It quickly becomes speculative and unproductive to discuss these issues further in general terms. In the second half of this chapter we illustrate some possibilities concretely in terms of a specific class or phase of design—layout—and a unique computational model and system for exploring layout design tasks—LOOS. We show that the LOOS approach takes advantage of existing technologies and human and computer strengths and integrates them in such a way that its architecture reflects an *exploration-based model of design* akin to that proposed in Smithers et al. (1989).

Insights from these research efforts confirm that determining the architectural features of a CSDE must be approached as a design problem itself with evolving goals. However, we believe that the major themes that must be addressed can be identified, and they are as follows:

1. that design is best modeled as an exploration process with human/computer cooperation;

2. that the immediate enhancement of the creative potential of human designers can be coupled with the evolutionary enhancement of the role of the computer toward that of a more autonomous, creative partner;

3. that design theory in domains and insights into creativity should be accumulated experimentally and empirically through the normal use of design systems; this will be enabled if there exist sophisticated knowledge structures (persistent memory), representations, and languages to elicit, accumulate, and refine design knowledge (including process knowledge) during single design tasks and across a set of tasks.

Besides being evolutionary in its behavior, the environment proposed is also an evolutionary step in terms of the history of development of computational design tools; a step that integrates formal problem solving and knowledge-based methods in a manner that allows it to display a gradual improvement in its behavior. The CSDE framework that we propose for conducting design research accommodates both 'creativity in the large' and 'creativity in the small.' What we mean by creativity in the large is the overall potential for producing superior results (innovative, creative, and custom design) that emerges through the integration of multiple human/machine processes and representation capacities, both long and short term. By creativity in the small we mean the focus on computationally modeling individual processes or mechanisms that potentially produce creative results such as mutation and modification operators, analogy, case-based-reasoning, and so forth.

We see these two levels of exploration and potential for creativity as compatible, indeed necessary to one another. A significant and important part of the evolution of a CSDE will be the introduction, refinement, and incorporation of more and more individual computational mechanisms for enhancing creativity comprising the gradual shift of design expertise from human to machine. At the same time our belief is that the focus on and development of CSDEs as a whole is necessary as an empirical testbed where such mechanisms can emerge as ideas, take-shape, and be tested.

13.2.4   Testing conjectures about design creativity

We now reexamine our conjecture specifying conditions for the occurrence of creative acts in design. *Briefly restated, our conjecture is that the potential for creative design occurring is increased when designers are provided with the capability to explore an expanded formulation space or more of a given solution space for a task.* In motivating and describing a computational model consisting of evolving CSDEs, we have also proposed the appropriate experimental environment in which to test our conjecture. The construction and planned evolution of such environments will provide the exact conditions necessary to promote our understanding of creativity, and achieve creative results for real design problems. We believe that any design research proposing conjectures about computational models of creativity must also specify the experimental environments in which to test them. This is in contrast to approaches that propose models for creativity and use computational implementation as a sufficient condition for validation without any (or very limited) verification of their purported behavior (Ohlsson, 1983; Bundy, 1983; Sharkey and Brown, 1985).

The next section describes how we can support a minimal CSDE that provides the conditions by which to evaluate our conjecture in the class of layout design tasks. We don't claim to verify the conjecture in the strong sense, but we clearly illustrate it in terms of examples of systematic exploration and task reformulation in layout design. Of course, we realize that in order to fully test the conjecture we should validate it across classes and domains of design tasks; layout design is just a beginning. Our proposal at the experimental level—constructing evolutionary CSDEs—will allow us to test for each of the conditions of the conjecture, and follow this approach in a number of design domains. Later we add a few further comments about each of the conditions in our conjecture by identifying some types of systematic exploration and task reformulation; these are by no means exhaustive but represent an interesting collection of possibilities. These examples are further illustrated in the next section.

Expanding the number of potential solutions examined
We note again the limitations of human designers in exploring and keeping track of multiple alternatives and the importance this attaches to constructing computational design systems that enable a designer to explore different options in parallel (Mittal et al., 1986; Mostow, 1985). As the following quote suggests, there is a connection between the ability of designers to explore a given design space more thoroughly and the potential to discover innovative solutions to a typical problem within a given problem space (Rychener, 1988):

> Past design work (which is largely done by people, with few ideas as to how to automate even its more routine aspects) has often been hampered by a failure to consider more than one or two main alternatives. This certainly excluded most truly innovative approaches. It has also meant that the search for alternatives has not been systematic and thorough.

In essence we advocate a more systematic examination of the potential solution space, at the appropriate levels of problem abstraction, as a means to expand the scope of exploration. Systematic generative capability effectively filtered through performance knowledge, and intelligent design history management will provide means to explore larger portions of a potential solution space than humanly(!) possible. Of course, such a design strategy is potentially combinatoric. However, systematic generation of alternatives does not necessarily imply an exhaustive enumeration but can be used to intelligently probe a solution space. Additionally, there exists at least one model for systematic generation of solutions that is tractable if certain conditions are met. *Hierarchical generate-and-test* permits pruning of candidate solutions that are only partially specified, and when a partial solution is pruned, an entire class of solutions corresponding to the description is eliminated from the generation process (Stefik et al., 1983). The LOOS system, presented in the next section, is an example of the implementation of this model in the domain of layout.

Expanding the exploration of task formulations
If purely syntactic generative mechanisms are proposed, the number of potential design descriptions can be large because they are missing an important part of the design task specification: performance constraints. Two sets of performance constraints with the same structural design descriptions correspond to two different formulations of the task. Performance constraints are an important means by which humans designers manage the complexity of exploring the solution space. By allowing a designer to incrementally define and manage sets of performance constraints, support for expanding the set of possible formulations of design tasks can be achieved. As the shortcomings in partial designs are detected, as a result of incomplete or faulty specification of the current set of constraints, the system could effectively aid the user in correcting the problem formulation. In this regard, design histories can also play a vital role in connecting the knowledge from previous attempts and solutions to the problem at hand. Modification of performance requirements is only one method of expanding the scope of exploration of the problem formulation.

Another important means by which the designer manages complexity is through problem decomposition using abstraction hierarchies. Design and performance constraints can be expressed at different levels of abstraction of the task. Any representational language for design, including generative ones, will have to provide mechanisms to allow for specification of task decompositions. The designer using these languages should be able to express decompositions and allow the computer to generate solutions at these levels. Alternative decompositions would also provide the opportunity for experimenting with differing formulations of a design task. Aid in managing possible sets of design task decomposition at various levels of detail can potentially allow for overcoming the tunnel vision behavior imposed by cognitive and temporal limitations.

Supporting and testing creative design hypotheses in evolving CSDEs
In the aforementioned discussion of our conjecture we *initially* assign the role of systematic (blind) generative capability and algorithmic solving methods to the computer due to its computational strengths while assigning the role of evaluator and specifier of rational objectives to the human. We expect a gradual change in these roles to take place in this integrated design environment based on the possibility of powerful computational variants of context sensitive human cognitive devices (abstraction, analogy, and learning), or purely computational techniques with no cognitive equivalence finding a stable use in the design environment. Techniques that are not used, or impose additional limitations on the ability to perform design, will fall out of the environment whereas others that enhance the power of the designer will find a niche in the environment sometimes proving useful beyond their originally intended use. We believe that we can use design environments constructed around these principles to enhance and understand the design process. As our understanding of the design process progresses, the role of the computer may evolve from that of an apprentice to a creative partner while in the initial stages they serve as amplifiers of human creative powers.

13.3   Layout design: A testbed for computer supported creative design

Layout design deals with many of the complex issues that typically arise in the design of artifacts that have to satisfy specified constraints and are composed of parts that have shape and take up space. Because layout involves the two-dimensional composition of objects into floor plans, site plans, and so forth, it is in some respects relatively less complex than some other design tasks. But layout design is interesting and important because it is a generic phase or process of many design disciplines. A design method for layout should be capable of dealing with many or all of these domains if its representation and overall architecture are general enough.

Layout design is also inherently difficult because of the large (potentially infinite) number of location and orientation combinations available for placing any single object. Furthermore, there are multiple interdependencies among the design objects imposed by their shapes, sizes, and the spatial relationships required to meet multiple performance requirements. For these reasons there is no known direct method that is guaranteed to produce feasible solutions without trial and error. Depending on the difficulty of the problem some amount of exploration of problem structure and search for candidate solutions is required whether in human or computer based approaches.

Recurring in the literature on layout design is the observation that due to cognitive limitations human designers do not have the capability of making systematic explorations of alternative arrangements (Liggett and Mitchell, 1981; Galle, 1986). A distinctive feature of layout problems is that decisions must simultaneously satisfy global requirements (e.g., usage of space) and local requirements (e.g., adjacency); an acceptable spatial arrangement results from a complex pattern of tradeoffs. Ideally, what is desired is a structured method for producing multiple alternative layout solutions where each proposed layout embodies tradeoffs that can be understood and justified, location decisions are made explicitly, and possible directions for variation are indicated. It is for these reasons that there have been severe drawbacks to the representation of spatial allocation problems in mathematical formulations such as quadratic-assignment or mixed-integer-programming. Typically, not enough is known up front about the constraints to formulate layout problems for this type of solver. These approaches may be suitable where the set of requirements is strictly limited (such as where distance or material flow is the overriding concern) but performance requirements impacted by considerations of adjacency, shape, size, alignment, relative location, and so forth, and their tradeoffs are very difficult or impossible to model apriori.

Because of its cross-disciplinary importance, its inherent complexity, the fact that only restricted 2-D representations are required, and the need to augment human methods, layout design is a remarkably suitable design task for the initial implementation and study of a CSDE. In this section we describe LOOS, an approach to supporting layout design, and its properties in relation to our conjecture and the requirements for an evolving CSDE.

13.3.1   The LOOS system: Human and machine cooperation

The following description of the LOOS system does not emphasize technical details or the current realization of all of its components (which are evolving). Rather, the intention is to provide the minimal explanation of the approach that will allow us to examine its basic organization of the design process. The primary design goal for LOOS was to build a partially-automated system combining human expertise with the systematic generative capability of computers. An initial system realizing that goal is implemented and running on real problems from several domains.

The core of LOOS is a process that composes a set of 2-D objects into one or more layouts of rectangles. This process is designed around a graph-based relational representation that facilitates the systematic generation of all candidate solution layouts and a separate tester that supports evaluation of candidate solutions over a wide range of criteria. Application of the system to a layout design task requires acquisition of a designers' knowledge and provides them with a set of alternatives that capture tradeoffs. The systems' components are a generator, a tester or evaluator, and a controller. Each was designed to be an independent module so that various evaluators and controllers are easily experimented with and replaced irrespective of and without disturbing the other components. For further technical detail, theory and prototype results see Flemming et al. (1989).

Representation and generation
The representation on which the approach is based uses the basic spatial relations *above, below, to the right,* and *to the left* to define the structure of a layout and represents this structure formally through a directed graph whose nodes represent the rectangles in a layout and whose arcs represent spatial relations between pairs of rectangles. Figure 13.1a shows an example, where solid arrows indicate *above/below* relations, half-tone arrows indicate *left/right* relations, and **E** is the distinguished exterior node that is above, right-of, left-of and below all nodes in a layout.

A set of generation rules has been developed to insert 'rectangles' into a graph, one at a time, and to construct in this fashion every set of realizable relations (for a given number of rectangles) as an alternative layout structure; a sample sequence of rule applications to generate partial layouts is shown in Figure 13.1b. The rules constitute a *generator* that is a formal grammar for the generation of 2-dimensional syntactically correct layouts of rectangles. The semantics of these layouts is established when objects from a given domain are attributed to these rectangles.

Spatial relations, as defined here, formulate a type of intermediate abstraction for describing layouts that reflects a separation of structural from dimensional concerns. Each representation suppresses the continuous dimensional properties of potential layouts and expresses the discrete spatial relations between objects. Each candidate layout thus represents a class of feasibly dimensionable layouts and the possibly infinite set of solutions is divided into a finite set of subsets that can, at least in principle, be enumerated. This representation captures a suitable notion of structure that can be used to define critical differences between alternative layouts and to

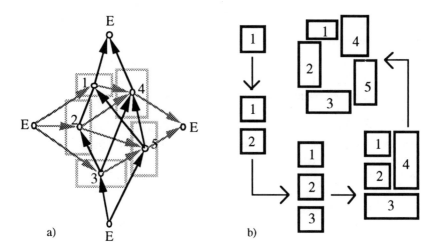

Figure 13.1. Formal representation and generation of arrangements of rectangles.

generate alternative structures; this allows the generation of a well-defined space of potential solutions. Higher-level concepts regarding the quality of layouts can be formulated based on this representation so it also serves as an explicit structure for queries, analysis, and evaluation.

The representation also supports the incremental monotonic specification of designs in terms of their structure. The formal properties of the generator insure that each partial layout generated is formally complete and distinct and that the spatial relations between objects already allocated will not change with the addition of further objects; alternative relationships between a given pair of objects will be found on other branches in the space of possible structures.

A restriction of the representation is its limitation to a rectilinear world. However, the representation achieves significant formalization and simplification given the present state of the art, and it permits numerous interesting applications at various levels of complexity across many design disciplines. Another potentially more serious restriction is that the representation, by itself, does not guarantee that the exploration of the potentially vast space of possible solutions will be efficient and computationally feasible. However the representation is extensible to support the hierarchic recursive processing of layout tasks through decomposition.

Layout task decompositions and their representation
A prime motivation for an extended representational framework is to deal

with scalability of the approach to larger problems and the combinatorics of the generation algorithm; the intent is to manage the complexity of problems both in the numbers of objects handled and in the amount of interactions and detail involved with those objects. To handle complexity, the experience of both human and automated methods suggests that a very important abstraction mechanism in layout design is a hierarchical decomposition of the objects it handles and of the tasks (or goals) it pursues. An approach, described later, has been implemented (Coyne, 1990) to achieve the decompositional structuring desired within the LOOS approach; this research is also converging with many of the other goals for creating a CSDE.

The system, as first developed, treats the underlying representation as *flat*: each node or rectangle represents a single, physical object at the same level of abstraction. In the extended framework, a loosely-packed arrangement of rectangles can represent layouts not only in different domains, but also at various scales and decompositions. A rectangle might represent a single unit or a cluster of rectangles each of which might again represent a cluster. The formal representation used in LOOS supports this recursive structure. In extending the representation to structured objects, each node, or layout component, also defines a layout *goal* or *task*, namely that of allocating the parts it contains. Decompositions in the domains of layout design can be understood in this dual function: they partition both the *object* and *process* of design. The merging of goals and design structure in terms of both function and hierarchy leads to the concept of a powerful integrated abstraction, a *goal-object* (GOB).

Each GOB is self-contained and represents a complete design task, and the knowledge, representation structures, and set of mechanisms with which to accomplish it. These include (but are not limited to) startup and terminating conditions, design method and control selection, evaluation criteria, and the structure and development of its own abstraction subtree (sub-GOBs). A layout task can now be planned as a decompositional hierarchy of subtasks corresponding to a nested tree of GOBs. The overall task is specified as a single top-level GOB. The decompositional structure for the layout task will partition this goal into subgoals at various abstraction levels. The design process will unfold as a *recursive, hierarchical* satisfaction of the layout goals. We elaborate on how this structure can be utilized in dynamically controlling the problem of decomposition and the solution process in the next section.

Evaluation and control
Controlling the syntactic generator.   Given that a well-defined space of potential solutions can be produced, LOOS employs a domain-dependent

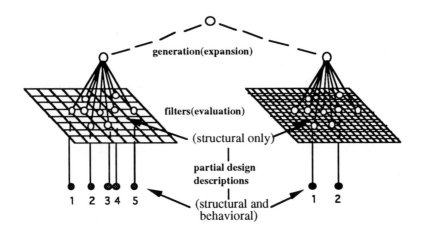

Figure 13.2. Generation and interpretation of partial solutions.

knowledge-based approach for evaluation. It discriminates among the generated candidates based on multiple criteria that capture the semantics for the quality of layouts in the particular domain and problem. This tester, which we also call a *semantic filter*, is designed to be built up incrementally as designers are stimulated to add, change, or withdraw criteria when confronted with partial layouts graphically displayed and rated.

The semantic filter in LOOS serves two critical purposes. First it completes the definition of partial design descriptions by adding behavioral interpretations to the structural alternatives proposed by the generator. Second, the filter must provide adequate knowledge for discriminating among alternatives so that the space of possible solutions is sufficiently reduced to make its exploration feasible and efficient. As is the case in most design tasks, the challenge is to fashion a set of criteria, neither overconstrained or underconstrained, balance the set the requirements or behavioral qualities that the designer is seeking; this may require tradeoffs among the criteria.

Figure 13.2 shows the expansion of a selected node (partial design) by the generator producing a set of alternatives, structurally defined, which represent the placement of another object in the layout in all possible ways. The figure also shows that with the same structural expansion the substitution of a different semantic filter (evaluative criteria) changes the descriptions of the partial alternatives produced.

The results of evaluation are stored in an *evaluation* record. In the current system this is an ordered three tuple consisting of the number of constraints, strong criteria and weak criteria violated. It also captures the relative ratings for partial designs in terms of individual requirements. Constraints indicate a requirement that a solution *must* satisfy in order to become acceptable; strong and weak criteria indicate desired properties of decreasing importance. Evaluation scores corresponding to the evaluation criteria for partial designs are ordered lexicographically in the tuple; that is, there is a relative left to right ordering of importance in the evaluation record. The arity of the tuple and assignment of importance of criteria to the elements in the tuple is up to the judgment of the designer using the system and is a matter for experimentation and knowledge-acquisition. Tradeoffs among design criteria are accommodated by their relative weighting as reflected in assignment to a category in the evaluation record.

A *controller* uses the results of evaluation and a simple branch-and-bound (BNB) strategy to steer the traversal of the space away from less promising alternatives deferring their development until it is certain that nothing better can be found. Using this strategy, the controller expands those and only those intermediate designs that are at least as good as any other design generated before (independent of its level of development in terms of number of objects placed), and prunes the space of candidate solutions.

The structure of the evaluation record, and the rating of partial designs in terms of it, facilitates the ordering of solutions with respect to *failing* requirements. The idea of a filter captures the notion of applying the semantics of the domain in question as a negative screen to the alternatives produced by the syntactic generator. This notion of guiding the expansion of the space of alternatives based on failure of requirements is an important one in design tasks involving multiple complex requirements with both global and local interactions. As a result of this strategy and exhaustive enumeration, LOOS is able to manage decision making and commitment in a unique and efficient way. As noted, it asserts the structural definition of candidates *monotonically* to produce new points in the potential solution space. Because all performance requirements are evaluated in terms of this structural definition, this guarantees that once a partial solution fails in terms of some performance test, it can never get better through further development and its performance is monotonically rated (as an increasingly negative score). Taken together, the representation, generator, tester, and controller of the LOOS approach implement a form of *hierarchical generate-and-test* (Stefik et al., 1983, p. 72). The architecture of LOOS and the domains for which it is intended satisfy the conditions that make this approach workable; in particular, the generator partitions the solution space in ways that allow early pruning, and partial solutions may be evaluated with certainty. This approach is effective in the face of multiple, complex interactions among the goals of layout, the global uncertainty of outcome until all objects are placed, and the need to systematically explore tradeoffs among multiple candidate solutions.

Controlling problem decompositions
The extended representation provides an opportunity both for decomposing an overall layout into components and for controlling the complexity of the representation at various levels or scales. Viewing GOBs (structured objects) alternatively as primitive objects or as subdesign tasks to be further developed provides a uniform protocol in controlling the layout task at different levels. For instance, in the layout of a building, placing 'rooms' within the building may be the final level desired, whereas in another design task the detail of the layout within each room may be needed; or, internals of some rooms may need to be placed while others are left undetailed. This provides designers great flexibility to represent (and experiment with) the degree of detail and level of completion desired in layout tasks. This decomposition strategy supports both top-down and bottom-up control of the design process, such as moving from coarser to finer scales or allocating parts that have been built from smaller components.

Many design systems advocate and depend on the strategy of decomposition or subgoaling to deal with complexity; however, very few deal with problems of recomposition, or the smooth integration of subgoals to solve an overall goal. To provide a method that allows dynamic, and flexible resolution of interaction between subtasks, the GOB architecture will allow some limited bottom-up processing to occur with the overall top-down control. For instance, this could happen opportunistically by pushing down a level of abstraction and querying/placing the subcomponents of a GOB in order to resolve an interaction at the higher level. The use of GOBs in this manner offers some opportunity for bounded negotiation and communication between 'leaky' subgoals to capture the advantages of subdividing a task while providing for realistic integration of design problems that are only 'nearly decomposable.'

13.3.2   The conjecture illustrated

We now examine the critical capabilities for the support of layout design in LOOS that begin to give it the character of a CSDE in which our conjecture can be tested.

Expanding the examination of given problem spaces for potential solutions
We have pointed out the limitations of human designers in exploring a large

space of solutions for a given problem. To overcome this, LOOS enables a designer to thoroughly examine the potential solutions for a given formulation of a layout problem. It does this by combining systematic generative capability and the abstract representation of partial designs with an evaluative knowledge-base. Leaving aside the development of the knowledge base(s) for a particular domain, once they exist, designers are enabled to easily look at many more potential solutions, and find distinct alternative solutions faster for a typical problem than they could using only their own resources. Depending on the complexity of the problem this could substantially reduce their expenditure of resources (conserving these for additional exploration of the design task at hand) while significantly increasing the number of distinct solutions considered. We believe that the capability for systematic examination, though not creative in itself, underlies the creative potential at a basic level; that is, it provides the grounds for its emergence rather than being the creative act itself.

Exploration of problem spaces through modification of evaluation criteria
Within LOOS's design process designers are also able to explore potential solutions for a given layout task in a variety of problem spaces. They are able to change the problem space within which they are working by changing the requirements or behavioral description of (partial) layouts in three ways:

1. by adding, changing, and withdrawing evaluative criteria;

2. by adding/changing measures of importance for particular evaluative criteria;

3. by adding or withdrawing categories of importance in the evaluation record (to which to assign the individual evaluative criteria).

Each of these can contribute to modifying the semantic filter through which the structurally defined and generated partial solutions are passed, as illustrated in Figure 13.2. Examples of evaluation requirements that might be added for a kitchen layout task are: 'The back of the refrigerator cannot be placed against a wall' and 'The sink has no space on either side for a work counter;' these might be assigned to different levels of importance in the evaluation record. The following list suggests additional levels of importance and corresponding categories of performance requirements that might be added to achieve finer grained discrimination of alternatives for a typical architectural layout task:

1. well-formedness tests, such as dimensional fit

2. code tests

3. good practice

4. client preference

5. office style or policy

6. designer preference

This possible extended hierarchy of requirement levels would be reflected in the extension of the evaluation record tuple. The significant thing about the elaboration of levels of possible evaluations is that those that reflect somewhat arbitrary constraints or criteria (designer preference) could contribute to balanced discrimination on problems that would otherwise be overconstrained or underconstrained. The LOOS approach will readily accommodate such customization, and its applicability will depend on the domain in question.

For particular domains of layout, the construction of a hierarchy of evaluative knowledge-bases, corresponding to the aforementioned levels, would provide a means for individuals or firms to create and store their 'intellectual design capital.' This possibility reflects the opportunity for designers to conveniently intermix a variety of personal and institutional evaluation and stopping rules in design. The same iterative generate-evaluate-modify cycle may be used to develop these knowledge bases or customize an existing one. We have more to say about the role that such knowledge-bases might play as part of design histories later.

The interaction of designers with a graphic display of partial designs is an important example of raising the abstraction level at which computer tools can provide external memory aids to the designer. The exploration of alternative problem spaces in a developing design task, with the close interconnection of long-term memory aids (from internal and external sources through a noticing and evoking process), might be considered a *creative process* in itself. At the very least it will have significant direct impact on the potential for producing *creative results* in the overall human/computer design environment.

Expanding the exploration of problem spaces through decomposition
Each GOB has a set of constituent objects, other (sub)GOBs, whose placement make up its layout task. A designer may experiment with alternative decompositions by assigning an object as a constituent of one GOB as opposed to another, or by making an object active in the layout at a different level of abstraction, for instance at the same level as a former 'parent' GOB.

In this way designers are afforded the flexibility to capture and experiment with the granularities of objects and layout tasks within a domain until they find a suitable decomposition relative to the constraints of their present task. This is a familiar process in many design domains where there is frequently the option to choose a standard structured object from a library or design database, or to custom build in context from a more primitive set of components. For specific critical GOBs it may be desirable to build up and record ordered alternative decompositions (sets of constituents) so that successive ones may be tried dynamically in the event that sufficiently good evaluations are not achieved by the prior one.

Initially within a domain, the human designer will develop the decomposition knowledge through experimentation and enter it into the system in the form of GOBs, their development levels and constituents. This involves knowledge elicitation and acquisition at the task decomposition level, and the potential for exploration of alternative problem spaces in terms of the structure of the task. Over time and problem runs a knowledge-base of GOBs will be accumulated in a domain and constitute accessible long term memory usable to help structure any given task, and of course customizable to the task. Experimentation with decompositions for a given task may lead to creative solutions.

13.3.3 Computer supported design and creativity in LOOS

In the LOOS approach to layout design the computer supplies the generative expertise and 'horsepower' whereas the human provides the evaluative judgment to formulate the interpretation of the syntactically proposed layouts and to structure and guide the overall process. Through this balance of capabilities the overall architecture of the LOOS system effectively addresses some of the long-standing fundamental problems of supporting layout design. In this section we summarize how LOOS illustrates features of an evolving CSDE that encompasses capabilities that incrementally and cumulatively enhance creativity in design. In doing so we answer, in large part, the following two questions that should be asked of any computational design environment that purports to enhance the creative capacities of human designers.

1. How does an integrated environment support the creativity of a human designer and make accessible essential knowledge and judgment that would be difficult (or impossible) to encode in an independent computational design system?

To support a computational design model that answers this question

LOOS provides the following design support features:

- The use of an independent syntactic solution generation capability. The strict separation of evaluation from formal syntactic generation enables a critical division of labor between machine and man, and also enables the approach to be applied to 'generic layout tasks' across multiple disciplines. (Generation of solutions)

- The incorporation of semantic concerns in a tester within a well-defined context for evaluation. Spatial relations provide an explicit structure for evaluation of partial designs in terms of a current full set of applicable criteria. (Encapsulation of evaluation criteria)

- The use of multiple representations and abstraction techniques and levels to mediate decisions and the processing of design goals to design specifications. Evaluations are enabled at different levels of abstraction. (Management of complexity)

- The facility to combine top-down and bottom-up reasoning with limited dynamic, automatic transitions between these modes on demand based on a limited commitment of resources. Control can also be managed interactively or automatically at all significant choice points. (Flexible control of reasoning)

- The computer performs constraint management and required bookkeeping as the design evolves, and can not only signal when constraints are violated, but is capable of keeping track of tradeoffs. (Short-term memory aid)

- The ability to use subjective evaluation and stopping rules (tradeoffs). This ultimately results in the compilation of this knowledge into evolving customizable knowledge-bases. The compilation of knowledge-bases helps the designer in experimenting with multiple sets of evaluation rules. (Long-term personalized repository of knowledge)

- The means for domain experts to make explicit their knowledge when confronted with a concrete solution in a familiar graphical display, as opposed to formulating their knowledge in general terms unrelated to a concrete case. (Communication through the language of a design task)

The LOOS architecture, in addition to supporting generative activity, also supports patching activity by serving as a diagnostic, evaluative system (in domains where an evaluation knowledge-base has been developed.) Designs, produced by either manual or automated means, are easily converted into LOOS's internal representation, submitted immediately for evaluation and the results displayed with an explanation of any violations. It would also be possible to remove a design object or objects deemed most responsible for a failure (by backward application of generation rules) and to resubmit the reduced configuration, along with the object(s) to be inserted, to the generator in order to obtain additional alternatives.

Along these lines, it is easy to imagine how an interactive environment for using the LOOS system in multiple ways could be constructed. The device of removing a (critical) piece from the layout and reinserting it in all possible ways could be developed into a form of *prototype adaptation* (Gero et al., 1988), and bears a strong relationship to the heuristic planning mechanism of *debugging an almost correct plan* (Sussman, 1975). This capability could be used in developing, learning, and teaching patching expertise.

2. How does this integrated environment evolve over time while providing the grounds for creativity? What does each agent gain? And how do their roles change, and so forth?

An evolving environment has to provide for a continual update of the division of labor. The system will have to acquire new design abstractions and evaluations from the interaction with the designer over large classes of problems. These capabilities would allow the system to propose design abstractions based on the specifications of the problem.

From our description of the LOOS it should be clear that we have illustrated an architecture that will support the evolution of computational knowledge, mechanisms, and interaction levels. Each GOB will be a relatively independent task with considerable local autonomy and ability to respond flexibly and dynamically to accomplishing its task. In a sense, each GOB represents the entire core LOOS system—and more—by providing an appropriate place to acquire, store, retrieve, and reason about the application of knowledge of layout design in many forms. For instance, each GOB will store its own semantic filter appropriate to its layout task and set of constituent objects; this will save in a structured way an evaluation knowledge-base that a designer develops and wants to store at the proper level of abstraction. Similarly, each GOB will have a slot for methods to achieve its task, of which the core systems' generative method will be only one option (albeit the prime one initially). Possible alternative methods are selecting from a pre-enumerated set, refining a prototypical arrangement, modifying an almost correct arrangement, constraint-directed generation, or heuristic or interactive constructive methods. Over time the system may learn to use particular methods in the context of particular layout subtasks. As knowledge and experience accumulate over design tasks in a domain, one would expect a shift to take place from generate-and-test to more direct methods, such as instantiating prestored generalized solutions. One can envisage that skeleton or prototypical layouts (for instance, generalized context-invariant layouts satisfying internal relationships only) are stored as a result of previous design sessions and used as a basis for creating or completing a desired layout in response to a current context.

With the model of design and the architecture for computational support presented in this chapter we can generate an understanding of classes of design problems that can be accumulated in the form of classified design histories. The LOOS CSDE integrates elements of search-based and knowledge-based systems as an evolutionary step toward an *exploration-based model of design* as cited earlier in Section 13.2.3. Iterations of generate-evaluate-modify converge on the desired formulation of the design task and produce not only the enumeration of all possible solutions given that formulation, but an implicit theory of layout design for that domain in the form of decomposition and evaluation knowledge-bases. Iterations over multiple problems in a domain can refine the knowledge-base and theory produced. We believe that such domain theories of design and further insights for research will emerge through the ordinary exercise of the system on design tasks. In this way, the process of abstraction and generalization of knowledge from particular design tasks will no longer be just implicit in the practice of human designers alone, but will become explicit in the evolving architecture and knowledge-bases of a CSDE. We believe that this environment will also provide the opportunity to introduce and experiment in context with a variety of mechanisms for learning, the use of analogy, modification, and patching operations, and other localized methods possibly related to design creativity or innovation.

We have shown that the LOOS system satisfies the basic requirements posed in our conjecture and begins to address the critical issues involved in the realization of an expanded computational model and experimental testbed for design and creativity—an evolving CSDE. We realize that the success of CSDEs is dependent on many other requirements that we have not discussed here, such as the development of sophisticated cooperative interaction models—including development of a well-structured interactive graphical display, high level languages, and so forth. These are needed to give a designer high-level access to and understanding of the developing content of knowledge structures and design representations without concern for their internal representation and implementation. These and related concerns form part of the critical research issues being formulated for the further development of the LOOS environment.

On a more general level, the structure of GOBs, and the overall structure of a CSDE to accomplish the goals outlined, is itself a design problem, the formulation of which requires experimentation and testing in context (see Section 13.2.3). The study of the required structure can be identified with the aim of understanding how to build design apprentices who accumulate experience and apply it to new tasks; this includes the compilation of expertise while retaining the flexibility to be creative. In motivating and describing the development of CSDEs such as LOOS, we propose using the computational medium both as a partially automated assistant to deal with real design tasks, and as a foundation for further research in design and creativity.

13.4 Conclusion

In this chapter we described an approach to the design of computational environments that can be used to study the conditions under which creativity can occur. We proposed a conjecture on creativity within an information processing theory of design. This conjecture, briefly stated, predicates the occurrence of creative design when a designer is provided the capability to explore an expanded problem formulation space or more of a given solution space for a task. We then characterized the realization of design environments to enhance creativity as a design task itself with evolving goals. Through LOOS, an architecture for layout design, we illustrated how the conditions of the conjecture could be supported in an evolving computer supported design environment. We also described how this architecture allows for the development of domain theories of design. Finally, we discussed the significance of our approach as a foundation for design research and its relation to existing areas of research in creativity and design.

Acknowledgments. The authors are grateful to Ulrich Flemming, David Steir, and the editors of this book for their helpful comments on earlier drafts of this chapter. Support for this work has come from the National Science Foundation through its funding of the EDRC.

References

Addanki, S., & Murthy, S. (1987). Prompt: An innovative design tool, *Proceedings of the Sixth National Conference on Artificial Intelligence*, AAAI'87, Morgan Kaufman, Los Altos, California.

Adelson, B., & Soloway, E. (1984). A cognitive model of software design, *Technical Report 342*, Department of Computer Science, Yale University.

Akin, O. (1986). *Psychology of Architectural Design*, Pion, London.

Baker, N., & Fenves, S. (1987). A knowledge acquisition study of structural engineers performing design, *Technical Report EDRC 12-19-87*, Engineering Design Research Center, Carnegie Mellon University, Pittsburgh.

Bundy, A. (1983). Nature of AI: Reply to Ohlsson, *Artificial Intelligence and Simulation of Behaviour Quarterly* (Summer): 24–25.

Coyne, R. F. (1990). Planning in design synthesis: Abstraction-based LOOS (ABLOOS), *PhD Thesis*, Engineering Design Research Center, Carnegie Mellon University, Pittsburgh.

Doyle, J. (1984). Expert systems without computers or theory and trust in artificial intelligence, *AI Magazine* 5(2): 59–63.

Doyle, J. (1988). On rationality and learning, *Technical Report CMU-CS-88-122*, Department of Computer Science, Carnegie Mellon University, Pittsburgh.

Eastman, C. (1969). Cognitive processes and ill-defined problems: A case study from design, *Proceedings International Joint Conference on Artificial Intelligence*, IJCAI.

Flemming, U. (1988). Rule-based systems in computer-aided architectural design, in, M. D. Rychener (ed.), *Expert Systems for Engineering Design*, Academic Press, San Diego, California, pp. 93–112.

Flemming, U. (1989). Some thoughts on creativity (unpublished paper), Department of Architecture, Carnegie Mellon University, Pittsburgh.

Flemming, U., Coyne, R. F., Glavin, T., Hsi, H., & Rychener, M. (1989). A generative expert system for the design of building layouts (final report), *Technical Report EDRC 48-15-89*, Engineering Design Research Center, Carnegie Mellon University, Pittsburgh.

Galle, P. (1986). Abstraction as a tool of automated floor-plan design, *Environment and Planning B: Planning and Design* 13: 21–46.

Genesereth, M. R. (1983). An overview of meta-level architecture, *Proceedings of the National Conference on Artificial Intelligence*, AAAI, pp. 119–124.

Gero, J. S., Maher, M. L., & Zhang, W. (1988). Chunking structural design knowledge as prototypes, in J. S. Gero (Ed.), *Artificial Intelligence in Engineering Design*, Elsevier/CMP, Amsterdam, pp. 3–21.

Goel, V., & Pirolli, P. (1989). Motivating the notion of generic design within information processing theory: The design problem space, *AI Magazine* 10(1): 18–36.

Hodges, A. (1985). *Alan Turing The Enigma of Intelligence*, Unwin, London.

Kalagnanam, J., & Subrahmanian, E. (1989). Learning to diagnose by doing, *Proceedings of the International Joint Conference on Artificial Intelligence, IJCAI'89*, Morgan Kaufmann, Los Altos, California, pp. 540–545.

Levesque, H. (1986). Making believers out of computers, *Journal of Artificial Intelligence* 30(2): 81–108.

Liggett, R. S., & Mitchell, W. J. (1981). Optimal space planning in practice, *Computer Aided Design* 13(5): 277–288.

Mittal, S., Dym, C. L., & Morjaria, M. (1986). PRIDE: An expert system for the design of paper handling systems, *Computer* (July): 102–114.

Mostow, J. (1985). Toward better models of the design process, *AI Magazine* 6(1): 44–57.

Newell, A., & Simon, H. A. (1972). *Human Problem Solving*, Prentice-Hall,

Englewood Cliffs, New Jersey.

Ohlsson, S. (1983). Mathematics, behavior, and creativity: A reply to Bundy, *Artificial Intelligence and Simulation of Behaviour Quarterly* (Summer): 25.

Orelup, M. F., Dixon, J. R., & Simmons, M. K. (1987). Dominic II: More progress towards domain independent design by iterative redesign, *WAM*, ASME, pp. 1–14.

Rich, E. (1984). The gradual expansion of artificial intelligence, *IEEE Computer* (May): 4–12.

Rychener, M. D. (1988). Research in expert systems for engineering design, *Expert Systems for Engineering Design*, Academic Press, San Diego, California, pp. 1–33.

Sharkey, N., & Brown, G. (1985). Why artificial intelligence needs an empirical foundation, *Artificial Intelligence: Principles and Applications*, Chapman Hall, New York, pp. 269–291.

Simon, H. A. (1973). The structure of ill structured problems, *Artificial Intelligence* **4**: 181–201.

Simon, H. A. (1981). *Sciences of the Artificial*, 2nd edn, MIT Press, Cambridge, Massachusetts.

Smithers, T., Conkie, A., Dohen, J., Logan, B., & Milligan, K. (1989). Design as intelligent behaviour: An AI in design research programme, *Technical Report DAI426*, Department of Artificial Intelligence, University of Edinburgh, Edinburgh.

Stefik, M. (1981). Planning and meta-planning (Molgen: part 2), *Artificial Intelligence* **16**(2): 141–170.

Stefik, M., Aikins, J., Balzer, R., Benoit, J., Birnbaum, L., Hayes-Roth, F., & Sacerdoti, E. (1983). Basic concepts for building expert systems, *in*, F. Hayes-Roth, D. A. Waterman, & D. B. Lenat (Eds), *Building Expert Systems*, Addison Wesley, Reading, Massachusetts, pp. 59–86.

Steinberg, L. (1987). Design as refinement plus constraint propagation: The VEXED experience, *Proceedings of the Sixth Annual Conference on Artificial Intelligence, AAAI'87*, Morgan Kaufmann, Los Altos, California, pp. 830–835.

Sussman, G. J. (1975). *A Computer Model of Skill Acquisition*, American Elsevier, New York.

Takewaki, T., Miyachi, T., Kunifuji, S., & Furukawa, K. (1985). An algebraic manipulation system using meta-level inference based on human heuristics, *ICOT Technical Report TR-140*, ICOT Research Center, Institute for New Generation Computer Technology.

Ullman, D. G., Dietterich, T. G., & Stauffer, L. A. (1988). A model of the mechanical design process based on empirical data, *AI EDAM* **2**(1): 33–52.

Zhao, F., & Maher, M. L. (1987). Using analogical reasoning to design buildings, *Engineering with Computers* **4**: 107–119.

14 Dynamic Associations for Creative Engineering Design

Mary Lou Maher and Fang Zhao

Creative design often features associations between seemingly unrelated concepts. Two essential elements involved in this association process are some form of an associated conceptual network that provides the basis of such associations and a reasoning mechanism that enables such associations. A collection of hierarchically organized prototypes can serve as the associated network. A system for generating design specifications dynamically using design prototypes as a resource provides an initial knowledge-based creative design environment.

14.1 A knowledge-based design model using analogy and mutation

The use of knowledge-based techniques has enabled new insights in engineering design research. The ability to model and implement design processes as reasoning systems has resulted in another look at design theory and methodology as potentially useful tools. There is activity that goes beyond CAD programs that facilitate visualization and analysis to the generation of design configurations. Most of the current knowledge-based design programs address routine design in narrow domains. In this chapter we consider the issue of creativity because rarely does a designer rely entirely on well known previous design solutions without consideration of change and adaptation. One way to support this change and adaptation is to look carefully at creativity strategies and design knowledge and model them using knowledge-based techniques.

Although creativity is not well understood, it has been the subject of much research. There are numerous publications identifying strategies to help humans be more creative. We consider these strategies as a basis for computer creativity. Specifically, we are interested in analogy and mutation as two strategies that show promise for computer implementation.

Analogy is a useful approach for solving an unfamiliar new problem without adequate or directly applicable knowledge. By analogy, relationships between a new problem and past experience or knowledge about design concepts can be found. This experience or knowledge can be used in a new situation so that the new problem can be better understood or a plan for solving the new design problem can be generated. Because analogy does not require the two episodes or concepts compared to be the same, it leaves room for creativity. In order to use analogy effectively a large amount of experience and knowledge is needed and techniques for relating past experience and new problems is essential.

Currently the analogy approach in computer programs is an active research area in artificial intelligence and its application (Prieditis, 1988; Keane, 1988). Various forms of analogical reasoning are under study. Based on the nature of the knowledge transfer from previous experience to new problem, the analogical reasoning approach can be classified into two categories: transformational analogy and derivational analogy (Carbonell, 1982, 1983, 1986; Carbonell et al., 1983). Transformational analogy adapts the solutions to the past problems for the new problem. Derivational analogy applies the past problem solving processes or methods to solve the new problem.

Mutation is the deliberate action of changing features or attributes of an object or concept in an unconventional manner. An unconventional manner is one in which the change is not restricted by conventional rules and constraints. The purpose of mutation is to find new properties, functions, and meanings of an old concept by looking at it from different perspectives. An example of a computer program that uses mutation is AM (Lenat, 1982; Lenat and Brown, 1983). Because mutation is knowledge intensive, it is difficult to obtain meaningful mutation operators. This may make mutation look arbitrary. Without appropriate control, applying mutation operators is opportunistic and success cannot be guaranteed.

A model for knowledge-based creative design using mutation and analogy is illustrated in Figure 14.1 (Maher et al., 1989). In this model, the design

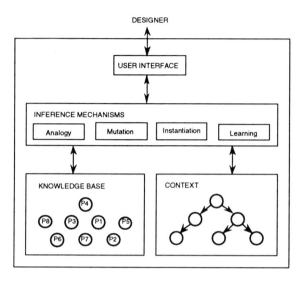

Figure 14.1. Model of knowledge-based design using mutation and analogy.

process is considered a search in a knowledge-base of design experience and concepts. The search for a design concept is based on analogy. In a non-routine design situation, the correspondence between the new design specifications and the design concepts based on previous experience may not be close. Upon selection of a design concept that appears to be interesting, mutation is used to transform the past experience to a form that is appropriate for application to the new design problem. Instantiation is the process through which the transformed knowledge is used to generate an unconventional design solution. In this model, the inferencing schemes are based on analogy, mutation, and instantiation; the knowledge-base is composed of design concepts based on previous experience; and the context contains the evolving information about the new design problem.

In this chapter we describe a memory organization for a knowledge-base that can support analogy and mutation. We propose the idea of a design prototype for memory organization. We look more closely at the analogy technique in the proposed model, specifically at the use of dynamic associations for generalizing a set of design specifications in order to avoid the automatic use of routine design concepts. We then discuss the implementation of these ideas in a computer program. Finally, we conclude and identify directions for further work.

14.2   Design prototypes as a basis for organizing memory

A conceptual schema, called a design prototype, has been developed to represent and organize design knowledge and experience. Prototypes are intoduced by Gero (1990) and their use in routine structural design is described by Gero et al. (1988). A prototype is a generalization of groupings of elements in a design domain that provides the basis for the commencement and continuation of a design. The prototype represents a class of elements from which instances of elements can be derived. It comprises the knowledge needed for reasoning about the prototype's use as well as about how to produce instances in a given design context. A prototype can also be related to others either as a specialization or generalization or as a component or system to which other prototypes are the components. A hierarchy of prototypes can therefore be constructed. A designer's design knowledge may be considered as being comprised of a set of prototypes in the designer's particular domain. Design using prototypes is a process in which suitable prototypes are sought for based on the given design specifications and are instantiated to produce instances that satisfy design goals and constraints.

In order to support creative design, we propose that it is necessary to represent design knowledge that includes function, structure, and behavior. Purely syntactic design knowledge, for example, what a particular design looks like, is not sufficient for reasoning about unconventional uses of design experience. To facilitate reasoning about a prototype's semantics as well as syntax in design, a prototype explicitly represents the following knowledge categories:

- **Functions** are the design goals or requirements that can be achieved by using the prototype.

- **Structure** attributes describe the prototype in terms of its physical existence or the conditions for such existence. These are typically design variables whose values will be determined during the instantiation process, as well as some generalized attributes that describe the prototype structure at a higher conceptual level.

- **Behaviors** are the expected reactions or responses of the prototype under the possible design environment. Performance attributes of the prototype are the behaviors of particular interest in evaluating the appropriateness and "goodness" of an instance of the prototype.

- **Design methods** are the design plans that can be executed to produce instances of the prototype for different design specifications. Design plans are available for various design situations. The results of executing a design plan will be the selection of a set of variables that are relevant in determining the structure and performance of the instance as well as the assignments of values to these variables.

Representing design knowledge as prototypes provides a framework for capturing the terminology and the meaning of the terms in a particular domain. For example the statement "design a rigid frame" brings forth the prototype associated with the label "rigid frame." This prototype includes the requirements of lateral load resistance, open bays, rigid connections, and the design parameters of bay width and height, material and size of beams and columns, and so on, even though none of these was mentioned explicitly in the prototype's label. When determining the size of beams and columns, their prototypes will be recalled to produce the beam and column instances using knowledge stored in these prototypes, respectively.

An example of a partially defined rigid frame prototype is given in Figure 14.2. An attribute may have, besides a value, several facets to describe itself. These facets provide information such as the valid data type of the value, the allowable range of the value, procedures to perform information processing specific to this attribute, and the relations between this and other attributes. In this example, only the constant values and ranges of attributes are shown. The difference between this representation of a rigid frame and a more general object oriented representation is the explicit categorization of the attributes as function, behavior, and structure allowing reasoning about the categories of attributes in addition to reasoning about the attributes themselves.

This explicit representation can support creativity because it goes beyond the representation of a physical description of classes of design elements. As shown in Figure 14.3, these knowledge categories are closely related, although many of the relationships are only implicitly understood. A set of design specifications can provide information in any of the categories, as indicated by the dotted lines. The dark arrows indicate mappings that are typically explicitly stated in current typical computer programs used during design. The mapping from function to structure represents available heuristics for producing design solutions that may be explicitly stated in knowledge-based expert system. The mappings from structure to behavior and behavior to performance are explicitly stated in available engineering analysis programs. The lighter arrows represent mappings that are not explicitly stated but are necessary for creative design. Being able to reason from function to structure via expected performances and behaviors allows the generalized routine function-structure mappings to be bypassed.

Functions	resist-load	lateral load, gravity load
	extend	2D, vertical
	provide	open bays
Behaviors	mechanism	bending
	stress	bending stress, shear stress, axial stress
	deformation	lateral deflection
	load path	
	max bending moment	
	max shear force	
	max axial force	
	lateral deflection	
	weight	
	cost	
Structure	geometry	2D, framed
	components	beams, column, rigid connections, supports
	loading condition	
	support condition	
	topology	
	material	range (steel concrete)
	number of stories	range (> 0)
	number of bays	range (> 0)
	bay sizes	range (> 0)
	has-columns	
	has-beams	
Methods	main plan (for control of instantiation)	
	calculate max-bending-moment	
	calculate max-shear-force	
	calculate max-axial-force	
	....	

Figure 14.2. A rigid frame prototype.

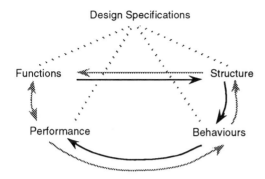

Figure 14.3. Knowledge categories in a prototype and reasoning directions.

Prototypes are an interesting conceptual scheme because of the breadth of the design knowledge included. Designers are capable of using prototypes in unexpected ways, as well as generating new prototypes. Operations on prototypes can be classified into three groups: prototype refinement, prototype adaptation, and prototype creation. This classification can be mapped on to routine and creative design and is further described later.

- **Prototype refinement.** Here the prototype is instantiated from its class and is found to be adequate so only values of the design variables are searched for within the limits defined. These values are such as to produce the required functions and performance. Routine design falls into the category of prototype refinement.

- **Prototype adaptation.** If the prototype instance is found to be inadequate in some sense, a number of opportunities are open to the designer or design system to adapt the prototype to make it more useful. Attempts may be made to change the behaviors of the prototype by changing its structure, or relax the constraints on the structure or performance variables so that new values for them may be found. Prototype adaptation is one means of producing innovative designs.

- **Prototype creation.** Creating new prototypes is the highest of the design endeavors and very little is known, in a formal sense, as to how this is done. A new prototype is usually recognized after it has been created and shown to be useful. Prototype creation may be considered an extension of prototype adaptation, where the adapted prototype is sufficiently different to be considered a new prototype. A new prototype is a post facto recognition of a creative design.

Whereas prototype refinement assumes that the selected prototype provides the design knowledge needed to produce an acceptable instance, prototype adaptation indicates that the selected prototype is inadequate in some way. A prototype is selected on the basis of a set of design specifications, in which the specifications are matched with the prototype's function, structure, and behavior attributes. In routine design, a prototype exists that closely matches the given set of specifications and prototype refinement follows. In creative design, the set of specifications is unusual in some way and the selected prototype cannot be simply refined so it must be adapted. In the following section, the idea of generating an unusual set of specifications using the categories of design knowledge in prototypes is explored.

14.3   Dynamically generating specifications for design

A design process begins with a set of specifications, identifying some of the characteristics of the design solution. These design specifications are used to find appropriate design concepts, in our case design prototypes, for application to the design problem. Therefore, design specifications describe a possible solution space for the design problem. Design is an iterative process, where the set of design specifications may be changed or elaborated as the design proceeds. As a result, the solution space also changes accordingly. In routine design, the specifications can be satisfied using past design experience in conventional ways, which means that a correspondence between fixed solution spaces and classes of design problems exists. Such direct correspondence makes routine design efficient. In creative design, however, knowledge about the desired artifact is inadequate, and there are no known relations between the design problem and the solution space. One aspect of creative design is to explore the possible solution spaces to allow creativity to occur. Dynamic generation of a set of design specifications is intended to partly simulate this exploration process. It requires little initial information and does not involve any explicitly stated rules for specifying the relevant information in a given design situation, thus avoiding the assumption of conventional design solutions from the beginning.

Creative design often features creative associations between not obviously related concepts (Schank, 1986). Two essential elements involved in this creative association process are some form of a conceptual network that provides the basis of such associations and a reasoning mechanism that enables such associations. We propose a collection of hierarchically organized prototypes can serve as the associated network. On the one hand they are concepts themselves. On the other hand, they provide connections between themselves and other concepts explicitly through the hierarchy and implicitly through the three categories of function, behavior, and structure. Given

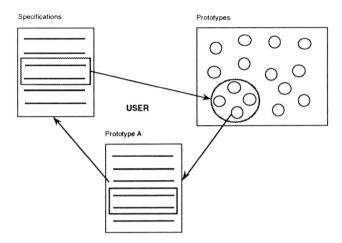

Figure 14.4. Dynamic associations in prototypes.

a prototype, relevant attributes can be identified, or vice versa; given an
attribute prototypes, that possess this attribute can also be identified. Attributes of a prototype are also connected through the simple fact that they
all belong to the same prototype. Classification of attributes into different
categories adds more semantic information to the connections implied by the
syntax between attributes of a prototype.

Using prototypes as the conceptual network, analogy can be applied as
the reasoning mechanism. The purpose of analogy here is to find design
prototypes associated with a given set of design specifications where the
specifications are represented in terms of the desired attributes and values
for the artifact. This connection does not need to be strong, which means
that analogy does not require a prototype to be a perfect match. This
relaxing of design requirements reflects the flexibility necessary in creative
design.

As illustrated in Figure 14.4, with prototypes and analogy, it is possible to
dynamically generate a set of design specifications using associations between
a given set of design specifications and the specification of prototypes that
share at least one attribute with the new design problem. The designer can
provide an initial set of specifications that may provide little information
about the artifact, at which point the creative design system searches for
prototypes using one of the specifications as an index. Among all the
prototypes found through the index, one is selected, possibly randomly, to
expand the set of specifications. The selected prototype is considered for one
of the knowledge categories, for example, structure, other than the category

of the index used to retrieve it, for example, function. The attributes associated with that category of the selected prototype are added to a set of potential design specifications. This process serves to broaden the initial set of specifications and to identify, dynamically, associations between the new design problem and previous experience. This process continues iteratively until an interesting set of specifications has been generated or an interesting prototype has been selected.

For example, an initial set of design specifications may contain a statement that a structure is needed to resist transverse load (function) and span a certain distance (structure). At this point we can focus on the structure attribute, span, ignoring the function attribute. Some prototypes in the knowledge-base that have this attribute are *beam*, *truss*, and *steel deck*. The truss is selected and the behavior attributes are chosen to be added to the set of potential specifications. These behavior attributes, such as axial stress, have no apparent relationship to the original set of specifications but may lead to other prototypes that do. Next, a function attribute may be selected as an index and the behavior attributes of a retrieved prototype may be used to expand the set of specifications. This continues until the designer wishes to stop searching for relevant prototypes upon retrieval of an interesting prototype or until a set of specifications is complete enough to look for a partial match for all specifications. In this example the categories of function, behavior, and structure are used to explore and expand a set of specifications so that the routine design spaces are not automatically used.

By using the semantics of prototypes, encoded as attributes associated with function, behavior, structure, and so forth, for identifying potential specifications, the system can dynamically generate associations between function and structure that were not anticipated. For example, the system could generate an association between the length of a truss and the span of a cable through the common behavior of axial stress. The next step is to make use of such associations for designing a specific artifact. This requires mutation and is beyond the scope of this chapter.

14.4   Implementation

The capability of dynamically generating design specifications has been implemented in a computer system using LISP and a frame language that is designed to support prototype representation developed at Carnegie Mellon University (Gero et al., 1988). The application domain for experimenting with these ideas is the design of structural systems for buildings. The prototypes stored in the current system's knowledge-base include: beam,

Extend

is-a	function			
values	horizontal	vertical	1D	2D
prototypes	(truss ...)	(column	(column ...)	rigid-frame ...)
		rigid-frame ...)		

Figure 14.5. Index "Extend".

cantilever-beam, column, truss, space-truss, vierendeel-truss, rigid-frame, braced-frame, steel-deck, flat-plate, tube core, bridge, arch-bridge, arch, and cable. As described in Section 2, the specification of a prototype consists of attributes grouped into different categories (see example in Figure 14.2). One additional category, *structure variables*, is added in the implemented prototype specification. The purpose is to distinguish structural variables that define an instance of a prototype from the *structure* category that provide higher level conceptual descriptions of the prototype structure. Examples of such structure attributes are the general geometry of an arch as two-dimensional and curve-shaped. Examples of structure variables are the span and height of an arch. Some attributes have predefined values, for instance *resist-load* in the *functions* group may have values of *lateral-load, gravity-load*, and so forth. The attributes that do not have predefined values, such as beam span and material type, may have predefined ranges. Some other attributes have neither values nor ranges, but predefined data types to which the values they assume have to conform.

To facilitate the search for prototypes given an attribute as an index, an indexing system is used. Each attribute, when considered as an index, is associated with the prototypes that include it among their attributes. Figure 14.5 shows how several prototypes are indexed under attribute *extend*, which is a function of the structural design prototypes. This scheme provides the connections from attributes (and their values) to prototypes. For example, given a design specification that the structure extends vertically in one dimension, some prototypes can be easily identified as *column, truss*, and *rigid-frame*. Among them, only *column* perfectly satisfies the specification; truss and rigid-frame partly satisfy the requirement because they extend in two dimensions instead one. This indexing system is generated when the prototypes are loaded into the system the first time and then saved into a file. They are changed or regenerated only when changes are made to the prototypes.

A weight is assigned to each specification to reflect the importance of the requirement where a higher value indicates a more important specification. This weight is currently assigned by the user. These weights are later used to evaluate the prototypes that are partial matches for the entire set of specifications. The evaluation of a prototype is made based on the number of requirements in the specifications it satisfies and the weight of the requirements. The higher the evaluation, the closer the match.

An operator is used in each specification to relate the attribute to its expected matching values. It states that a prototype that has the attribute and satisfies that relation is a match. Valid operators and their meanings are:

- = simultaneous satisfaction: A prototype is a match if it has the attribute as well as all the values that follow the = symbol for that attribute.

- **NOT-IN** exclusion: All the values following **NOT-IN** should not appear in a prototype that is a match for the specified attribute.

- **IN** selective satisfaction: If a set of values is related to an attribute by **IN**, then a prototype possesses the attribute and any of these values is considered a match.

- <> selective exclusion: A prototype is a match if it has the attribute and not all the values that follows the <> symbol are the values for that attribute.

The operators = and **NOT-IN** are stronger than **IN** and <>. It is more often in non-routine design to use the latter two because strict constraints hinders creative thinking. The system provides the user with the options of relaxing requirements by substituting **IN** for =, and <> for **NOT-IN**. A requirement can also be relaxed by using **any** as a value for an attribute. In this case, it only matters that a prototype has the attribute, not what values this attribute may assume.

The steps for dynamically generating specifications are described as the following.

1. A set of specifications are provided by the user.

2. One specification is used as an index to retrieve a set of prototypes.

3. One prototype is selected to serve as the basis for expanding the set of specifications.

4. A category is selected for expansion.

5. The attributes of the prototype in the selected category are added to the potential set of specifications.

6. The user may prune the set of specifications.

7. The second through seventh steps are repeated until termination.

The process of generating design specifications terminates in two situations:

- **Involuntary termination.** This happens when the selection of any one specification as an index does not retrieve attributes that have not already been considered as potential specifications. In other words, the knowledge-base of prototypes and associated attributes has been exhausted.

- **Voluntary termination.** The user indicates that a prototype that has been retrieved using an index is suitable for possible mutation and instantiation or that the current set of specifications is suitable for finding prototypes that are partial matches of the entire set of specifications.

An example of a session using the described system for generating an expanded set of specifications is shown later. Texts surrounded by {} are later annotations.

```
{ The system starts by creating a new design problem }
Please enter the name of the new problem >> First National Bank
{ The user generates the following initial set of design
specifications }
Initial design specifications:
        Functions
1.  RESIST-LOAD = LATERAL-LOAD      (8)
2.  EXTEND      = 2D                (8)

Would you like to expand this set of specifications?
(Y or N) y

Please select one of the above specifications as the new index
for expanding the design specifications >> 1

The following prototypes are found through index
        RESIST-LOAD = LATERAL-LOAD
1.  BRACED-FRAME
2.  RIGID-FRAME
3.  CORE
```

```
4.  TUBE
5.  ARCH
6.  BRIDGE
Are you particularly interested in any of the above prototypes?
(Y or N) y
Please specify by its number >> 2

Use prototype RIGID-FRAME for subsequent design or as a source of
additional specifications?
1.  START DESIGN
2.  AS A SOURCE
>> 2

Use Prototype RIGID-FRAME as a source of additional
specifications.

In which information category of RIGID-FRAME are you interested?
1.  BEHAVIORS
2.  STRUCTURE
3.  STRUCTURE VARIABLES
4.  PERFORMANCE
5.  ANY OF THE ABOVE
>> 5

Category STRUCTURE VARIABLES is randomly selected.
Please specify by number(s) which of the following are to be
added into the design specifications:
1.  LENGTH
2.  HEIGHT
3.  NUMBER-OF-STORIES
4.  NUMBER-OF-BAYS
5.  BAY-SIZE
6.  STORY-HEIGHT
7.  MATERIAL-TYPE (STEEL CONCRETE)
8.  NONE OF THE ABOVE
>> 3 5

Would you like to associate any value(s) with attribute NUMBER-
OF-STORIES?
(Y or N) y

Valid operators to associate the attribute with its value(s) or
range:
    = <>  IN   NOT-IN
Please choose one >> =

Please select appropriate value for NUMBER-OF-STORIES
```

```
>> 5

Please enter a weight in [0 , 20] for this requirement.
>> 13

Would you like to associate any value(s) with attribute BAY-SIZE?
(Y or N) y

Valid operators to associate the attribute with its value(s) or
range:
    =  <>  IN  NOT-IN
Please choose one >> in

Please select appropriate range for BAY-SIZE
*     >=  150  <=  200  ft
*

Please enter a weight in [0 , 20] for this requirement.
>> 11

Would you like to expand the set of specifications?

          Current Specifications        Potential Attributes

               Functions                Structure Variables
1.  RESIST-LOAD = LATERAL-LOAD  (8)   5.  LENGTH
2.  EXTEND      = 2D            (8)   6.  HEIGHT
                                      7.  NUMBER-OF-BAYS
          Structure Variables         8.  STORY-HEIGHT
3.  NUMBER-OF-STORIES = 5       (13)  9.  MATERIAL-TYPE
                                          (STEEL CONCRETE)
4.  BAY-SIZE IN [150 , 200]    (11)

(Y OR N) >> y
Please specify by number which of the above indices you are
interested in to use as the new index >> 4

The following prototypes are found through index
                BAY-SIZE IN [150 , 200]
1.  BRACED-FRAME
2.  RIGID-FRAME
Are you particularly interested in any of the above prototypes?
(Y or N) y
Please specify by its number >> 1

Use prototype BRACED-FRAME for subsequent design or as a source of
additional specifications?
```

```
1.  Start design
2.  As a source
>> 2
```

Use prototype BRACED-FRAME as a source of additional
specifications

In which information category of BRACED-FRAME are you interested?
```
1.  FUNCTIONS
2.  BEHAVIORS
3.  STRUCTURE
4.  PERFORMANCE
5.  ANY OF THE ABOVE
>> 2
```

Please specify by number(s) which of the folowing are to be added
into the design specifications:
```
1.  MECHANISMS (BENDING COMPRESSION/TENSION)
2.  STRESS (AXIAL-STRESS)
3.  DEFORMATION (LATERAL-DEFLECTION)
4.  NONE OF THE ABOVE
>> 2
```

Would you like to associate any value(s) with attribute STRESS?
(Yor N) y

Valid operators to associate the attribute with its value(s) or
range:
```
    = <>  IN  NOT-IN
Please choose one >> =
```

Please specify any values associated with STRESS:
```
1.  AXIAL-STRESS
>> 1
```

Please enter a weight in [0 , 20] for this requirement.
```
>> 9
```

Would you like to expand the set of specifications?

Current Specifications		Potential Attributes	
Functions		**Behaviors**	
1. RESIST-LOAD = LATERAL-LOAD	(8)	6. MECHANISMS (BENDING COMPRESSION/TENSION)	
2. EXTEND = 2D	(8)	7. DEFORMATION (LATERAL-DEFLECTION)	

```
           Behaviors                         Structure Variables
3.  STRESS = AXIAL-STRESS      (9)    8.  LENGTH
    Structure Variables               9.  HEIGHT
4.  NUMBER-OF-STORIES = 5      (13)  10.  NUMBER-OF-BAYS
5.  BAY-SIZE IN [150, 200]     (11)  11.  STORY-HEIGHT
                                     12.  MATERIAL-TYPE
                                          (STEEL CONCRETE)
```

(Y OR N) >> y
Please specify by number which of the above indices you are
interested in to use as the new index >> 3

The following prototypes are found through index
          STRESS = AXIAL-STRESS
 1. COLUMN
 2. CABLE
 3. TUBE
 4. CORE
 5. ARCH
 6. BRACED-FRAME
 7. RIGID-FRAME
 8. SPACE-TRUSS
 9. TRUSS
10. VIERENDEEL-TRUSS
11. ARCH-BRIDGE
Are you particularly interested in any of the above prototypes?
(Y or N) y
Please specify by its number >> 2

Use protytype CABLE for subsequent design or as a source of
additional specifications?
1. Start design
2. As a source
>> 2

Use prototype CABLE as a source of additonal specifications.

In which information category of CABLE you are interested?
1. FUNCTIONS
2. STRUCTURE
3. STRUCTURE VARIABLES
4. PERFORMANCE
5. ANY OF THE ABOVE >> 2

Please specify by number(s) which of the following are to be added
into the design specifications:

```
1.  GEOMETRY (2D CURVED)
2.  NONE OF THE ABOVE
>> 1

Would you like to associate any value(s) with attribute GEOMETRY?
(Y or N) y

Valid operators to associate the attribute with its value(s) or
range:
  =  <>  IN  NOT-IN
Please choose one >> =

Please specify any values associated with GEOMETRY:
1.  2D
2.  CURVED
>> 1 2
```

	Current Specifications			Potential Attributes
	Functions			Behaviors
1.	RESIST-LOAD = LATERAL-LOAD (8)		7.	MECHANISMS (BENDING COMPRESSION/TENSION)
2.	EXTEND = 2D (8)		8.	DEFORMATION (LATERAL-DEFLECTION)
	Behaviors			
3.	STRESS = AXIAL-STRESS (9)			Structure Variables
			9.	LENGTH
	Structure		10.	HEIGHT
4.	GEOMETRY = (2D CURVED) (7)		11.	
			12.	STORY-HEIGHT
			13.	MATERIAL-TYPE (STEEL CONCRETE)
	Structure Variables			
5.	NUMBER-OF-STORIES = 5 (13)			
6.	BAY-SIZE IN [150 , 200] (11)			

14.5   Discussion of implementation and example

The implementation is a simple experiment in partial matching and retrieval of categorized attributes of design prototypes. This experiment provides some insight into the value of the dynamic associations approach to exploring design spaces through the use of design prototypes. The example session is discussed here to highlight the capabilities of the implementation and to make explicit the amount of interaction between the designer and the computer program.

The example session starts with a vague set of specifications in which the designer indicates that the design solution is to be a lateral load resisting system that is two-dimensional. This is a rather vague specification as most buildings have two-dimensional lateral load resisting systems and the problem is usually further defined by additional specifications.

The designer chooses to expand the set of specifications by considering prototypes that have the function of resisting lateral load, ignoring the requirement that the structural system be two-dimensional. Using this attribute as an index, six prototypes are found, of which a rigid frame is selected for expanding the specifications. The computer randomly selects the structure variables as the source of expansion and the designer chooses the number of stories and the bay size as the attributes to be used for further specification of the current design problem. Now the set of specifications is considered in two parts: current and potential. The current specifications are those that the designer has indicated are of interest, the potential specifications are those that are associated with a selected prototype but were rejected by the designer.

The designer then chooses to expand the set of specifications again, this time using the bay size as an index. In a structural system for buildings, a rigid frame is a fairly routine design solution. The bay size is one of the structure variables of the rigid frame. The use of bay size as an index produces two prototypes, the rigid frame (again) and the braced frame. The designer chooses the braced frame this time, and then chooses the behavior of the braced frame as a source of additional specifications. The behavior of a braced frame is described by three attributes, of which the designer chooses axial stress. This introduces a specification that is inconsistent with a rigid frame, but because the rigid frame prototype is not the only source of design knowledge, this inconsistency can be supported.

Using the axial stress attribute as an index, 11 potential prtotoypes are found, of which the cable prototoype is selected. Again, the cable serves as a source of specifications. The designer chooses the geometry of the cable to expand the set of specifications. This is where the example session ends. What has been illustrated is that the designer started with a vague and potentially routine set of specifications for the design of a lateral load resisting system for a building. Through the associations of prototypes in the knowledge-base, the set of specifications was intially expanded towards the use of a routine design solution, the rigid frame. Adding further specifications, such as axial stress (not indicative behavior of a rigid frame), the designer ended up specifying the use of a cable structure for the lateral load resisting system. This is not a conventional use of cables.

The associations described earlier are illustrated in Figure 14.6, where the left side of the figure shows the set of specifications and the right side shows the prototypes used as the sources of the attributes. The progression of the expanding set of specifications is from the top of the figure to the bottom. The set of specifications for the structural system is illustrated in Figure 14.7.

14.6   Conclusions and directions

Prototypes are a rich and flexible organization for design knowledge. This is demonstrated by the capability of the system to dynamically generate design specifications, which has been achieved at very low computational cost with the facilitation of the indexing system. The problem of hard coded rules that makes the modification and updating of expert systems difficult is reduced in this system, because the relevance of design knowledge is determined by associations and not by rules, and the procedure for making these associations is rather simple. Taking advantage of prototype hierarchy and information grouping, irrelevant information can be left out. This is important in creative design, because at the initial stage the system and the designer may know very little about the form or function of the final design.

The implementation and expermiment described in this chapter indicate that dynamic associations can be made between prototypes using function, behavior and structure as the basis for grouping indeces into the knowledge-base. In our experiments, the value of the associations has been decided by the designer rather than by the computer program. Encoding this value as explicit knowledge is a difficult and interesting research question.

Once a set of specifications and an associated prototype are decided on, the design process then involves determining which of the prototype's atttributes are relevant and how values can be assigned to the variables. This is not a trivial question because the prototype only provides knowledge for its routine use. However it is expected that mutation may provide a means for combining relevant prototypical knowledge. Computational models for mutation of prototypes is a current focus of our research.

In this chapter we have addressed the use of a knowledge-base for the part of the design process in which a design problem is specified. The use of computers during design usually assumes that the design problem is completely specified and the computer program is used either to facilitate the development or description of a solution for the design specification.

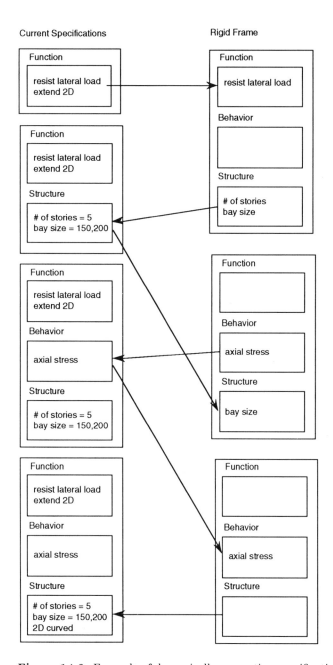

Figure 14.6. Example of dynamically generating specifications using prototypes.

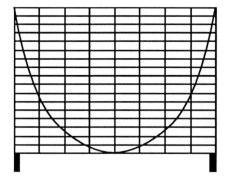

Figure 14.7. Illustration of generated specifications.

Although it appears that our implementation and experiments have not yet addressed the development of a creative design, we have addressed the role of computers in developing specifications that potentially lead to creative design solutions. What we have not addressed is the development of the set of specifications into a feasible design solution. This is the focus of our current work.

Acknowledgments. Many of the ideas reported in this chapter were initiated and enhanced through conversations with John Gero. The work is supported in part by the National Science Foundation through grant DMCE 8811877.

References

Carbonell, J. G. (1982). Towards a computational model of metaphor in common sense reasoning, *Proceedings of the Fourth Annual Meeting of the Cognitive Science Society.*

Carbonell, J. G. (1983). Learning by analogy: Formulating and generalizing plans from past experience, *in* R. S. Michalski, J. G. Carbonell, & T. M. Mitchell, (Eds), *Machine Learning: An Artificial Intelligence Approach*, Tioga, Palo Alto, California.

Carbonell, J. G. (1986). Derivational analogy: A theory of reconstructive problem solving and expertise acquisition, *in* R. S. Michalski, J. G. Carbonell, & T. M. Mitchell (Eds), *Machine Learning II: An Artificial Intelligence Approach*, Morgan Kaufmann, Los Altos, California.

Carbonell, J. G., Larkin, J. H., & Reif, F. (1983). Towards a general scientific reasoning engine, *Technical Report CIP No. 445*, Department of Computer Science, Carnegie Mellon University, Pittsburgh.

Gero, J. (1990). Design prototypes: A knowledge representation schema for design, *AI Magazine* **11**(4): 26–36.

Gero J. S., Maher, M. L., & Zhang, W. (1988). Chunking structural design knowledge as prototypes, *in* J. S. Gero (Ed.), *Artificial Intelligence in Engineering: Design*, Elsevier/CMP, Amsterdam, pp. 3–21.

Keane, M. T. (1988). *Analogical Problem Solving*, Ellis Horwood, Chichester.

Lenat, D. B. (1982). An artificial inteligence approach to discovery in mathematics as heuristic search, *in* R. Davis, & D. B. Lenat (Eds), *Knowledge-Based Systems in Artificial Intelligence*, McGraw-Hill, New York.

Lenat, D. B., & Brown, J. S. (1983). Why AM and Eurisko appear to work, *Proceedings AAAI-83*, Pittsburgh, pp. 236–240.

Maher, M. L., Zhao, F., & Gero, J. S. (1989). A knowledge-based model for creative design, *Proceedings of the NSF Engineering Design Research Conference*, University of Massachusetts, pp. 333–346.

Prieditis, A. (1988). *Analogica*, Pitman/Morgan Kaufmann, Los Altos, California.

Schank, R. C. (1986). *Explanation Patterns: Understanding Mechanically and Creatively*, Hillsdale, New Jersey.

Subject Index

ambiguous figures, 33
analogy, 129, 237, 304, 330, 337
argumentation, 247
ATMS, 160
behavior, 116, 332
CAD, 29, 296, 302
cognitive models, 212, 298
combination, 127
computer, 260, 261
concentration, 3
connectionist models, 186, 192
constraints in design, 11, 163, 276, 279
construction kits, 242, 243
creative design, 3, 115, 122, 140, 274, 303, 335
creative persons, 50
creative process, 4, 45, 47, 63, 74, 92, 112, 268, 301
creative product, 4, 44, 52, 85
creativity, definition of, vii, 44, 46, 91, 93, 141, 236, 297
critics, 246, 247, 248
design environments, 242, 306
design grammars, 113, 222
design knowledge, 149
design problems, 144

design process, 144
design prototypes, 118, 149, 277, 323, 332
design schemas, 184
design space, 217, 237
designing, 26, 94
dynamically generating specifications, 336
emergent schemas, 197
emergent shapes, 29, 223
emergent value, 52, 76, 84
exploration, 147, 170, 181, 270, 299, 307
first principles, 130, 275
functional organization of brain, 99
generate-and-test, 213, 317
genetic design analogy, 217
goal-directed design, 41
human-computer interaction, 260
index of opportunity, 18
indexing, 339
induction, 280, 290
innovative design, 2, 114, 140, 274
inventing the wheel, 281
layout design, 195
learning, 290
limitations of human designer, 300

memory, 181, 331

monotonicity, 275, 317

mutation, 128, 141, 220, 223, 329

natural evolution, 215

network model of creativity, 102

neural networks, 98, 186

nonroutine design, 2, 26, 273

optimization, 274, 275

reminding, 68

routine design, 2, 26, 113, 140, 273, 335

rules, 221, 264, 268

search, 141, 213

semantic filter, 316

shape algebra, 28

shape grammars, 38, 268

shape recognition operators, 30

social, opportunity, 14

strategic support, 158

structure, 115, 332

systematic generation, 310

tactical support, 160

transformation, 3